BIOLOGY 203

HUMAN ANATOMY AND PHYSIOLOGY — A MODERN SYNTHESIS, LABORATORY PRACTICES

FALL 2017

REGINA SHANNON, LAB COORDINATOR
C. DAVID BRIDGES, PROFESSOR
STUART MICHAEL

PURDUE UNIVERSITY

macmillan learning
curriculum solutions

Printed in the United States of America

10 9 8 7 6 5 4 3 2 1

ISBN 978-0-7380-9579-0

Macmillan Learning Curriculum Solutions
14903 Pilot Drive
Plymouth, MI 48170
www.macmillanlearning.com

Shannon 9579-0 F17

macmillan learning
curriculum solutions

Sustainability
Hayden-McNeil's standard paper stock uses a minimum of 30% post-consumer waste. We offer higher % options by request, including a 100% recycled stock. Additionally, Hayden-McNeil Custom Digital provides authors with the opportunity to convert print products to a digital format. Hayden-McNeil is part of a larger sustainability initiative through Macmillan Learning. Visit http://sustainability.macmillan.com to learn more.

bedford/st. martin's • hayden-mcneil
w.h. freeman • worth publishers

TABLE OF CONTENTS

INTRODUCTION

COURSE INFORMATION

BIOLOGY 203 RECITATION AND LABORATORY POLICIES

FALL 2017

Welcome to Biology 203—Human Anatomy and Physiology

THE COURSE

The material covered in the laboratory is intended to provide hands-on exercises related to the lecture component of the course. Lab activities are arranged to follow the organization of the lecture manual but the lab moves through the material quicker. Therefore, the lab portion of the course tends to be ahead of the lecture.

STUDY MATERIALS

Items 1 through 5 are required.

1. Lecture notes. C. David Bridges; Hayden-McNeil, 2017, ISBN: 978-0-7380-9569-1. On sale at bookstores. Required text.

2. Laboratory manual, Regina Shannon, C. David Bridges, Stuart Michael; Hayden-McNeil, 2017, ISBN: 978-0-7380-9579-0. On sale at bookstores. Required text.

3. Di Fiore's *Atlas of Histology* with functional correlations, either:

   • 12th ed., Victor P. Eroschenko, Lippincott, Williams, and Wilkins, 2012, ISBN-13: 978-1-4511-1341-9, or

   • 11th ed., Victor P. Eroschenko, Lippincott, Williams, and Wilkins, 2008, ISBN-13: 978-0-7817-7057-6, or

   • This text is a required text for BIOL 203 students, optional for BIOL 201 students.

4. Scientific, non-graphing, non-programmable calculator.

5. i>clicker.

THE RECITATION

Class attendance is expected. Recitations meet on Fridays 10:30–11:20 am, 11:30 am–12:20 pm, and Mondays 10:30–11:20 am, 11:30 am–12:20 pm, and 2:30–3:20 pm. If you have a time conflict with your scheduled recitation, you may attend one of the other recitations in the sequence with the **Lab Coordinator's** permission. Other than rescheduling to another recitation within a given sequence, NO MAKEUPS are allowed. **It is your responsibility to make contact!**

Most recitations, there will be a 20-point multiple choice quiz given at the end of the period. NO MAKEUPS are allowed. These quizzes will use the i>clicker system mentioned below. Of the 11 quizzes, 10 will count and one will be extra credit. **None** will be dropped.

You will be required to purchase an i>clicker remote for in-class participation. i>clicker is a response system that allows you to respond to questions I posed during class, and you will be graded on that participation. Each clicker has a unique serial number on the back of the remote. Place a piece of scotch tape over that bar code and ID to preserve it. In order to receive credit on your quizzes you will need to register your i>clicker remote online on **Blackboard** (NOT the i>clicker site) within the first TWO weeks of class. To do this, go to the course **Blackboard site**. At the bottom of the home page you will see a link marked "register your I Clicker here." Click on that, and enter your remote ID in the field that appears on the next page. Then simply click on the register button. The remote ID is the series of numbers and sometimes letters found on the bottom of the back of your i>clicker remote. The i>clicker response system will be used in EVERY recitation, and IT IS YOUR RESPONSIBILITY to bring it with you. If you do not bring your i>clicker remote to recitation, and opt to write your responses on paper, **you do so at your own risk**.

THE LAB

LAB READING ASSIGNMENTS

When you come to lab each week, you should have completed the readings in the lab manual chapter as well as readings indicated at the beginning of the lab manual chapter. Readings indicated at the beginning of the lab manual chapter include chapters in the lecture notes. You will be tested on this material during the lab. Any or all of the background readings are fair game for quizzes and exams.

HISTOLOGY TEXT

The histology text will help you complete the lab exercise using the prepared histology slides. Please review the lab chapters that are identified as those requiring the text. BRING YOUR HISTOLOGY TEXT TO CLASS ON THE APPROPRIATE LAB as indicated at the beginning of the lab chapters.

LAB WORKSHEETS

Ten-point **online** worksheets over the given laboratories are due by the night before your lab. The questions **MUST** be answered in your own words. Full credit will be given if the worksheets are turned in on time. The assignment is due by midnight the night BEFORE your lab. If the assignment is late, **no credit** will be given—no exceptions.

LAB REPORTS

Due dates for lab reports will be announced in class and are listed in the laboratory schedule. The assignment is due by at the beginning of your lab; **half credit** will be given for those assignments turned in late but within **24 hours** of your deadline. If more than 24 hours elapse, **no credit** will be given—no exceptions or extensions will be given. Since data for the lab reports may only be collected during the week the experiment is run, students who miss lab will **not** be able to make up the lab report for *any* reason.

LAB QUIZZES

A twenty-point in-lab quiz will be given during each laboratory session. **The test will cover material from the previous week's topic (50%) as well as material for the present week's lab topic (50%).** This **includes** material from the corresponding topics found in the **Lecture Manual**. Test questions come in the form of multiple choice, matching, labeling, short answer, and fill in the blank. Histology slides **will** appear on weekly quizzes. Of the 12 in-lab quizzes, all of them will count. **None** will be dropped. There will also be 15-point weekly post-lab online quizzes. Of the 12 post-lab quizzes, all of them will count. **None** will be dropped. There will be a 95-point midterm exam covering Labs 1–7 and a 95-point lab final exam covering Labs 8–13.

ALL WRITTEN ASSIGNMENTS

We ask that you RETAIN A COPY OF ALL WRITTEN ASSIGNMENTS YOU HAND IN and RETAIN ALL GRADED WORK until after final grades are received at the end of the semester. We will not be responsible for an apparently lost assignment or error in recorded grades if you do not have a copy of the work that is in question.

OPEN LABS (help sessions)

During the week, there will be several open lab sessions. These are actually help sessions/office hours that are staffed by the graduate teaching assistants. It is your opportunity to receive additional assistance outside your assigned laboratory session. Slides and demos will be available for viewing should you want to study them. **NO LABS OR QUIZZES may be made up during the Open Labs without the written permission of the Assistant Lab Coordinator!**

DISABLING CONDITIONS

Any student who, because of a disabling condition, may require special arrangements in order to meet course requirements for either the recitation AND/OR the lab should contact the Lab Coordinator by the third week of class in order to make necessary accommodations. Students who do not contact the Lab Coordinator by the third week of class, or as soon as they know they have a disabling condition, forfeit their rights to special accommodations. Students must work with the Dean of Students Office in order to receive special accommodations for this class.

HAVING PROBLEMS?

If you are experiencing difficulties with this course, or have some personal problems or emergencies which are affecting your performance in this course, please speak with Regina Shannon or Lisa Kolo as soon as possible.

ACADEMIC DISHONESTY

A. CHEATING

This is an uncomfortable but necessary topic to cover.

> "The commitment of the acts of cheating, lying, and deceit in any of their diverse forms (such as the use of substitutes for taking examinations, the use of illegal cribs, plagiarism, and copying during examinations) is dishonest and must not be tolerated. Moreover, knowingly to aid and abet (directly or indirectly) other parties in committing dishonest acts is in itself dishonest." (University Senate Document 72–18, December 15, 1972)

Cheating includes looking at a neighbor's paper, *for any excuse or reason whatsoever* **(e.g., "time management"), and** *irrespective* **of whether any advantage has been gained from this action.**

The vast majority of students are honest. Unfortunately, it has been our experience that there are often one or two students in our class of 700–900 individuals who are prepared to cheat in order to elevate their grades. It just isn't worth it. We will apply **zero tolerance** to any act of dishonesty, **irrespective** of whether any advantage has been gained from this action. It doesn't matter whether the cheating incident involves a 350-point exam, a 20-point quiz, an online assignment, or a take-home assignment. All will be treated with equal severity. **The penalties are very severe indeed, and** *can* **involve being given a failing grade for the entire course.**

If the case is of an unusually serious nature or magnitude, requires further investigation, or calls for a stronger penalty than punitive grading, the matter will be turned over to the Office of the Dean of Students for possible **additional** action.

B. PLAGIARISM POLICY

Purdue prohibits "dishonesty in connection with any University activity." Plagiarism is an example of dishonesty. **Plagiarizing is the copying of published works, submitting parts or all of previous course papers/projects, or paraphrasing others' ideas or words** *without proper attribution*. Proof of guilt will result in a lowered or failing grade for the course.

Put no more than **10% direct quotes (using quotation marks and the reference) in your report.** If your report contains more than 10% from another author, your work is no longer original. PURDUE PLAGIARISM POLICIES WILL BE ENFORCED. PLAGIARISM IS REASON ENOUGH TO GET A FAILING GRADE IN BIOL 203/204.

LAB ATTENDANCE/TARDINESS

In order to receive full credit for each laboratory session, you must

- arrive **on time** and
- attend the session **until it is dismissed by your TA.**

Anyone leaving early for any reason without permission will receive a **zero on their quiz, half credit on their worksheet and any other assignments handed in that week** and **may also jeopardize their TA points.**

Anyone arriving to lab **after** the class has started will have their work counted as being late and will receive **half credit**. Anyone arriving to class between 15 minutes–1 hour 49 minutes late will have the above penalty and must reschedule a time with the Assistant Coordinator to attend another lab section. No one will be permitted to stay in the lab who is more than 14 minutes late. **It is your responsibility to make contact!** Anyone arriving to class after their regularly scheduled lab is over is considered to have been absent instead of tardy and will be treated accordingly.

If you miss your assigned laboratory session due to illness, accident, or some other unavoidable circumstance, you must contact the **Assistant Lab Coordinator within 24 hours** of the missed class. **It is your responsibility to make contact!** To receive full credit you must verify the circumstances for the missed class and have them approved by the Assistant Coordinator. Any arrangements for turning in late work must be arranged through the Assistant Coordinator and **not your TA.** Data for lab reports may be collected **only** during the week scheduled. Therefore, lab reports will not be accepted from anyone who was unable to attend a lab the week the data was collected.

If you are approved for ANY type of make-up, you MUST turn in a copy of the e-mail stating the approval.

Homework due dates are *not* adjusted if you are ill. If you cannot make it to class, arrange for a classmate or friend to deliver your homework for you. You may arrange to leave work with the Assistant Lab Coordinator.

If you know you will be absent from a lab, you MUST contact the **Assistant Lab Coordinator** by NO LATER than the Friday before. All quiz make-ups must be completed within TWO weeks of the missed lab.

The Assistant Lab Coordinator, Lisa Kolo, may be contacted by e-mail at lkolo@purdue.edu (which is preferred), **or** by phone **4-1356. Leave a message** on voice mail if she is not available.

There will **NOT BE A MAKE-UP LAB.** Unexcused lab absenteeism cannot be made up.

When contacting the **Assistant Lab Coordinator**, be sure to include ALL of the following information:

- Your current lab section (CRN or Day/Time)
- The date of the expected absence
- The reason for your absence
- The lab section (CRN or Day/Time) you would like to attend. You can find the lab schedule on Blackboard.

COURSE POINT DISTRIBUTION

The point distribution for the course is as follows:

3 lecture exams @ 350 pts. each	=	1050	**A:**	2040–2400 points
25 online lecture quizzes @ 10 pts. each	=	250	**B:**	1800–2039 points
10 recitation quizzes @ 20 pts. each	=	200	**C:**	1560–1799 points
13 online worksheets @ 10 pts. each	=	130	**D:**	1320–1559 points
11 in-lab quizzes @ 20 pts. each	=	220	**F:**	below 1320 points
1 in-lab quiz @ 10 pts.	=	10		
12 online post-lab quizzes @ 15 pts. each	=	180		
Lab Reports	=	130		
Midterm/Final	=	190		
TA evaluation pts.	=	40		
Total points for BIOL 203	=	2400		

STAFF

1. Instructor

C. David Bridges, Ph.D., D.Sc.,

Professor of Biological Sciences,
Adjunct Professor of Physiology and Biophysics
(Indiana University School of Medicine)
Telephone 494-8153
Home phone 463-7334
Lilly Hall of Life Sciences, room 1-230
E-mail: **bridgesc@purdue.edu**

2. Laboratory Coordinator

Regina M. Shannon
Telephone 494-9224
Lilly Hall of Life Sciences, room 1-232 (office)
E-mail: **rmshanno@purdue.edu**

3. Assistant Laboratory Coordinator

Lisa Kolo
Telephone 494-1356
Lilly Hall of Life Sciences, room B-213
E-mail: **lkolo@purdue.edu**

4. Course Secretary

Merissa Kessler
Telephone 494-8518
Lilly Hall of Life Sciences, room G-110
E-mail: **kessler7@purdue.edu**

5. Course Web Site

http://www.itap.purdue.edu/tlt/blackboard/
Log in using Purdue username and password

6. Course Lab Portal Site

BIO203L.courses.haydenmcneil.com

These policies in their entirety are subject to change. See the course Web site
(**http://www.itap.purdue.edu/tlt/blackboard/**) for up-to-date lab policies.

LABORATORY SCHEDULE

BIOLOGY 203

Fall Semester, 2017

Week	Date	Topic	Weekly test covering	Homework covering
1	Aug. 22–24	Lab 1: Introduction to Anatomy and Physiology	none	
2	Aug. 29–31	Lab 2: Cell Biology and the Cell Cycle Diffusion/Osmosis Experiment	Lab 1, 2	LAB 1 & 2
3	Sept. 5–7	Lab 3: Tissues I: Epithelial Tissue	Lab 2, 3	LAB 3
4	Sept. 12–14	Lab 4: Tissues II: Connective Tissue and the Integumentary System	Lab 3, 4	LAB 4 Lab report 1
5	Sept. 19–21	Lab 5: Skeletal System and Joints	Lab 4, 5	LAB 5
6	Sept. 26–28	Lab 6: Tissues III: Muscle Tissue, Muscular System and Levers, EMG Experiment	Lab 5, 6	LAB 6
7	Oct. 3–5	Lab 7: Nerve–Muscle Interaction Frog Leg Experiment	Lab 6, 7	LAB 7
8	Week of Oct. 9	Lab Midterm	Labs 1–7	none Lab report 2
9	Oct. 17–19	Lab 8: The Nervous System I	Lab 7, 8	LAB 8 Lab report 3
10	Oct. 24–26	Lab 9: The Nervous System II Brain and Reflexes Experiment	Lab 8, 9	LAB 9
11	Oct. 31–Nov. 2	Lab 10: Special Senses: Vision, Hearing, and Balance	Lab 9, 10	LAB 10
12	Nov. 7–9	Lab 11: Cardiovascular System I	Lab 10, 11	LAB 11 Lab report 4
13	Nov. 14–16	Lab 12: Cardiovascular System II	Lab 11, 12	LAB 12 Lab report 5
	Nov. 21–23	Thanksgiving Break		
14	Nov. 28–30	Lab 13: Cardiovascular System III ECG and Circulation Experiment	Lab 12, 13	LAB 13 Lab report 6
15	Week of Dec. 4	Lab Final	Labs 8–13	Lab report 7

	Written Work Due
Lab Report 1	Sept. 12–14
Lab Report 2	Oct. 11–13
Lab Report 3	Oct. 17–19
Lab Report 4	Nov. 7–9
Lab Report 5	Nov. 14–16
Lab Report 6	Nov. 28–30
Lab Report 7	Dec. 7

RECITATION SCHEDULE

BIOLOGY 203

Fall Semester, 2017

Week	Date	Topic	Quiz
1	Aug. 21	Course Info, Introduction, and Lab 1	—
1	Aug. 25	Course Info, Introduction, and Lab 2	—
2	Aug. 28	Lab 2: Cell Biology and Life Cycle of the Cell	1
2	Sept. 1	Lab 3: Tissues I: Epithelial Tissue	1
3	Sept. 4	Labor Day–NO CLASS	—
3	Sept. 8	Lab 4: Tissues II: Connective Tissue and the	2
4	Sept. 11	Integumentary System	
4	Sept. 15	Lab 5: Skeletal System and Joints	3
5	Sept. 18		
5	Sept. 22	Lab 6: Tissues III: Muscle and Nervous Tissue	4
6	Sept. 25	Muscle System and Levers	
6	Sept. 29	Lab 7: Nerve–Muscle Interaction	5
7	Oct. 2		
7	TBA	Lab Midterm Review	
8	Oct. 9	NO CLASS	
8	Oct. 13	Lab 8: The Nervous System I	
9	Oct. 16	Lab 8: The Nervous System I	6
9	Oct. 20	Lab 9: The Nervous System II	7
10	Oct. 23		
10	Oct. 27	Lab 10: Special Senses: Vision Hearing and Balance	8
11	Oct. 30		
11	Nov. 3	Lab 11: Cardiovascular System I	9
12	Nov. 6		
12	Nov. 10	Lab 12: Cardiovascular System II	10
13	Nov. 13		
13	Nov. 17	Lab 13: Cardiovascular System III	11
14	Nov. 20	Thanksgiving Break—NO RECITATION	
14	Nov. 24	Thanksgiving Break—NO RECITATION	
15	Nov. 27	Lab 13: Cardiovascular System III	11
15	TBA	Lab Final Review	

LECTURE SCHEDULE

BIOLOGY 203

Fall Semester, 2017

Date	Topic
Aug. 22	Lecture 1—Introduction to the Course and to the Human Body
Aug. 24	Lecture 2—Introduction to the Course and to the Human Body, continued
Aug. 29	Lecture 3—Basic Chemistry and Biochemistry
Aug. 31	Lecture 4—Biology of the Cell
Sept. 5	Lecture 5—Cell Metabolism I
Sept. 7	Lecture 6—Cell Metabolism II
Sept. 12	Lecture 7—Tissues of the Body
Sept. 14	Lecture 8—Membranes Found in the Body
Sept. 19	Lecture 9—Bones and Joints
TBA	Lecture Exam 1
Sept. 26	Lecture 10—Muscle I
Sept. 28	Lecture 11—Muscle II
Oct. 3	Lecture 12—Neurophysiology I
Oct. 5	Lecture 13—Neurophysiology II
Oct. 10	October Break—NO CLASS
Oct. 12	Lecture 14—Neurophysiology III: Somatic Sensory Receptors
Oct. 17	Lecture 15—Central Nervous System I: Spinal Cord, Spinal Reflexes
Oct. 19	Lecture 16—Central Nervous System II: Meninges Ventricles, Cerebrospinal Fluid, Brain Stem
Oct. 24	Lecture 17—Central Nervous System III: Cerebral Cortex and Basal Ganglia
Oct. 26	Lecture 18—Central Nervous System IV: Neurotransmitters; Cerebellum
Oct. 31	Lecture 19—Central Nervous System V: Integration of Sensation, Motor Function, Motivation
TBA	Lecture Exam 2
Nov. 7	Lecture 20—The Autonomic Nervous System
Nov. 9	Lecture 21—Special Senses I: The Eye, Olfaction, and Taste
Nov. 14	Lecture 22—Special Senses II: The Ear—Hearing and Balance
Nov. 16	Lecture 23—Cardiovascular System I: Function, Basic Arrangment, Blood Vessels, the Heart
Nov. 21	Lecture 24—Cardiovascular System II: Cardiac Cycle, Energy Supply, Cardiac Output
Nov. 23	Thanksgiving—NO CLASS
Nov. 28	Lecture 25—Cardiovascular System III: Electrical Properties of the Heart, the Electrocardiogram, Dysrhythmias
Nov. 30	Lecture 26—Cardiovascular System IV: Blood Vessels, Capillaries, and the Control of Blood Pressure
Dec. 4	Lecture 27—Cardiovascular System V: Exercise, Hemorrhage, Hypertension, Atherosclerosis, Coronary Cirulation
Dec. 7	Lecture 28—Cardiovascular System VI: Heart Disease
TBA	Lecture Exam 3

PERSONAL GRADE RECORD SHEET

Name _____

Lab CRN _____   T.A._____

Lab, Day & Time _____   _____

Recitation Quizzes 20 points each	In-Lab Quizzes 20 points each	Post-Lab Quizzes 15 points each	Worksheets 10 points each	Lab Reports/TA Points	
1	1	1	1	Lab report 1: Osmosis (15)	
2	2	2	2	Lab report 2: Intro to LabTutor (15)	
3	3	3	3	Lab report 3: EMG (20)	
4	4	4	4	Lab report 4: Frog Leg (20)	
5	5	5	5	Lab report 5: Reflexes (20)	
6	6	6	6	Lab report 6: Frog Heart (20)	
7	7	7	7	Lab report 7: ECG (20)	
8	8	8	8	TA evaluation points (40)	
9	9	9	9	Sum	
10	10	10	10	Midterm Exam: Labs 1–7 (95)	
Sum	11	11	11	Final Exam: Labs 8–13 (95)	
	12 (10 pts)	12	12	Sum	
	Sum	Sum	13		
			Sum		

Recitation quizzes subtotal (200)	
In-lab quizzes subtotal (230)	
Online worksheets subtotal (130)	
Online post-lab quizzes subtotal (180)	
Lab reports, TA points subtotal (170)	
Midterm and Lab Final (190)	
Lab Total Points (1100)	

PERSONAL GRADE RECORD SHEET FOR LECTURE

Name _____

Column 1	
Title	Score
Lecture 4 online quiz (10 pts)	
Lecture 5 online quiz (10 pts)	
Lecture 6 online quiz (10 pts)	
Lecture 7 online quiz (10 pts)	
Lecture 8 online quiz (10 pts)	
Lecture 9 online quiz (10 pts)	
Lecture Exam 1 (350 pts)	
Lecture 10 online quiz (10 pts)	
Lecture 11 online quiz (10 pts)	
Lecture 12 online quiz (10 pts)	
Lecture 13 online quiz (10 pts)	
Lecture 14 online quiz (10 pts)	
Lecture 15 online quiz (10 pts)	
Lecture 16 online quiz (10 pts)	
Total for Column 1 (out of 480 pts)	

Column 2	
Title	Score
Lecture 17 online quiz (10 pts)	
Lecture 18 online quiz (10 pts)	
Lecture 19 online quiz (10 pts)	
Lecture Exam 2 (350 pts)	
Lecture 20 online quiz (10 pts)	
Lecture 21 online quiz (10 pts)	
Lecture 22 online quiz (10 pts)	
Lecture 23 online quiz (10 pts)	
Lecture 24 online quiz (10 pts)	
Lecture 25 online quiz (10 pts)	
Lecture 26 online quiz (10 pts)	
Lecture 27 online quiz (10 pts)	
Lecture 28 online quiz (10 pts)	
Lecture Exam 3 (350 pts)	
Total for Column 2 (out of 820 pts)	
Total for Column 1	
Total for **BOTH** Columns	

FORM FOR CALCULATING YOUR GRADE STATUS DURING THE SEMESTER (USE THIS IF YOU NEED A GRADE CHECK)

FALL 2017

Name _____

Your points are listed on Blackboard.

Be aware that bonus points are a privilege, not a right.

	Points obtained (include bonus points, if any) (a)	Maximum points possible (b)
Lecture Exam 1		
Lecture Exam 2		
Lecture Exam 3		
Lecture Online Quizzes		
Recitation		
Laboratory		
Bonus Points (e.g., i>clickers)		— — —
Totals	(= a)	(= b)
You currently have 100a/b percent =	% (grade =)	
Points remaining = 2400 – b =		

Grade	Total points	Percentage of remaining points you must get to obtain indicated grade
A	2040	$100 \times (2040 - a/2400 - b) =$
B	1800	$100 \times (1800 - a/2400 - b) =$
C	1560	$100 \times (1560 - a/2400 - b) =$
D	1320	$100 \times (1320 - a/2400 - b) =$

LABORATORY

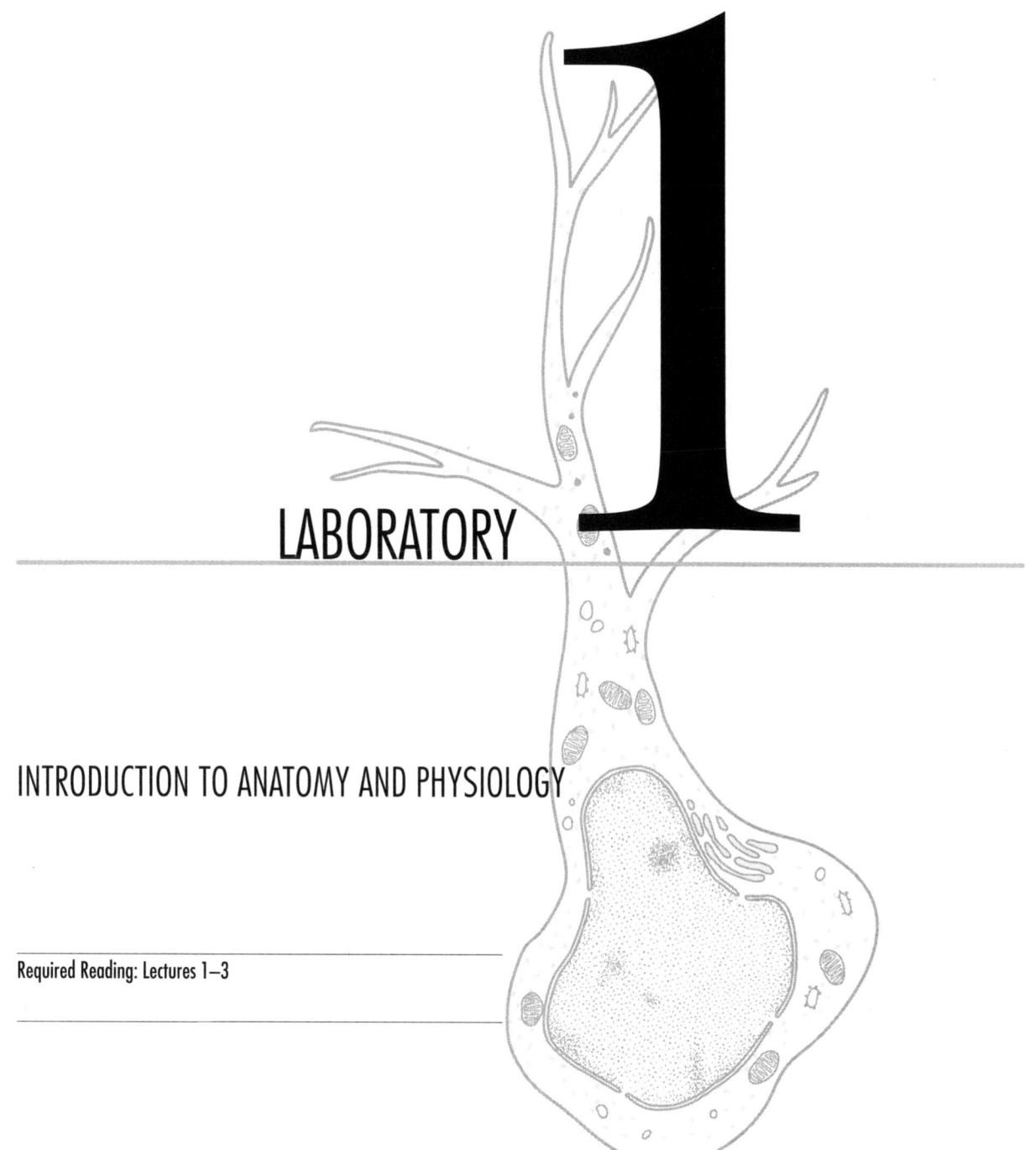

INTRODUCTION TO ANATOMY AND PHYSIOLOGY

Required Reading: Lectures 1–3

Objectives

1. Explain the concept of homeostasis and explain its importance in survival and disease states.

2. List six factors that are under homeostatic control in the body.

3. List and explain the five levels of organization of the body.

4. List the major body cavities and state their locations.

5. List the organs found in each major body cavity.

6. List the membranes associated with the thoracic and abdominopelvic cavities.

7. List the major organ systems, their function and the organs comprising each of them.

8. Give examples of how the terms that describe relative positions, body sections (planes), and body regions are used.

9. Define what is meant by an inorganic substance and list the major inorganic substances found in cells.

10. Define what is meant by an organic substance, and describe four major groups of organic substances and their role in the cell.

11. Define a carbohydrate: name three classes of carbohydrates and give an example of each.

12. Define a lipid, name three classes of lipids and give examples of each.

13. Define a protein and list at least three examples of proteins.

14. Describe what is meant by denaturation and what can cause it.

15. List the three components of a nucleotide.

16. Describe the basic structure of nucleic acids.

17. Know the simple chemical formulas of the inorganic substances listed.

18. Know the simple chemical formulas and/or structural formulas of glucose, sucrose, triglycerides, phospholipids, cholesterol and the general structure of an amino acid.

19. Correctly use the terms that describe relative positions, body sections and body regions.

20. List and explain the **planes** of the body.

21. Understand the basic structure of a microscope, and become proficient in its **use**.

I. Structure and Properties of Matter

You need to read your lecture notes. The following headings cover all the topics in the lecture notes.

A. Matter, Elements, and Atoms

B. Atoms Are Composed of Protons, Neutrons, and Electrons

C. What Is Meant by Isotopes?

D. Molecules—Combinations of Atoms

E. How Atoms Bond with Each Other and How Ions Are Formed

F. Molecules and Chemical Compounds—How Their Compositions and Arrangements Are Expressed in Terms of "Formulas"

1. **Simple formulas.**

2. **Structural formulas.**

G. Chemical Reactions—The Making and Breaking of Bonds between Atoms, Ions, or Molecules

H. Acids, Bases, Salts, and Electrolytes

I. The Concept of pH—A Measure of Acidity or Alkalinity

II. Chemical Composition of Cells

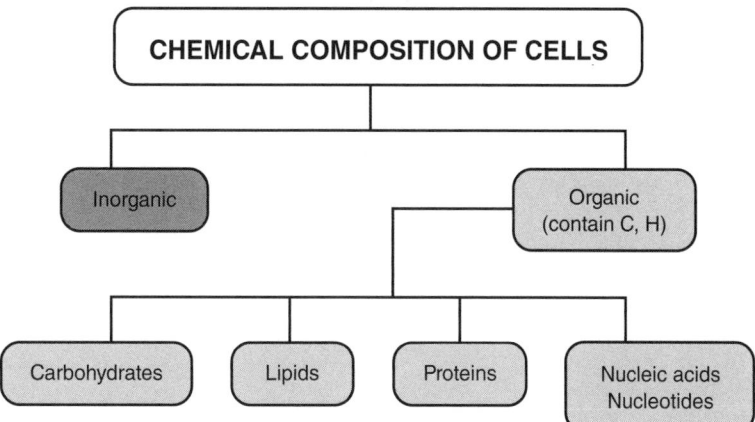

Figure 1-1. Chemical composition of cells.

A. Inorganic Substances

B. Organic Substances in Cells

1. Carbohydrates

Carbohydrates always contain carbon, hydrogen and oxygen. A few may have other elements such as nitrogen.

Carbohydrates include compounds called sugars, which are burned by the cells of the body to produce energy.

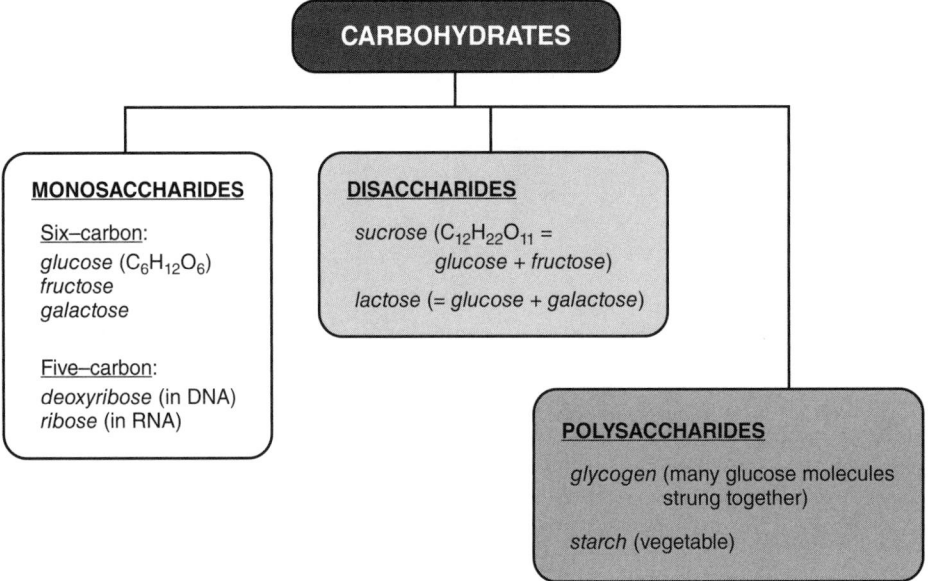

Figure 1-2. Carbohydrates.

Biochemistry of Carbohydrates

Monosaccharides

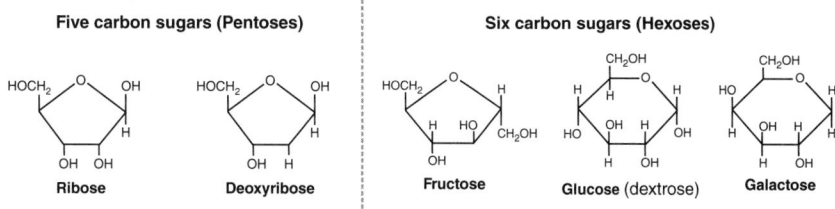

Disaccharides

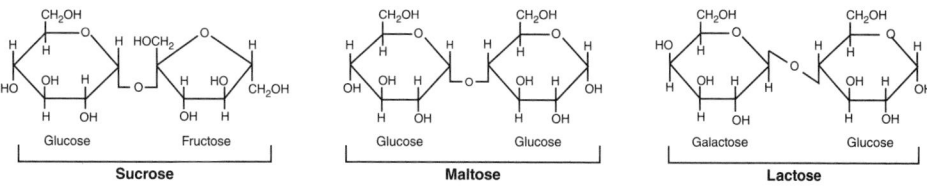

Polysaccharides

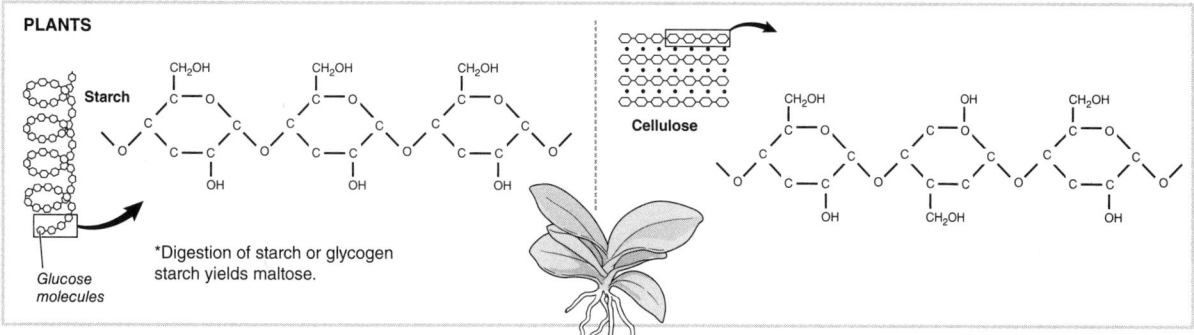

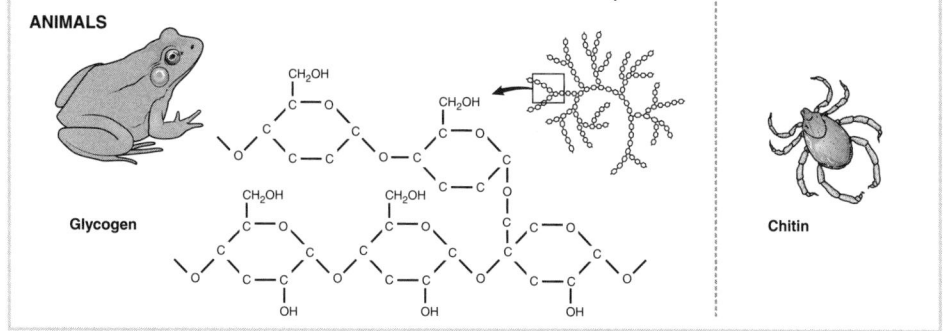

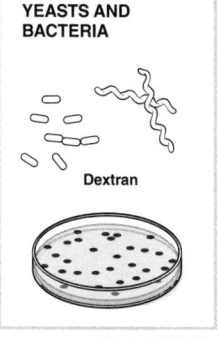

©Hayden-McNeil, LLC

Figure 1-3.

2. Lipids

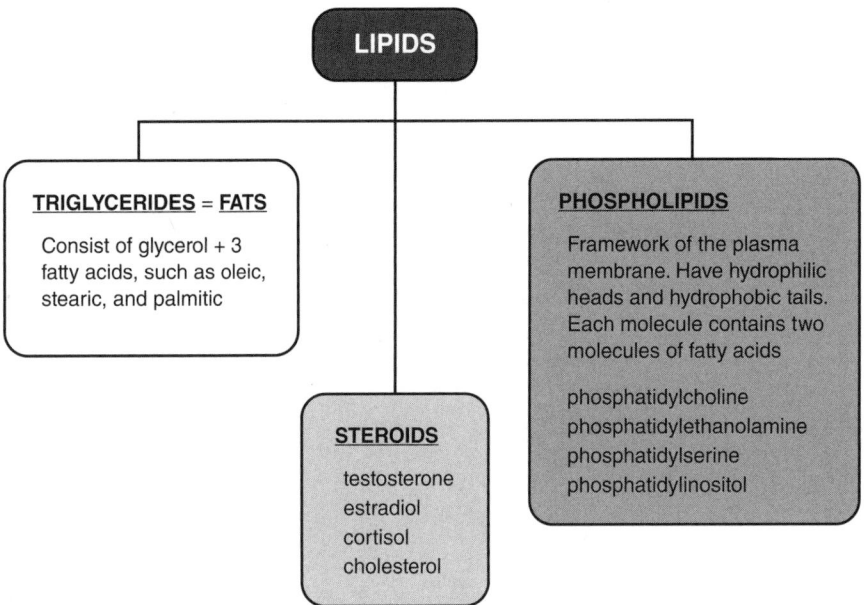

Figure 1-4. Lipids.

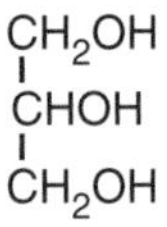

Glycerol

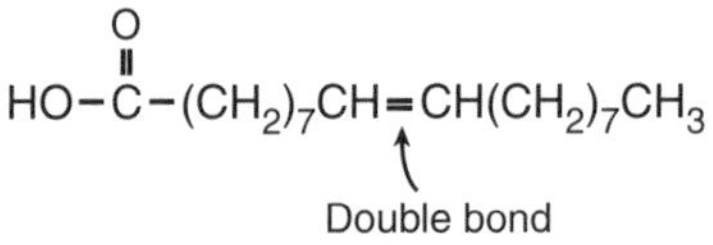

Unsaturated fatty acid

Note: *The three fatty acids are different*

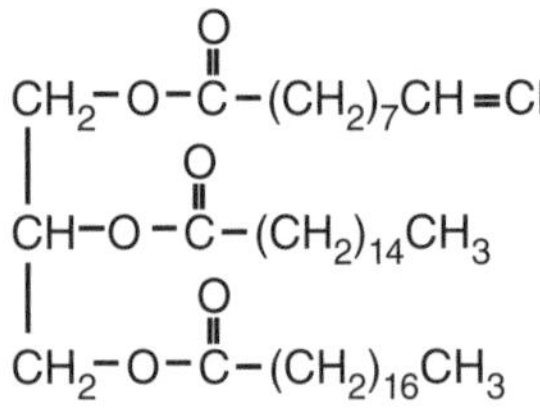

Triglyceride

Figure 1-5.

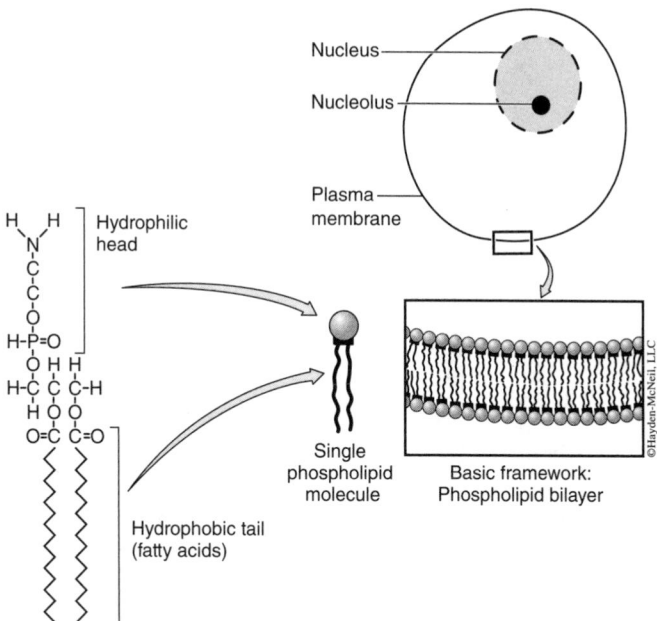

Figure 1-6. Phospholipids. The plasma membrane of the cell is built up around a framework consisting of a phospholipid *bilayer.* *Proteins* (not shown here) are then attached or inserted into this bilayer.

Phosphatidylcholine

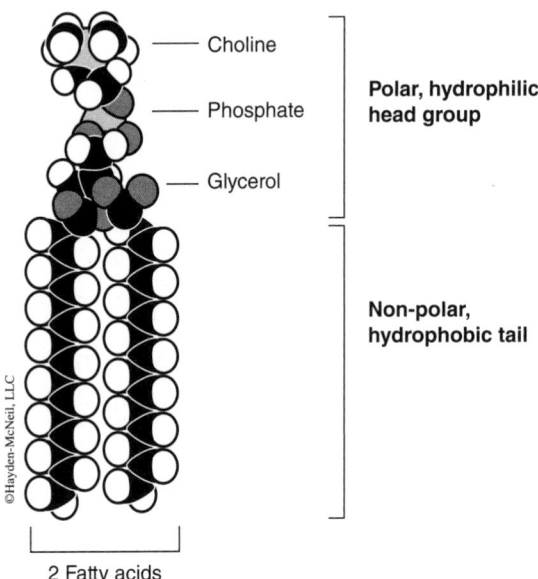

Phosphatidylcholine

Triglyceride

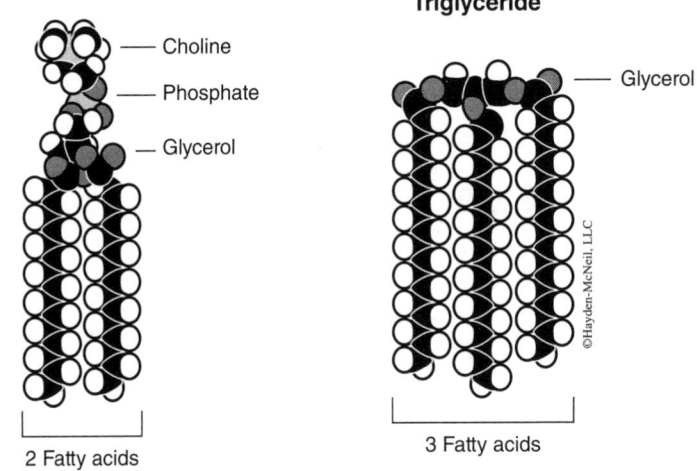

Figure 1-7. Molecular structures of phosphatidylcholine and a triglyceride.

3. Proteins

Proteins make up more than half of the dry weight of the cells in your body. They are vitally important in the cell's structure, in its metabolism, and in many other functions of the cell. *Albumin, hemoglobin, collagen, amylase* and 99% of all *enzymes* are proteins.

Proteins are linear assemblies (chains) of *amino acids*. An amino acid has an $-NH_2$ group *(amino group)* at one end, and a $-COOH$ group *(carboxyl group)* at the other. In proteins, the amino acids are joined via covalent bonds between the amino and carboxyl groups. These bonds are called *peptide* bonds. There are about 20 common amino acids found in various sequences in different proteins. *Leucine, alanine, glycine, phenylalanine, serine, cysteine, histidine, arginine, methionine, lysine, tryptophan* and *tyrosine* are examples of amino acids.

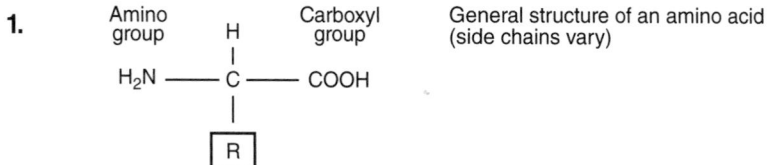

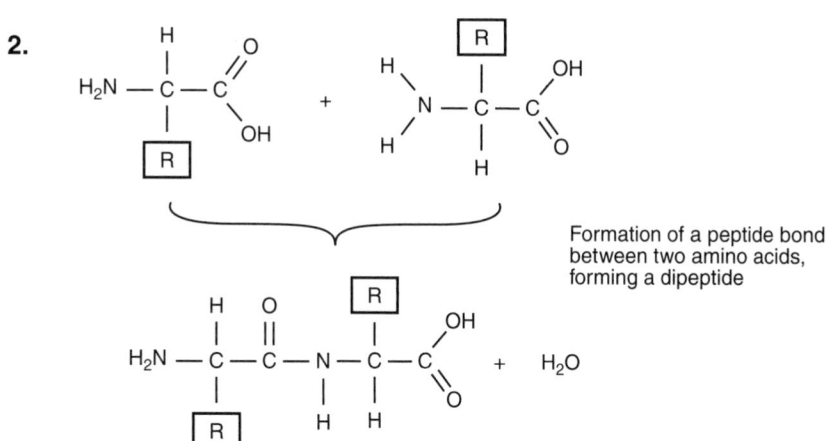

Figure 1-8. Molecular structures of cholesterol and an amino acid (1 and 2), formation of a peptide bond (3). R = side chain.

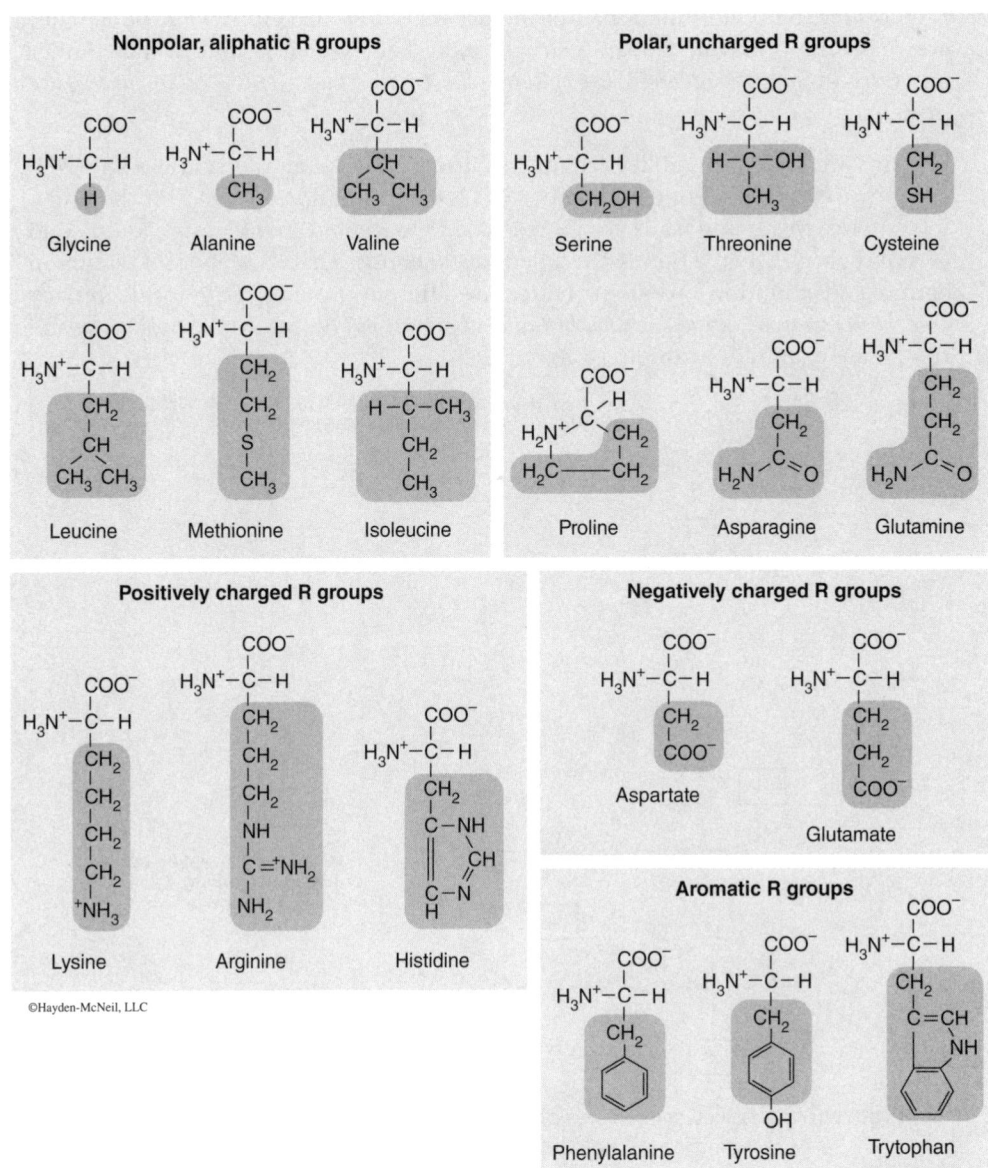

Figure 1-9. Structures of the 20 amino acids used to construct
all the proteins in the human body.

The *amino acid sequence* of a protein is unique to that protein (although large families of proteins with similar functions are sometimes found to have similar sequences, or even regions with identical sequences). The amino acid sequence is important in determining the properties of the protein and how it folds to achieve its final shape (e.g., globular, ellipsoidal). The amino acid sequence also determines the occurrence of various *structural domains* within the protein (e.g., alpha helix, pleated sheets, random coil).

4. **Nucleic Acids and Nucleotides**

Nucleic acids include the very large molecules **DNA** (*deoxyribonucleic acid*) and **RNA** (*ribonucleic acid*).

DNA and RNA are made up of chains of **nucleotides** joined together by covalent bonds. A nucleotide consists of the following three components.

- *A nitrogen-containing base*

  - **adenine** (A), present in DNA and RNA
  - **guanine** (G), present in DNA and RNA
  - **cytosine** (C), present in DNA and RNA
  - **thymine** (T), present in DNA
  - **uracil** (U), found instead of thymine in RNA

- *A 5-carbon sugar (pentose)*

  - ribose (in RNA, ribonucleic acid)
  - 2-deoxyribose (in DNA, deoxyribonucleic acid)

- *One or more phosphate groups*

  - the nucleotides of DNA and RNA have **one** phosphate group,
  - ATP has **three phosphate** groups

Nucleotides have many functions in addition to being building blocks for DNA and RNA. A really important nucleotide is **ATP** (*adenosine triphosphate*), which consists of the nitrogen-containing base adenine, the 5-carbon sugar ribose, and three phosphates.

We will come back to DNA, RNA and ATP later in these lectures. They are all very important molecules in the functioning of the cell.

Nucleotides and Nucleic Acids

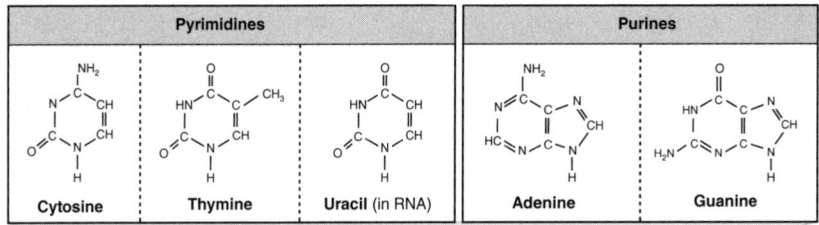

Pyrimidines			Purines	
Cytosine	Thymine	Uracil (in RNA)	Adenine	Guanine

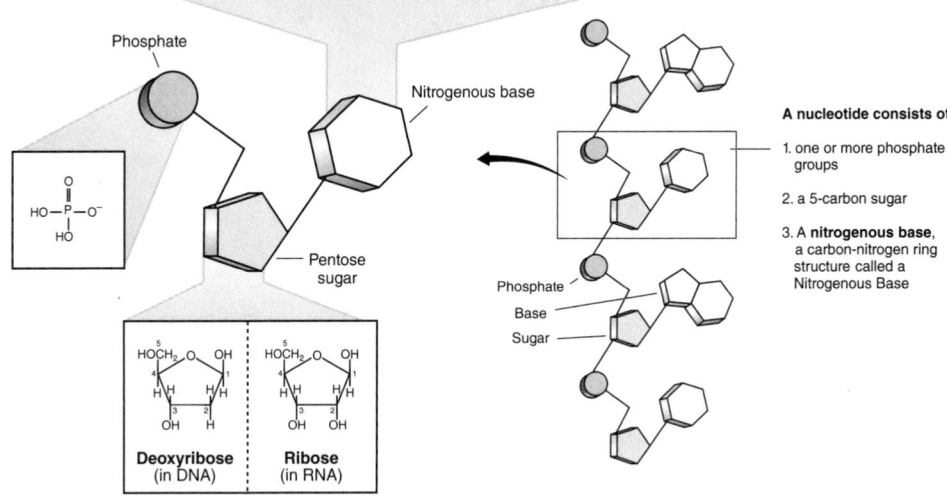

A nucleotide consists of:

1. one or more phosphate groups

2. a 5-carbon sugar

3. A **nitrogenous base**, a carbon-nitrogen ring structure called a Nitrogenous Base

Deoxyribose (in DNA)   Ribose (in RNA)

©Hayden-McNeil, LLC

Single Nucleotide Molecules

Single nucleotide molecules have two critical functions in the human body:

1. Capture and transfer energy in high-energy electrons or phosphate bonds

2. Aid in cell-cell communication

NUCLEOTIDE	BASE		SUGAR		PHOSPHATE GROUPS		OTHER COMPONENTS
ATP	Adenine	+	Ribose	+	3 phosphate groups		
ADP	Adenine	+	Ribose	+	2 phosphate groups		
NAD	Adenine	+	2Ribose	+	2 phosphate groups	+	Nicotinamide
FAD	Adenine	+	Ribose	+	2 phosphate groups	+	Riboflavin
cAMP	Adenine	+	Ribose	+	1 phosphate groups		

III. The Human Body—From Atoms to Organ Systems (Levels of Organization)

The human body is composed of **atoms** of oxygen, hydrogen, carbon, nitrogen etc. These atoms are organized progressively into:

1. **Molecules** (e.g., water, two atoms of hydrogen linked to one atom of oxygen) and macromolecules (= "large molecules," e.g., DNA)

2. **Cells** (e.g., white blood cells, muscle cells, nerve cells), which contain cell organelles (e.g., mitochondria, little powerhouses that produce energy for the cells)

3. **Tissues**, made up of cells (e.g., muscle tissue, nerve tissue)

4. **Organs**, groups of tissues (e.g., liver, heart, kidney)

5. **Systems**, groups of organs designed to do a specific job (e.g., the digestive system, reproductive system, nervous system).

Atoms, molecules and macromolecules represent the most basic level of organization of the human body—the chemical level.

IV. The Human Body—Major Features—Cavities, Organ Systems, and Membranes That Line the Cavities and Cover the Organs

A. Cavities

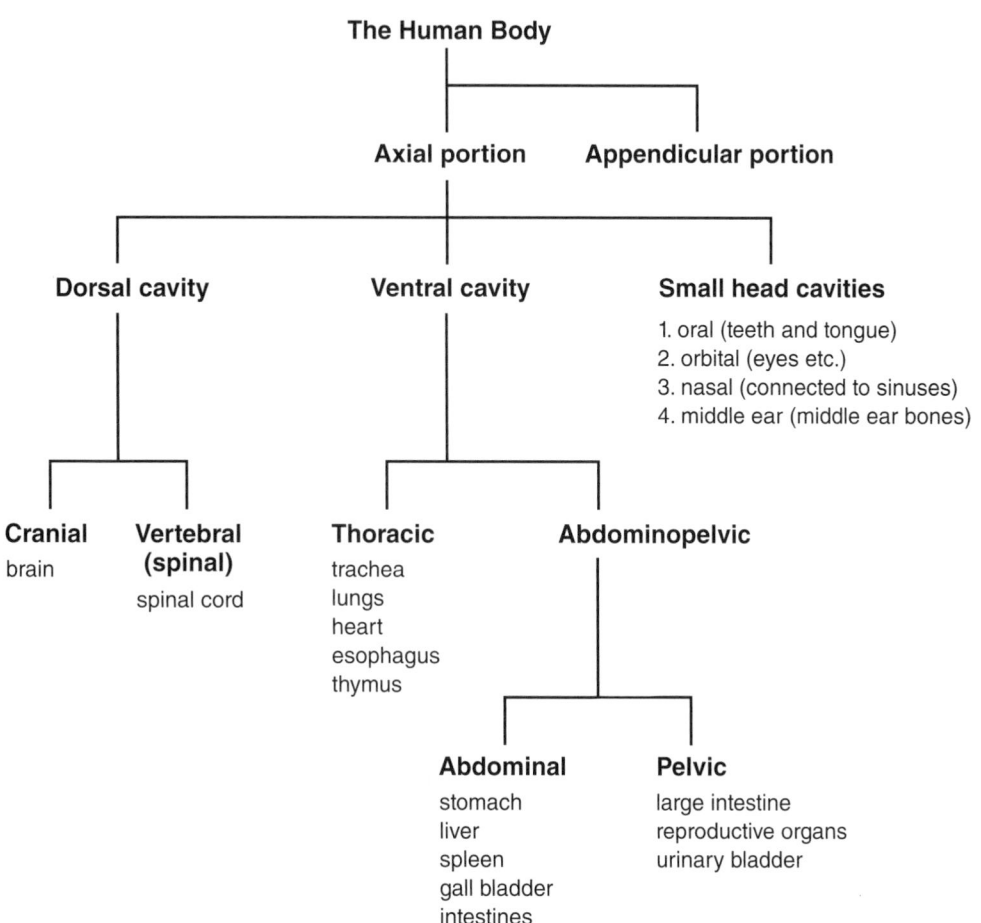

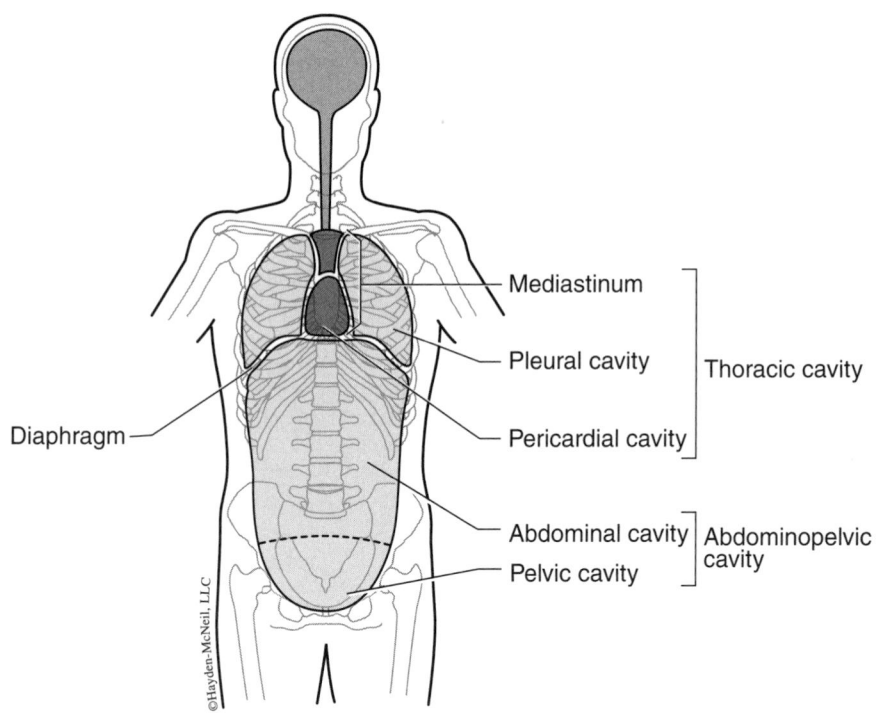

Body cavities - anterior view

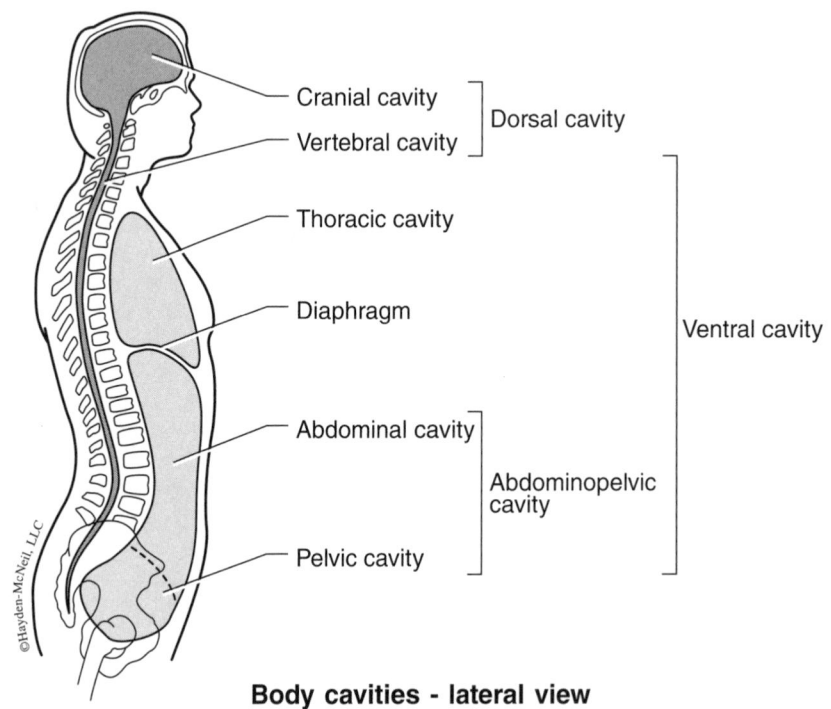

Body cavities - lateral view

B. Membranes

Membranes

Thoracic cavity

Abdominopelvic cavity

Pleural
lines thoracic cavity
and covers lungs

Pericardial
surrounds heart and
covers its surface

Peritoneal
lines abdominopelvic cavity
and covers organs inside
(stomach, intestines, etc.)

Inflammation of the pleural, pericardial, and peritoneal membranes is called **pleuritis**, **pericarditis**, and **peritonitis**. The part of a membrane that lines the walls of the cavity is called the parietal part. The part of a membrane that covers the surface of an organ is called the visceral part. Spaces between the parietal and visceral portions of these membranes are called pleural, pericardial, and peritoneal.

C. Organ Systems

1. Body covering — **integumentary** system

2. Support, protection, and movement — **skeletal** system
    - **muscular** system

3. Integration and coordination — **nervous** system
    - **endocrine** system

4. Processing and transporting — **digestive** system
    - **respiratory** system
    - **circulatory** system
    - **lymphatic** system
    - **urinary** system

5. Reproduction — **reproductive** system

V. Some New Language

A. Relative Positions of Body Parts

1. **Superior/inferior**

   superior = toward the head: "the thorax is superior to the abdomen"

   inferior = away from the head: "the legs are inferior to the trunk"

2. **Anterior/posterior**

   anterior (ventral) = toward the front: "the nipples are on the anterior side of the body"

   posterior (dorsal) = toward the back: "the kidneys are posterior to the intestines"

3. **Medial/lateral**

   medial = toward the midline: "the heart is medial to the lungs"

   lateral = toward the side: "the ears are lateral to the head"

   ipsilateral = same side

   contralateral = opposite side

4. **Proximal/distal**

   proximal = toward the main mass of the body: "the knee is proximal to the foot"

   distal = away from the main mass of the body: "the hand is distal to the elbow"

5. **Superficial/deep**

   superficial = toward the surface of the body: "the skin is superficial to the muscles"

   deep = away from the surface of the body: "a deep wound"

6. **Central/peripheral**

   central = at the center: "the brain and spinal cord are part of the central nervous system"

   peripheral = around the outside: "the popliteal nerve is part of the peripheral nervous system"

B. Sections Cut Through the Body or an Organ

You will often see references to *sagittal, transverse,* and *coronal* body sections. These are just words that are used to define cuts along various parts of the body, and the directions the cuts are made. Sections that divide a body or organ exactly in half use the prefix mid- (e.g., mid-sagittal).

Sagittal—divides the body into left and right portions. A mid-sagittal cut divides the body into equal right and left halves. The word derives from the Latin for arrow (the Zodiac sign for Sagittarius is a half-human with a bow and arrow). The left and right parietal bones of the skull are joined at the sagittal suture.

Transverse (across, horizontal)—any cut that divides the body into superior ("upper") and inferior ("lower") segments.

Coronal (= **frontal**)—a cut that divides the body into anterior ("front") and posterior ("back") portions.

Long tubular structures (such as the aorta) can be cut transversely, longitudinally, or obliquely.

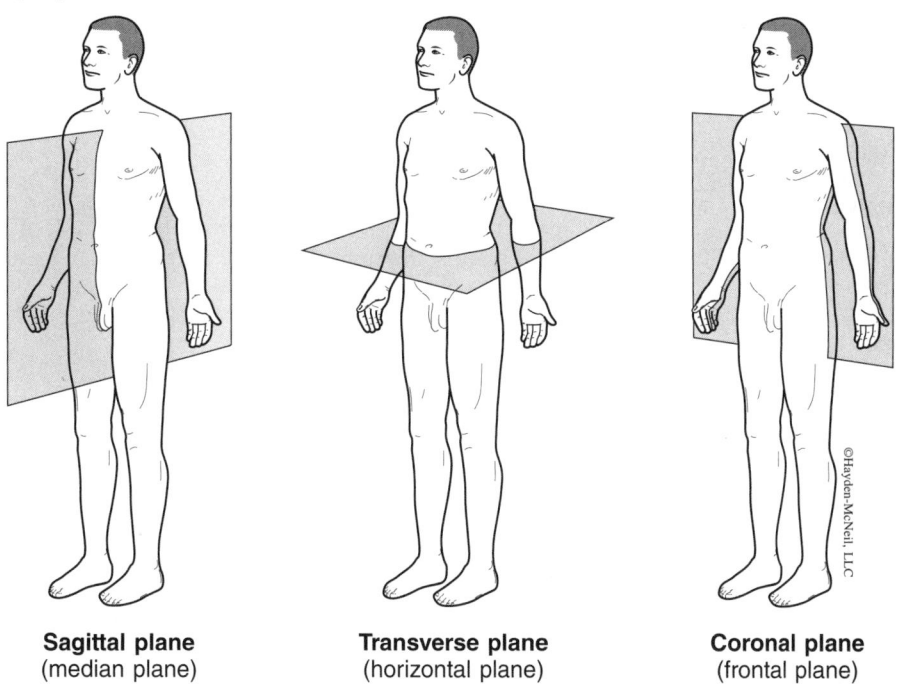

Sagittal plane	**Transverse plane**	**Coronal plane**
(median plane)	(horizontal plane)	(frontal plane)

Body planes

C. Regions of the Body

There are numerous terms used to define various regions of the body. A few examples are:

abdomen	you can figure that one out (abdominal pain)
acromial	point of the shoulder (from Greek "akron," meaning peak)
brachial	upper arm
antebrachial	forearm
antecubital	space in front of elbow (antecubital fossa, an indentation in this region where blood is sometimes withdrawn)
axillary	armpit (axillary glands, axillary hairs)
buccal	cheek (the buccal cavity is the mouth cavity enclosed by the cheeks)
carpal	wrist (think of carpal tunnel syndrome)

cephalic	head
cervical	neck (cervical dislocation)
costal	ribs (intercostal space)
cubital	elbow (the ancient measure of length called the cubit was based on the distance from the elbow to the tip of the middle finger = usually about 18 inches but sometimes 21 inches or more)[1]
digital	finger (= digit)
frontal	forehead (frontal bone of the skull)
genital	reproductive organs
lumbar	lower back
mammary	breast (mammary glands; mammals, animals that suckle their young at the breast)
nasal	nose
oral	mouth
pelvic	region above genitalia
pectoral	chest (pectoral muscles, "pecs")
pedal	foot (bicycle pedals; where you place your feet when riding a bicycle: quadruped, four-footed animal: biped, two-footed animal)
plantar	sole of foot
umbilical	navel (umbilical cord)
vertebral	the vertebra or spinal column (intervertebral discs)

The **abdominal** area is subdivided into 9 regions, three down the left side, three down the center and three down the right side.

Right side (superior to inferior regions)	Center (superior to inferior regions)	Left side (superior to inferior regions)
Right hypochondriac	Epigastric	Left hypochondriac
Right lumbar	Umbilical	Left lumbar
Right iliac	Hypogastric	Left iliac

Some people just divide the abdominal area into quarters, or quadrants. These are designated as right upper, right lower, left upper, and left lower quadrants.

---

[1] *"And there went out a champion out of the camp of the Philistines, named Goliath of Gath, whose height was six cubits and a span."* (I Samuel 17)

VI. Introduction to the Microscope

Cells cannot be seen with the unaided eye, and must be viewed with a microscope.

A. The Compound Microscope

The compound microscope is one of the most important working tools of the biologist. The upper limit of magnification for a high quality compound microscope is approximately 2000×. Microscopes commonly used in student laboratories magnify approximately 1000×. The primary optical parts of a compound microscope are the two lenses; an objective lens, and an ocular lens (eyepiece). Magnification occurs in two stages: (1) the objective lens first forms a real, inverted, and magnified image of the object; (2) the ocular lens further magnifies this image.

The compound microscope uses light to visualize objects. The **phase contrast microscope** uses light to display refractive differences in cellular components. Substances that have been tagged with fluorescent markers (e.g., proteins) are visualized by **fluorescence microscopy**. In **electron microscopy**, an electron beam is used instead of a light source and magnets are used instead of lenses. A magnification of 200,000× or more can be achieved.

1. The Parts of a Compound Microscope

On the microscope at your work station, locate the parts indicated in the diagram below.

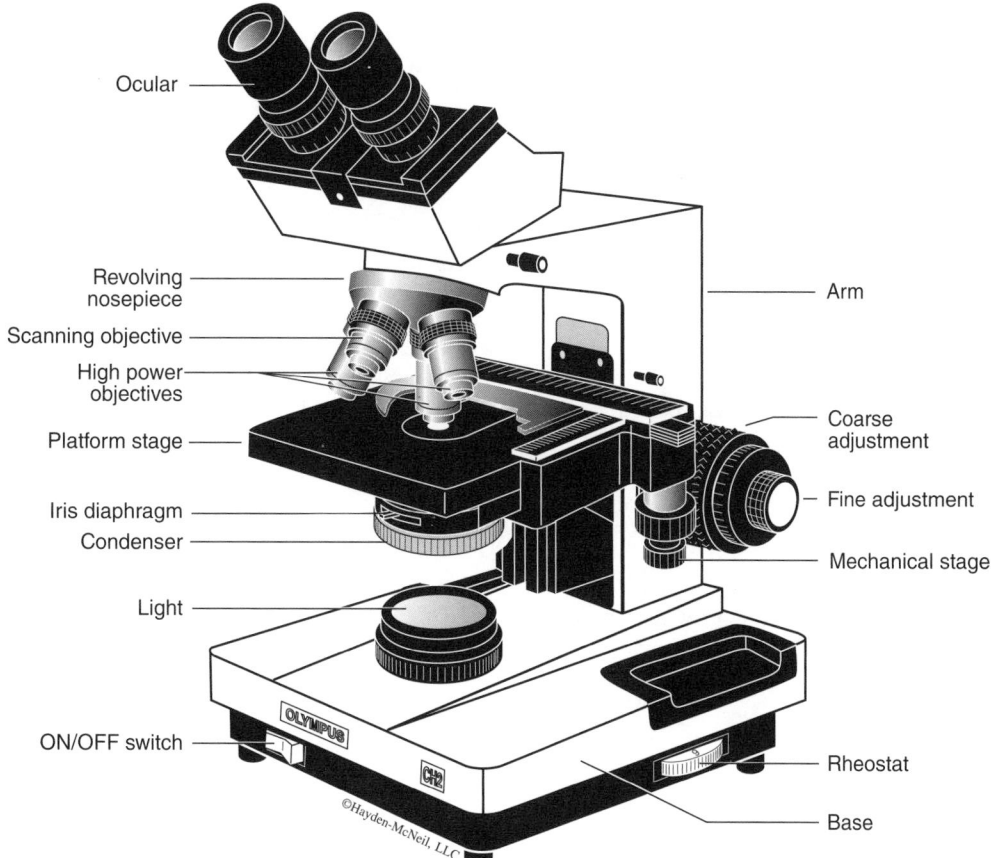

Figure 1-10. The compound microscope.

2. Magnification and Resolution

Resolving power is the minimal distance between two points that can still be seen as two separate points. If the distance is less than the resolving power, the two points cannot be distinguished and merge into one. The greater the **resolving power** of a microscope, the more detail can be seen in the specimen being viewed.

Magnification: magnification is calculated by multiplying the magnifications of the individual lenses. The total magnification of any specimen is the product of the magnification of the ocular lens and objective lens. Magnification can be expressed by the following formula:

MAGNIFICATION = Magnification of Ocular $\times$ Magnification of Objective.

Calculate the total magnification for the various lens combinations for the microscope you will be using. In most cases, the power of the ocular lens is **10$\times$**. The power of the objective lens is engraved on the surface (e.g., $\times$**40**).

3. General Rules for Care and Use of the Microscope

a.   Carry the microscope upright with **two** hands—one hand on the arm and one under the base of the microscope.

b.   Clean the lenses with **lens paper** (**NOT** Kleenex or Kimwipes).

c.   **Always** have the scanning objective lined up with the light source and the stage all the way up **before** inserting a slide. Using the coarse adjustment knob (**for the scanning and low power objectives only**), focus on the specimen by moving the stage away from the objective lens.

d.   **Never** bring the stage **upward** with the **coarse** adjustment knob while looking through the microscope. You may overdo it and ram the objective into the slide, cracking the slide and damaging the expensive objective.

e.   Learn to examine the specimen by focusing up and down through the specimen with the fine adjustment.

f.   Always return the microscope with the scanning objective in place and the stage as far up as it will go. Clean the ocular and objective lenses with **lens paper** prior to covering the microscope. Microscopes **must** be covered and the light turned **off** when your work is finished.

4. Proper Use of the Microscope

Before placing a slide on the microscope stage, turn on the lamp and move the **scanning objective** (4×) in line with the light source. Turn the coarse adjustment knob on the microscope **while observing from the side**, until the stage is all the way up. Place the slide on the stage and view it through the eyepiece. Slowly turn the coarse adjustment knob to lower the stage of the microscope until the specimen is seen, first fuzzy, and then finally sharp and clear. If you turn the adjustment knob too rapidly and miss the object, it is better to bring the stage back up while **watching** the objective to avoid hitting the lens with the specimen. **Never use the coarse adjustment knob to move the stage upwards while looking through the eyepieces.** The image formed by the compound microscope is inverted. Therefore, the object will be seen upside down and reversed so that the right side is on the left. If the slide with the specimen is moved, the image will move in the opposite direction. In time, adjustments to the reversal become natural.

After the specimen is in focus, some readjustment might be necessary to improve the lighting. If there is too much light (so that the specimen cannot be easily seen against the glare), slowly turn the iris diaphragm to a smaller opening. In general, the opening of the diaphragm should be about the same size as the opening on the front lens of the objective. Raising or lowering the condenser may also adjust the amount of light hitting the specimen.

Greater magnification is accomplished by using lenses of higher power. The field of vision for the high-power lens is smaller than that seen with the scanning lens. When the low power is in focus, it is possible to turn the next higher power objective into position by rotating the nosepiece. When you rotate from the low to high-power objective lens, the microscope should remain in focus. That is, the lenses are **parfocal**. If better focusing is needed, only use the fine adjustment knob. **Never use the coarse adjustment knob with the high power objective for fear of breaking the microscope slide and/or the objective lens.**

Oil immersion objective—the space between the objective and the slide must be filled with immersion oil so that the light can be directed through the lens efficiently. A **single** drop of oil is placed on the slide in the area being viewed, and the oil immersion objective is slowly swung into place. Oil must **always** be removed from the microscope and the slide after use. Use a solvent or lens paper—do not use paper towel or Kleenex. Be sure oil is not on any other objective. The oil can ruin the other objectives. The oil immersion lens will only be used for demonstrations, and is **not** for student use.

5. Fixing and Staining

Fresh tissue must be fixed, sectioned and stained before being viewed under the microscope. The piece of tissue is first immersed in a fixing solution that contains formaldehyde or glutaraldehyde. This process hardens and preserves the tissue, so maintaining its structure. The fixed tissue is then impregnated with a substance such as paraffin wax, which allows it to be sectioned with a microtome. The result is very thin slices that are transferred to glass slides. The wax is then removed, and the section is stained, frequently with a mixture of hematoxylin and eosin (H&E). With this stain, the nucleus looks blue and the cytoplasm pale pink. There are many other stains that are used as well. Some of them stain specific structures or substances such as collagen, fat or glycogen.

Exercise A

Insert a prepared slide of the letter "e" on the stage of the microscope and focus under the scanning objective. It may be necessary to change the amount of light by adjusting the iris diaphragm or condenser. Examine the slide first under the scanning objective, low power, then under high power. When you rotated from one lens to another, the print should remain in focus. If it did not, some **fine** adjustment may be necessary. Using the course adjustment **will cause damage to the microscope and/or break the slide.**

Sketch the letter "e" in the circle provided below, approximating its shape, size, and position with respect to each of the three optical fields.

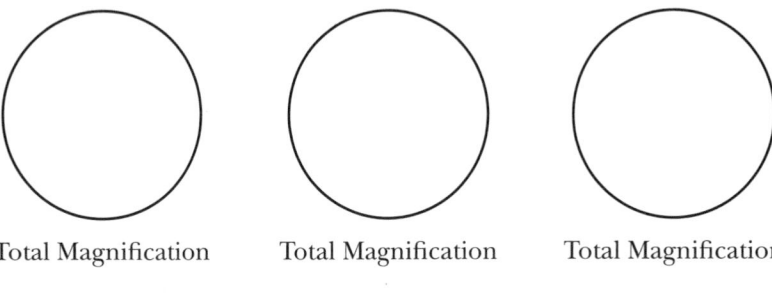

Total Magnification   Total Magnification   Total Magnification

_____   _____   _____

What happens to the orientation of the image as it passes through the microscope lenses?

While viewing the stage move the slide from left to right. Which way does the image move?

Exercise B

Observe a prepared slide of "microfilm." Adjust the text into view using the scanning objective. Notice the amount of text in view. Now, change to the low power objective. A slight adjustment using the **coarse adjustment** knob may be necessary.

Can you read more text or less?

Finally, change to the high power objective. A slight adjustment using the fine adjustment knob may be necessary.

Why can't you use the coarse adjustment knob?

Can you read more text or less?

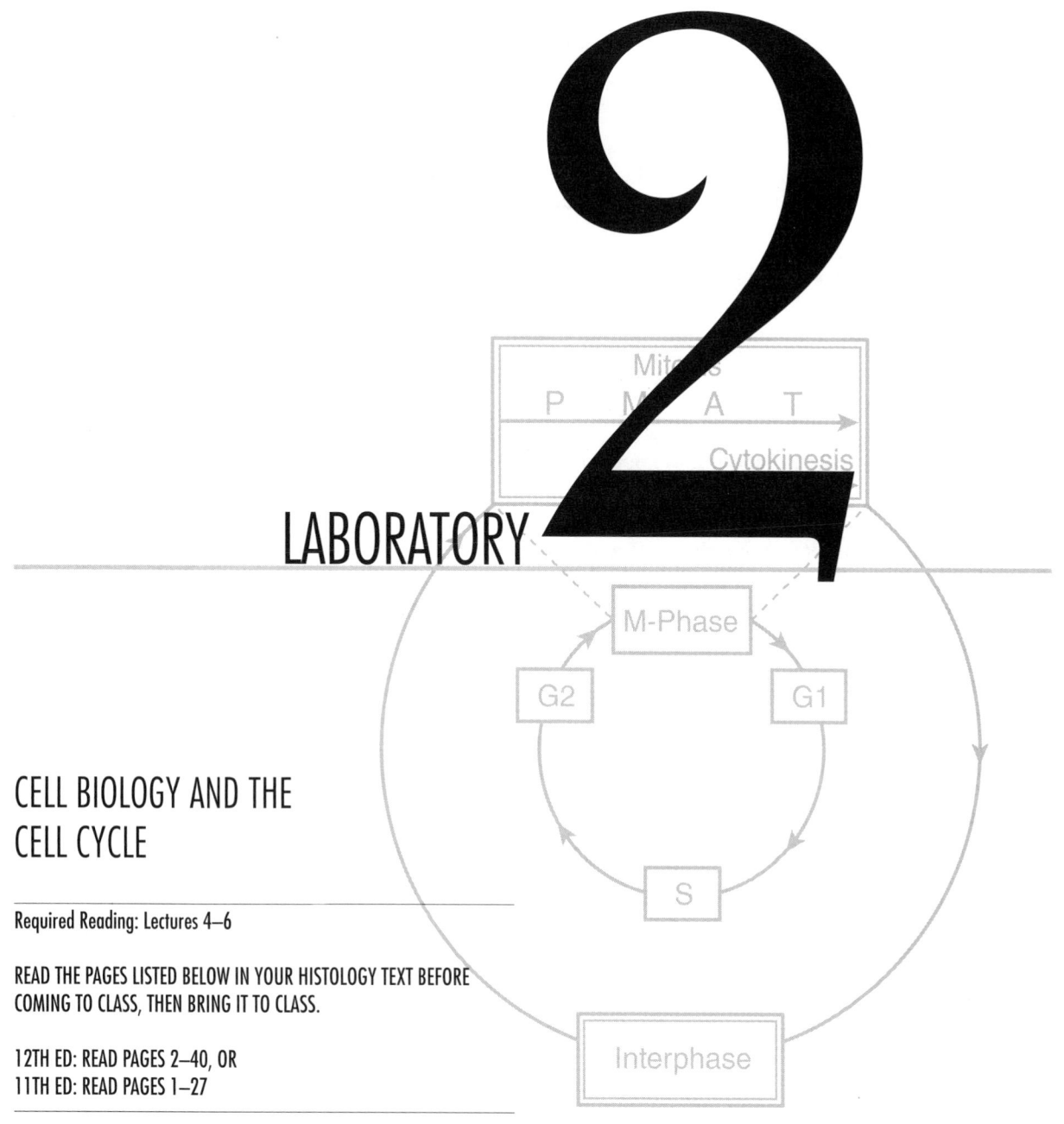

LABORATORY 2

CELL BIOLOGY AND THE CELL CYCLE

Required Reading: Lectures 4–6

READ THE PAGES LISTED BELOW IN YOUR HISTOLOGY TEXT BEFORE
COMING TO CLASS, THEN BRING IT TO CLASS.

12TH ED: READ PAGES 2–40, OR
11TH ED: READ PAGES 1–27

Objectives

1. From memory, draw a cell and label the plasma membrane, nucleus, nuclear membrane, nucleolus, endoplasmic reticulum (rough and smooth), Golgi apparatus, and mitochondria.

2. Draw a diagram illustrating the molecular architecture of the plasma (cell) membrane.

3. List and describe the function of each of the organelles and other structures found in the cell cytoplasm or associated with the cell surface.

4. Name and describe the three types of junctions found between certain cells.

5. Describe the structure of the nucleus and what it contains.

6. Explain what is meant by chromatin, and describe a chromosome.

7. List the three ways in which substances can pass across the plasma membrane without the need for energy expenditure by the cell.

8. List and describe three ways in which substances pass across the plasma membrane with the aid of energy provided by the cell.

9. List and describe three types of endocytosis.

10. Define what is meant by cell differentiation, and what this means in terms of gene expression. Explain what is meant by stem cells.

11. Describe the ways in which cells differ from each other.

12. Draw a circular diagram to illustrate the life cycle of a dividing cell.

13. Describe the four stages of mitosis.

14. Explain the importance of having cell cycle checkpoints.

15. Define apoptosis, and give one example.

16. Describe how necrosis differs from apoptosis.

I. The Cell

The cell is the smallest functional unit of the body, which contains about seventy-five trillion cells. Cells vary in size, shape, and function. They also vary in their mobility and in their ability to multiply. However, all cells consist of a nucleus surrounded by a jelly-like cytoplasm containing a variety of organelles (e.g., mitochondria), all enveloped in the plasma membrane.

A. The Plasma Membrane (Cell Membrane)

1. Structure of the plasma membrane.

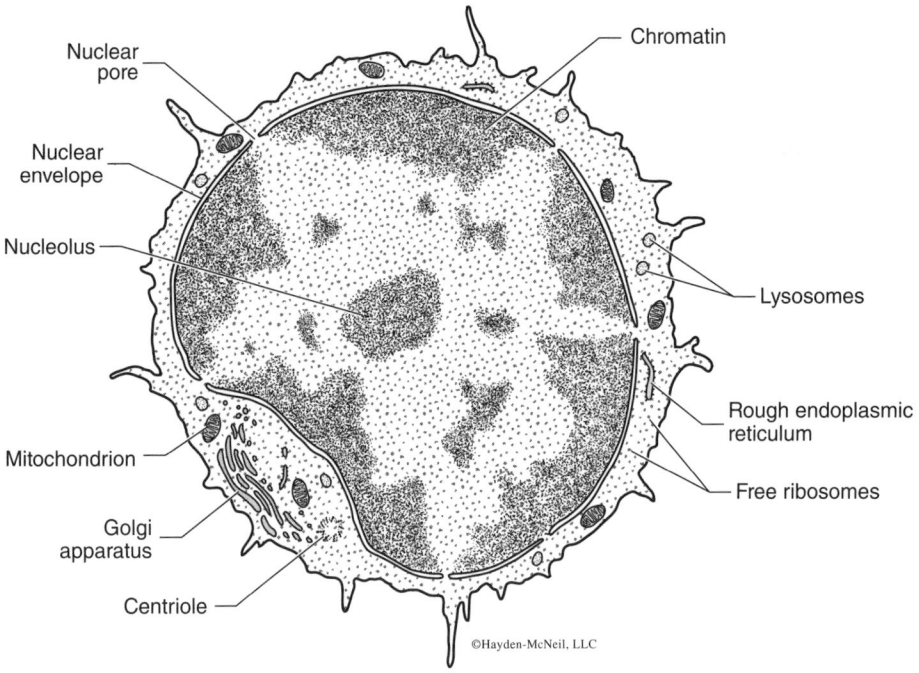

"Resting" lymphocyte

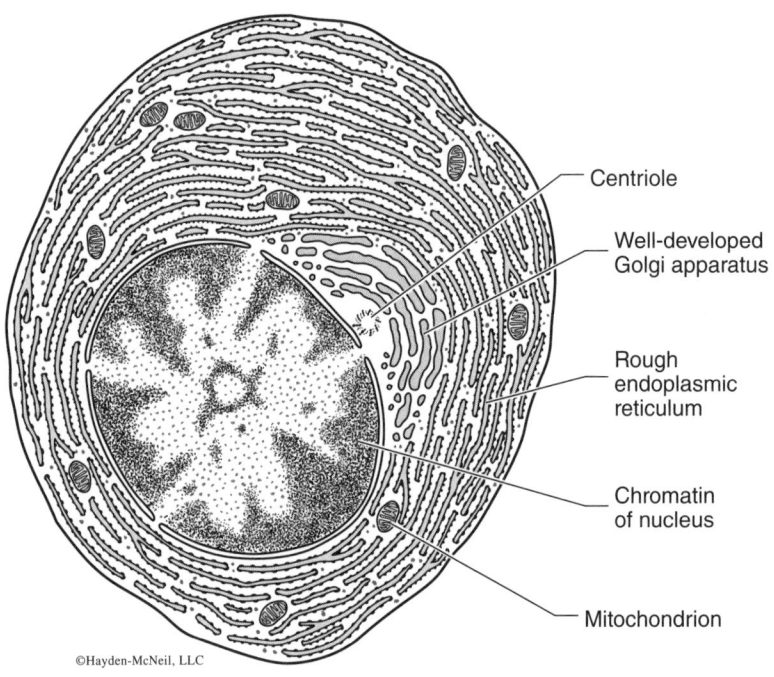

Activated B-lymphocyte
Synthesizing and secreting
antibodies

Figure 2-1. A resting white blood cell and another white cell synthesizing and secreting large quantities of proteins called antibodies. Note the enormous increase in rough endoplasmic reticulum and the increased size of the Golgi in the lower cell.

Table 1. Cytoplasmic Organelles/Membrane Structures

Organelle	Structure	Function
Endoplasmic reticulum (smooth and rough)	Network of membranes forming sacs and canals.	Transports materials within the cell, provides attachment for ribosomes, and synthesizes lipids.
Ribosomes	Particles composed of protein and ribosomal RNA.	Synthesize proteins.
Golgi apparatus	Group of flattened, membranous sacs.	Packages and processes proteins and other macromolecules for secretion or for transport to other parts of the cell. In this context it can be thought of as similar to a post office; it packages and labels "items" and then sends them to different parts of the cell.
Mitochondria	Derived evolutionarily from bacteria.	Oxidize carbon fuels, the energy released being packaged in ATP molecules.
Lysosomes	Membranous vesicles.	Represent the cell's garbage disposal system. Contain enzymes capable of digesting substances that enter cells and worn-out organelles such as mitochondria.
Peroxisomes	Membranous vesicles.	Contain enzymes.
Centrosomes	Nonmembranous structures composed of two rod-like centrioles.	Help distribute chromosomes to daughter cells during cell reproduction and initiate formation of cilia.
Cilia, flagella	Hair-like projections from the cell surface that contain microtubules and can move back and forth.	Cilia and flagella are motile.
Microvilli	Fingerlike protrusions of the plasma membrane.	Increase surface area.
Vesicles	Membranous sacs.	Contain various substances that recently entered the cell and store newly synthesized molecules.
Microfilaments and microtubules	Structures that sometimes form a meshwork in the cytoplasm.	Support cytoplasm and help move substances and organelles within the cytoplasm.
Inclusions	Examples include lipid droplets, glycogen and melanin granules.	Storage of triglycerides, carbohydrates: melanin granules, which cause skin pigmentation.

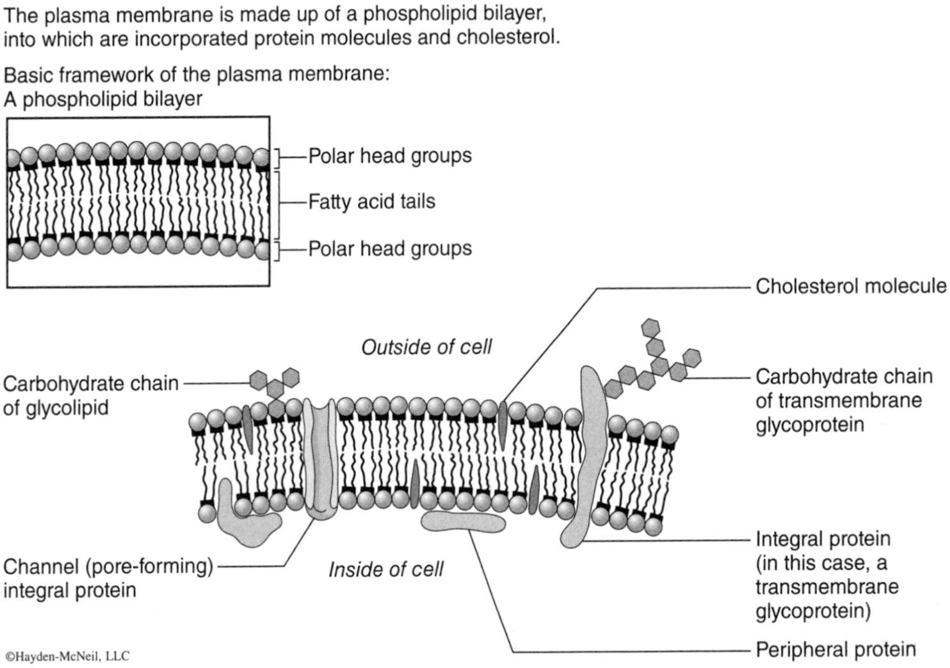

The plasma membrane is made up of a phospholipid bilayer, into which are incorporated protein molecules and cholesterol.

Basic framework of the plasma membrane:
A phospholipid bilayer

©Hayden-McNeil, LLC

Figure 2-2. The cell membrane.

B. The Cytoplasm

C. The Nucleus

The nucleus is surrounded by the nuclear envelope, which contains nuclear pores that allow passage of large molecules between the nucleus and cytoplasm.

1. **nucleolus**—produces ribosomes that travel from the nucleus into the cytoplasm

2. **chromatin**—molecules of DNA that contain the information needed for protein synthesis

3. **nuclear matrix**—consists of a variety of molecules that play a role in gene expression.

II. Movement of Substances Through the Cell Membrane

Passage of material into and out of the cell occurs via two types of processes

- **Physiological processes** require energy. Examples are active transport, endocytosis, and exocytosis.

- **Physical processes** do not require the expenditure of energy. They include simple diffusion, **facilitated diffusion**, and osmosis. Substances move down their concentration gradients. That is, they move from an area where the concentration of the substance is high to an area where the concentration of the substance is low.

Osmosis is the term used for the diffusion of water through the cell membrane. Since phospholipids do not permit water to diffuse through them, water passes through special channels formed by proteins called **aquaporins**.

If the concentration of solutes is different on each side of the membrane, **water will osmotically cross the selective membrane** and tend to equalize the concentrations of solute on each side. Solutions with a high concentration of solute have low water potential; and solutions with a low concentration of solute have a high water potential. Water flows from regions with a high water potential to regions with a low water potential.

Consider a cell that is impermeable to solute but permeable to water and place it in a solution where the solute concentration outside the cell is greater than the solute concentration inside the cell. That is, the cell is placed in a solution where the water potential inside the cell is higher than outside. In other words, the solution is hypertonic with respect to the cell. By osmosis, water will flow from inside the cell, where the water potential is high, to the outside of the cell, where the water potential is lower. The cell therefore loses volume and shrinks.

Now suppose we place the cell in a solution where the solute concentration outside the cell is less than the solute concentration inside the cell. That is, the cell is placed in a solution where the water potential is higher than inside the cell. In other words, the solution is hypotonic with respect to the cell. By osmosis, water will flow from outside the cell, where the water potential is high, to the inside of the cell, where the water potential is lower. The cell therefore gains volume, swells, and may burst or lyse.

high solute concentration	low water potential
low solute concentration	high water potential

Water flows from high water potential to low water potential.

If the cell is in a hypertonic solution	solution has lower water potential than cell interior, water flows out of cell
If the cell is in a hypotonic solution	solution has higher water potential than cell interior, water flows into cell
If the cell is in an isotonic solution	solution has same water potential as cell interior, no net flow of water into or out of the cell

Clinical Application. Treatment for a person who has lost blood volume as a result of injury or hemorrhage is to replace his or her blood volume via intravenous transfusion of fluid. You mustn't use pure water. Pure water is hypotonic, and the red blood cells (RBCs) will expand and perhaps burst (hemolysis) as water moves into them. You obviously cannot use seawater since it is hypertonic to human cells. If RBCs are placed in a hypertonic solution they will shrink (crenate) as water moves out of the cells. Therefore, the transfusion fluid must be **isotonic**. That is, the fluid contains the same concentration of solutes as the inside of the blood cell. Therefore, there is no net flow of water across the cell membrane and the cell maintains its correct shape. Note: A 0.9% sodium chloride solution is isotonic for human cells, and is called isotonic saline or normal saline.

**Define each solution in which the cell is immersed:
hypertonic, hypotonic, and isotonic**

Insert arrows to show direction of water movement (if any).

- Water molecule
O Large impermeable molecule

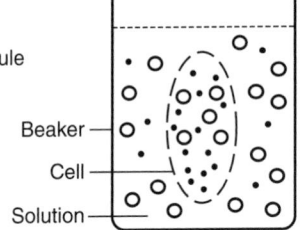

Beaker—
Cell—
Solution—

Beaker = high concentration of O
Cell = low concentration of O

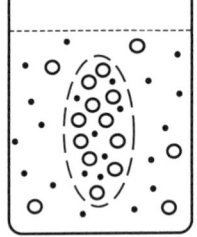

Beaker = low concentration of O
Cell = high concentration of O

NOTE: The pores in the membrane are big enough for the water molecules to pass through, but too small for the larger molecules to pass through.

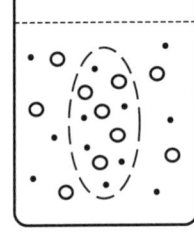

Beaker and cell = equal concentrations of O

III. Life Cycle of the Cell

Different types of cells have different life cycles. It is particularly important to note that **NOT ALL CELLS DIVIDE IN THE MATURE ADULT.**

1. **Skeletal** and **cardiac muscle** cells *rarely* do.

   Differentiated **neurons** are also in this category.

2. Other cells continuously divide. One example is the cells that form the stratum germinativum in the skin.

3. Yet other cells can be regarded as *quiescent*—that is, they have opted out of the cell cycle after mitosis. Liver cells are a particularly interesting example. Normally, liver cells do not go on dividing after adulthood has been reached. However, if it is damaged in any way, the liver is unique in that the hepatocytes start to divide. They continue to do so until the mass of the liver is restored.

Dividing cells pass through the **M phase** when they are dividing, followed by **interphase** when they are growing and synthesizing DNA, followed by the M phase again.

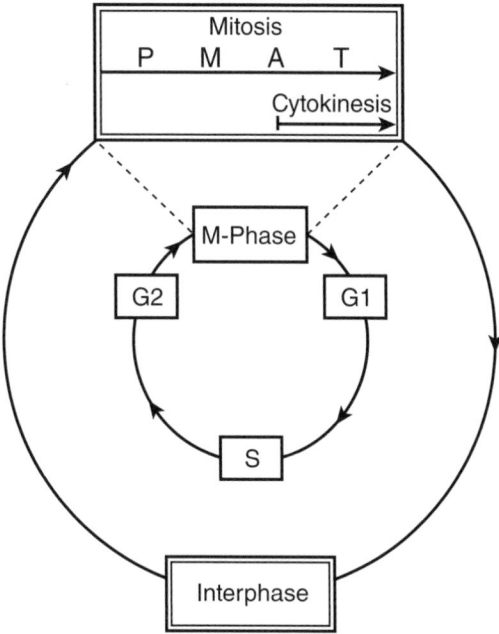

Figure 2-3. The cell cycle.

A. Interphase

During the first part of interphase, known as G1 or gap 1, the chromosomes **decondense**, and there is a large increase in the biosynthetic activity of the cell, which was virtually shut down during the M phase. The next part of the interphase, known as S, involves DNA synthesis (**replication**) and continues until all the 46 single chromosomes have been replicated. During the next cell division, each replicated chromosome will be seen as a twinned structure consisting of the two "sister" chromatids. During this time the centrosome is replicated. After S phase, the cell enters G2 (gap 2) phase, where it prepares for the onset of a new M phase and another round of division.

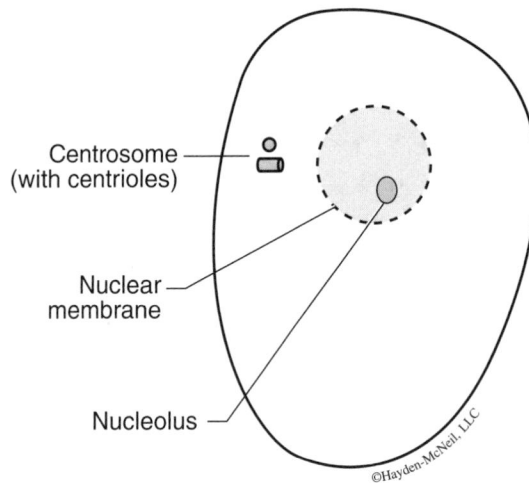

Centrosome
(with centrioles)

Nuclear
membrane

Nucleolus

©Hayden-McNeil, LLC

Figure 2-4. Interphase.

B. M Phase

Mitosis

Mitosis is divided into **prophase, metaphase, anaphase**, and **telophase**. Below is a description of each of these phases.

1. **Prophase**—The first stage, prophase, is characterized by changes in both the nucleus and the cytoplasm. The chromatin in the nucleus begins to condense and form visible chromosomes. While the chromosomes are condensing, the nucleolus disappears.

    Each chromosome appears to consist of two halves joined by a button-like structure known as a **centromere**. Each half, called a **chromatid**, is actually a complete chromosome.

    The centrosomes (each made up of two centrioles) begin to separate, moving toward opposite poles of the cell. As the centrosomes separate, microtubules extend from one pair to the other forming a structure called the mitotic spindle. Eventually, the centrosomes will be at opposite ends of the cell, with the mitotic spindle stretched between them.

    While this has been going on, the nuclear membrane has begun to disappear by breaking up into small vesicles and dispersing itself about the cytoplasm.

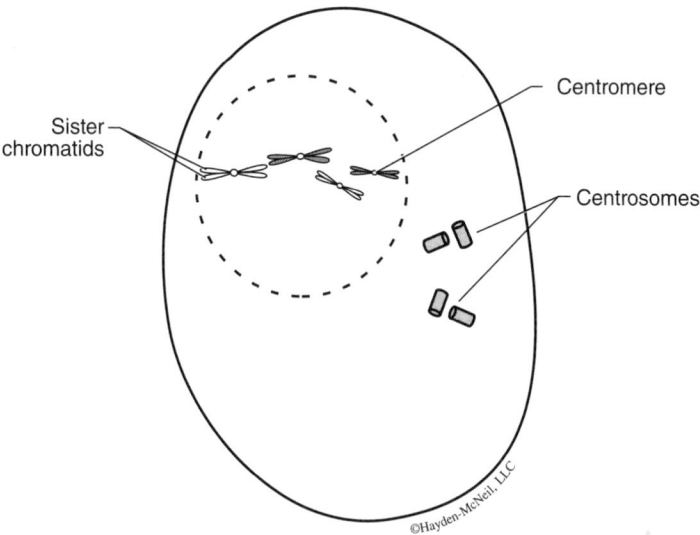

Figure 2-5. Prophase.

2. **Metaphase**—In metaphase, there is no recognizable nucleus, but the mitotic spindle is stretched across the cell, and the chromosomes are clearly discernible. The centromere for each chromosome becomes attached to a spindle fiber, and the chromosomes move, so as to lie across the middle of the spindle. This is sometimes called the **metaphase plate** or **equatorial plate**.

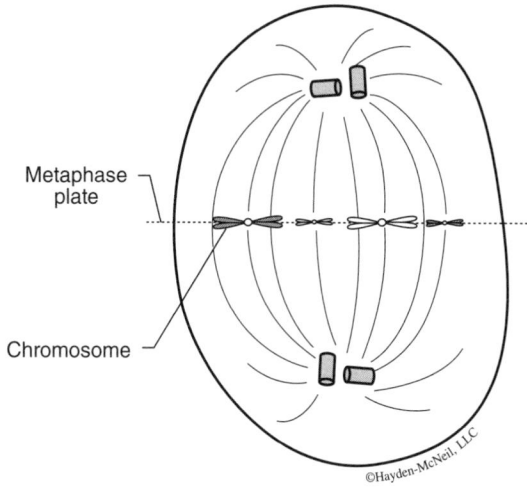

Figure 2-6. Metaphase.

3. **Anaphase**—In anaphase, the centromeres divide, so that there is one for each chromatid. One centromere is attached to a spindle fiber that leads to one end of the cell and the other is attached to a fiber leading to the other end. The chromatids separate from each other. The microtubules draw the centromeres, each with a chromosome attached, away from the center of the cell toward one centrosome or the other. Toward the end of anaphase, there are identical clusters of chromosomes at opposite ends of the cell.

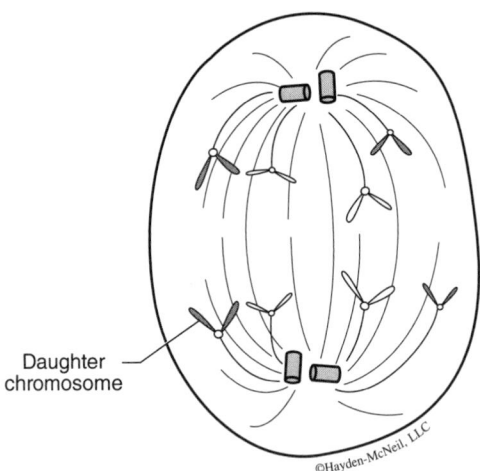

Daughter chromosome

©Hayden-McNeil, LLC

Figure 2-7. Anaphase.

4. **Telophase**—Telophase is the final stage of mitosis. During this phase, the nuclear membrane reforms, the nucleus reforms, the chromosomes unwind and disperse, the nucleolus reappears, and a new cell cycle begins for the two daughter cells.

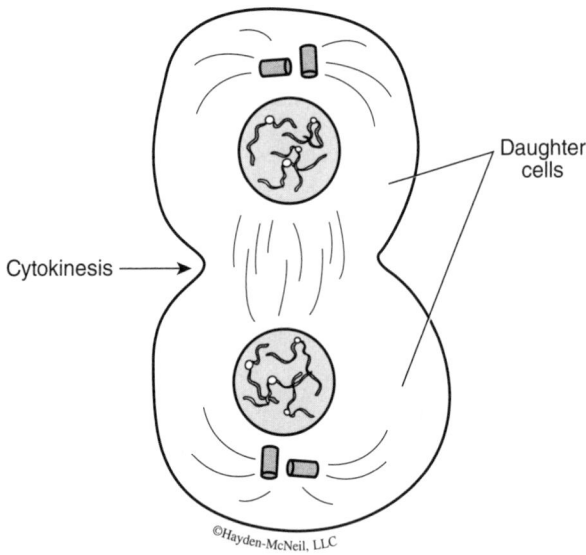

Daughter cells

Cytokinesis

©Hayden-McNeil, LLC

Figure 2-8. Telophase.

Cytokinesis

Mitosis is nuclear division. **Cytokinesis** starts in the middle of anaphase and represents cytoplasmic division. During anaphase a contractile ring forms around the middle of the cell. It forms over the former location of the metaphase plate. The contraction of a ring of actin microfilaments progressively squeezes the cell into two new cells. The cytoplasm and organelles are distributed equally between these two cells. The end of cytokinesis signals the end of the M phase.

C. Cell Differentiation

All the cells of your body originated from a single fertilized egg cell (oocyte). During development, this cell has divided many times. At some point, the daughter cells start to look different from one another. Some become skin cells, others become bone cells, and still others become nerve cells and so on. This process is called **differentiation**. During this process, some cells **withdraw from the cell cycle** (i.e., cease to divide), while others continue to divide throughout life.

D. Cell Cycle Checkpoints

E. Apoptosis—Cell Suicide or Programmed Cell Death

Exercise A

Demonstration of hypertonic/hypotonic and isotonic solutions: observing **the movement of water** across a selectively permeable membrane.

Osmosis—Although we cannot obtain a cell big enough to measure the effects of osmosis, in this class we can simulate these processes. Dialysis tubing is an artificial membrane with microscopic pores similar in size to those in your kidney. Today, we will fill dialysis tubing with different solutions to observe osmosis.

Using dialysis tubing you will **investigate the movement of WATER** across a selectively permeable membrane. We will test the dialysis tubing for the movement of water by observing a change in weight. THE SOLUTE USED IN THIS STUDY **CANNOT MOVE ACROSS THE SELECTIVELY PERMEABLE MEMBRANE!**

1. Obtain three 10–15 cm lengths of dialysis tubing, 6 tubing closures, and 3 beakers. Clip one end of each piece of tubing tightly with the tubing closure. The clip works best if approximately 1 cm of tubing extends beyond the clip.

"Artificial Cell"

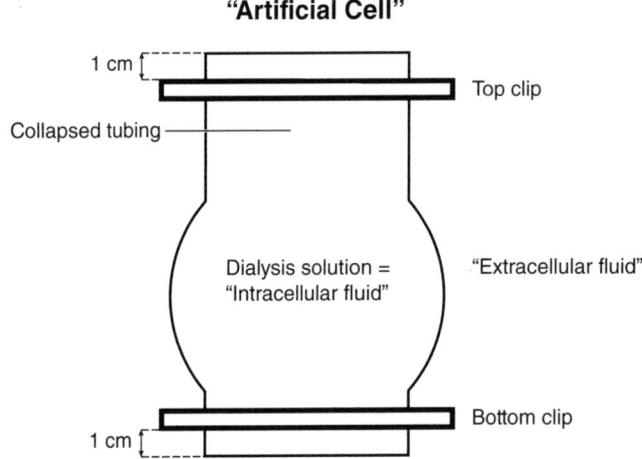

2. Fill the **tubes** according to the following schedule. Be certain no water is in the tube before you start. Work with your partner to add the solution and remove the excess air as in the figure below. Clip the top of the tube with a second closure (~1 cm from end). This will leave an area of collapsed tubing, YOU MUST HAVE AN AREA OF COLLAPSED TUBING.

	Tubing Contents (20–25 ml)	Beaker Contents
Setup A	solution X	solution A
Setup B	solution X	solution B
Setup C	solution X	solution C

3. With the tubes all filled, rinse the outside of the bags (= artificial cell) gently with distilled water. Thoroughly dry it with paper towels and weigh the dried bags filled with solution ("intracellular fluid"). Record the weight on your data sheet.

4. Fill the beakers using the schedule above with 200 ml of the given solutions. Place the appropriate clipped and weighed bag in the solution. The bag must be completely immersed in the solution. Record your start time for each setup in the space provided below.

5. After 60–80 minutes have elapsed, remove the bag from the beaker. We want to find out if water osmotically moved across the selectively permeable membrane. Dry and reweigh the bags. Record your results in the space provided below.

Exercise A: Data Collection

Setup 1:

Start time: _____   Finish time: _____

Initial weight of bag ("intracellular"): _____(indicate units)

Final weight of bag ("intracellular"):_____(indicate units)

Weight change of bag ("intracellular"): _____(increase or decrease?)

Setup 2:

Start time: _____   Finish time: _____

Initial weight of bag ("intracellular"): _____(indicate units)

Final weight of bag ("intracellular"):_____(indicate units)

Weight change of bag ("intracellular"): _____(increase or decrease?)

Setup 3:

Start time: _____   Finish time: _____

Initial weight of bag ("intracellular"): _____(indicate units)

Final weight of bag ("intracellular"):_____(indicate units)

Weight change of bag ("intracellular"): _____(increase or decrease?)

Exercise B

Observe a General Animal Cell at high power. Draw one of the cells in view. Label the cell membrane, nucleus, and cytoplasm. Can you identify any organelles? Why/why not?

Exercise C

Obtain a prepared slide of a whitefish blastula that shows the stages of the cell cycle. Begin by examining the slide under low power. You should be able to see differences among some of the cells as you scan the slide. Now, switch to high power when you are located over cells actively dividing (in mitosis). Continue to search the slide locating the four different stages of mitosis among the cells. Identify the stage and obtain your TA's verification if you are unsure. Remember, you may see a slide like these again on a test. You may be asked to show your notes/drawings for participation points. You will be asked to identify the mitotic stage of the cell in view.

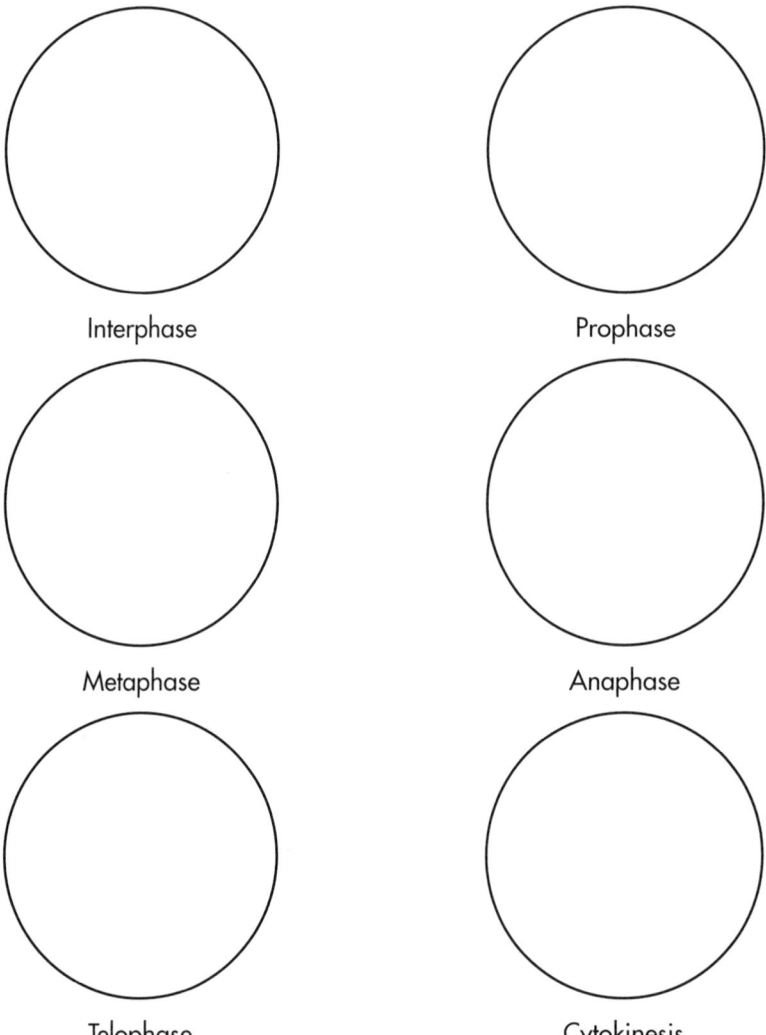

Interphase	Prophase
Metaphase	Anaphase
Telophase	Cytokinesis

LABORATORY

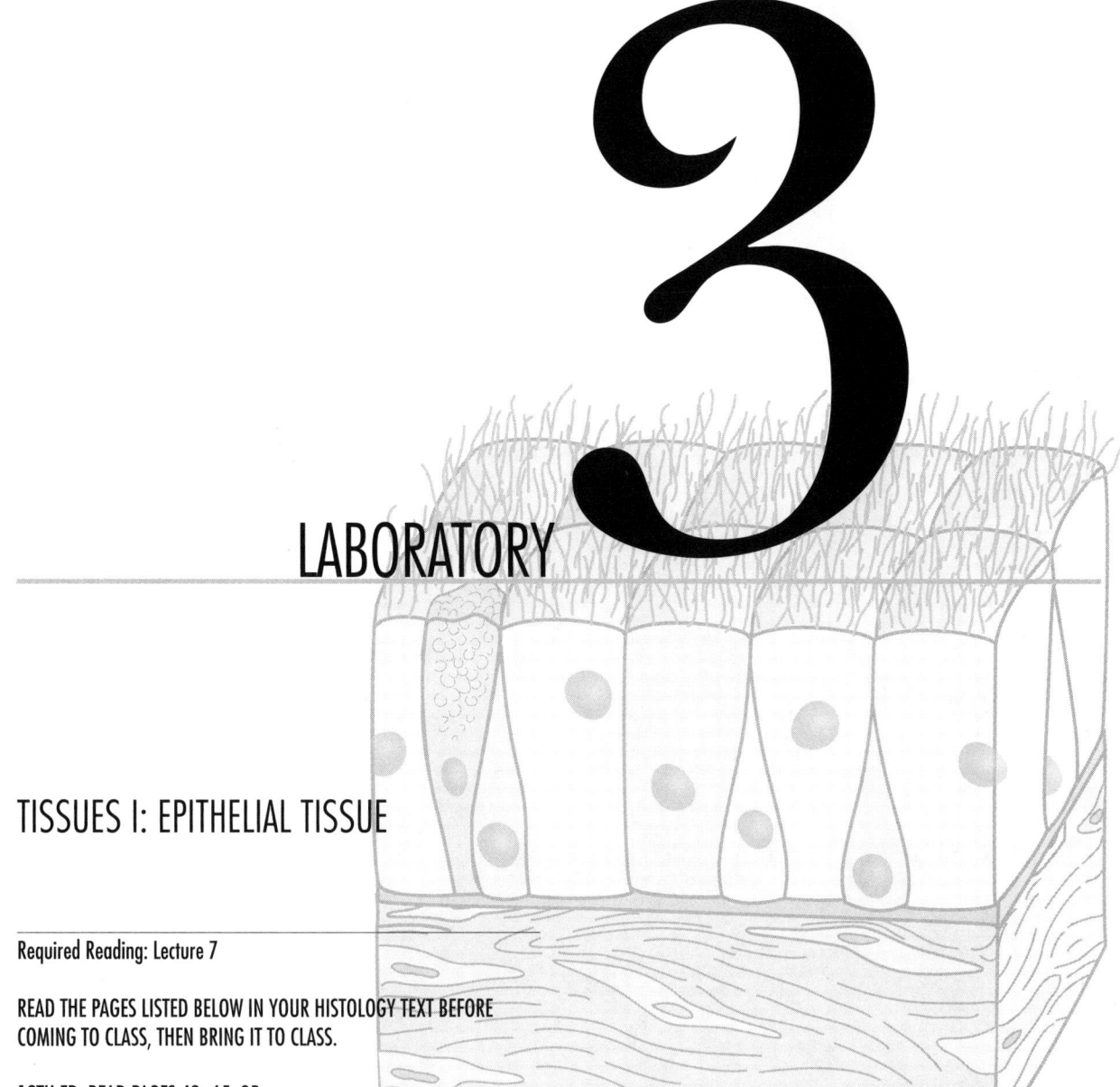

TISSUES I: EPITHELIAL TISSUE

Required Reading: Lecture 7

READ THE PAGES LISTED BELOW IN YOUR HISTOLOGY TEXT BEFORE
COMING TO CLASS, THEN BRING IT TO CLASS.

12TH ED: READ PAGES 42–65, OR
11TH ED: READ PAGES 28–52

Objectives

1. To understand the **structure–function** relationship between the different types of **epithelial cells**.

2. To be able to name and **visually identify histological** preparations of **epithelial cells**.

3. To be able to list where a particular epithelial cell may be found and how it **functions** at that particular **location**.

4. Draw and label a diagram to show the **general layout** of an epithelium.

5. List and describe the seven types of **epithelium**, and state the **organs** in which they are found.

I. Tissues of the Body

Tissues are made up of many cells and are classified into four types.

In today's lab, we are going to concentrate on **epithelial tissue**. The other three tissue types that we will be discussing over the next several weeks will be **connective**, **muscle**, and **nervous** tissue.

A. Epithelial Tissue

Epithelial tissue covers all surfaces in the human body. These surfaces include the outer surface of the body (skin), the linings of the body's cavities and also the linings of hollow organs such as the gut. Additionally, endocrine and exocrine glands develop from epithelial tissue.

Despite the differences in function, certain characteristics are common to all epithelial tissue. Epithelial cells are structurally polarized; one end of the cell is a free surface that borders the space that the epithelium lines. The opposite end of the cell is anchored, usually to connective tissue, by the **basement membrane**, which contains collagen IV, laminin, and proteoglycans. There are no blood vessels within epithelial tissue. However, the underlying connective tissue is well supplied with blood vessels.

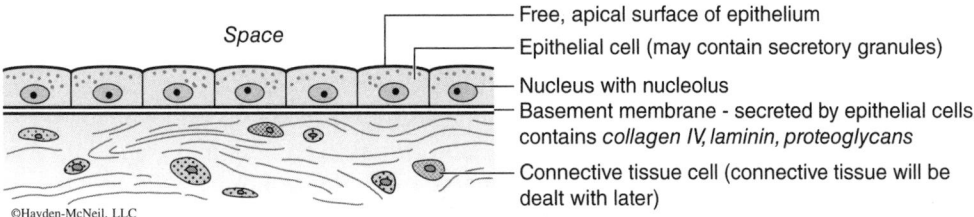

©Hayden-McNeil, LLC

Figure 3-1. Structure of epithelium.

Classification of Epithelial Tissue

The cells that make up epithelial tissue have various arrangements and shapes. There are three ways the **cells** of **epithelial tissue** can be **arranged**:

1. **simple**—a single layer

2. **stratified**—two or more layers on top of one another

3. **pseudostratified**—appears stratified but really only a single layer of cells.

There are three basic cell shapes:

1. **squamous**—thin, flat cells like floor tiles

2. **cuboidal**—like dice

3. **columnar**—width of cell shorter than height.

So, putting together the adjectives for arrangement and shape, we have our types of epithelial tissue. For example, a single layer of cube shaped cells would be called **simple cuboidal**. Or, columnar cells which appear stratified but are really in a single layer would be called **pseudostratified columnar**. If these same cells would have cilia present, the name changes to **pseudostratified ciliated columnar**.

1. **Simple Squamous Epithelium**—This type of epithelium is composed of flattened, irregularly shaped cells arranged in a single layer. Substances diffuse easily through it. As a result, simple squamous epithelium is located in the alveoli of the lung (the site where the exchange of oxygen and carbon dioxide occurs), and also in that part of the kidney that is responsible for the filtration of blood. It can also be found lining the blood vessels, lining body cavities, and covering visceral organs.

   The simple squamous epithelium lining blood vessels is called **vascular endothelium**, while that which lines body cavities and covers the viscera is called **mesothelium**.

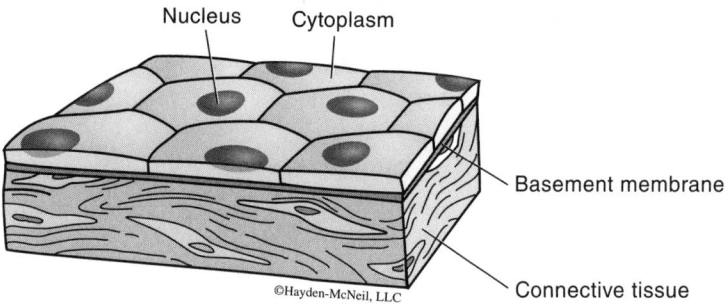

Figure 3-2. Simple squamous epithelium.

2. **Simple Cuboidal Epithelium**—This epithelial type is made up of a single layer of cube-shaped cells that function toward absorption, secretion, and excretion. As a result, it can be found covering the surface of the female ovaries, lining the capsule of the lens of the eye, and forming the tubule system in the kidneys where it is involved in the reabsorption of water. It can also be found lining small ducts and glands where secretion is involved.

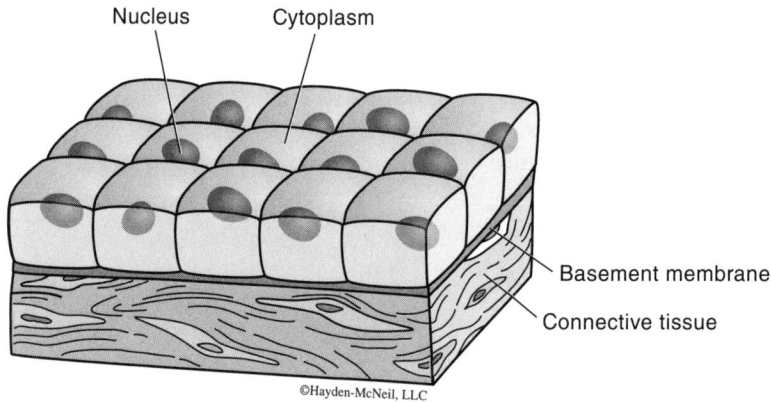

Figure 3-3. Simple cuboidal epithelium.

3. **Simple Columnar Epithelium**—A single layer of cells that appear elongated or rectangular make up this type of epithelium. Each cell contains a nucleus that is located near the basement membrane. Depending on the site and function of this tissue, certain modifications may or may not be present. For example, simple columnar cells that line the small intestine exhibit tiny projections called **microvilli** that extend into the lumen of the small intestine. The microvilli function to increase the surface area of the columnar cells that function to absorb nutrients as they pass through the small intestine. Also among the columnar cells of the small intestine are mucus-secreting **goblet cells**, so called because the mucus accumulates at one end of the cell causing it to bulge out giving it the appearance of a wine glass. The mucus, when secreted, serves as a lubricant between the wall of the small intestine and the food passing through it. A third modification is **cilia** that are found on the columnar cells of the upper respiratory tract and in the female's uterus and Fallopian tubes.

   Simple columnar epithelium can also be found in the stomach, nasal sinuses, and the central canal of the spinal cord.

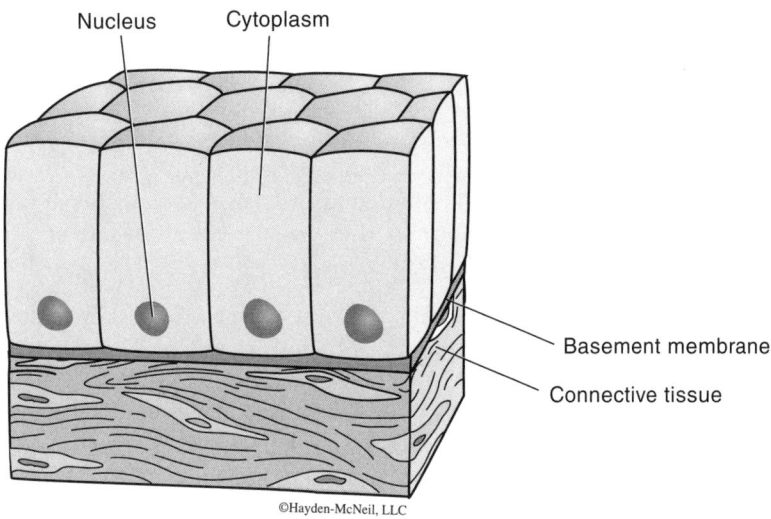

©Hayden-McNeil, LLC

Figure 3-4. Simple columnar epithelium.

4. **Pseudostratified Columnar Epithelium**—As the name suggests, this type of epithelium is made up of columnar cells that appear stratified. In reality, however, each cell of this epithelial type makes contact with the basement membrane and therefore has a simple arrangement. The reason that it appears stratified is because the nuclei of the cells occur at varying depths within the cell. Both cilia and goblet cells are present among these cells; the cilia constantly sway back and forth and the goblet cells secrete mucus. This type of tissue is found in the upper respiratory tract (the trachea) and also in some parts of the male reproductive system. In respiration, this epithelium functions to entrap foreign particles in the mucus and then to remove such substances through the action of the cilia that propel the entrapped particles upward out of the respiratory tract. In the reproductive system, the cilia aid in the movement of sex cells from one region to another.

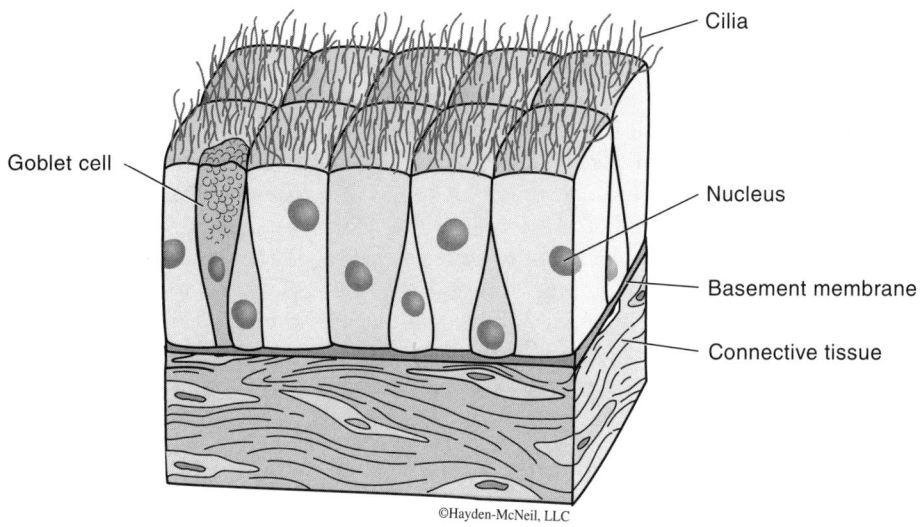

©Hayden-McNeil, LLC

Figure 3-5. Pseudostratified ciliated columnar epithelium.

5. **Stratified Squamous Epithelium**—This type of epithelium is comprised of many layers of cells. However, it is only the cells of the upper layers that take on the squamous shape. The other cells located deeper, nearer to the basement membrane, can sometimes take on a cuboidal-shaped appearance. It is at this depth that cell division occurs. As new cells are formed, they push their way upward so as to replace older cells that have been sloughed off.

Stratified squamous epithelium forms the outer layer of the skin (called the epidermis) and lines the mouth, throat, esophagus, vagina, and anal canal. There is one major difference between the stratified squamous cells of the epidermis and the cells of the other sites mentioned. In the skin, as new cells push their way to the upper layers, the accumulation of the protein **keratin** causes them to harden and die. As a result, they form a tough, protective barrier which prevents the drying out of underlying tissue and which acts as a first line of defense against invading microorganisms. In those sites other than the skin, the accumulation of keratin does not occur, leaving these cells alive.

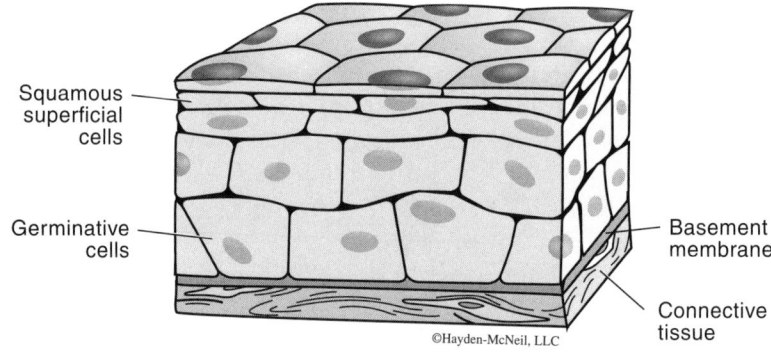

©Hayden-McNeil, LLC

Figure 3-6. Stratified squamous epithelium.

6. **Transitional Epithelium**—Transitional epithelium is constructed similarly to non-keratinized stratified squamous. The only difference is that the outer cells of transitional epithelium are not flat but rather cuboidal in shape. It is called transitional because the shape of these cuboidal cells can change under the influence of pressure. For this reason, it is located in areas where the tissue must be stretched in response to increased tension—like the urinary bladder and other parts of the urinary tract (the ureters and the urethra). So, in the contracted state, this tissue appears as several layers of cuboidal-shaped cells. In the distended state, or under the influence of pressure, the tissue will stretch as the cuboidal cells flatten out.

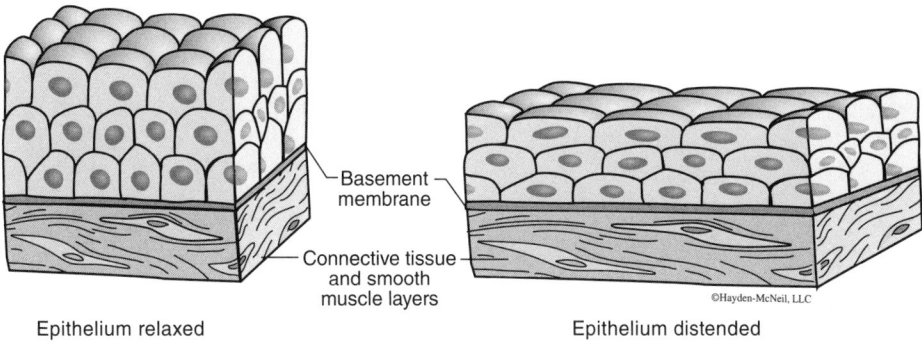

Epithelium relaxed

Epithelium distended

Basement membrane

Connective tissue and smooth muscle layers

©Hayden-McNeil, LLC

Figure 3-7. Transitional epithelium.

7. **Glandular Epithelium**—Very often, cuboidal or columnar cells form what are called **glands**—a single cell or a group of cells that secrete substances produced within the cell or group of cells into ducts, onto surfaces, into tissues, or into the blood.

The glands of the human body are of two types—exocrine and endocrine. The **exocrine** glands are those that secrete their cellular products into ducts that lead to a free surface, be it the skin or the lumen of a hollow organ. Such glands include the **sweat glands** that release perspiration in an attempt to cool the body, the **salivary glands**, and the **goblet cells**. An **endocrine** gland does not have a duct or conduit through which the secretions travel; rather these secretions are dumped directly into the bloodstream. The secretions of the endocrine glands are called hormones, chemical messengers that regulate many of the physiological processes of the human body.

Exercise A

Observe the six slides of epithelial tissue. In each case, begin your observation using the low power objective, then switch to high power. Following is space for you to draw what you observe. Make sure you are thorough with this exercise; these slides will most likely appear on a test. You may be asked to show your notes/drawings for participation points.

1. **Simple Squamous**

    cytoplasm
    nucleus
    cell membrane

Function: _____

_____

_____

_____

_____

_____

Location: _____

_____

_____

2. **Simple Cuboidal**

    cuboidal cells
    nucleus of cell
    cell membrane
    lumen of tubule

Function: _____

_____

_____

_____

_____

_____

Location: _____

_____

_____

3. **Simple Columnar**

    goblet cells
    nucleus of columnar cell
    cell membrane
    brush border (microvilli)

Function: _____

_____

_____

_____

_____

_____

Location: _____

_____

_____

4. **Pseudostratified Columnar**

    cilia
    nucleus of cell
    pseudostratified columnar cells
    goblet cells

Function: _____

_____

_____

_____

_____

_____

Location: _____

_____

_____

5. **Stratified Squamous**

   stratified squamous layer
   loose connective tissue
   basement membrane

Function: _____

_____

_____

_____

_____

_____

Location: _____

_____

_____

6. **Transitional**

   transitional cell layer
   loose connective tissue
   lumen

Function: _____

_____

_____

_____

_____

_____

Location: _____

_____

_____

LABORATORY 4

TISSUES II: CONNECTIVE TISSUE AND THE INTEGUMENTARY SYSTEM

Required Reading: Lectures 7–8

READ THE PAGES LISTED BELOW IN YOUR HISTOLOGY TEXT BEFORE
COMING TO CLASS, THEN BRING IT TO CLASS.

12TH ED: READ PAGES 66–85, 108–141, 260–283, OR
11TH ED: READ PAGES 54–97, 212–233

Objectives

1. List the **functions** of connective tissue.

2. With a diagram, illustrate the three components of generalized connective tissue.

3. Name five **cell** types found in connective tissue, and describe their functions.

4. Name two varieties of **fiber** found in connective tissue (based on the major protein found in the fibers).

5. What is a major component of the ground substance in many forms of connective tissue?

6. Name **types** of **connective tissue proper**—describe each of them, their subclasses (if any), and where they are found.

7. Name the types of **specialized connective tissue**—describe each of them, their subclasses (if any), and where they are found.

8. Understand the **structure–function relationship** between the different types of connective tissues.

9. Be able to name and describe microscopically the different connective tissues.

10. Define what is meant by a **cutaneous membrane**.

11. List the five important **physiological functions** of the **skin**.

12. With a diagram, describe the **structure** of the skin, showing all its layers.

13. In what skin cells do we find melanin and what cells produce it?

14. Stratified squamous epithelium can be non-keratinized and keratinized. Explain the difference. Explain in detail the sequence of keratinization in the layers of the skin. To what **group** of chemical substances does keratin belong?

15. Describe the structure of the dermis and hypodermis.

16. List the **accessory** structures of the skin and describe them in detail.

17. Describe the structure of a **hair follicle**.

18. Describe the types of glands in the skin.

I. Connective Tissue

Abundant throughout the body.

1. Binds structures together.

2. Supports and protects.

3. Serves as a framework.

4. Fills up spaces.

5. Stores fat.

6. Generates blood cells.

7. Protects against infections.

8. Helps repair tissue damage.

Consists of **cells** and **matrix**. The matrix consists of **fibers** and **ground substance**. The ground substance is an amorphous, homogeneous material in which the cells and fibers are embedded. Some types of connective tissue are flexible, while others (such as bone) are quite rigid.

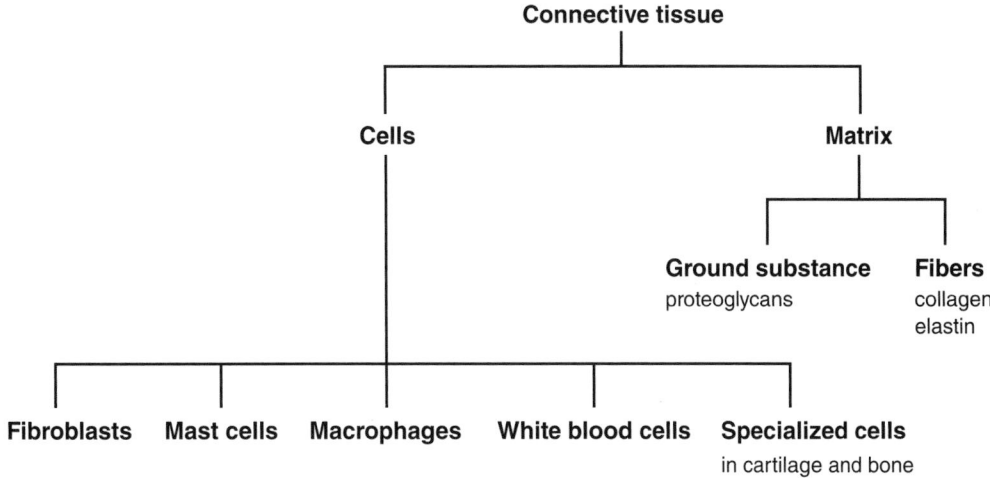

Figure 4-1. Connective tissue outline.

A. Cells of Connective Tissue

Five different cell types occur in connective tissue:

1. **Fibroblasts**

2. **Macrophages**

3. **Mast cells**

4. **White blood cells**

5. **Specialized cells**—found in cartilage and bone.

B. The Matrix of Connective Tissue

The cells of connective tissue are embedded in a matrix consisting of **ground substance** and **fibers**.

1. Two Types of Fiber

    a. **Collagenous fibers**—white fibers composed of **collagen**.

        Networks of very thin collagen fibers are sometimes spoken of as being made up of **reticular** fibers.

    b. **Elastic fibers**—yellow fibers composed mainly of the protein elastin, but also contain a protein called **fibrillin**.

2. Ground Substance

    The **ground substance** of connective tissue is usually a gel-like material composed of special protein molecules to which are attached large amounts of carbohydrates. These molecules are called **proteoglycans**. They are present in all tissues and organs. They bind water, and play an important role in maintaining the **hydration** of a tissue.

Table 1. Components of Connective Tissue—Summary

Component	Characteristic	Function
Fibroblasts	Widely distributed, large cells.	Secrete proteins (collagen, elastin) that become fibers.
Macrophages	Motile phagocytic cells.	Clear foreign particles from tissues. Part of the immune system and important in inflammation.
Mast cells	Large cells packed with granules, usually located near blood vessels.	Release substances that help prevent blood clotting and promote the inflammatory response.
White blood cells	e.g., phagocytic neutrophils	Move into connective tissue during the inflammatory response.
Specialized cells	Found in the lacunae of cartilage (chondrocytes) and bone (osteocytes).	Synthesis and maintenance of cartilage and bone.
Collagenous fibers (white fibers)	Thick fibers of collagen with great tensile strength. Thin fibers of collagen that form networks.	Form strong structures such as ligaments, reinforce connective tissue. "Reticular fibers" form supportive networks in various organs.
Elastic fibers (yellow fibers)	Composed of elastin (associated with the protein fibrillin), thinner than collagen fibers.	Found in structures subject to stretch (such as the yellow ligaments between vertebrae).

C. Classification of Connective Tissue

There are **nine** types of connective tissue.

Connective Tissue Proper

1. Loose (areolar)

2. Adipose

3. Dense Regular

4. Dense Irregular

5. Elastic

6. Reticular

Specialized Connective Tissue

7. Cartilage

   a. hyaline cartilage

   b. elastic cartilage

   c. fibrocartilage

8. Bone

9. Other types—some people include blood

II. Connective Tissue Proper

A. Loose Connective Tissue

Loose connective tissue (also called areolar connective tissue) is one of the most abundant types of connective tissue in the human body. It is composed of collagenous and elastic fibers randomly dispersed in the matrix. Numerous fibroblasts are present.

Areolar tissue exhibits both flexibility and strength. It binds tissues together yet allows flexibility and elasticity. It is found surrounding blood vessels and nerves, muscle fibers and muscle groups, and binding skin to underlying muscles.

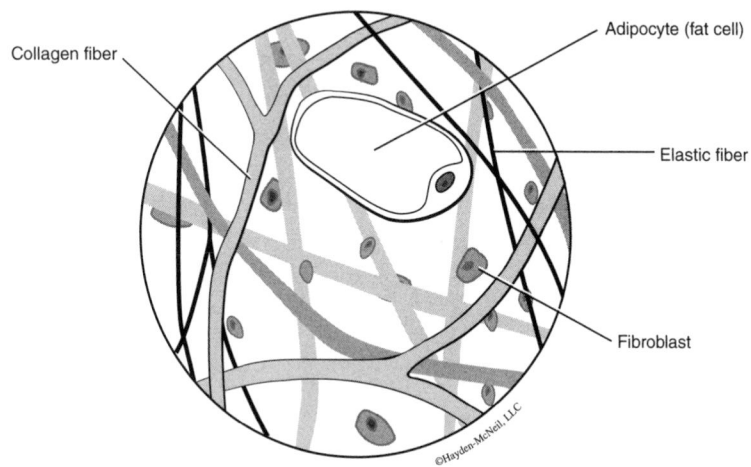

Figure 4-2. Loose connective tissue.

B. Adipose Tissue

Adipose tissue contains large numbers of cells called adipocytes. These cells, which initially resemble fibroblasts, store triglycerides (fat). The nucleus of the cell gets pushed to one side as the amount of fat increases, and the tissue takes on a characteristic foamy appearance. Adipose tissue contains no fibers. Triglycerides stored in adipose tissue represent the body's most important energy resource.

In addition to storing triglycerides, adipose tissue fills spaces, cushions and holds organs in place, acts as a shock absorber, insulates, and gives shape to the body surfaces. As a result, adipose tissue can be found just below the skin, around many organs (especially the heart and kidneys), around the eyes, and at the joints.

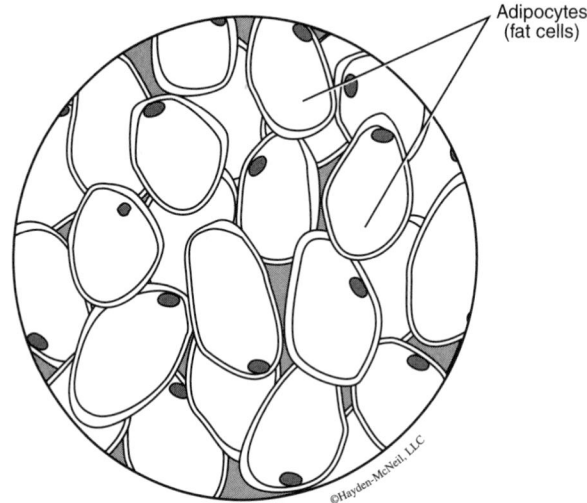

Figure 4-3. Adipose tissue.

C. Dense Regular Connective Tissue

The matrix is predominantly **collagen fibers**. They are densely packed and arranged parallel to the direction of the force. Interspersed among the collagen fibers are elastin fibers, but they are few in comparison. This tissue has a poor blood supply that makes the healing process very slow.

Dense regular connective tissue forms **tendons** (which attach muscle to bone); **ligaments** (which attach bone to bone); and **aponeuroses** (sheet-like tendons connecting one muscle with another or with bone).

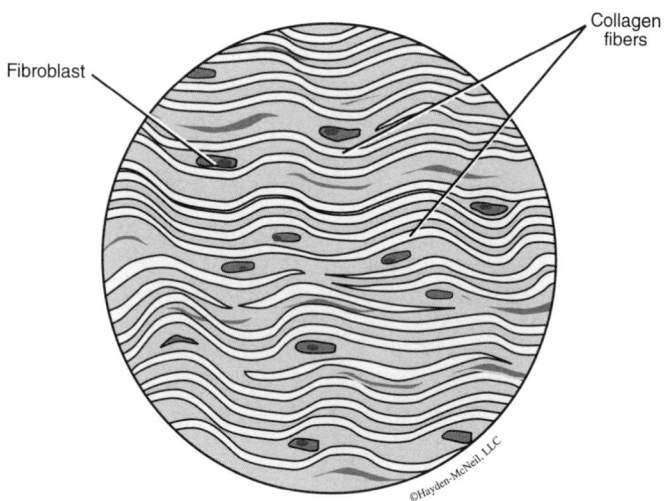

Figure 4-4. Dense regular connective tissue.

D. Dense Irregular Connective Tissue

The matrix is also predominantly **collagen fibers**. They are densely packed and are interwoven in three dimensions rather like a basket weave. Interspersed among the collagen fibers are elastic fibers, but they are much fewer in comparison. This arrangement provides strength in all directions as opposed to **one** direction as in dense regular connective tissue. This tissue also has a limited blood supply that makes the healing process very slow.

Dense irregular connective tissue is found in the **dermis** of the skin, in **sheaths** covering muscles, nerves, and in the **adventitia** of blood vessels. It is also found forming **capsules** covering various organs and joints, making up the sclera of the eye and the **membrane** covering cartilage (**perichondrium**) and bone (**periosteum**).

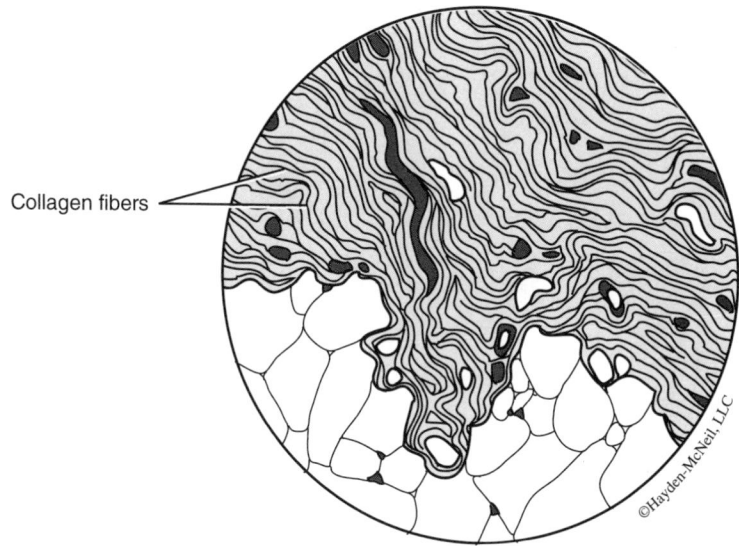

Figure 4-5. Dense irregular connective tissue.

E. Elastic Connective Tissue

The fibers are composed of the protein elastin, arranged parallel or in irregular branching patterns. A few collagen fibers may be present, together with a small amount of the important protein fibrillin. This tissue can be stretched to about one and a half times, and can return to its original length by elastic recoil. It is present in the walls of arteries, in the trachea and lungs, in the larynx, and between adjacent vertebrae (yellow ligaments or **ligamenta flava**).

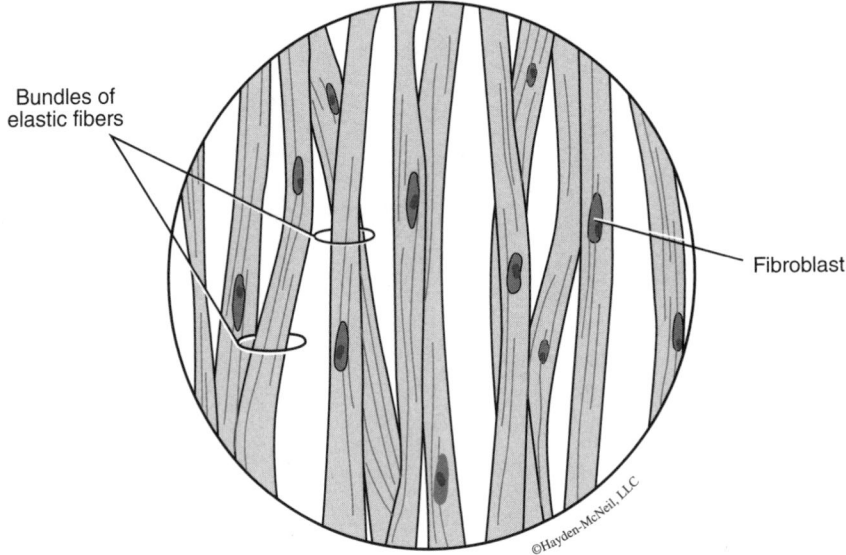

Figure 4-6. Elastic connective tissue.

F. Reticular Connective Tissue

Reticular connective tissue is made up of a network of thin collagen (reticular) fibers. It provides a supporting framework for a number of organs, including the liver, spleen, and lymph nodes.

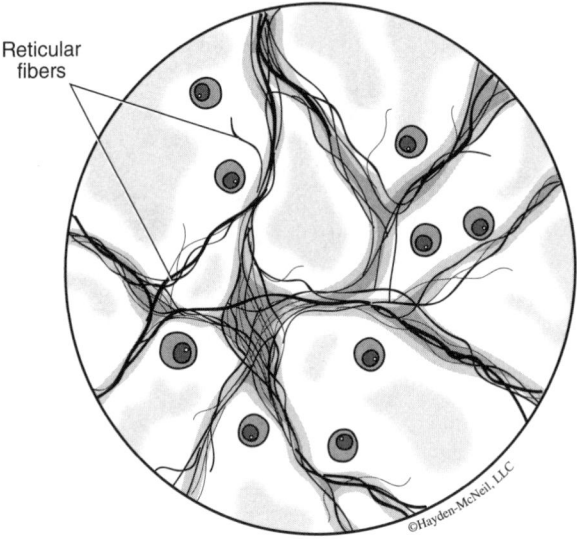

Figure 4-7. Reticular connective tissue.

III. Specialized Connective Tissue

A. Cartilage

Cartilage is avascular (contains no blood vessels) and therefore heals very slowly when torn or damaged. Nutrients are supplied from blood vessels in the perichondrium, a layer of dense irregular connective tissue that covers its surface.

Cartilage contains collagen and elastic fibers, which are produced by **chondrocytes**. These cells occur either singly or in groups within cavities in the cartilage matrix called **lacunae**.

The three types of cartilage—hyaline, elastic, and fibrocartilage—are distinguished by the type of fibers they contain.

1. Hyaline Cartilage

If anyone has ever eaten a steak and bit into a piece of gristle, you have encountered hyaline cartilage. Found at the end of bones (articular cartilage), in the nose, larynx, trachea, ribs, and respiratory tubes, this type of cartilage is the most common of the three. It is comprised of a matrix containing **collagenous** fibers. Only chondrocytes embedded in lacunae in the matrix are visible under the microscope because the collagenous fibers are very fine.

2. Elastic Cartilage

Very similar to hyaline cartilage except that **elastic** fibers predominate. This tissue can be found in the larynx and in the ear flaps.

3. Fibrocartilage

Fibrocartilage has tensile strength, weight-bearing properties, and is resistant to stretch and compression. It has many, microscopically visible **collagenous** fibers. Fibrocartilage is found in areas of the body where it can act as a shock absorber. Pads of fibrocartilage are found between the vertebrae and in joints such as the knee.

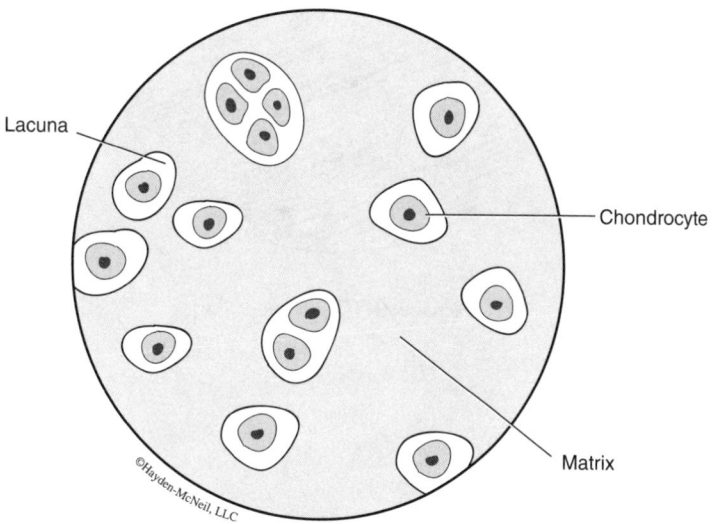

Figure 4-8. Hyaline cartilage.

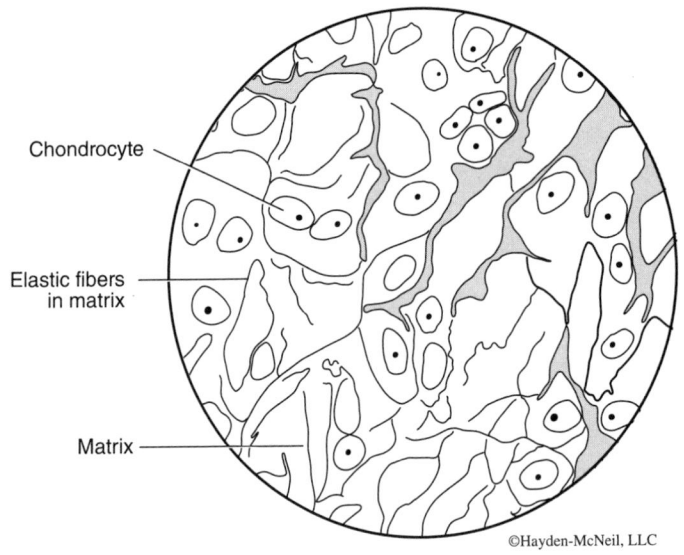

©Hayden-McNeil, LLC

Figure 4-9. Elastic cartilage.

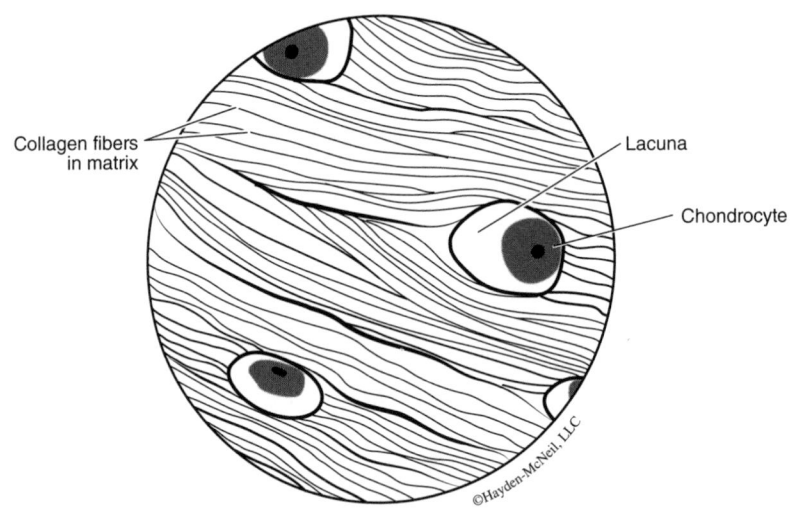

©Hayden-McNeil, LLC

Figure 4-10. Fibrocartilage.

B. Bone

The unit of compact (cortical) bone is the osteon. The center of an osteon contains a Haversian (osteonic, central) canal containing blood vessels and nerve fibers. Surrounding the Haversian canal, rather like the rings of a tree, are deposited successive layers of matrix called **lamellae**. Between the lamellae are spaces called **lacunae** which house the **osteocytes**. Each osteocyte is in contact with other osteocytes and to the blood vessels of the osteonic canal via small canals, called **canaliculi**.

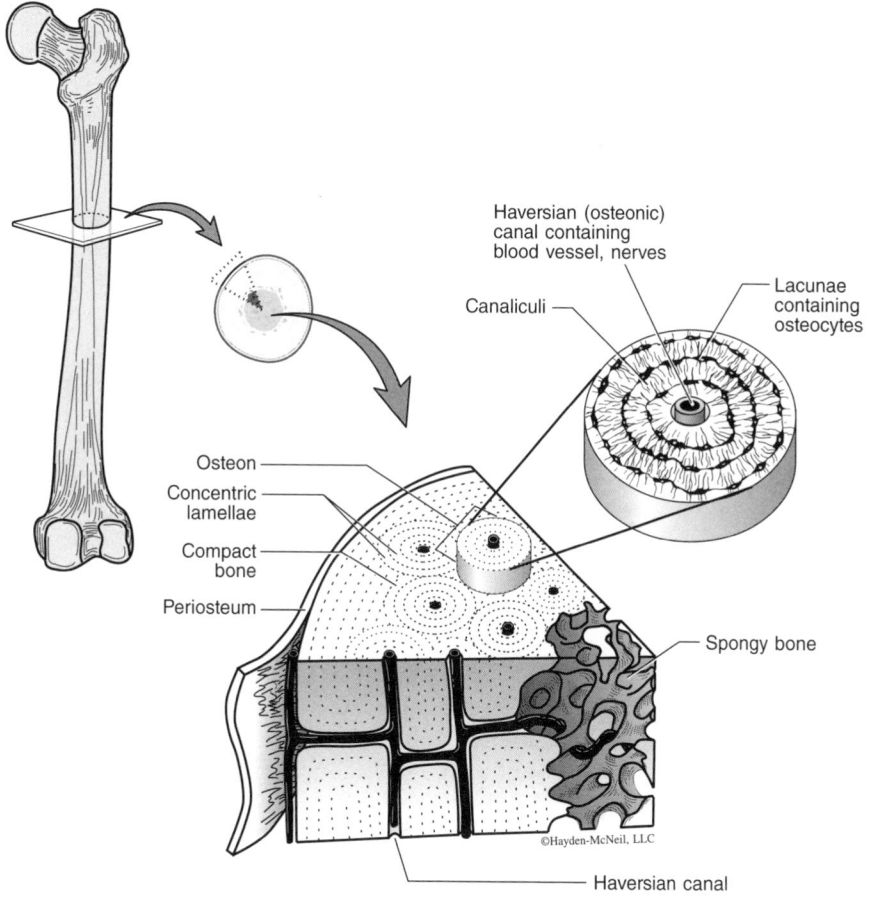

Figure 4-11. Bone.

C. Other Types—Blood

Blood is sometimes regarded as connective tissue.

IV. The Skin

The skin (together with hair and nails) is also known as the **cutaneous** membrane.

The skin is called an organ because it consists of several tissues structurally joined together to perform specific activities. Its surface area is large, about 2 square meters or 3,000 square inches.

Five Physiological Functions of the Skin

1. **Regulation of body temperature**

2. **Protection**—protects the underlying tissues against bacterial invasion, abrasion, dehydration, and ultraviolet radiation.

3. **Sensation**

4. **Excretion (minor function)**

5. **Synthesis of vitamin D**—vitamin D3 or cholecalciferol is synthesized in the skin when its precursor (7-dehydrocholesterol) is exposed to ultraviolet radiation.

Structure

Skin is divided into three layers:

1. **Epidermis**—the outer layer, is stratified squamous epithelium. As with all epithelium it has no blood vessels. A group of specialized cells called **melanocytes** produce the dark pigment **melanin**. Melanin protects deeper layers from the damaging effects of ultraviolet radiation. In some people, melanin tends to form patches called freckles. People who cannot synthesize melanin are called albinos.

   The epidermis is subdivided into four layers. From the outside, they are as follows.

   a. The **stratum corneum** is the outermost layer of the skin. It consists of a tough layer of tightly packed, flattened, fully-keratinized dead cells (about 25–30 cells thick). These cells are continually lost by abrasion.

   b. The **stratum granulosum (granular cell layer).**

   c. The **stratum spinosum (prickle cell layer).** Bundles of keratin filaments traverse the cells and are inserted into the *desmosome* junctions between them.

   d. The **stratum basale** (= **stratum germinativum, basal cell layer**) is the innermost layer. It consists of dividing cells that gradually push older cells nearer the outer surface where they finally form the stratum corneum. These older cells go through a process called *keratinization*, where they progressively die and become packed with a tough, fibrous, waterproof protein called **keratin**.

In healthy skin, new cells are produced in the stratum basale at roughly the rate at which they are lost from the stratum corneum. Normally, it takes 2–4 weeks for a cell from the basal layer to reach the stratum corneum and be lost by shedding.

In the condition known as **psoriasis** the rate of basal cell proliferation is accelerated, the epidermis thickens; cells do not have time to keratinize properly, and are shed within a week.

Excessive **rubbing** of the skin can also over stimulate cell division in the stratum basale, causing overproduction of the stratum corneum. The result is a callus or corn.

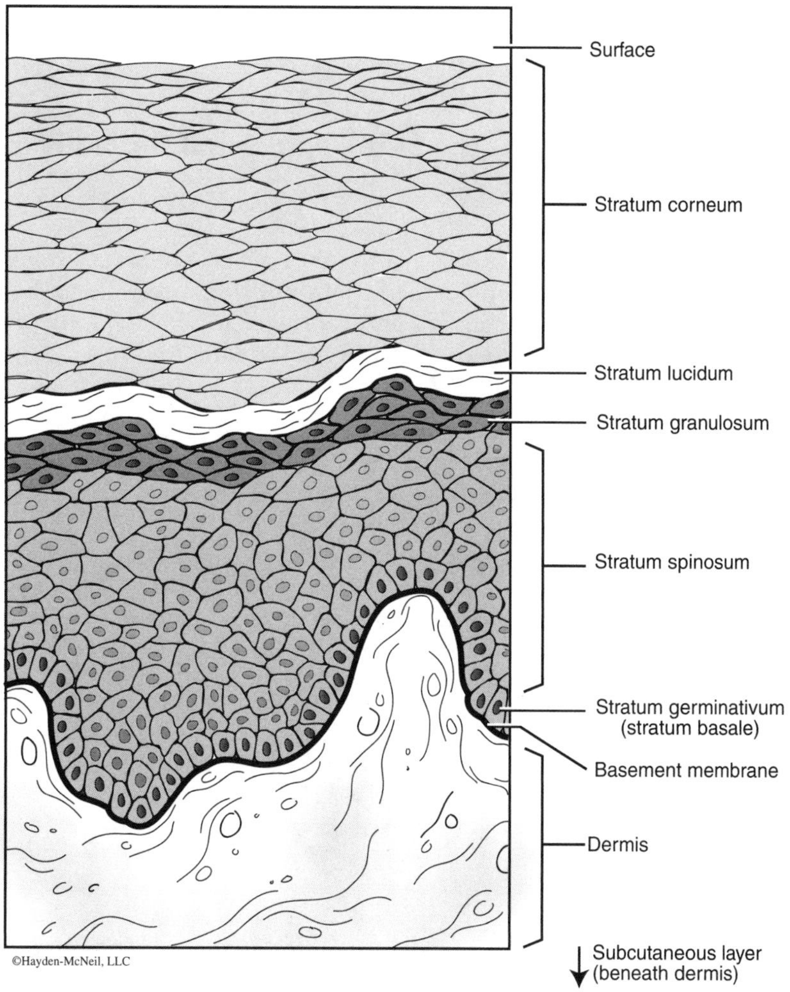

Figure 4-12. Layers of the skin.

2. The **dermis** is relatively thick. It consists mainly of dense, irregularly arranged connective tissue containing interlacing bundles of collagenous and elastic fibers. This arrangement allows the skin to stretch (e.g., during pregnancy, or when limbs are flexed at joints such as the knee and elbow). The dermis projects up into the epidermis in little humps called **dermal papillae**.

The dermis contains blood vessels and sometimes smooth muscle fibers (e.g., the skin enclosing the testes, the scrotum, and those that cause the hairs to "stand up").

Nerve fibers course through the dermis. Some are "motor," and carry signals to the dermal muscles and glands. Others have a sensory function, and carry impulses to the central nervous system after stimulation of specialized dermal sensory receptors for pressure, touch, pain, temperature, etc. (these will be discussed later).

Hair follicles and **glands** occur at various depths in the dermis, and will be discussed in the next section.

3. **Subcutaneous layer**—lies beneath the dermis. Fibers from the dermis anchor the skin to the subcutaneous layer, which is in turn attached to the underlying tissues and organs. The subcutaneous layer consists largely of loose connective tissue and adipose tissue. This layer also contains nerve fibers, and blood vessels. The adipose tissue acts as a heat insulator.

V. Accessory Structures of the Skin—Epidermal Derivatives

A. Hair Follicles

Hair follicles are structures from which hairs arise. Hair can be an insulator, but is also protective. The eyelashes protect the eyes from flying insects, for example. Hairs in the nose and ears protect the airways and external ear canal from particles and insects. Touch receptors are associated with hair follicles, and respond if the hair is gently touched.

Note that the technique of electrolysis destroys the hair-generating bulb of the hair follicle. A depilatory just removes the hair.

A smooth muscle, called the **arrector pili** extends from the dermis to the side of the hair follicle. When the muscle contracts under the stresses of fright, fear, cold, and emotions, the hair stands on end. In humans, this contraction gives "goosebumps" or "gooseflesh," because the skin around each hair shaft forms an elevation. In animals such as the cat, it causes the fur to stand on end (particularly in the tail) and makes the animal look larger and more threatening.

A **sebaceous** or oil gland is connected to the hair follicle, and is discussed next.

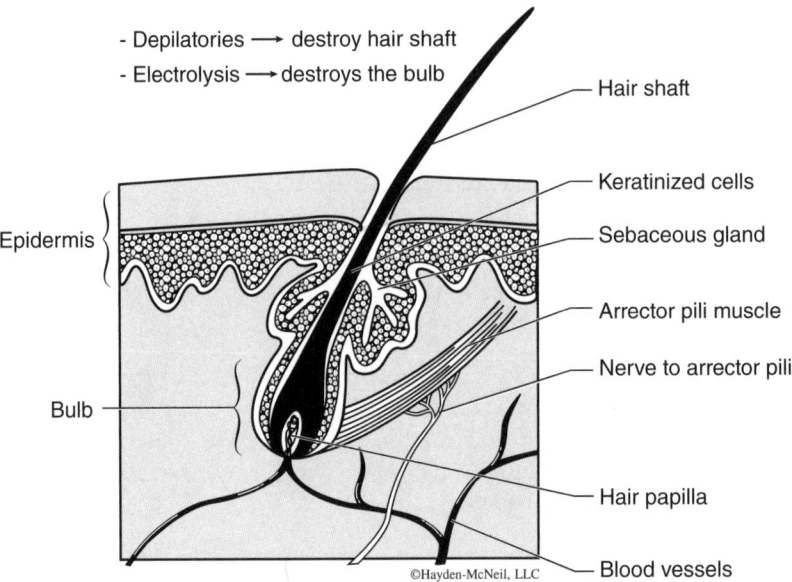

Figure 4-13. Layers and accessory structures of the skin.

B. Glands

There were supposedly three different ways glands of the skin could secrete. They were characterized based on this method.

- Holocrine glands: secretion is made up of disintegrated cells and their contents.

- Apocrine glands: cells release small parts of cell that then release their contents.

- Merocrine glands: cells produce and release secretion while remaining intact.

However, transmission electron microscope (TEM) studies suggest that apocrine glands actually release their secretion by merocrine secretion.

There are three types of glands associated with the skin.

1. **Sebaceous** glands—these are holocrine glands that are almost always associated with hair follicles. They secrete an oily material called sebum that keeps the hairs and the skin soft and pliable, forms a protective film that prevents excessive evaporation of water, and inhibits the growth of certain bacteria.

   Sometimes the sebaceous glands become enlarged because of accumulated sebum, and acne lesions called blackheads develop. Pimples or boils often develop, because sebum contains nutrients for certain bacteria. The blackhead is black because it contains melanin and oxidized oil from the sebum.

2. **Sweat (sudoriferous)** glands—these glands are divided into two types, **apocrine** sweat glands and merocrine sweat glands. In the skin, these merocrine glands have a special name: **eccrine** sweat glands.

   Eccrine sweat glands are much more common on the body surface, and their secretion is more watery than that from apocrine sweat glands. They are present everywhere except for the margins of the lips, nail beds, glans penis, glans clitoris, labia minora, and eardrums. Eccrine glands are most numerous in the skin of the palms and soles. Hence "sweaty palms" when you are under emotional stress. The sweat from eccrine sweat glands is a very dilute solution of sodium chloride (with minor proportions of other inorganic salts), lactic acid and several nitrogen-containing compounds such as urea, ammonia, amino acids, and uric acid. Other substances that need not concern us are also present in trace amounts.

   Apocrine sweat glands are mainly in the skin of the axilla, pubic region, and pigmented areas (areolae) of the breasts. The ducts of apocrine sweat glands open into hair follicles. Apocrine secretions have an odor, hence the use of deodorants, most of which are applied to the axillary region of the body.

   Eccrine glands release sweat as a secretory product. Granules fuse with the membrane of the secretory cell and release the contents. The sweat then travels up the duct, aided by myoepithelial cells between the secretory cells, where it eventually releases at the surface of the skin. Because of the bleb-like protrusions in the apical part of secretory apocrine cells, it was once thought that the product simply pinched off the membrane (apocrine secretion). Even though they are not thought to secrete by apocrine secretion, they are continued to be called apocrine sweat glands to avoid confusion with the eccrine glands.

3. **Ceruminous** glands—modified sweat glands found only in the external ear canal. The combined secretion of the ceruminous and sebaceous glands in the external ear canal forms the earwax. This material acts as a sticky barrier that prevents the entrance of foreign bodies (such as the odd bug or whatever).

C. Nails

Each nail consists of a nail **plate** (body) that overlies a surface of skin called the nail **bed**. The nail is produced by epithelial cells that reproduce and undergo keratinization in the half-moon (lunula) region of the nail.

Exercise A

You and your partner need to pick up 10 slides of connective tissue. In each case, begin your observation using the low power objective, then switch to high power. Following is space for you to draw what you observe. You may be asked to show your notes/drawings for participation points. Make sure you are thorough with this exercise; these slides will most likely appear on a test.

1. **Loose Connective** (areolar)

   elastic fibers—thin
   collagenous fiber—thick
   various cells

   Function: _____

   _____

   _____

   _____

   _____

   _____

   Location: _____

   _____

   _____

2. **Adipose**

   adipose cells
   nuclei of adipose cell
   artery/capillary

   Function: _____

   _____

   _____

   _____

   _____

   _____

   Location: _____

   _____

   _____

3. **Dense Regular Connective**

collagenous fiber—thick
nuclei not visible

Function: _____

_____

_____

_____

_____

_____

_____

Location: _____

_____

_____

4. **Dense Irregular Connective**

collagenous fiber—thick
nuclei not visible

Function: _____

_____

_____

_____

_____

_____

_____

Location: _____

_____

_____

5. **Elastic Connective**

(Ligamentum nuchae)
elastic fibers—thin
fibroblasts

Function: _____

_____

_____

_____

_____

_____

_____

Location: _____

_____

_____

6. **Reticular Connective**

    collagenous fibers
    fibroblast

Function: _____

_____

_____

_____

_____

_____

Location: _____

_____

_____

7. **Hyaline Cartilage**

    chondrocyte in lacuna
    nucleus
    differentiating chondrocytes
    collagenous fibers not seen

Function: _____

_____

_____

_____

_____

_____

Location: _____

_____

_____

8. **Fibrocartilage**

    chondrocyte in lacuna
    collagen fibers

Function: _____

_____

_____

_____

_____

_____

Location: _____

_____

_____

9. **Elastic Cartilage**

   elastic fibers
   chondrocytes
   nuclei of chondrocyte
   lacuna

Function: _____

_____

_____

_____

_____

_____

Location: _____

_____

_____

10. **Bone**

   canaliculi
   osteocyte in lacuna
   central (Haversian) canal
   lamellae
   lacunae

Function: _____

_____

_____

_____

_____

Location: _____

_____

_____

Exercise B

Observe the two slides of human skin. Begin your observation using the low power objective, then switch to high power. Below is space for you to draw what you observe. Identify the three layers of the skin, sebaceous glands, sweat glands, and hair follicles. Make sure you are thorough with this exercise; this slide will most likely appear on a test.

Exercise C

Introduction to LabTutor Activity

LABORATORY 5

SKELETAL SYSTEM AND JOINTS

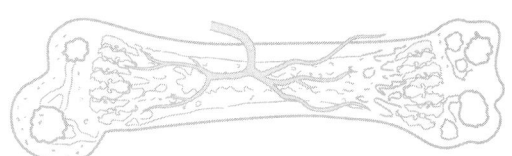

Required Reading: Lecture 9

READ THE PAGES LISTED BELOW IN YOUR HISTOLOGY TEXT BEFORE
COMING TO CLASS, THEN BRING IT TO CLASS.

12TH ED: READ PAGES 122–141, OR
11TH ED: READ PAGES 79–97

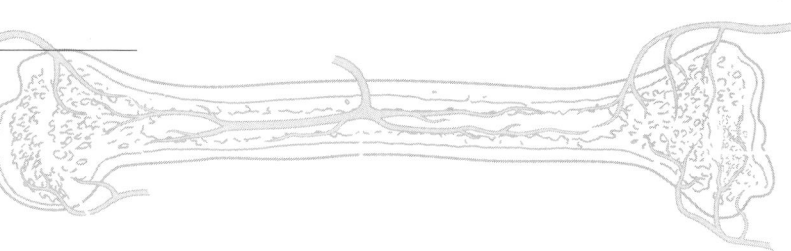

Objectives

1. Classify bones according to their shapes and name an example from each group.

2. Describe IN DETAIL the structure of the femur (include the medullary cavity, red bone marrow, types of bone in different locations, articular cartilage, periosteum, etc.) and wherever possible list the functions of the parts.

3. Explain why bone is similar to reinforced concrete. What substances are involved in bone?

4. Describe (with a diagram) the microscopic organization of compact bone. Include all features of the osteon.

5. Sketch the stress lines in the spongy bone at the head of the femur.

6. List and describe IN FULL DETAIL the four types of cells found in bone and their interrelationships. What cells give rise to osteoclasts, and how might they relate to the immune system?

7. Describe the **osteocyte-lacuno-canalicular** network, and how it is believed to function in the response of bone to stress.

8. Describe the process of ossification and distinguish intramembranous and endochondral ossification. What bones are produced by these two processes?

9. Describe the stages in the ossification of a long bone.

10. Describe how a long bone increases in length during development.

11. Describe and discuss the five important factors that are important in bone development, growth, turnover and repair. Explain in detail, with the names of its precursors, how the active form of vitamin D (calcitriol) is produced and in what tissues it is produced.

12. Lack of vitamin D causes what disease in infants? What is the condition called in adults?

13. Describe the changes in the skeleton that take place in men and women as they age.

14. Describe the cells and molecules involved in osteoporosis.

15. How is osteoporosis prevented and treated (know the difference between osteoporosis from osteopetrosis).

16. Describe three major types of joints and the structures that hold them together. List the subtypes of these joints, where applicable.

17. Describe the structures that make up a synovial joint.

18. Name two components of synovial fluid, and describe the properties of synovial fluid (use a graph).

19. Describe three types of structure associated with the knee joint.

20. List the seven types of synovial joints, giving an example of each.

21. List the major bones that make up the axial and appendicular parts of the skeleton.

22. Locate and identify the bones and the major features of the bones that make up the skull, vertebral column, thoracic cage, pectoral girdle, upper limb, pelvic girdle, and lower limb.

23. Explain how skeletal muscles interact with the skeleton to produce movements at joints.

24. Describe the following joints and explain how their articulating parts are held together: shoulder joint, elbow joint, hip joint, knee joint.

I. Introduction

Bone is similar to reinforced concrete, which consists of concrete (providing *compressional* strength) containing steel rods (providing *tensile* strength).

1. **Collagen** fibers (= steel rods) provide tensile strength.

2. **Calcium phosphate**, mainly in the form of the mineral **hydroxylapatite**, $Ca_{10}(PO_4)_6(OH)_2$ (= concrete), provides **compressional** strength (some calcium carbonate and other compounds are also present—see lecture 9).

The skeleton serves as a **support** structure and to **protect**. The bones of the skull and the vertebrae protect underlying nervous tissue while the ribs of the rib cage enclose the organs of the thoracic cavity. The bones also serve as **levers** to amplify muscle contractions. The red bone marrow of adult bones is the site where the various cells of the blood are formed, a process called **hemopoiesis** or **hematopoiesis**. The yellow marrow stores triglycerides, which are an important source of energy. The skeleton also represents the body's largest reserve of calcium, which is important in blood clotting, muscle contraction, release of neurotransmitter and hormones, and as an intracellular signaling element.

II. Bone Structure

Bones can be divided on the basis of their shapes.

1. **Long** bones are bones that are longer than they are wide. Due to their shape, these bones are located in areas of the body where they must act as levers. Examples include the bones of the arm (humerus, radius, ulna, metacarpals), of the leg (femur, tibia, fibula, metatarsals), and of the fingers and toes.

2. **Short** bones are bones that are just about equal in length and width, somewhat like a cube. Such bones can be found in confined places where they generally function to transfer forces. An example would be the bones of either the wrist or of the ankle.

3. **Flat** bones include the bones of the skull, the ribs, and the scapulae of the shoulder girdle. They are somewhat broad and thin are called flat bones. These bones, due to their shape, allow for the attachment of muscle and also for protection of underlying tissue.

4. **Irregular** bones are so called because of the wide variety of shapes that they can take. They often have projections that serve as attachment sites for muscle. Examples of this type of bone include the vertebrae.

5. **Round** or **sesamoid** bones include some bones in the wrist and the patella (knee-cap). These bones are most often round in shape and occur within tendons at joints that endure a lot of pressure.

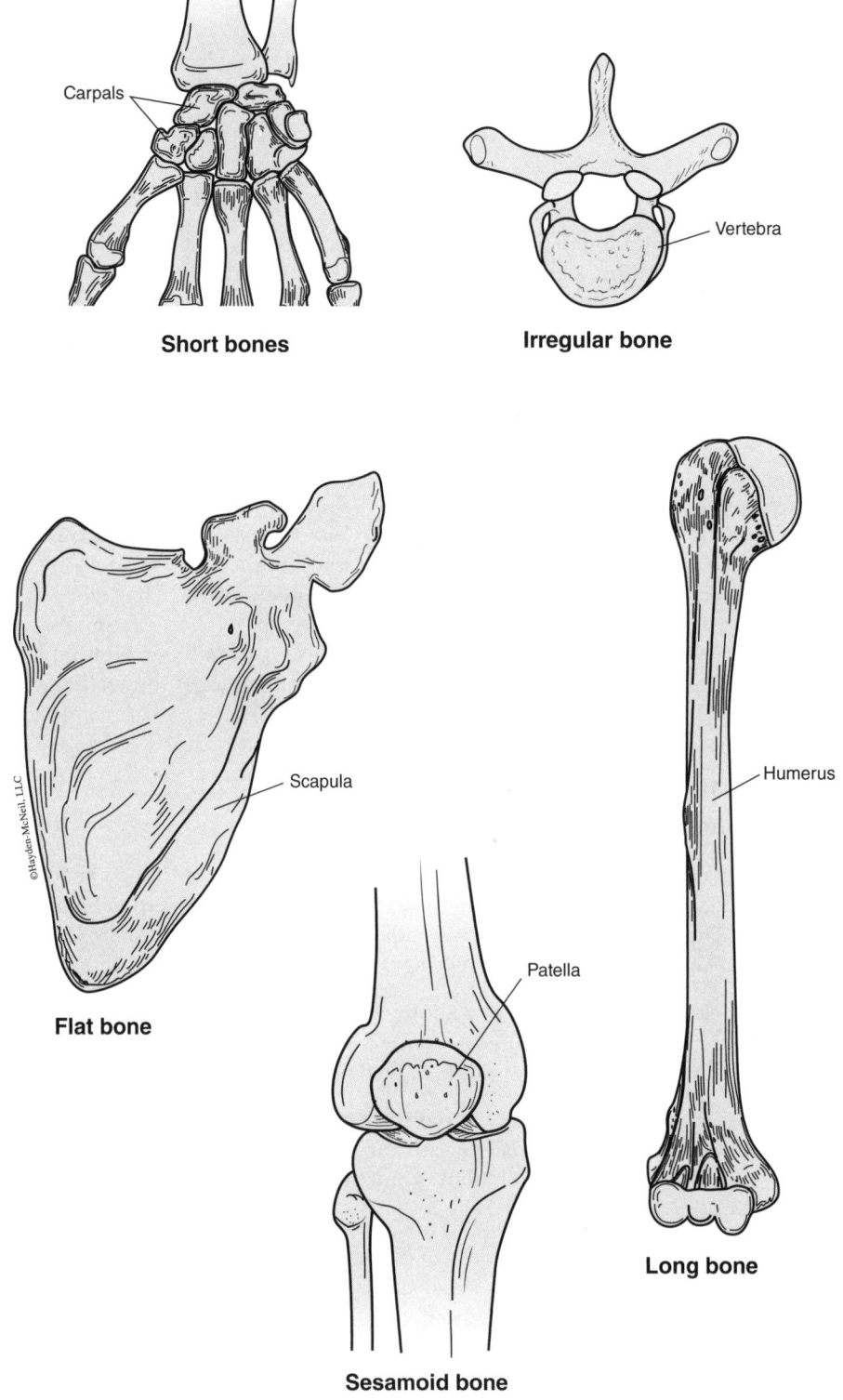

Figure 5-1. Classification of bones.

A. Anatomy of a Long Bone

The shaft, or long portion of the bone, is called the **diaphysis**. At each end of the diaphysis are the **epiphyses**, each covered by a thin layer of hyaline cartilage called **articular cartilage**. Dense irregular connective tissue, called **periosteum**, covers the remainder of the surface of the bone.

The wall of the **diaphysis** is made up of what is called **compact bone**. Compact bone enables the bone to resist bending under the stress of the weight of the body. We have already studied the structure of compact bone (Lab 4). Its functional unit is the osteon. The **epiphyses**, on the other hand, are composed mainly of spongy bone. Red bone marrow, a type of specialized connective tissue that produces blood cells, is found in the spongy bone. It is found in all the bones of infants, and is restricted to the skull bones, vertebrae, ribs, sternum, clavicles, and pelvic bones of adults. Most bones contain both compact and spongy bone.

The center of the diaphysis is hollow, and is called the **medullary cavity**. This cavity is continuous with the spongy bone of the epiphyses and is lined with a layer of cells that make up the **endosteum**. Fat-storing yellow marrow is found in the medullar cavity.

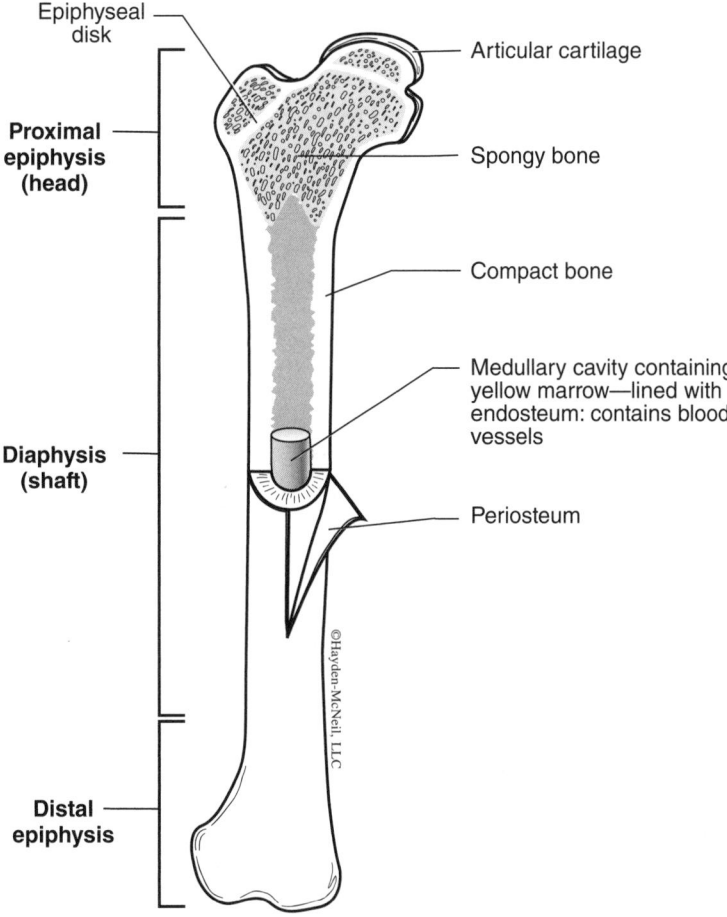

Figure 5-2. Major parts of the long bone (femur).

III. Bone Development

Bones start to form around the sixth or seventh week of embryonic life. Either fibrous connective tissue or hyaline cartilage is progressively replaced by bone, a process called **ossification**. Ossification is said to be intramembranous if it occurs in fibrous connective tissue or endochondral if it occurs in hyaline cartilage. The process involves the synthesis of collagen fibers by osteoblasts followed by calcium phosphate deposition on these fibers.

Intramembranous bones include the flat bones of the skull, the mandible and bones such as the clavicle (collarbone). These bones begin as layers of vascularized fibrous connective tissue. **Osteoblasts**, bone-forming cells, differentiate from **osteoprogenitor** cells and begin to deposit a bony calcified matrix around themselves. Eventually, as more and more matrix gets deposited, the osteoblasts become totally surrounded by the matrix and are left within small cavities called lacunae. They are now called **osteocytes**. The bone that forms is spongy bone.

However, most of bone in your body started out in embryonic life in the form of a cartilage model of your future skeleton, and bones were formed by endochondral ossification. In the case of a long bone, such as the tibia, there was a tightly regulated sequence of events depending on the expression of several genes. The process depends on a series of gene-protein interactions that form a "feedback loop" controlling chondrocyte differentiation. See Figure 5-3.

1. In the beginning, the cartilaginous model tibia is ensheathed in perichondrium.

2. Then a periosteal collar forms—a primary ossification center develops, where bone replaces cartilage. A marrow cavity appears.

3. Nourishing blood vessels invade from the perichondrium, penetrating the marrow cavity. The cartilage model continues to grow at its ends.

4. The periosteal collar thickens and lengthens due to the activity of osteoblasts in the periosteum. Secondary ossification centers appear at the epiphyses, when spongy bone is laid down.

5. The cartilage remains as hyaline cartilage in the epiphyseal plate (= epiphyseal disk) and as articular cartilage on the articulating surfaces of the epiphyses.

6. As long as the chondrocytes in the epiphyseal plate remain active, a long bone will continue to grow in length.

7. When the chondrocytes finally stop dividing, the cartilage in the epiphyseal plate is replaced by bone, and growth in **length** stops.

8. However, bones grow in **thickness** due to bone-manufacturing osteoblasts adding bone at the surface (just below the periosteum). In parallel, the marrow cavity is enlarged by the bone-dissolving osteoclasts.

9. Note that this system is an ingenious way of starting out with a basic cartilage design, partially converting it to bone (which is needed once you have been born), but at the same time allowing for the enormous amount of growth that occurs during development from infancy through adolescence. For example, the long bones of an infant lengthen by 50% during the first year after birth.

Bones undergoing ossification are continually undergoing remodeling.

Remodeling is the replacement of old bone tissue with new bone tissue, a process that involves balancing the activities of bone-making **osteoblasts** and bone-dissolving **osteoclasts.** These cells also play an important role in the healing of fractures.

Even after bones have reached their adult shapes and sizes old bone is perpetually destroyed and new bone is formed in its place. As much as 15% of the total bone mass is turned over each year. This turnover is not evenly distributed throughout the skeleton, however. The distal portion of the femur (thighbone) is totally replaced every four months, although the bone in certain areas of the shaft will not be replaced during one's lifetime.

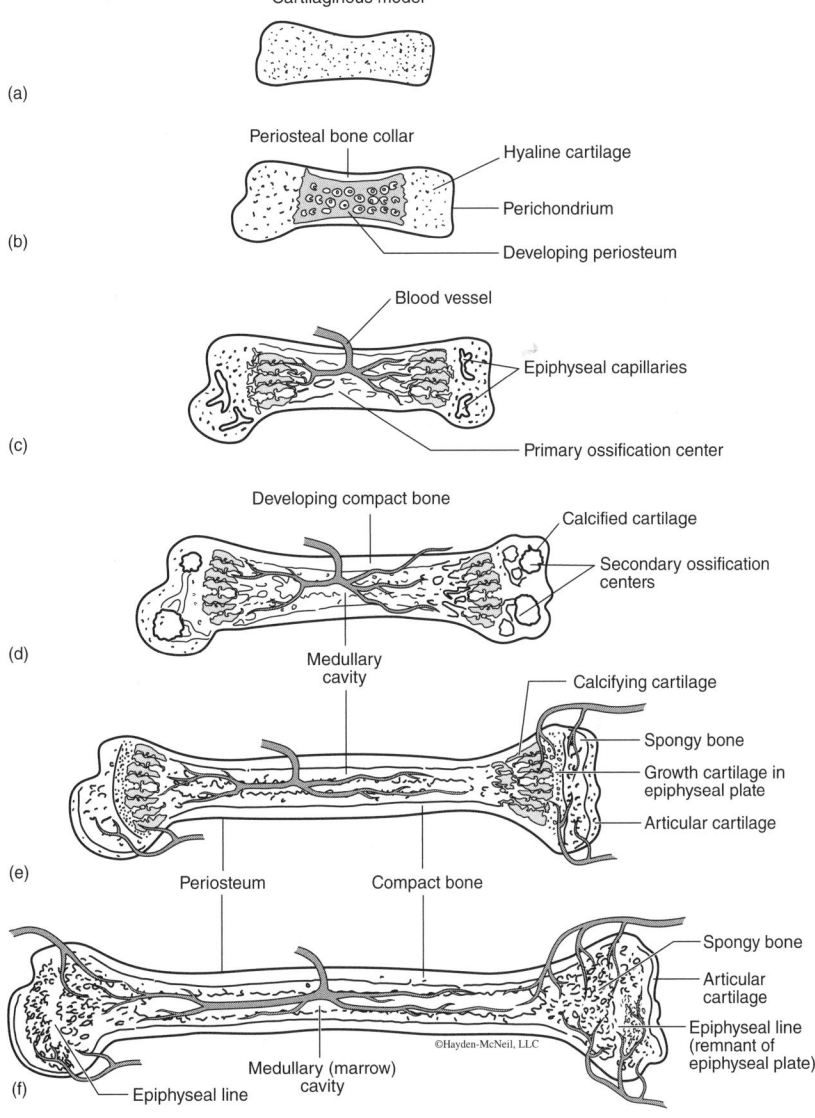

Figure 5-3. Bone growth and development—endochondral ossification.

Clinical Application. To determine if a person's bones are still growing, a physician will often times take an X-ray and look to see if there is still an epiphyseal disk (plate) between the diaphysis and epiphyses of long bones.

A. Factors Which Affect Bone Growth and Development

1. **Nutrition—minerals**: There must be adequate intake of **calcium, phosphorus** in the form of phosphate, and other elements including **boron** and **manganese**.

2. **Nutrition—vitamins: Vitamin D** is required for the proper reabsorption of calcium in the small intestine—calcium that is used as the matrix material for bone tissue. When calcium becomes deficient, the bones tend to become weak and deformed and can actually bend under the weight or stress of the human body. In children, this condition is called **rickets**; in adults, **osteomalacia**. Both eggs and fortified milk products provide adequate sources of Vitamin D. **Vitamin A** is needed for the bone resorption that occurs during normal bone development. **Vitamin C** is required for the proper formation of collagen. If either is deficient, the bones become slender and fragile.

3. **Hormones**

   a. **Growth hormone**: A hormone released by the anterior pituitary gland that promotes growth of cartilage at the epiphyseal disk. If it is deficient or absent during growth, the resulting condition is called **dwarfism**. Just the opposite, **gigantism**, occurs if growth hormone release is in excess before ossification of the epiphyseal disk.

   b. **Calcitonin:** secreted by the thyroid gland. In many animals it influences calcium metabolism by its ability to inhibit the activity of osteoclasts in bone tissue. At the present time, it is thought not to be very important in humans.

   c. **Sex Hormones:** Hormones secreted by the gonads (ovaries and testes) are called the sex hormones. Among their other functions, they function to promote bone formation during early childhood, bone growth at the onset of puberty, and, after a while, they prompt the closure of the epiphyseal disks resulting in the cessation of bone growth. Anabolic steroids will also promote closure of the epiphyseal disks.

   d. **Parathyroid hormone:** secreted by the parathyroid gland and functions to increase the amount of calcium ions in the blood. One of the ways this is accomplished is by stimulating the activity of the osteoclasts found in bone tissue. This acts to stimulate bone resorption.

   e. **Thyroid hormones:** Among their other functions they stimulate bone resorption.

4. **Exercise**

   Exercise puts physical stress on the bones to which skeletal muscles are attached. As a result of this stress, the bones are stimulated to become thicker and stronger by deposition of mineral salts and production of collagen fibers. On the other hand, bones of persons who are inactive tend to be weak and much thinner.

5. **Aging**

   a. **Osteoporosis:** A disorder in which there is excessive loss of bone mass and mineral content. It is particularly serious in women after menopause.

IV. The Skeleton

The human skeleton is divided up into the axial and the appendicular skeletons. The axial skeleton includes the bones that support and protect the organs of the head, neck, and trunk; the appendicular corresponds to the bones of the limbs, and the bones of the pectoral and pelvic girdles.

A. The Axial Skeleton

The human skull (the combination of the cranium and the facial bones) is made up of twenty-two bones, some of which are paired and some of which are not. For the most part, the bones of the skull articulate at immovable joints called sutures, the one exception being the lower jawbone. The cranium is made up of eight bones—one **frontal**, two **temporal**, two **parietal**, one **occipital**, one **sphenoid**, and one **ethmoid** bone. The other fourteen bones make up the facial skeleton. We will not identify all of the facial bones, but we are interested in the jawbones—the upper **maxilla** and the lower **mandible**, and the cheekbone, the **zygomatic**. Three small bones that many forget to include as bones of the skull are the ossicles of the middle ear. These three bones, the **malleus, incus,** and **stapes,** function to transmit sound vibrations from the external to the inner ear.

The **hyoid bone** is located in the neck between the mandible and the larynx. Held in position by many muscles and ligaments, it functions as the attachment site for muscles that move the tongue and that are involved in swallowing. It can be felt approximately a finger's width above the anterior prominence of the larynx (the Adam's apple).

The vertebral column, or spine, is composed of a series of thirty-three bones called vertebrae. It encloses and protects the spinal cord, supports the head, and serves as an attachment for the ribs and muscles of the back. The vertebrae are distributed as follows: the first seven are called the **cervical** vertebrae, then there are twelve **thoracic**, five **lumbar**, five **sacral** that are fused together to form the **sacrum**, and four **coccygeal** that are fused together to form the **coccyx**. Two cervical vertebrae of particular importance are the **atlas** and **axis**. The atlas is actually the first vertebra and it functions toward the support of the head. The second vertebra, the axis, allows the head to rotate (pivot) from side to side against the atlas, due to a projection of the axis called the **odontoid process.**

The vertebrae of the spinal column can vary greatly from one area to another. There are, however, several characteristics that are common among all vertebrae. Each vertebra possesses what is called a **body**, which forms the thick part of the bone. Projecting from the vertebrae in several directions are processes that serve as sites for muscle and ligament attachment. These include the **spinous** process, and the **transverse** processes. (See Figure 5-9—atlas-axis joint.)

What type of tissue is sandwiched between two adjacent vertebrae and what function does it serve?

The thoracic cage, or rib cage, is twelve pairs of bones that encase the vital organs of the thoracic cavity, thus protecting them. The first seven pair of ribs are called the **true ribs** because they articulate both anteriorly (with the sternum via **costal cartilage**) and posteriorly (with the vertebral column). The next five pair are called **false ribs** due to the lack of a direct anterior articulation—their costal cartilage does not reach the sternum directly. Of the false ribs, the costal cartilage of the first three pair join with the cartilage of ribs just above. The remaining two pairs, however, are called **floating ribs**, because they have no attachment at all.

The true ribs articulate anteriorly with the sternum, a bone which is made up of three parts—the upper **manubrium**, the middle elongated **body,** and the lower **xiphoid process.**

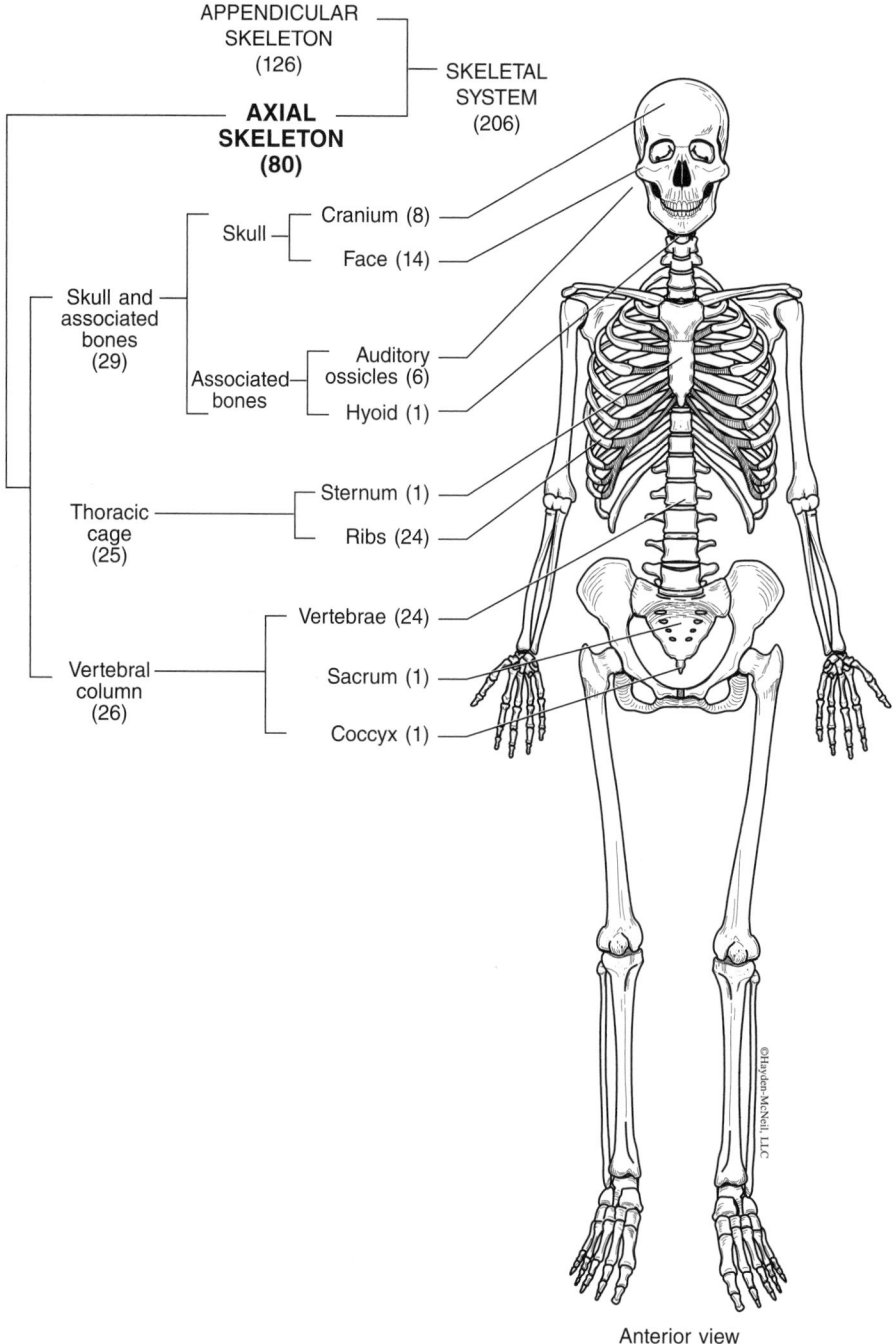

Anterior view

Figure 5-4. Axial skeleton.

B. The Appendicular Skeleton

The upper limbs are attached to the trunk by the **pectoral (shoulder) girdle**. The pectoral girdle consists of the **scapula** and the **clavicle**. It is very light and extremely mobile allowing for a wide range of movement. The **scapula**, better known as the shoulder blade, is a flat triangular bone. The **clavicle**, or collarbone, is a long, curved bone placed immediately over the first rib. It articulates with the manubrium medially, and with the top of the shoulder laterally.

The upper extremities consist of the bones of the upper and lower arms and hands. The **humerus**, or upper arm bone, articulates proximally with the scapula. The distal end articulates with the bones of the lower arm, the **radius** and the **ulna**. The proximal end of the ulna forms one part of the elbow joint and articulates with the radius. At its distal end, it becomes quite thin where it articulates with the radius and the bones of the wrist. Lateral to the ulna is the radius. Proximally, it articulates with the humerus and ulna, distally with the wrist bones, the **carpals.** There are eight carpals in the wrist that are joined together by cartilage. At their distal surface, they articulate with the five **metacarpals**. The fingers, then, are formed by the fourteen **phalanges**—three for each finger, two for the thumb.

The pelvic girdle, the site of attachment of the lower limbs, is a bony ring composed of two bones. Each bone of the pelvic girdle is comprised of three segments. The union of the three occurs at a depression on the hipbone called **acetabulum**. Of the three parts, the **ilium** is the largest. Its crest can be felt along the upper border of the hipbone. The lower portion of the hipbone is the **ischium**. It functions to support the body when it is in a sitting position. The anterior part of the hipbone is the **pubis**. The two pubic bones form a slightly movable joint called the **pubic symphysis**.

The lower extremities consist of the bones of the leg and feet. The **femur** is the longest and the strongest bone of the human skeleton. Proximally, it is described as having a head, which is directed towards the midline of the body and which articulates with the acetabulum of the pelvis. The distal end of the femur presents articulating surfaces for the kneecap (patella) and for the tibia. The **patella** is a sesamoid bone developed within the tendon of a muscle. It serves to protect the front of the knee joint. The **tibia** is situated at the medial side of the leg. Its proximal end articulates with the femur, the distal end with the bones of the ankle. The **fibula** lies lateral to the tibia. It is smaller than the tibia, and its proximal end does not articulate with the femur but only with the tibia. Distally, it meets with the bones of the ankle. The bones of the foot are somewhat analogous to the bones of the hand. There are seven **tarsal** bones, the largest being the **calcaneus** (the bone of the heel). Then there are five **metatarsals**, and fourteen **phalanges**—three for each toe, two for the great toe.

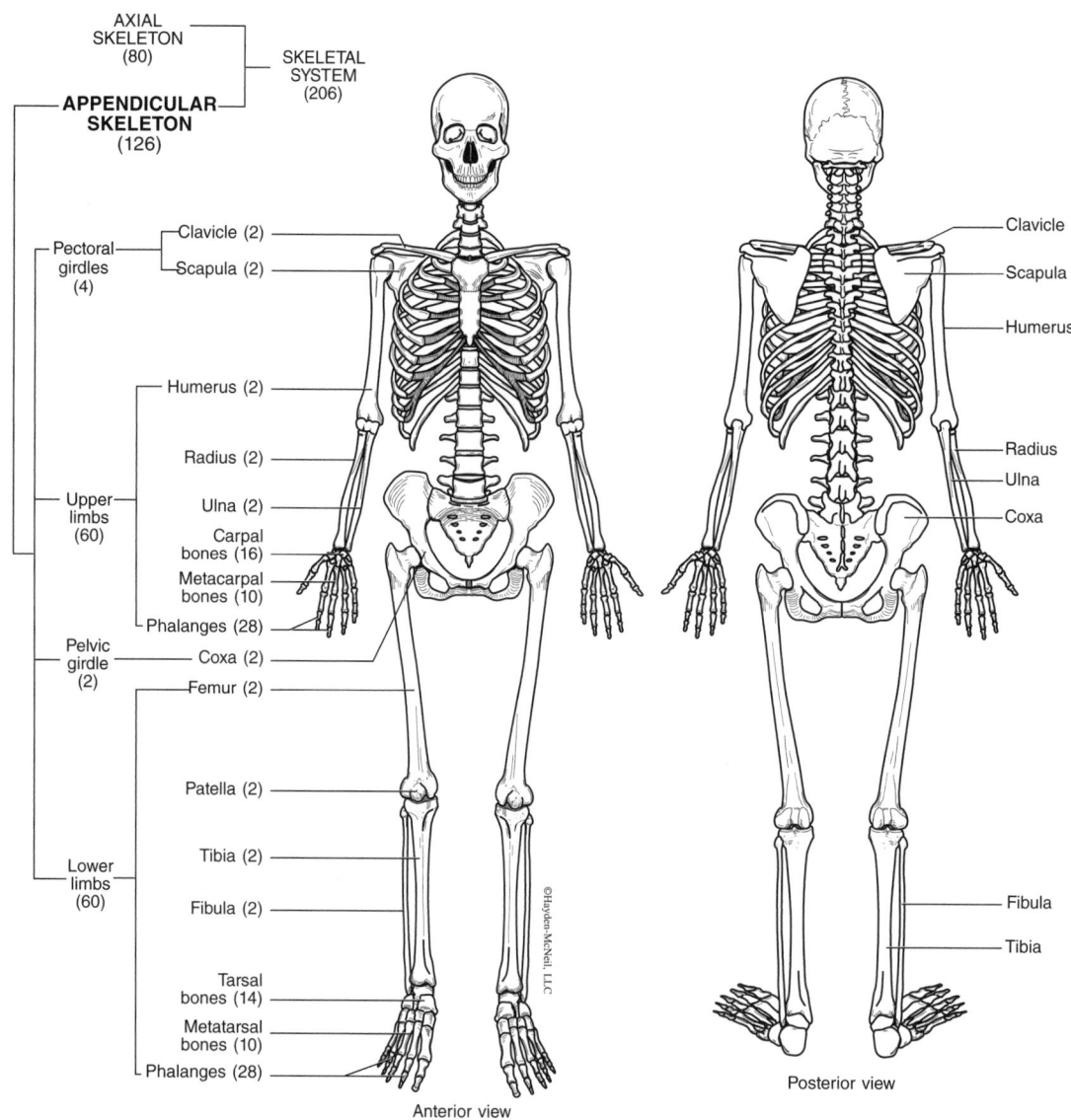

AXIAL
SKELETON
(80)

SKELETAL
SYSTEM
(206)

**APPENDICULAR
SKELETON**
(126)

Pectoral
girdles
(4)
— Clavicle (2)
— Scapula (2)

Upper
limbs
(60)
— Humerus (2)
— Radius (2)
— Ulna (2)
— Carpal
bones (16)
— Metacarpal
bones (10)
— Phalanges (28)

Pelvic
girdle
(2)
— Coxa (2)

Lower
limbs
(60)
— Femur (2)
— Patella (2)
— Tibia (2)
— Fibula (2)
— Tarsal
bones (14)
— Metatarsal
bones (10)
— Phalanges (28)

Clavicle
Scapula
Humerus
Radius
Ulna
Coxa
Fibula
Tibia

©Hayden-McNeil, LLC

Anterior view

Posterior view

Figure 5-5. Appendicular skeleton.

Bones to Know

(Names and location)

1. **The Axial Skeleton**
   a. Skull
      1. **cranium:** one frontal, two temporal, two parietal, and one occipital, sphenoid, ethmoid
      2. **facial:** maxilla, mandible, zygomatic
      3. **middle ear:** malleus, incus, and stapes

   b. Hyoid Bone

   c. Vertebral Column
      1. 7 **cervical** vertebrae (atlas & axis)
      2. 12 **thoracic** vertebrae
      3. 5 **lumbar** vertebrae
      4. 5 **sacral** vertebrae fused to form the **sacrum**
      5. 4 **coccygeal** vertebrae fused to form the **coccyx**

   d. Thoracic Cage: 24 ribs and the sternum (breastbone)
      1. **true ribs (14)**
      2. **false ribs (10)**
      3. **sternum (breastbone): manubrium, body and xiphoid process**

2. **Appendicular Skeleton**
   a. Pectoral Girdle
      1. **clavicle**
      2. **scapula**

   b. Arm
      1. **humerus**
      2. **ulna**
      3. **radius**

   c. Hand
      1. **carpal bones (8):** wrist
      2. **metacarpal bones (5):** palm
      3. **phalanges (14):** fingers

   d. Pelvic Girdle
      1. **ilium:** hipbone
      2. **ischium:** seat, supports body when sitting
      3. **pubis:** anterior portion

   e. Leg
      1. **femur**
      2. **tibia**
      3. **fibula**
      4. **patella**

   f. Foot
      1. **tarsal bones (7):** ankle
      2. **metatarsal bones (5):** sole
      3. **phalanges (14):** toes

V. Joints

A joint is where two or more bones meet. There are two different ways of classifying joints: **degree of movement allowed,** and their **structure**.

Based on the degree of movement that is permitted, joints are classified into three groups—**synarthrosis, amphiarthrosis,** and **diarthrosis**.

You will sometimes see joints classified according to the degree of **movement** they allow.
1. Immovable — *synarthrosis*
2. Slightly movable — *amphiarthrosis*
3. Freely movable — *diarthrosis*

Based on their structure, joints are classified into three groups—**fibrous, cartilaginous,** and **synovial**.

Fibrous joints occur where two bones come in very close contact with each other. Between the two bones exists a layer of fibrous connective tissue that binds the two bones together allowing for little to no movement between the bones. The three types of fibrous joints include the **syndesmosis** (distal end-tibia/fibula), **suture** (skull), and **gomphosis** (teeth) joints.

Cartilaginous joints occur where two bones are connected to each other by either hyaline or fibrocartilage. Within this category are two types—**synchondrosis** (as with rib to sternum articulation) and **symphysis** (intervertebral disks, symphysis pubis).

Lastly, the joint that allows for the freest movement: the synovial joint. The structure of a synovial joint is much more complex than that of the previous two. With the synovial joints, the ends of the bones involved are capped by **articular cartilage** (hyaline cartilage) that functions to reduce friction between the two bones and to convey body weight to underlying tissue. Surrounding the joint is the **joint capsule.** It has two parts, an outer layer of dense connective tissue that attaches itself to the periosteum of the bones, and an inner layer of loose connective tissue called the **synovial membrane**. This membrane covers all areas of the joint capsule except for those that are covered by articular cartilage. Secreted from the membrane and into the **synovial (or joint) cavity** is a clear, thick fluid called synovial fluid which functions to moisten and lubricate the surfaces of the joint. Because of the differences in the shapes of the bones involved with the synovial joints, they have been classified into seven categories—**ball-and-socket, condyloid (ellipsoidal), gliding, hinge, pivot, saddle,** and **bicondylar.** An example of each of the first six is diagrammed on the next page. The seventh class of synovial joints, bicondylar, is not mentioned in your text and is found in only one place in the human body and that is the knee joint. It is a hinge joint with limited rotation.

Table 1. Classification by Degree of Movement

Degree of Movement Category	Description	Qualifying Structural Category

Synarthrosis	No movement	Fibrous
		    Suture
		    Gomphosis
		Cartilaginous
		    Synchondrosis

Amphiarthrosis	Slight movement	Fibrous
		    Syndesmosis
		Cartilaginous
		    Symphysis

Diarthrosis	Free movement	Synovial All

Table 2. Classification by Structure

Structural Category	Type of Joint	Qualifying Degree of Movement Category
Fibrous Joints	Suture Gomphosis Syndesmosis	Synarthrosis Synarthrosis Amphiarthrosis
Cartilaginous Joints	Synchondrosis Symphysis	Synarthrosis Amphiarthrosis
Synovial Joints	All	All Diarthroses

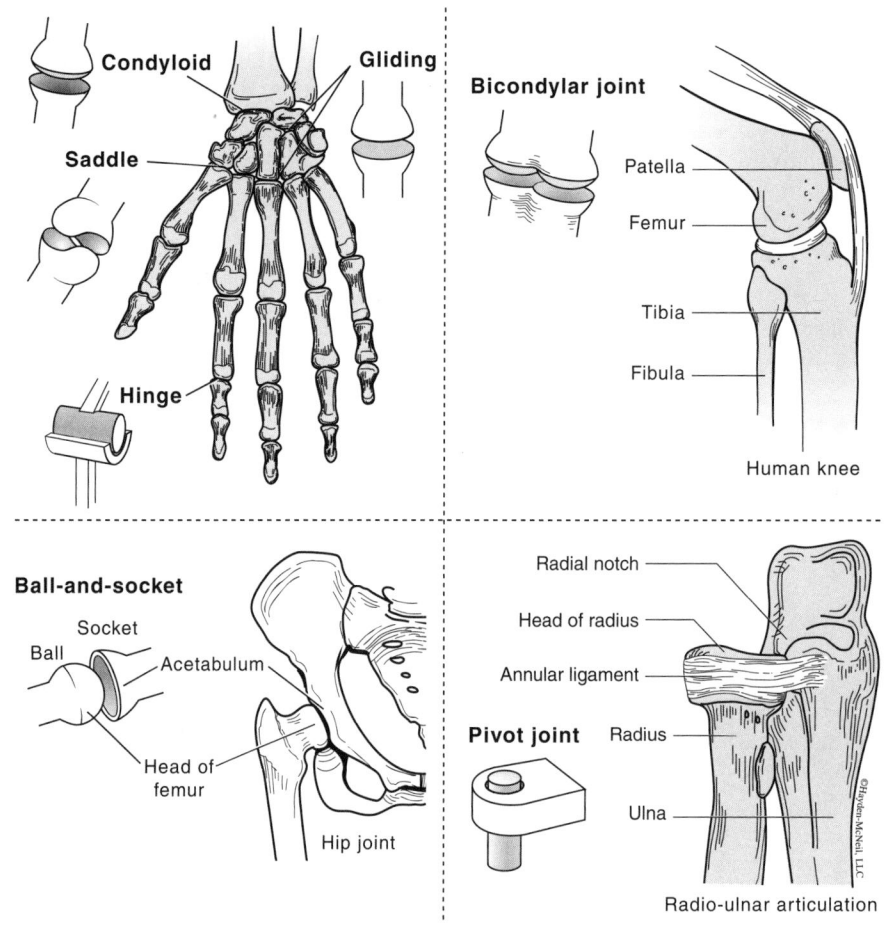

Figure 5-6. Examples of synovial joints.

Simple Model That Demonstrates Joint Motion

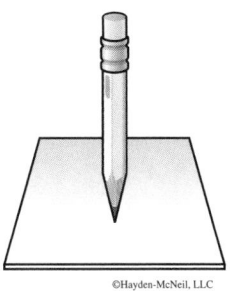

©Hayden-McNeil, LLC

Take a pencil and stand it upright on the surface of a desk or table. The pencil represents the bone, and the desktop represents an articular surface. There are only three ways to move the pencil. Considering them offers a way to analyze complex movements.

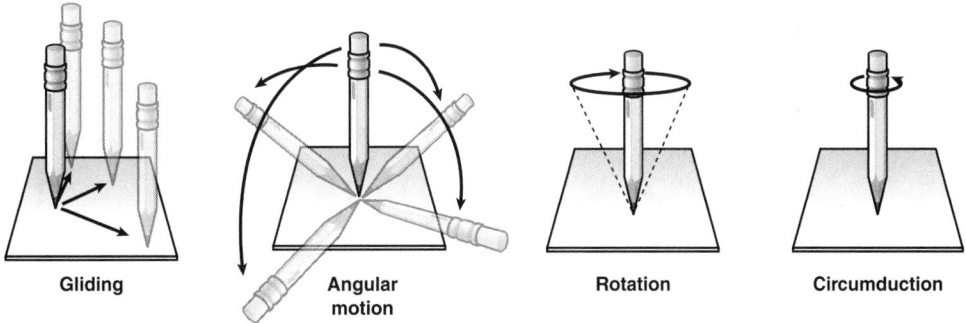

| Gliding | Angular motion | Rotation | Circumduction |

Exercise A

On the next two pages are skeleton figures in which none of the bones have been identified. Your task is to identify all of the bones of the axial and appendicular skeletons. Only name those bones which are listed above or which were identified by your TA during the skeleton review. We are giving you two skeleton figures, one for doing now, another to use as a review for the test.

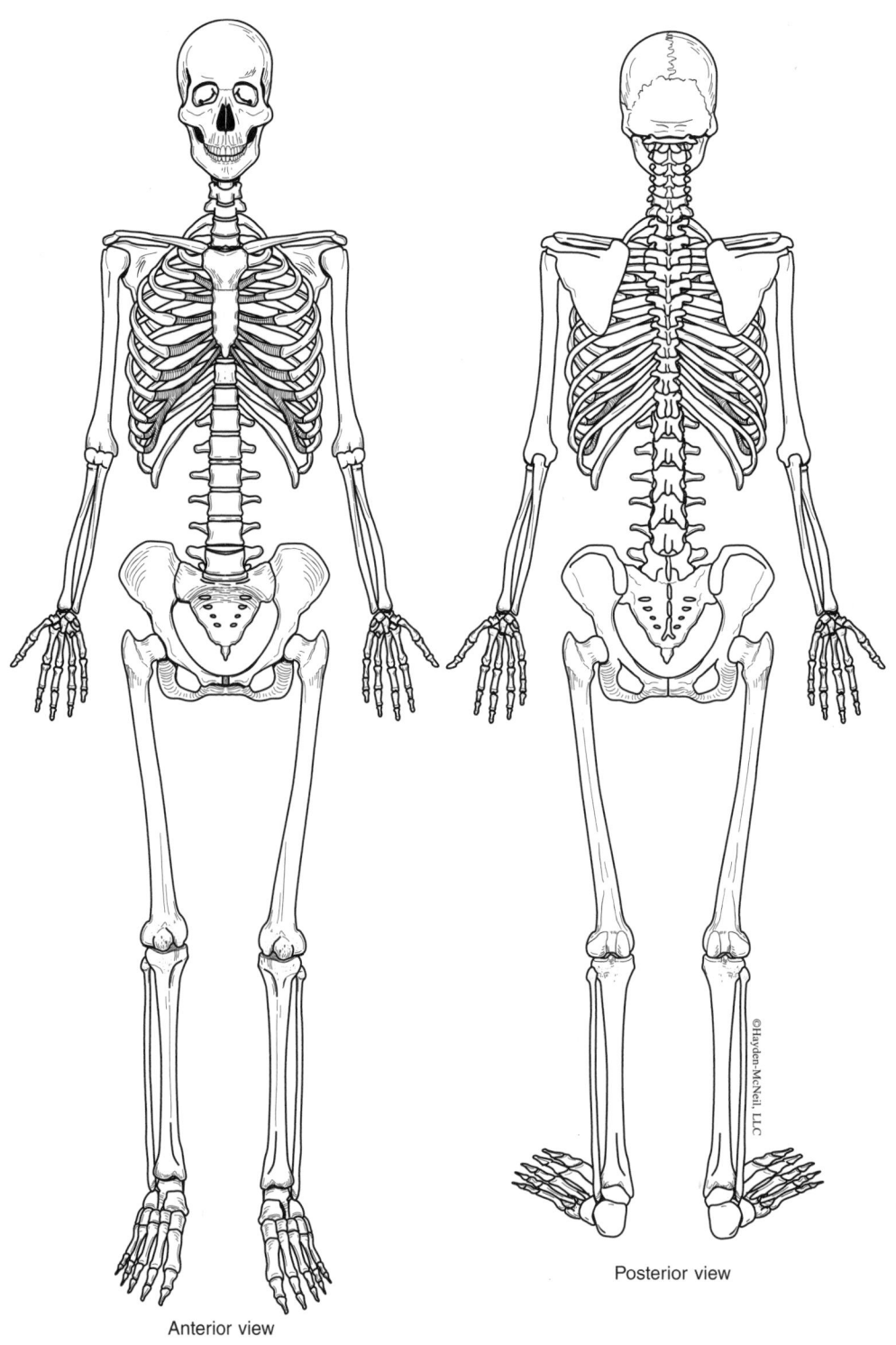

Anterior view

Posterior view

©Hayden-McNeil, LLC

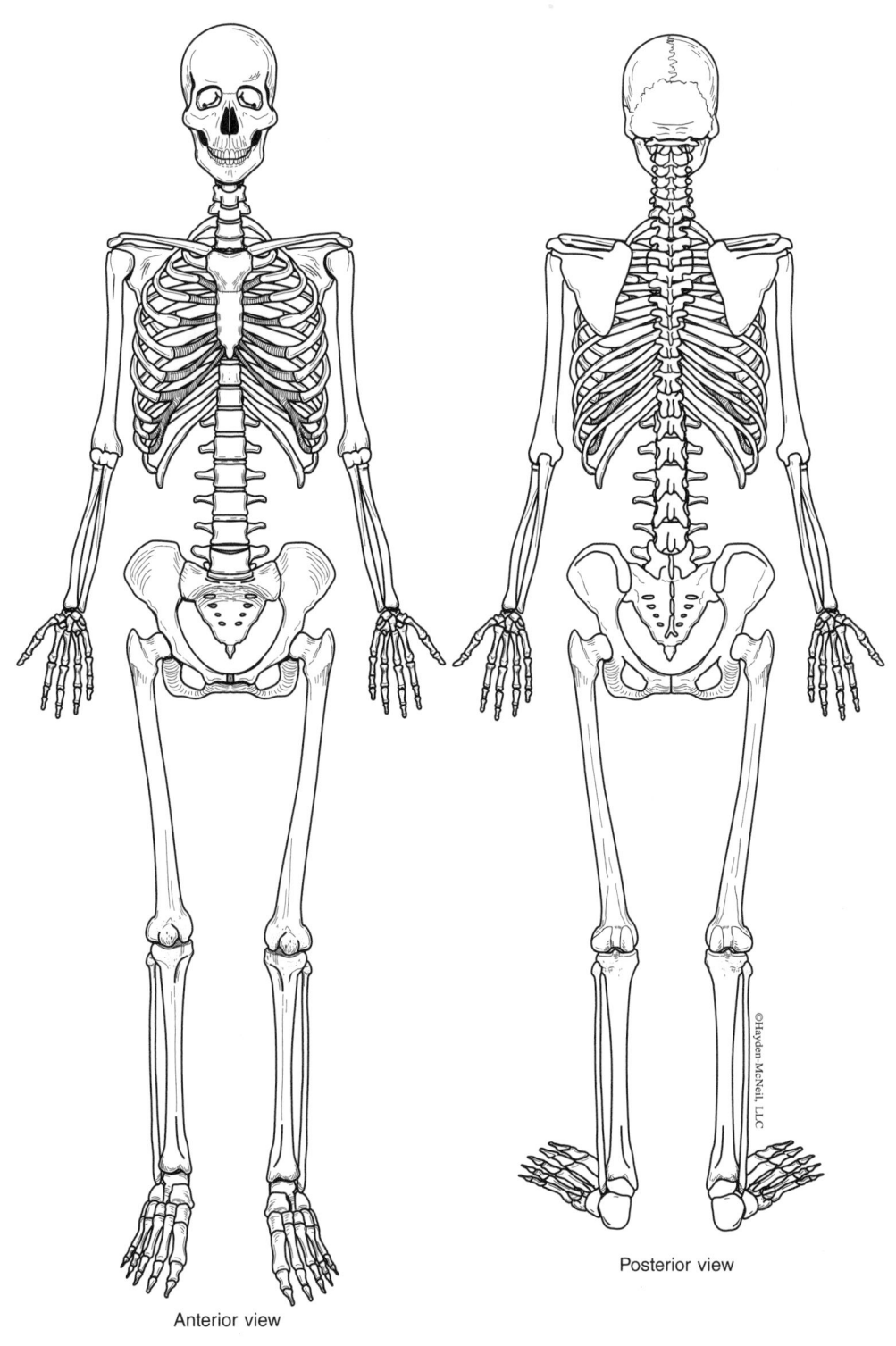

Anterior view

Posterior view

©Hayden-McNeil, LLC

Exercise B

Obtain a prepared slide of a long bone undergoing osteogenesis. In the slide of the developing bone, you should be able to recognize the epiphyseal plate. Because this is **an endochondral bone,** what type of connective tissue do you expect to see? Below is room for you to draw what you observe.

- chondrocytes in lacunae

- perichondrium

- zone of proliferating cartilage

- spicules of bone

- zone of ossification

Exercise C

Situated at different stations around the room are models of three different synovial joints—the shoulder joint, the knee joint, and the atlas-axis joint. Your task is to go to each station and, using the diagrams below, learn the main anatomical features of each joint. Identify each of the structures listed. Check them off when you are able to identify them comfortably. **Do not use excessive force when handling these models. They can be quite fragile**. Also, do not mark on them with anything.

1. Shoulder Joint

What type of synovial joint is this? _____

Structure	
clavicle	
humerus	
scapula	
coracoid process	
acromion process	
articular capsule	
ligaments:	
coracoclavicular ligament	
acromioclavicular ligament	
coracoacromial ligament	
coracohumeral ligament	

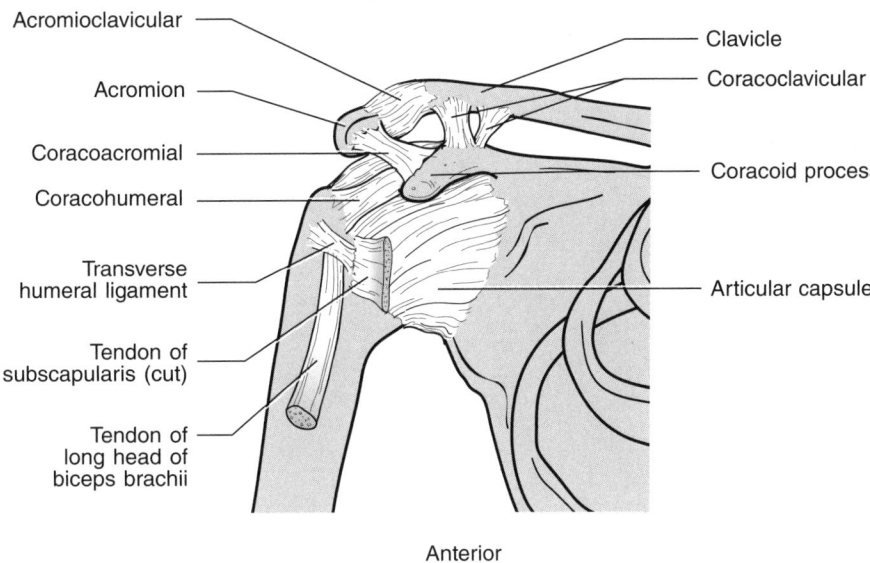

Anterior

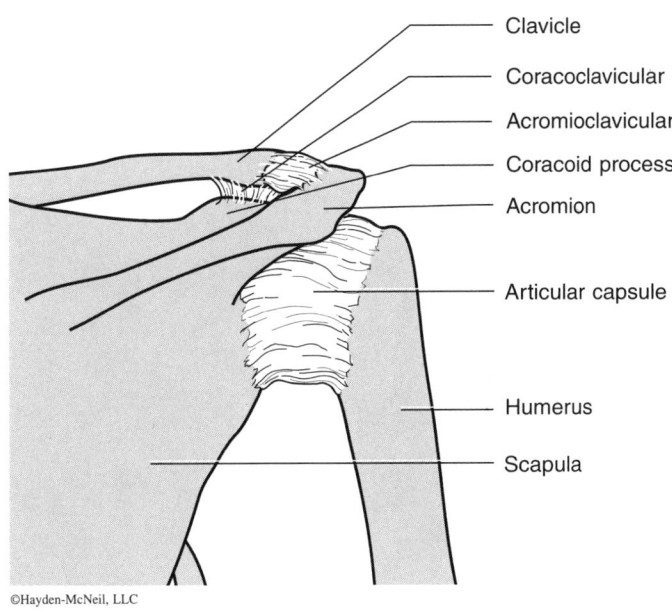

©Hayden-McNeil, LLC

Posterior

Figure 5-7. Shoulder joint.

2. Knee Joint

What type of synovial joint is this? _____

Structure	
femur	
tibia	
fibula	
patellar ligament	
patella	
lateral meniscus	
medial meniscus	
lateral (fibular) collateral ligament	
medial (tibial) collateral ligament	
anterior cruciate ligament	
posterior cruciate ligament	

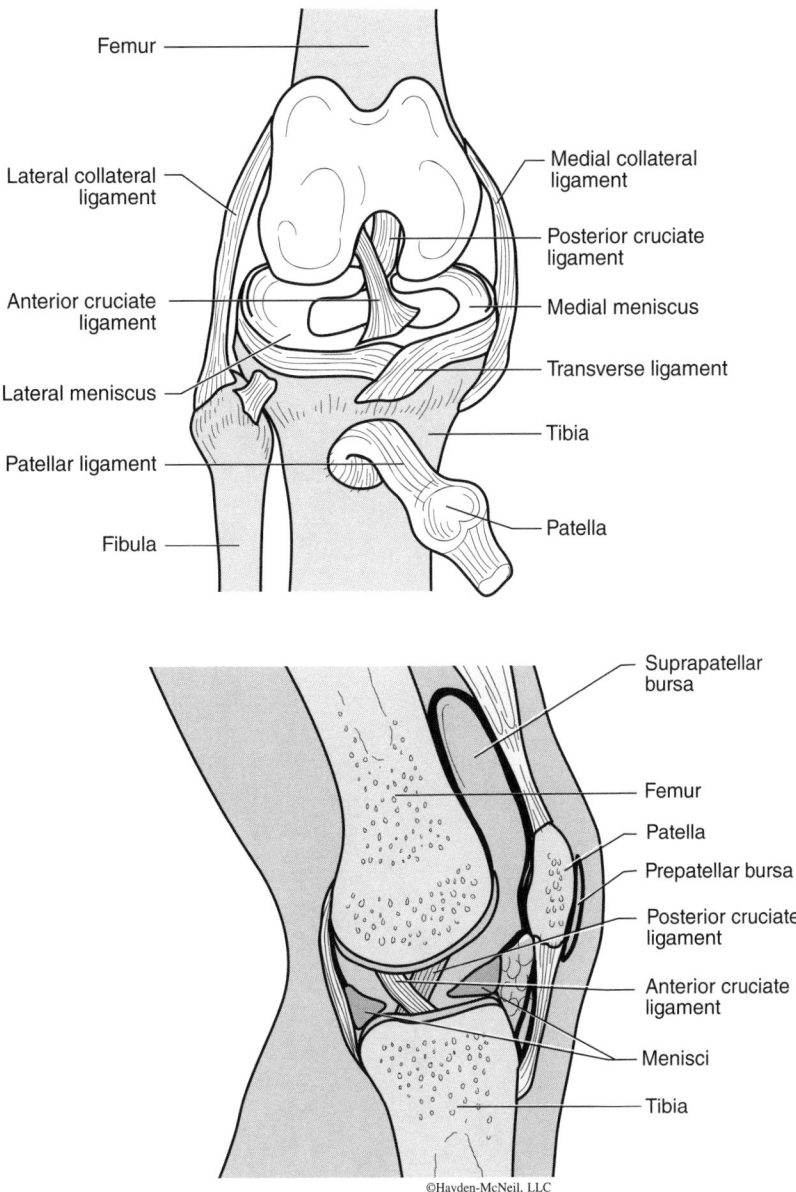

©Hayden-McNeil, LLC

Figure 5-8. Top: Anterior view of the knee joint (patella reflected downward). Bottom: Posterior view.

3. Atlas-Axis Joint

What type of synovial joint is this? _____

What type of movement does this allow? _____

Locate the:

atlas _____ axis _____

Gently lift the atlas, separating it from the axis. Can you see the odontoid process?

With the vertebral arteries (in red) passing through the transverse foramen of the cervical vertebrae, it is difficult to do, but try rotating the atlas over the surface of the axis to give you a better idea how this particular joint allows for the movement you have listed above.

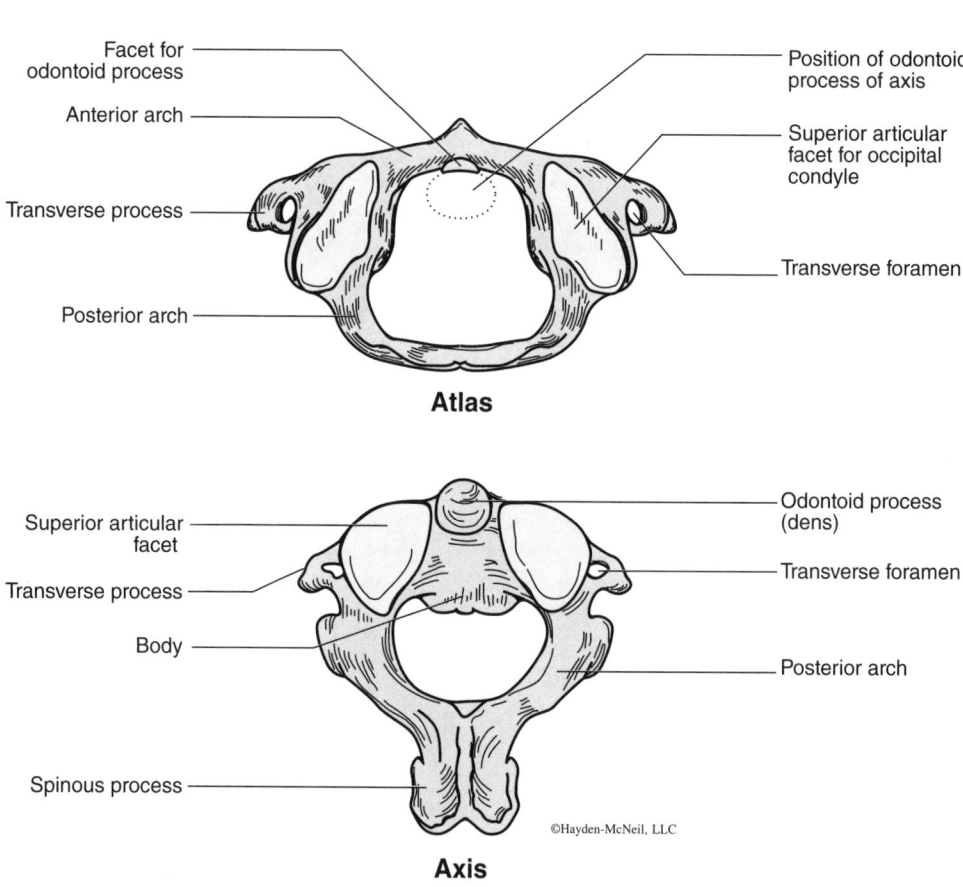

Figure 5-9. Atlas-axis joint.

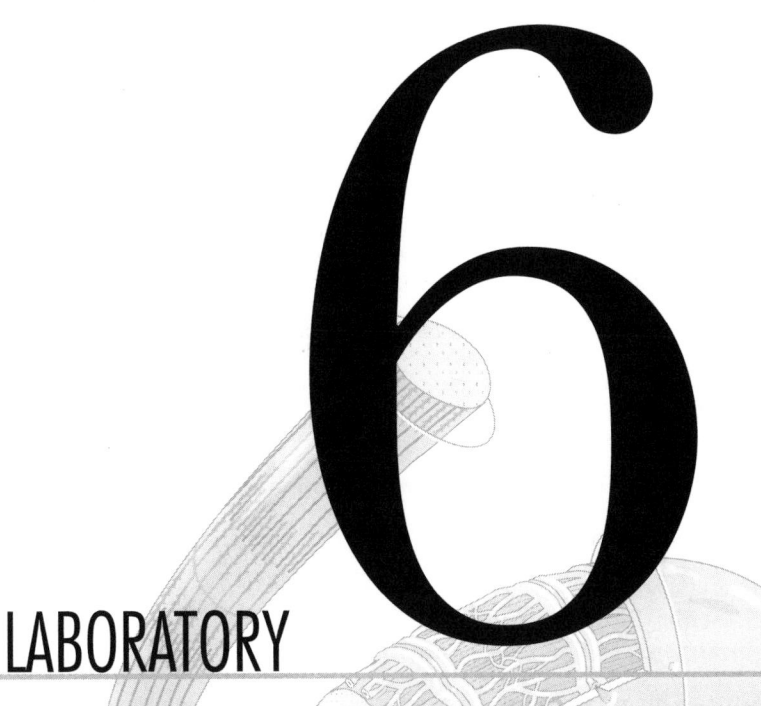

LABORATORY 6

TISSUES III: MUSCLE TISSUE, MUSCULAR SYSTEM AND LEVERS

Required Reading: Lectures 10–11

READ THE PAGES LISTED BELOW IN YOUR HISTOLOGY TEXT BEFORE COMING TO CLASS, THEN BRING IT TO CLASS.

12TH ED: READ PAGES 142–169, 190–197, 199, OR
11TH ED: READ PAGES 116–133, 151–153, 155

Objectives

1. Describe the three types of muscle, where they are found, and their function.

2. Describe the **connective tissue** in a skeletal muscle.

3. Describe how a skeletal muscle fiber develops.

4. Draw the structure of a skeletal muscle fiber.

5. Sketch a **myofibril**.

6. Describe and sketch the **neuromuscular junction**.

7. Name the **neurotransmitter used at the neuromuscular junction, and the enzyme** involved in its removal after it has acted.

8. Describe all the ways in which neuromuscular transmission can be blocked (e.g., myasthenia gravis, nerve gases).

9. Draw a **diagram** showing how the thin and thick filaments are organized in the sarcomere, and list the five steps involved in the contraction of a muscle fiber.

10. Describe the role of ATP in item #9 above.

11. Define what is meant by **excitation–contraction coupling**, and with a diagram describe how it works.

12. Describe how excitation–contraction coupling in **cardiac** muscle is slightly different from skeletal muscle (think calcium).

13. Describe muscle **relaxation (calsequestrin, calcium ATP-ase)**.

14. List the proteins found in muscle.

15. List the biochemical processes that provide **energy** for contracting muscle. Draw a composite diagram from memory. Distinguish anaerobic and aerobic processes.

16. Explain why an athlete might take a **creatine** dietary supplement and how this relates to the **phosphagen** system.

17. Describe the **sources of oxygen** for contracting muscles.

18. Discuss how aerobic and anaerobic processes and the phosphagen system all interact during exercise.

19. Explain what is meant by EPOC.

20. List the **energy systems** used in various sports (e.g., 100-meter dash, 200-meter dash, 800-meter run, marathon).

21. Construct a table contrasting the properties of **fast** and **slow** muscle fibers.

22. Give the proportions of fast and slow muscle fibers in the gastrocnemius and soleus muscles.

23. Give an explanation for the difference in the ratio of fast and slow muscle fibers in these two muscles. Indicate the difference in the proportions of fast and slow muscle fibers in the quadriceps femoris muscle group of a marathoner and a sprinter.

24. Summarize the cause of **heat stroke** in athletes.

25. List the **41 muscles** you are expected to know. List their origins and insertions, and the movements associated with them. Identify them on a diagram of the body's musculature.

26. Describe the two ways in which smooth muscle is organized, and relate this to function.

27. Describe the mechanism of smooth muscle contraction and note where it differs from skeletal muscle.

28. List four factors that control smooth muscle contractions.

29. Summarize in a table the similarities and differences between skeletal, smooth, and cardiac muscle.

30. Explain the ways in which different groups of skeletal muscles (agonists, etc.) interact to produce smooth, coordinated movements.

31. Describe the various types of skeletal muscle groupings and their functions.

32. Describe with diagrams what is meant by a first class lever, and give examples.

33. Describe with diagrams what is meant by a third class lever, and give examples.

34. Explain mathematically the advantage of having a lever system in the body. Illustrate with a diagram how the lever system activated by the biceps brachii muscle operates: discuss and **calculate** its advantages and disadvantages.

I. Overview

Muscle is involved in all movements occurring in the body, whether it is using your hand to write the answer to a question in an examination, whether it is the movements of the stomach that make a growling noise when you are hungry, or whether it is the contractions of your heart that make it go pit-pat when you get excited. Muscle is also important in maintaining posture.

In this laboratory, you will study the **structure** of cardiac, smooth, and skeletal muscle. You will discuss how muscles contract and how ATP is required for contraction in cardiac, smooth, and skeletal muscle. Skeletal muscle is under voluntary control, and we will consider how this is carried out by neurons of the nervous system. We will also study how the body uses bone levers to amplify muscle contraction.

A. Cardiac Muscle

1. **Location**—Only in the walls of the heart.

2. **Structure**—The muscle cells (muscle fibers) have cross-striations, and are joined end-to-end in branching networks. At the junction of two cardiac muscle fibers we find a structure called an **intercalated disc**. Each muscle fiber has a single nucleus. In other respects, cardiac muscle fibers are very similar to skeletal muscle fibers (see below). They contain the **proteins actin, myosin, troponin,** and **tropomyosin**.

3. **Properties**—The molecular events occurring during cardiac muscle contraction are very similar to those occurring in skeletal muscle (see below). Cardiac muscle is an involuntary muscle, and requires no nervous input to contract. It contracts and relaxes rhythmically entirely on its own. However, in the intact heart, the rate and force by which these contractions occur is increased by sympathetic nerve impulses, and the rate is reduced by parasympathetic nerve impulses.

B. Smooth Muscle

1. **Location**—Smooth muscle occurs in the walls of the gastrointestinal tract, blood vessels, and many other parts of the body.

2. **Structure**—Smooth muscle fibers are shorter than skeletal muscle and cardiac muscle fibers. Smooth muscle fibers contain actin and myosin arranged in myofibrils that extend along the length of the fibers. However, they are not well organized as in cardiac and skeletal muscle, so that smooth muscle fibers lack cross-striations. Also, smooth muscle cells lack T-tubules.

3. **Properties**—The contractions of smooth muscle are not under voluntary control, as is the case with skeletal muscle. Smooth muscle contraction can be controlled by sympathetic and parasympathetic nerve impulses, by hormones such as oxytocin and epinephrine, by substances such as carbon dioxide and hydrogen ions, and even by mechanically stretching it (as might occur in the intestines or the urinary bladder).

C. Skeletal Muscle

1. **Location**—With few exceptions skeletal muscle is attached to the bones of the skeleton.

2. **Structure**—A skeletal muscle consists of many long, narrow muscle cells bound together with connective tissue. You must know the following terms from the lecture notes—**fascia, aponeurosis, tendon, fascicle, epimysium, perimysium,** and **endomysium**.

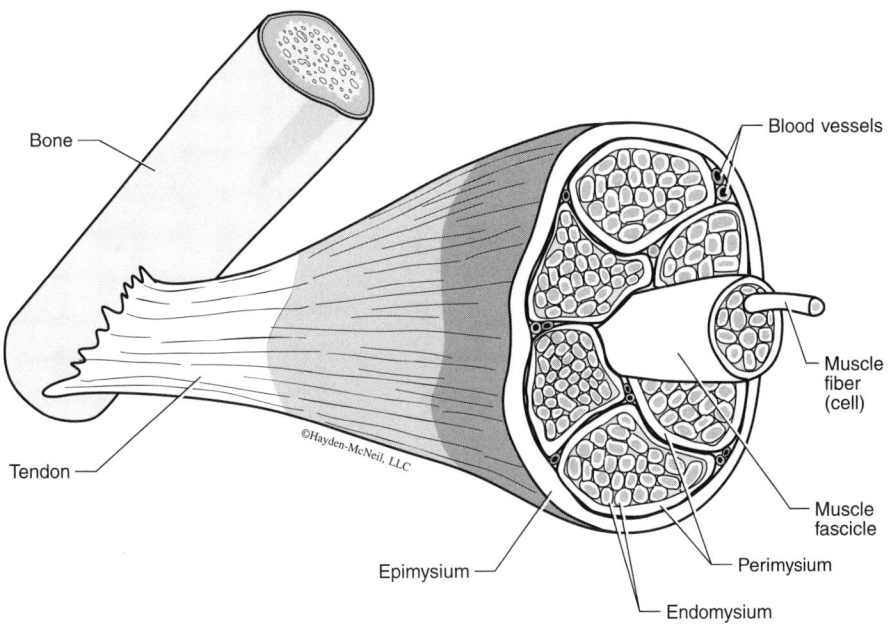

Figure 6-1. Skeletal muscle section.

Because a single muscle cell is such an elongated structure, it is usually referred to as a **muscle fiber** (**myofiber**). Each muscle fiber is unusual in that it contains many nuclei, rather than just the single one found in most other cells. This is because during development of the skeletal muscle system, muscle fibers were formed by the fusion of many individual cells called **myoblasts**.

The plasma membrane of a muscle fiber is called the **sarcolemma**, and its cytoplasm is called **sarcoplasm**. The sarcolemma is invaginated at many points to form structures called transverse tubules or **T-tubules**. The sarcoplasm contains many mitochondria. The endoplasmic reticulum is called **sarcoplasmic reticulum**.

The sarcoplasm contains **myofibrils** composed of thick filaments of **myosin** molecules and thin filaments of **actin** molecules. The thin filaments are associated with two other proteins called **troponin** and **tropomyosin**. Other proteins present in skeletal muscle are listed in section D.

The arrangement of these large protein molecules and the myofibrils in which they occur is so regular that it gives the skeletal muscle fiber a cross-striated appearance. These cross-striations have various designations. They include the Z-line, the A-band, and the I-band. The Z-line represents a point at which the ends of the thin filaments are attached (See lecture notes). That part of a myofibril between two Z-lines is called a **sarcomere**.

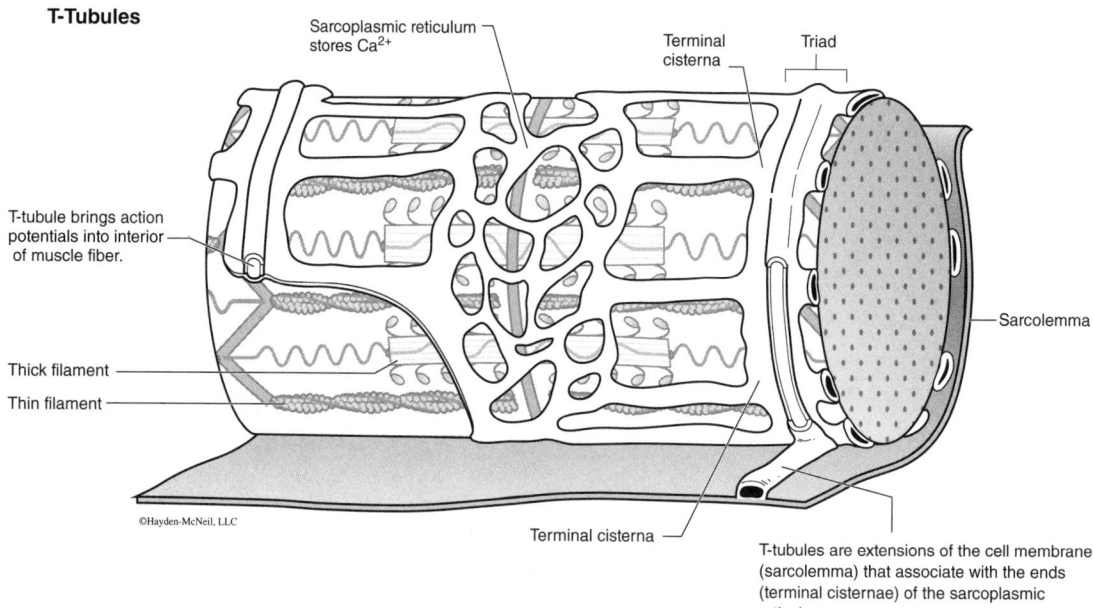

Figure 6-2. Interior of muscle fiber (cell).

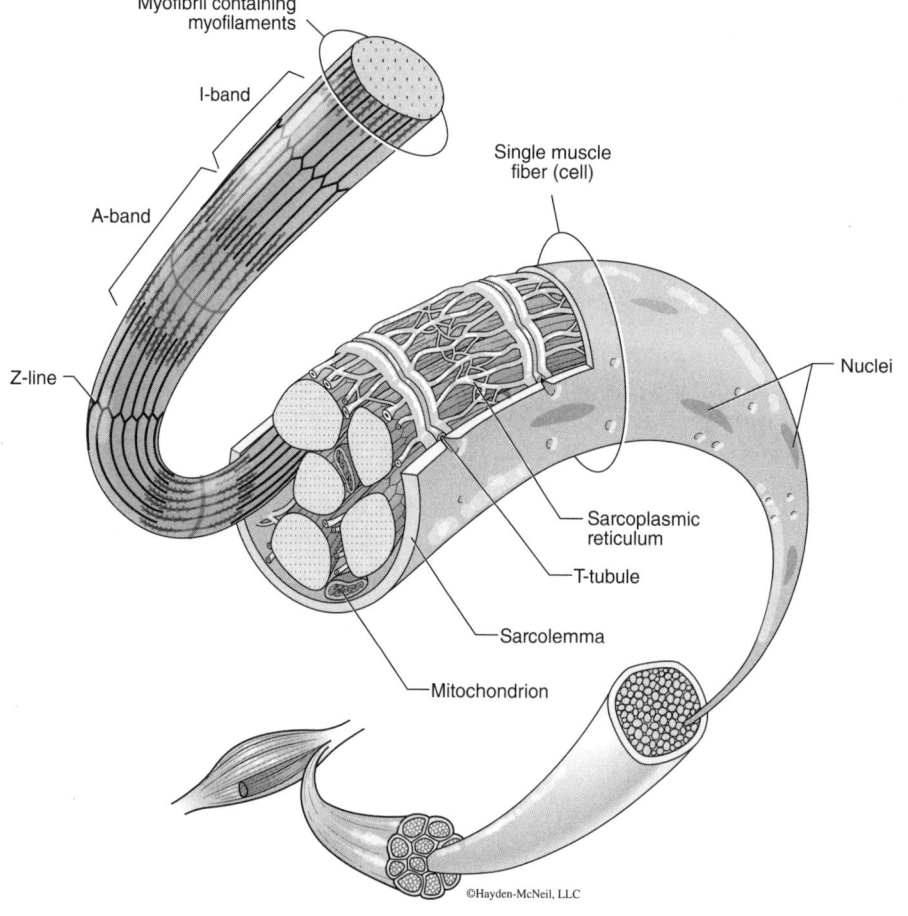

Figure 6-3. Skeletal muscle fiber (cell).

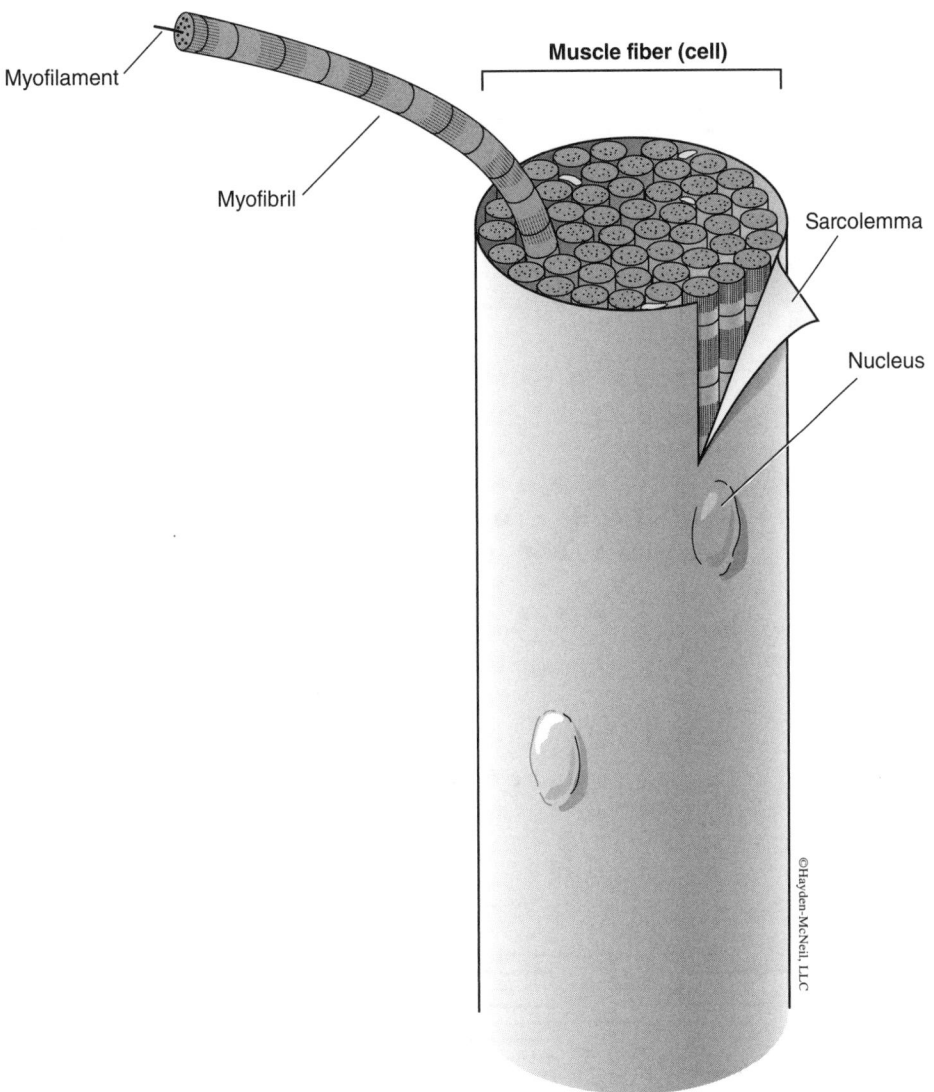

Figure 6-4. Skeletal muscle fiber (cell).

3. **Properties**—Skeletal muscle enables us to carry out a variety of voluntary movements, to maintain the body's posture and balance, and to produce heat. It is often said that skeletal muscle comes under voluntary control. That is true insofar as we can deliberately contract every skeletal muscle in our bodies. However, the complex contractions that occur in our postural muscles when the body is thrown off balance occur reflexively, and involve neurons in the spinal cord and parts of the brain. In a moment, we will consider how these neurons are wired to skeletal muscles.

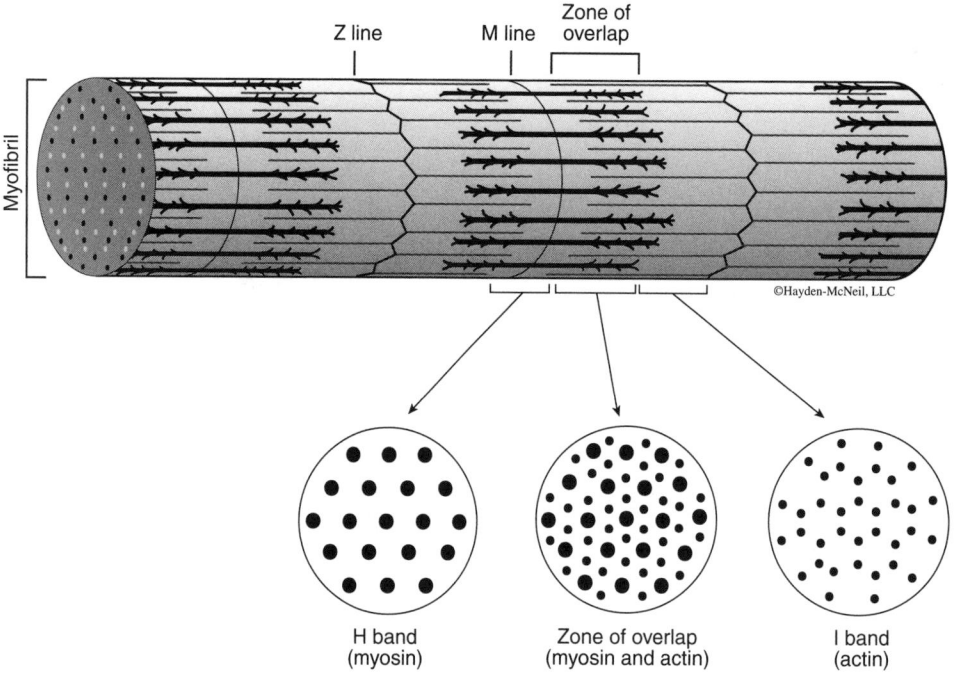

Figure 6-5. Myofibril.

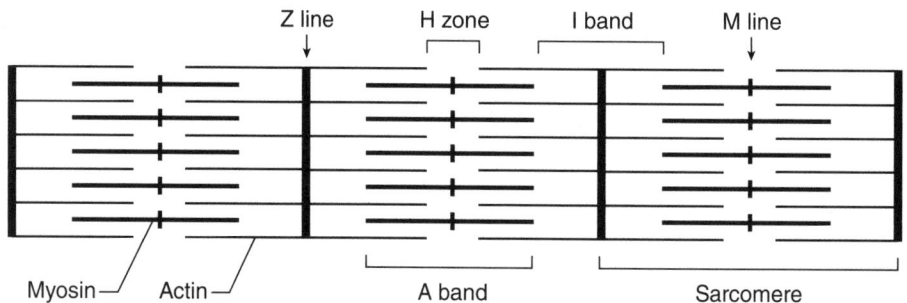

Figure 6-6. Sarcomere.

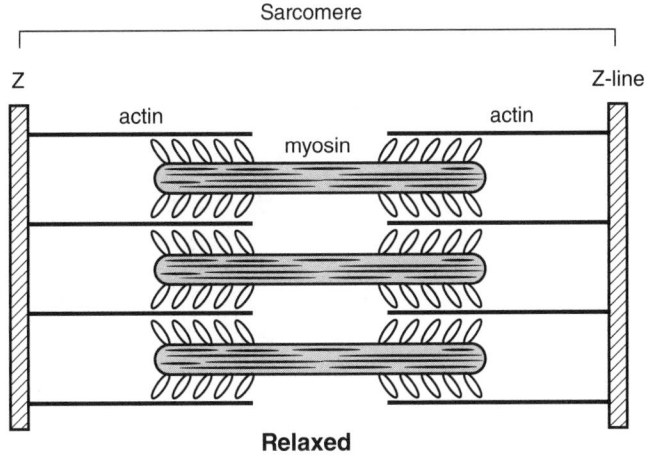

Relaxed

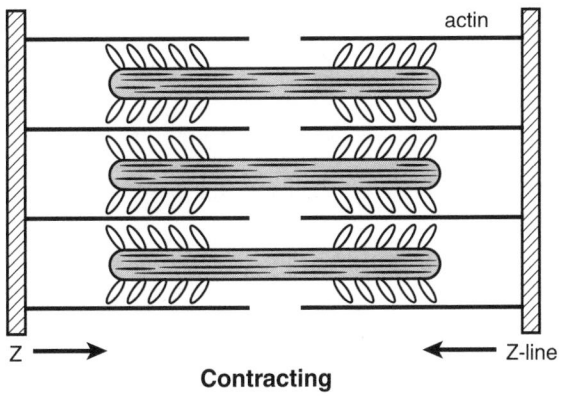

Contracting

thin filaments - actin
thick filaments - myosin

Figure 6-7. Sarcomere.

D. Proteins in Muscle (Cardiac and Skeletal)

Contractile	Excitation-contraction coupling	Sarcomeric skeleton	Cytoskeletal	Membrane-associated
Actin	Troponin	Titin	Desmin	Dystrophin
myosin	tropomyosin	nebulin	Mictrotubule proteins	

Also: *Calsequestrin, creatine phosphokinase, myoglobin*

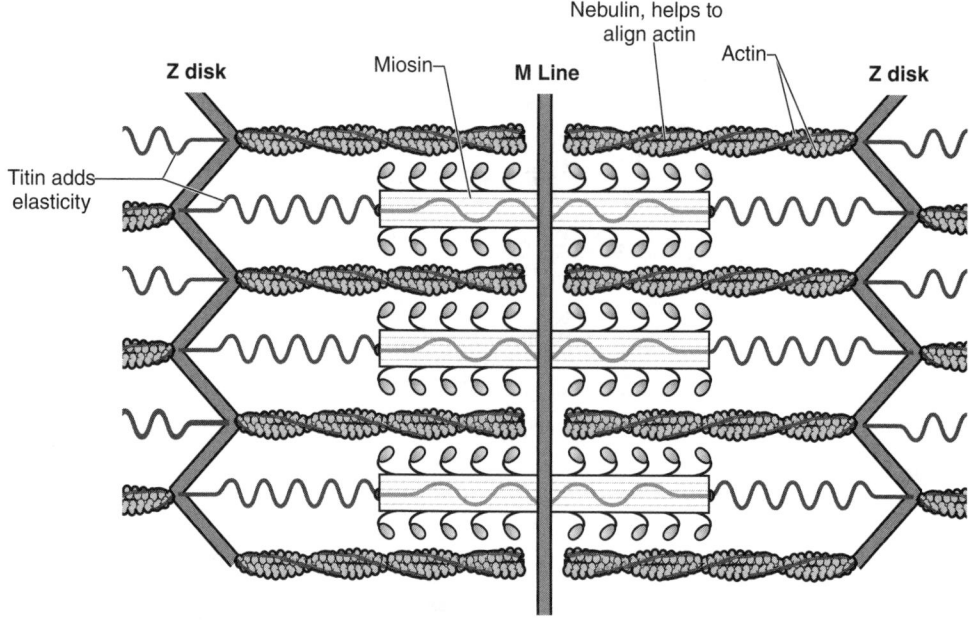

Titin and nebulin are giant accessory proteins. Titin spans the distance from one Z disk to the neighboring M line. Nebulin, lying along the thin filaments, attaches to a Z disk but does not extend to the M line.

Figure 6-8. Sarcomere anatomy.

E. How Muscles Contract

The contraction of smooth muscle, cardiac muscle, and skeletal muscle is powered by ATP and has its basis in the interaction of actin and myosin. However, in resting skeletal and cardiac muscle, actin and myosin cannot interact because the myosin binding sites on actin are masked by tropomyosin. Troponin is closely associated with both tropomyosin and actin, and plays an important function in initiating contraction, as discussed below.

Smooth muscle has actin and myosin, but does not have troponin and tropomyosin. You **must** read about further details on smooth muscle contraction from the lecture notes.

Contraction of skeletal and cardiac muscle is initiated when a wave of electrical depolarization spreads over the sarcolemma. This wave of electrical depolarization penetrates into the interior of the muscle fibers by means of the T-tubules. In skeletal and cardiac muscle, this leads to the release of calcium ions (stored within the sarcoplasmic reticulum) into the sarcoplasm.

In cardiac muscle, but not skeletal muscle, a large amount of calcium also enters the sarcoplasm from the extracellular fluid by passing through special channels in the T-tubules.

In cardiac and skeletal muscle, these calcium ions bind to troponin, which then causes a shape change in the molecules of tropomyosin. The adjustments that tropomyosin makes as a result of this shape change exposes the previously masked myosin-binding sites on actin. Actin and myosin are then free to interact (read lecture notes), and the muscle starts to contract.

The energy for contraction is provided by ATP, which binds to the head of the myosin molecule. The myosin molecule hydrolyses the ATP to ADP and phosphate. In the process, the energy of the ATP is transferred to the myosin molecule.

The myosin molecule acts rather like the oar of a rower. The procedure is as follows (see diagram).

1. Resting condition, the myosin is primed and ready for action.

2. Attachment of myosin head to actin (= dipping oar in water).

3. Power stroke (= rower pulling on oar).

4. Detachment and reorientation (= rower raises oar and brings it forward again).

5. Preparation and priming for next attachment step (Not shown in diagram).

This whole cycle is associated with the hydrolysis of ATP to ADP and an inorganic phosphate group (P_i). If you look at the diagram, you will see that ATP binds to the myosin head in the detachment and reorientation step (4). In the resting, primed condition (1), this ATP has been hydrolyzed (actually, by the ATP-ase activity of the myosin heads) and the products ADP and P_i remain bound to the myosin head.

It is during this hydrolysis that the energy of the ATP molecule becomes locked up in the myosin molecule, which is now primed and ready for action.

Sources of ATP are glycolysis (in the sarcoplasm) and oxidative phosphorylation (in the mitochondria). Additionally, some ATP can be formed from ADP and creatine phosphate. Creatine phosphate is part of the so-called "phosphagen" system, and is available to provide a burst of energy on demand.

ATP hydrolysis drives muscle contraction

1. Resting (ATP has been hydrolyzed to ADP and inorganic phosphate, which remain attached to myosin head—only one myosin head shown)

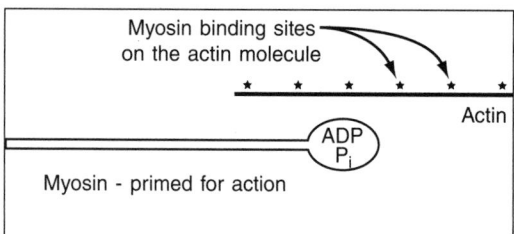

2. Inorganic phosphate (P_i) dissociates from myosin head—attachment

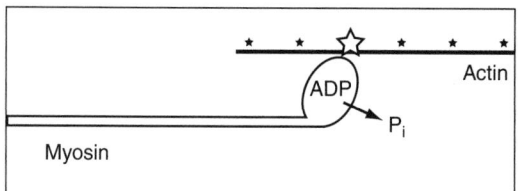

3. ADP dissociates from myosin head, followed by power stroke

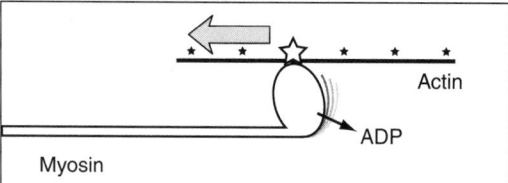

4. ATP binds to myosin head, followed by detachment and reorientation

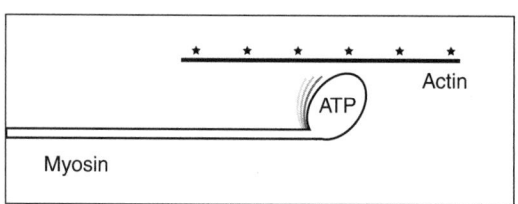

5. ATP is then hydrolyzed to ADP and inorganic phosphate (P_i). The myosin molecule is then primed for a return to step 1 and the cycle is repeated. ATP hydrolysis by the myosin head is catalyzed by actin.

Figure 6-9. Actin-myosin interactions.

Movement Type	Action
Flexion	decreases the angle at a joint
Extension	increases the angle at a joint
Abduction	moves a bone away from the midline of the body
Adduction	moves a bone toward the midline of the body
Elevation	produces an upward movement
Depression	produces a downward movement
Supination	palm is turned upward or anteriorly
Pronation	palm is turned downward or posteriorly
Protraction	pushes bone forward
Retraction	pulls bone backwards (from protraction)
Dorsiflexion	flexes ankle, moving foot inferiorly
Plantar Flexion	extends ankle, moving foot inferiorly
Compression	reduction of the volume or mass of something by applying pressure
Rotation	moves a bone around its longitudinal axis
Tension	makes a body part more rigid
Sphincter	decreases the size of an opening

F. Most Movements Involve Muscle Groups

Our brain normally visualizes a *movement* before it is made. Skeletal muscles usually function in groups to produce coordinated movements. Additionally, **most** skeletal muscles are arranged in opposing pairs. That is, flexors/extensors, abductors/adductors, etc.

Most movements are coordinated by several skeletal muscles acting in groups rather than individually. A muscle that is primarily involved in a movement is called the **prime mover** or **agonist**. In the case of flexing the forearm at the elbow, the prime mover is the biceps brachii.

In the above case, while the prime mover is contracting another muscle called the **antagonist** is relaxing. In the present example, this muscle is the triceps brachii.

Note that when the movement is changed so that the forearm is extended at the elbow instead of being flexed, the triceps brachii is the prime mover and the biceps brachii is the antagonist and must be relaxed.

The roles of the two muscles in the above example therefore depend on which movement is being made.

When the prime mover contracts it often acts in concert with other "helper" muscles that also contract. These muscles are called **synergists**. These muscles may smooth out the movement and help the prime mover to function more efficiently.

Synergists may also serve to stabilize the origin of a prime mover muscle. For example, the scapula is a freely movable bone that serves as the origin for several muscles that move the arm. To do this, however, the scapula must be held steady. This is accomplished by certain synergist muscles that hold the scapula firmly against the back.

In abduction of the arm, the deltoid muscle is the prime mover. It pulls on the humerus to abduct the arm. The supraspinatus muscle aids it synergistically. Since the origin of the supraspinatus is the scapula, and one of the origins of the deltoid muscle is also the scapula, other synergists must contract to hold the scapula steady and firm. At the same time, the antagonist muscle group (pectoralis major, latissimus dorsi, and teres major) to this action must be relaxed, so that the movement is unopposed.

On the following pages is a list of some of the major muscles of the human body. The origin of a muscle is the attachment site that is stationary or most fixed. The insertion is the attachment site that moves. The action is self-explanatory. You are responsible for knowing the information. Also, be able to locate them physically on a model or diagram.

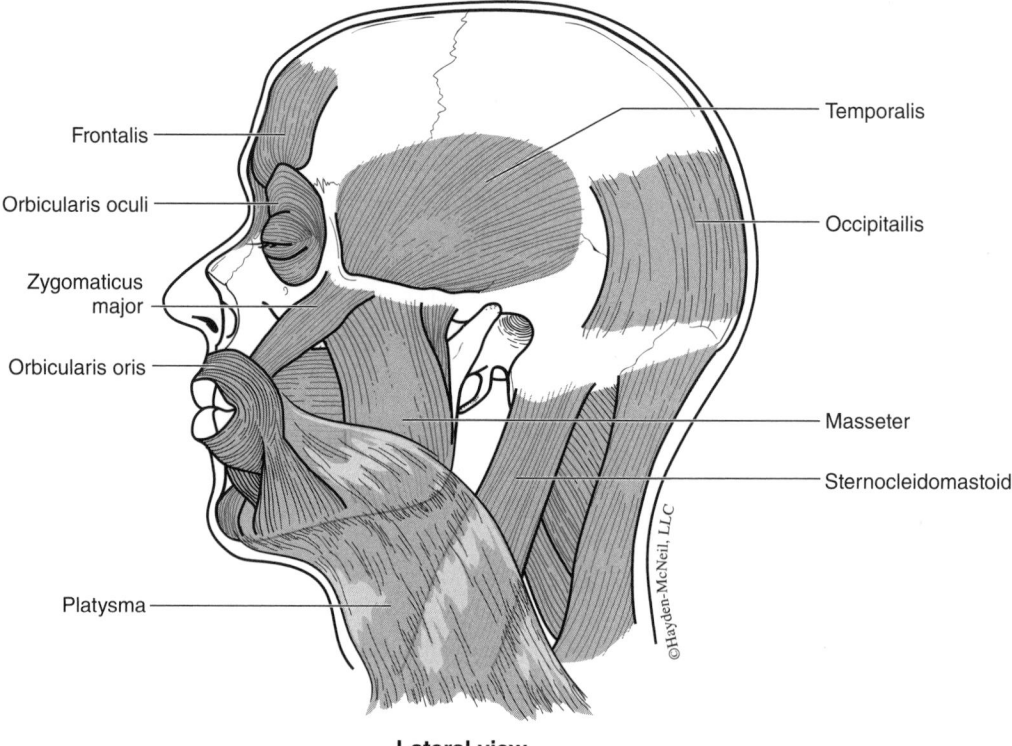

Lateral view

Figure 6-10. Lateral view

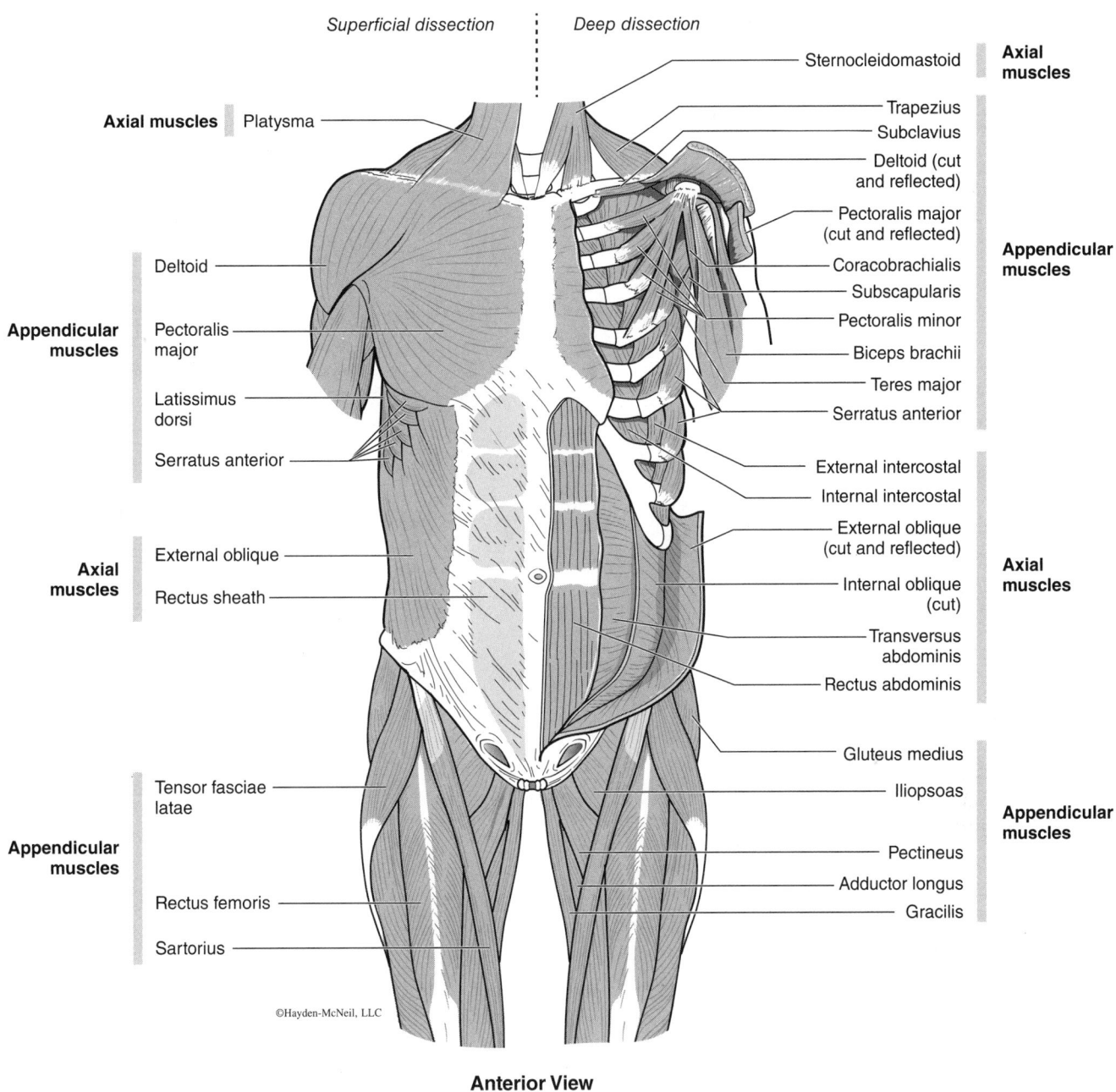

Anterior View

Figure 6-11. Muscles anterior view.

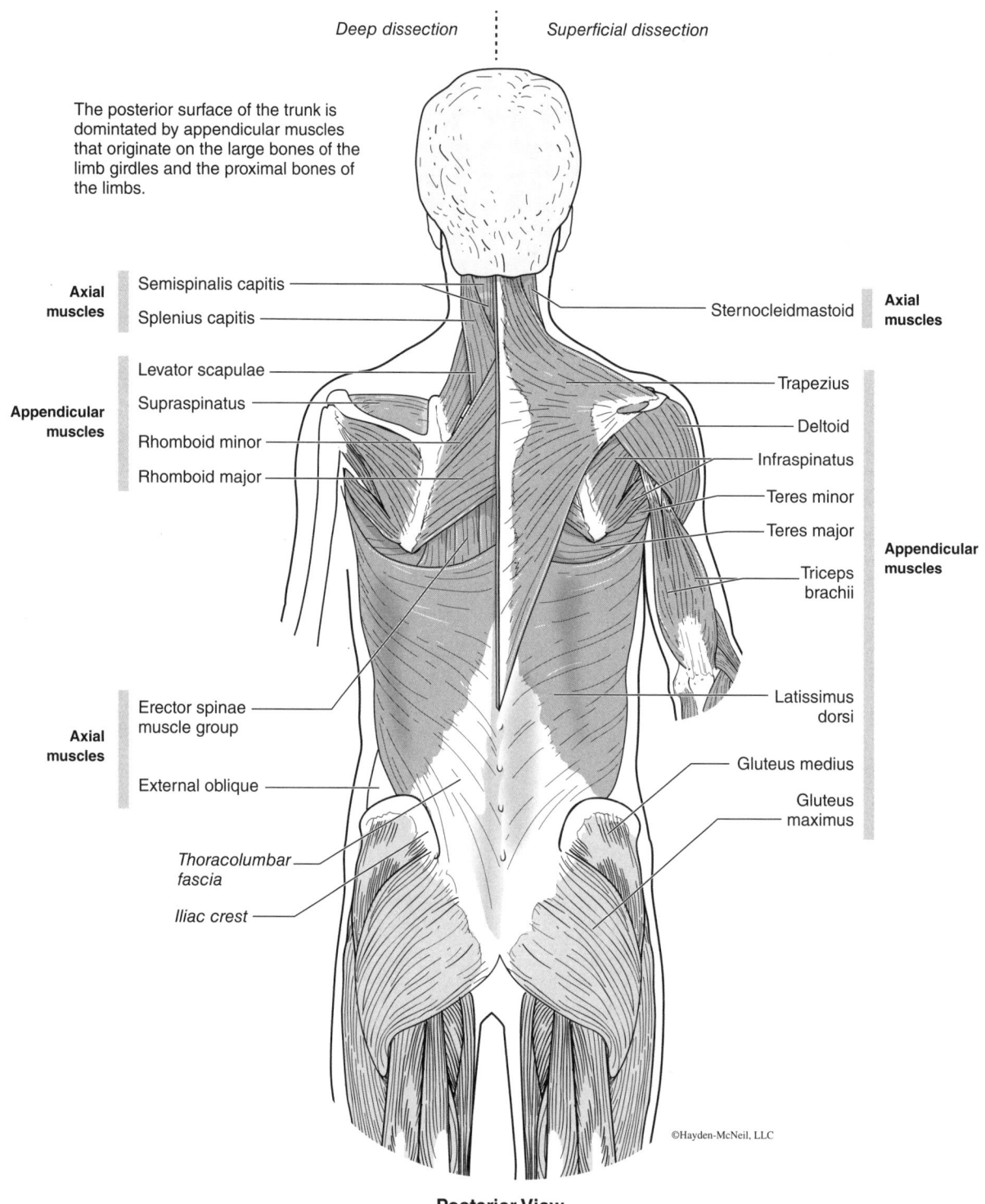

Deep dissection ┊ *Superficial dissection*

The posterior surface of the trunk is domintated by appendicular muscles that originate on the large bones of the limb girdles and the proximal bones of the limbs.

Axial muscles
- Semispinalis capitis
- Splenius capitis

Appendicular muscles
- Levator scapulae
- Supraspinatus
- Rhomboid minor
- Rhomboid major

Axial muscles
- Erector spinae muscle group
- External oblique
- *Thoracolumbar fascia*
- *Iliac crest*

Axial muscles
- Sternocleidmastoid

Appendicular muscles
- Trapezius
- Deltoid
- Infraspinatus
- Teres minor
- Teres major
- Triceps brachii
- Latissimus dorsi
- Gluteus medius
- Gluteus maximus

©Hayden-McNeil, LLC

Posterior View

Figure 6-12. Muscles posterior view.

Muscles That Position the Pectoral Girdle

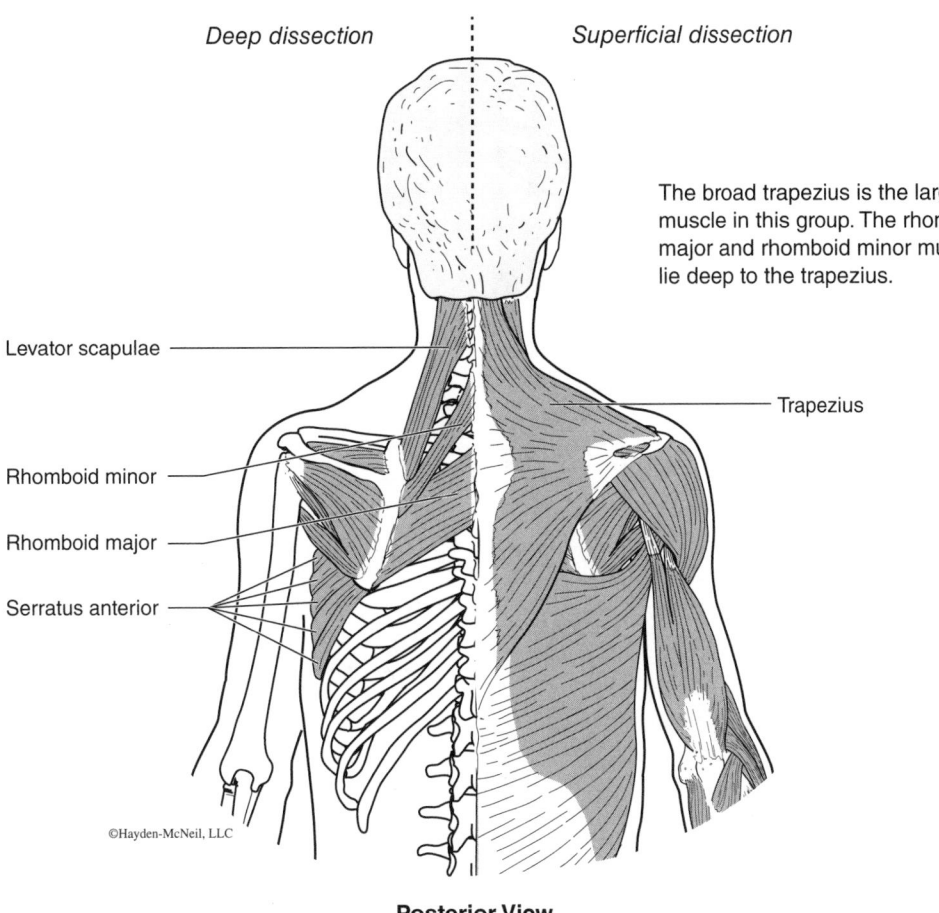

Deep dissection   *Superficial dissection*

The broad trapezius is the largest muscle in this group. The rhomboid major and rhomboid minor muscles lie deep to the trapezius.

Levator scapulae

Trapezius

Rhomboid minor

Rhomboid major

Serratus anterior

©Hayden-McNeil, LLC

Posterior View

Figure 6-13. Muscles posterior view—deep vs. superficial.

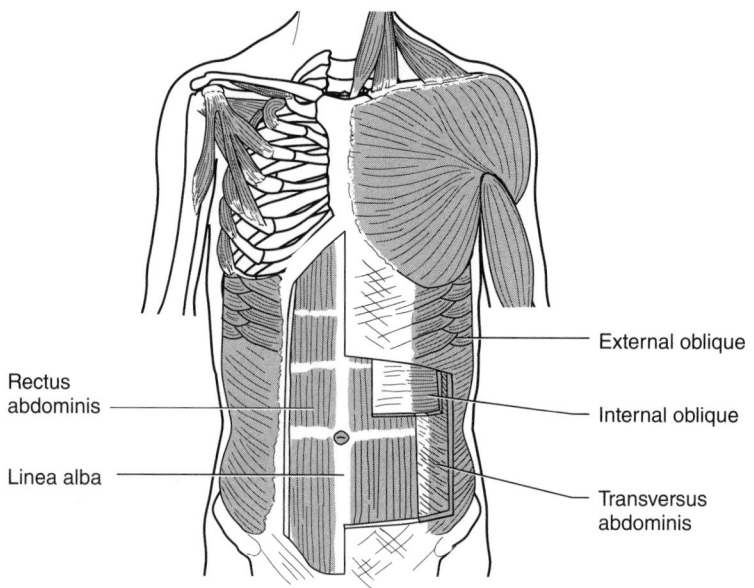

Rectus abdominis

Linea alba

External oblique

Internal oblique

Transversus abdominis

Note: The aponeuroses (tendons) of the three lateral abdominal muscles join to form the fascial sheath surrounding the rectus abdominis

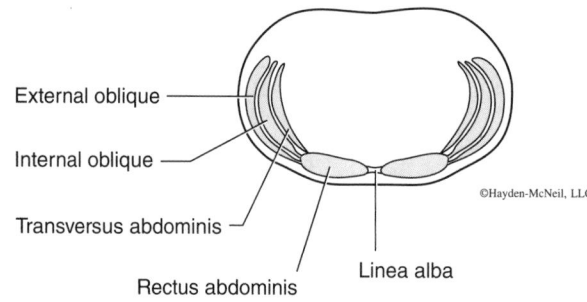

External oblique

Internal oblique

Transversus abdominis

Rectus abdominis

Linea alba

©Hayden-McNeil, LLC

Figure 6-14. Abdominal muscles. Trunk—anterior and cross-sectional views.

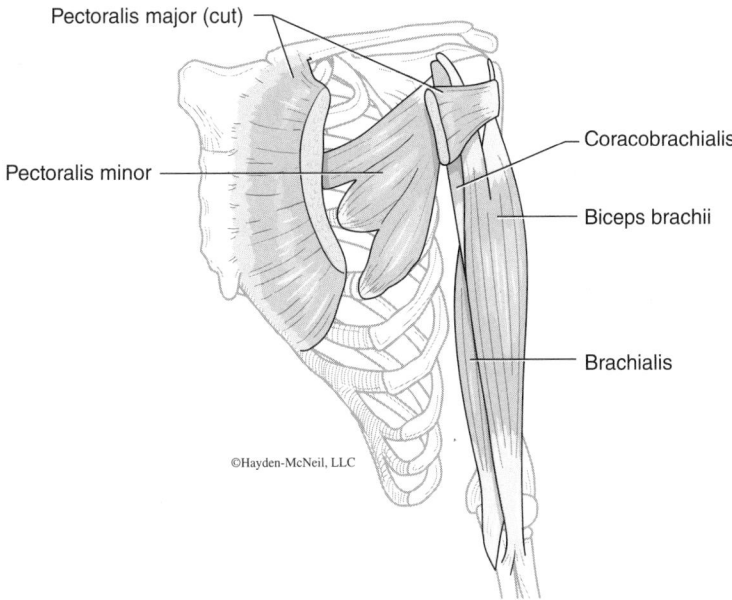

Figure 6-15. Muscles of the anterior chest and arm. Shoulder—anterior view.

Muscles That Position the Pectoral Girdle

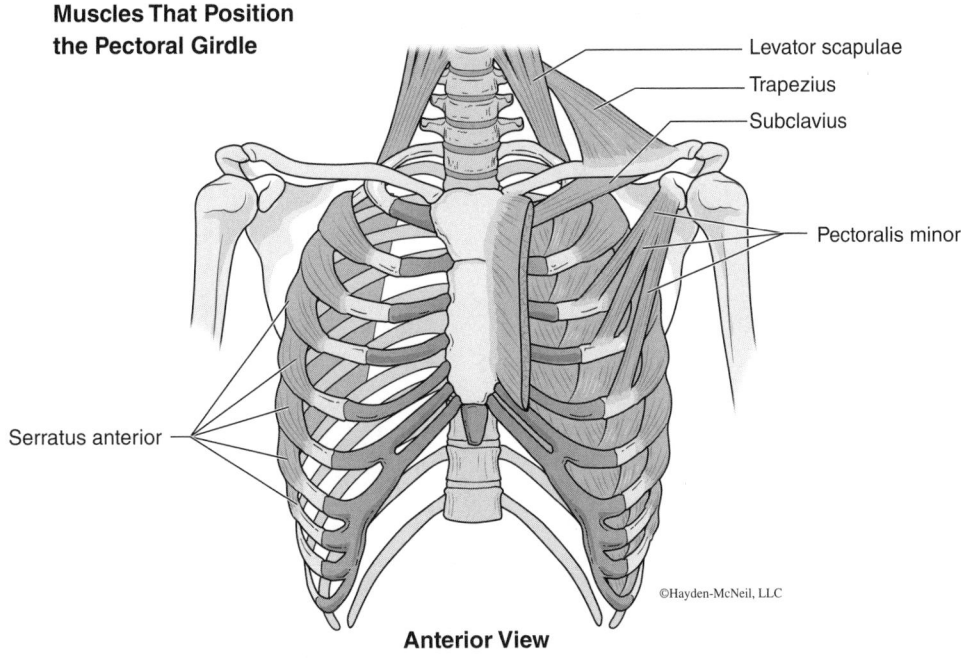

Anterior View

Figure 6-16. Muscles—close-up anterior view.

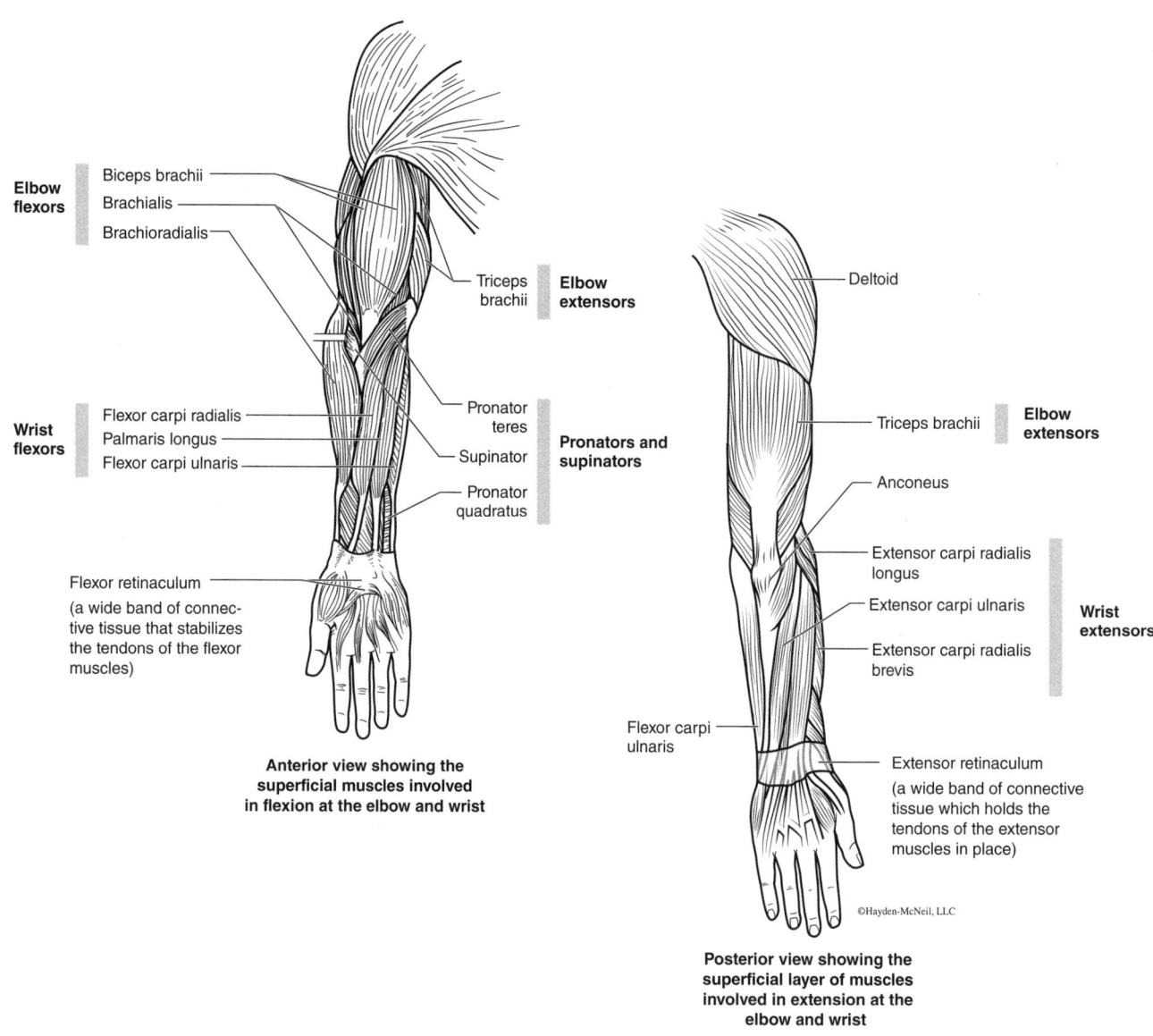

Elbow flexors
- Biceps brachii
- Brachialis
- Brachioradialis

Wrist flexors
- Flexor carpi radialis
- Palmaris longus
- Flexor carpi ulnaris

Flexor retinaculum

(a wide band of connective tissue that stabilizes the tendons of the flexor muscles)

Triceps brachii — **Elbow extensors**

Pronator teres
Supinator — **Pronators and supinators**
Pronator quadratus

Anterior view showing the superficial muscles involved in flexion at the elbow and wrist

Deltoid

Triceps brachii — **Elbow extensors**

Anconeus

Extensor carpi radialis longus
Extensor carpi ulnaris — **Wrist extensors**
Extensor carpi radialis brevis

Flexor carpi ulnaris

Extensor retinaculum

(a wide band of connective tissue which holds the tendons of the extensor muscles in place)

©Hayden-McNeil, LLC

Posterior view showing the superficial layer of muscles involved in extension at the elbow and wrist

Figure 6-17. Muscles anterior/posterior view—arm and hand.

Muscles that Move the Arm

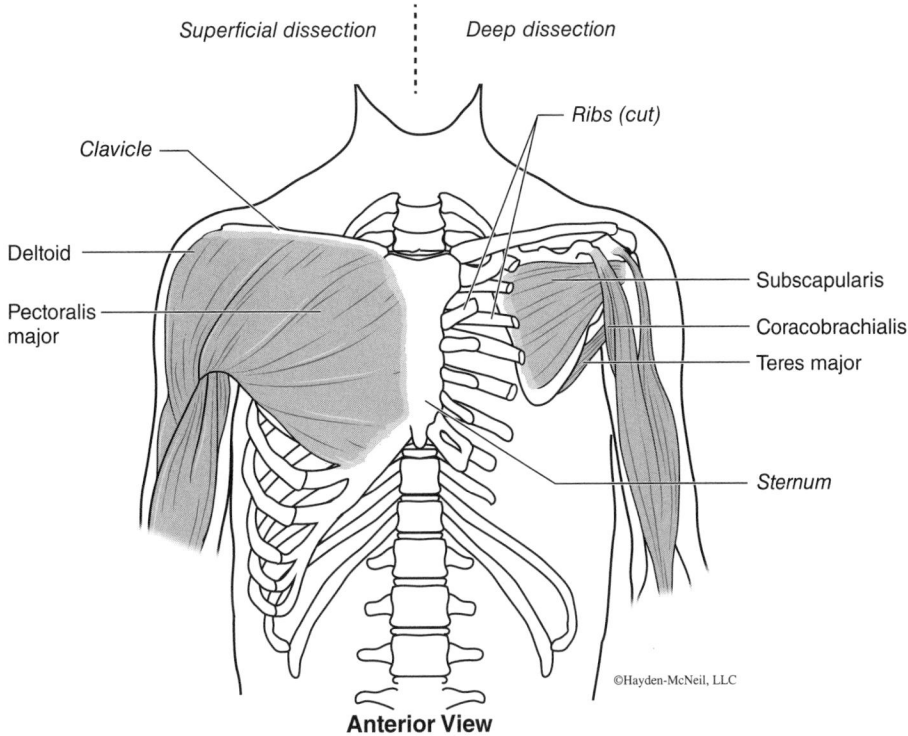

Figure 6-18. Muscles—anterior view torso—deep vs. superficial.

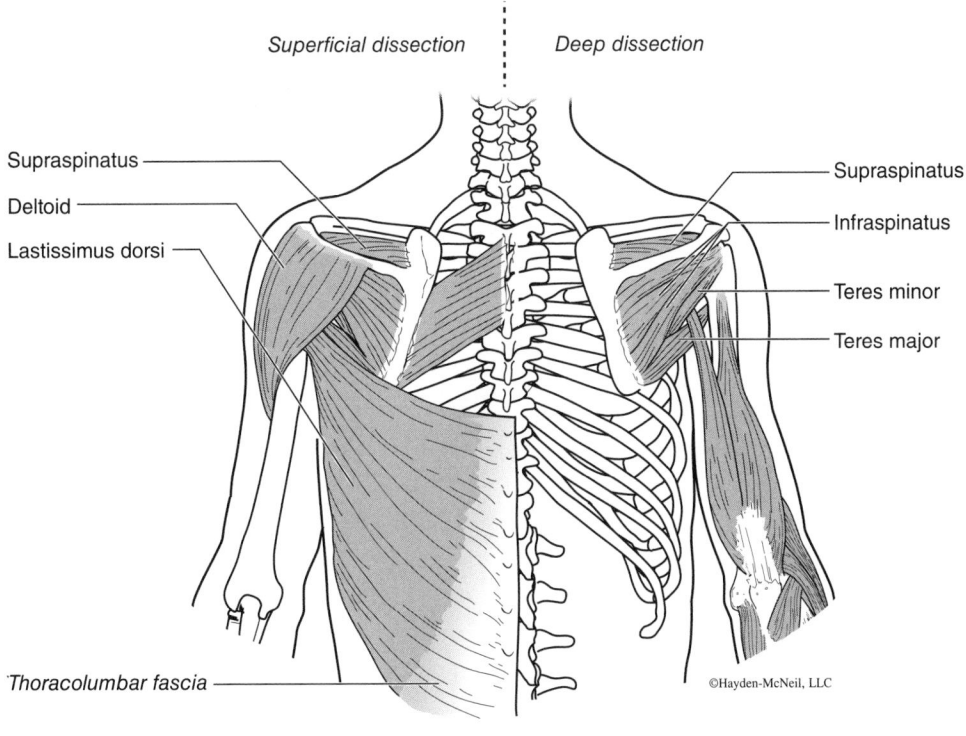

Figure 6-19. Muscles—posterior view torso—deep vs. superficial.

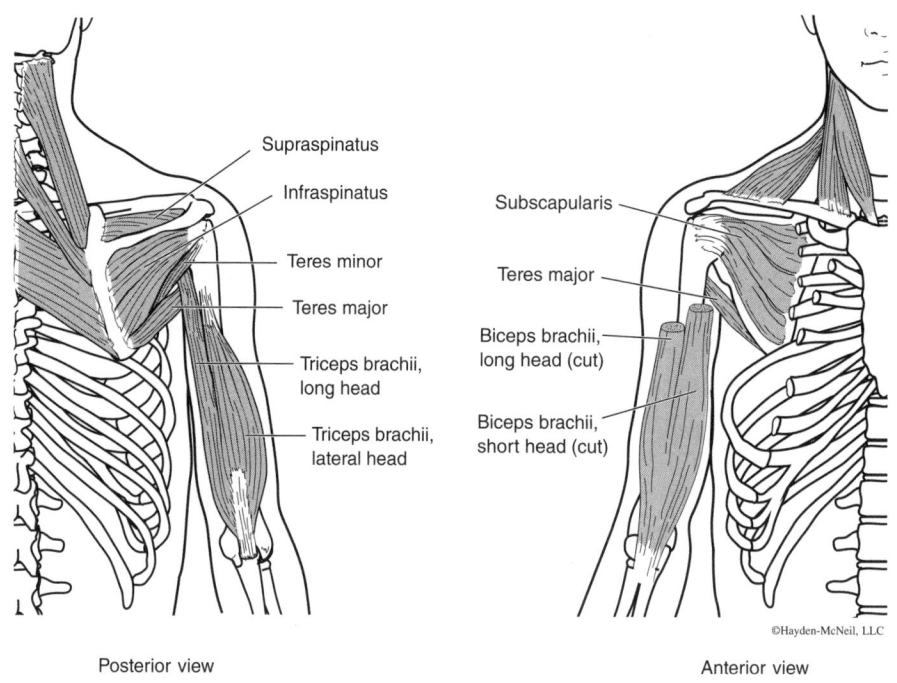

Posterior view

Anterior view

Figure 6-20. Muscles of the scapula and upper arm.

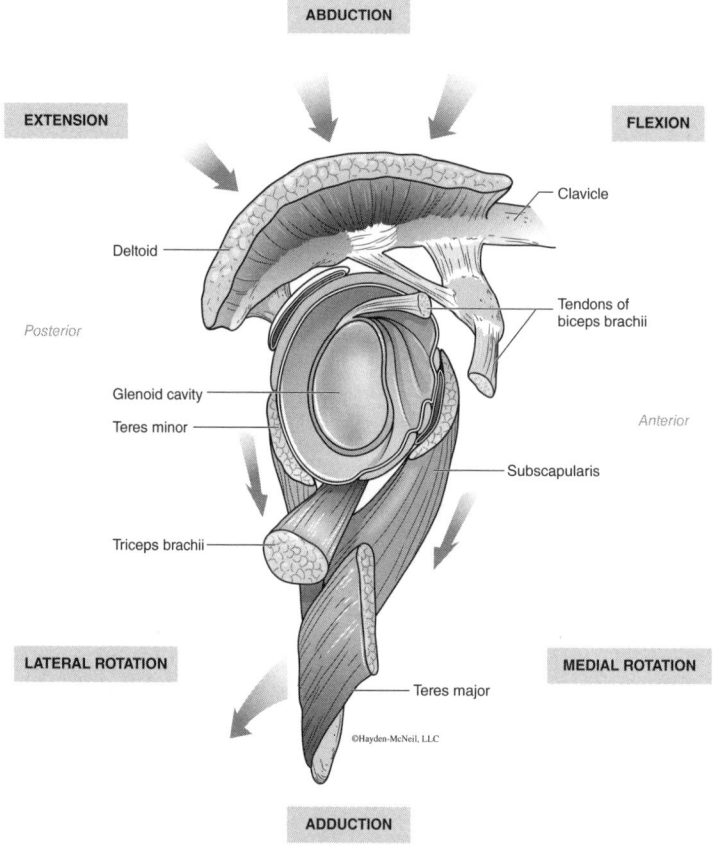

Figure 6-21. Muscles rotator cuff.

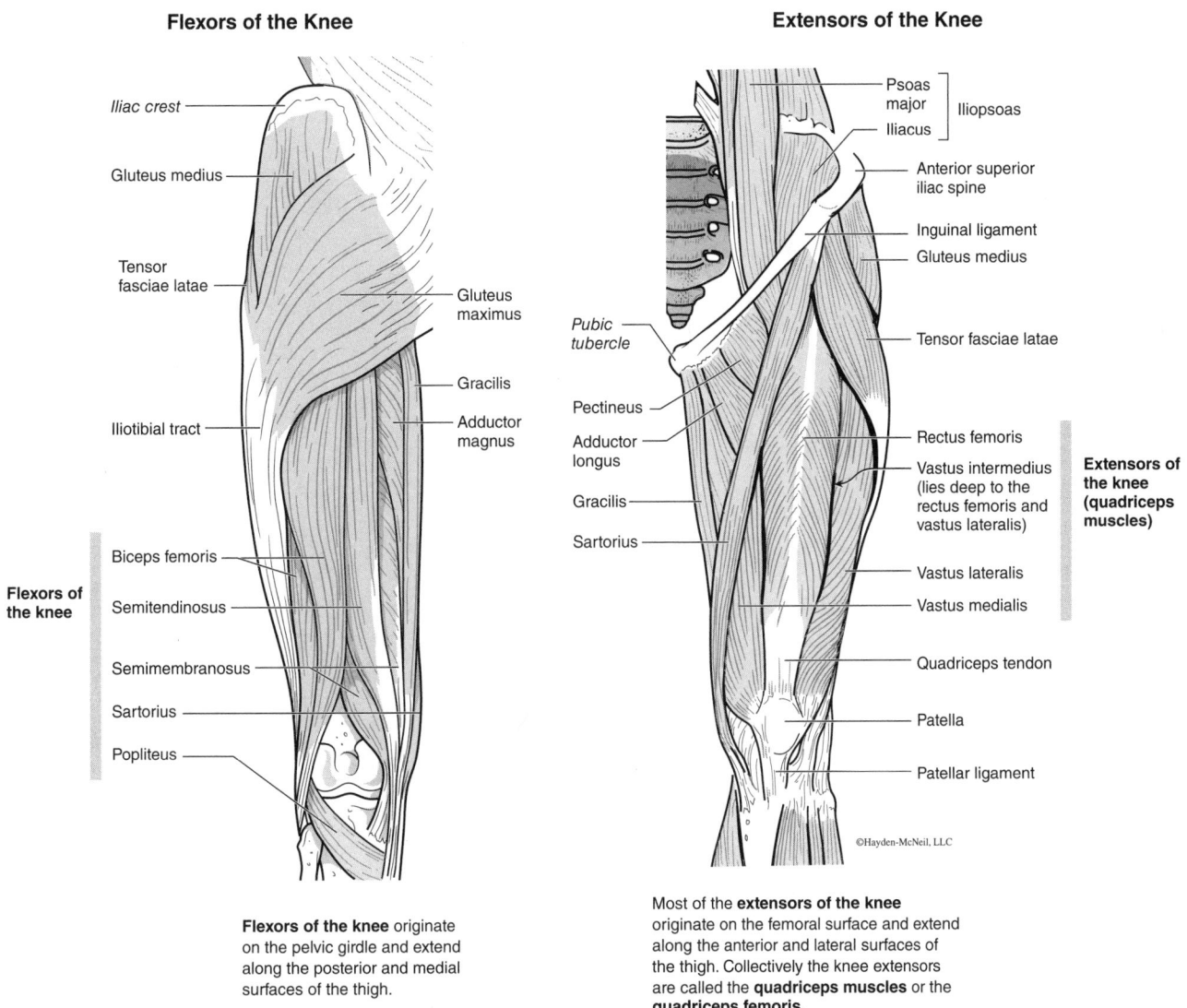

Flexors of the Knee

Iliac crest

Gluteus medius

Tensor fasciae latae

Gluteus maximus

Gracilis

Adductor magnus

Iliotibial tract

Flexors of the knee

Biceps femoris

Semitendinosus

Semimembranosus

Sartorius

Popliteus

Extensors of the Knee

Psoas major
Iliacus
Iliopsoas

Anterior superior iliac spine

Inguinal ligament
Gluteus medius

Pubic tubercle

Tensor fasciae latae

Pectineus

Adductor longus

Rectus femoris

Vastus intermedius (lies deep to the rectus femoris and vastus lateralis)

Extensors of the knee (quadriceps muscles)

Gracilis

Sartorius

Vastus lateralis

Vastus medialis

Quadriceps tendon

Patella

Patellar ligament

©Hayden-McNeil, LLC

Flexors of the knee originate on the pelvic girdle and extend along the posterior and medial surfaces of the thigh.

Most of the **extensors of the knee** originate on the femoral surface and extend along the anterior and lateral surfaces of the thigh. Collectively the knee extensors are called the **quadriceps muscles** or the **quadriceps femoris.**

Figure 6-22. Muscles anterior/posterior view—flexors vs. extensors.

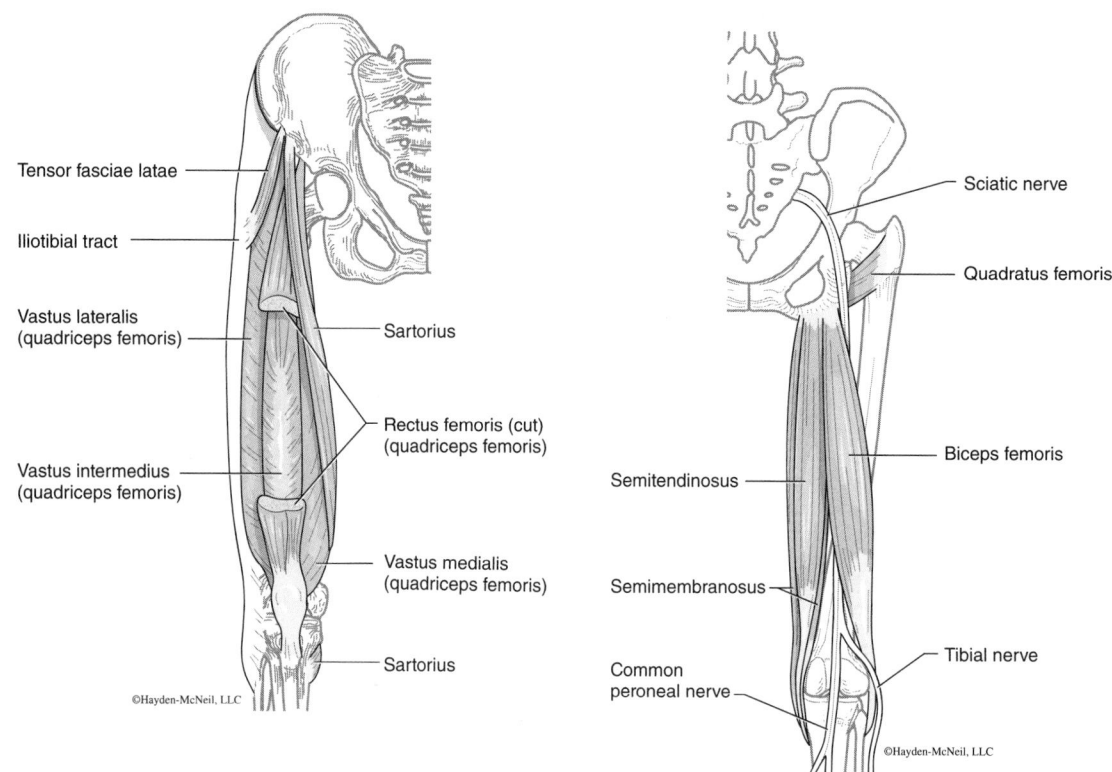

Figure 6-23. Muscles of the anterior thigh. Hip and thigh—posterior view.

Figure 6-24. Hamstring muscles. Hip and thigh—posterior view.

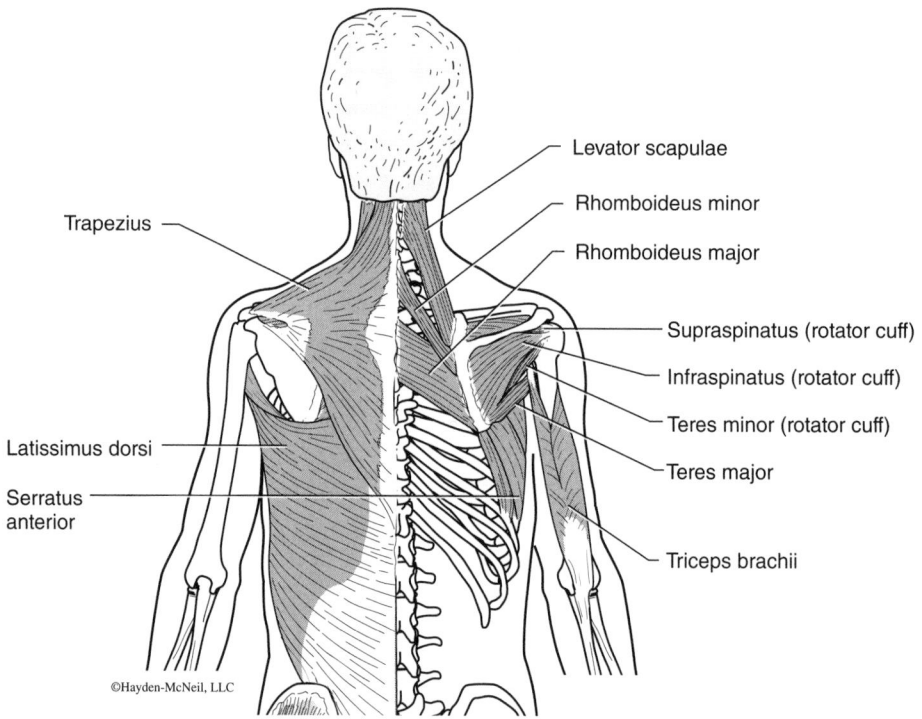

Figure 6-25. Posterior back, shoulder, and arm muscles. Trunk—dorsal view.

II. Levers and Muscle Action

The skeleton provides a system of levers that are moved by skeletal muscle contractions. Levers serve to amplify muscle contraction (see notes). Full details are given in your notes, and you should be familiar with them.

Consider the bones and muscles of our arms. The muscles in the upper arm move the forearm by pulling on the forearm bones. The contracting muscle provides the **in-force**. The in-force creates an **out-force** at the end of the arm nearest the hand. The out-force produces movement or lifts weights. In other muscle lever systems (e.g., the legs) the out-force can be involved in resisting gravity. The **fulcrum** is the point about which the lever moves. This is usually the joint. In our example the fulcrum is the elbow.

Levers are categorized depending on where their components are positioned. (See Figure 6-27.)

First-class levers: The components of this lever system are arranged so that the **fulcrum is between** the in-force and the out-force. This is a common arrangement for muscles that produce extension of body parts (e.g., extension of the forearm by the triceps or lifting of the head).

Second-class levers: There are no good examples of these in the human body.

Third-class levers: The components of this lever system are arranged so that the **in-force is between** the out-force and the fulcrum. This is a very common kind of lever in the body.

Long bones act as levers to amplify muscle contraction

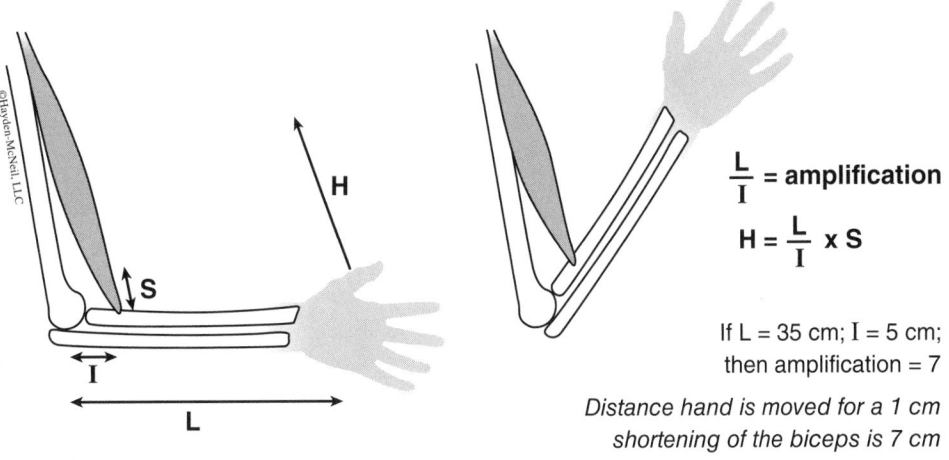

$$\frac{L}{I} = \text{amplification}$$

$$H = \frac{L}{I} \times S$$

If L = 35 cm; I = 5 cm; then amplification = 7

Distance hand is moved for a 1 cm shortening of the biceps is 7 cm

Figure 6-26. Calculation involving levers.

©Hayden-McNeil, LLC

First class lever

Third class lever

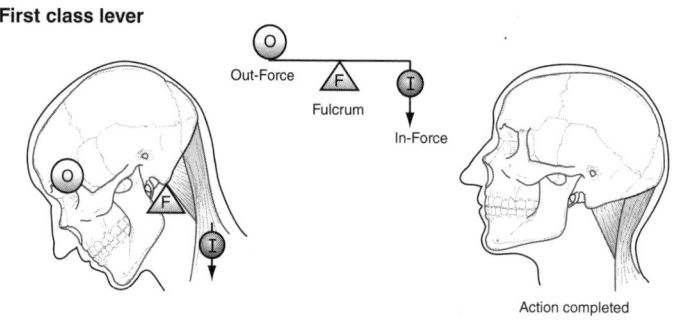
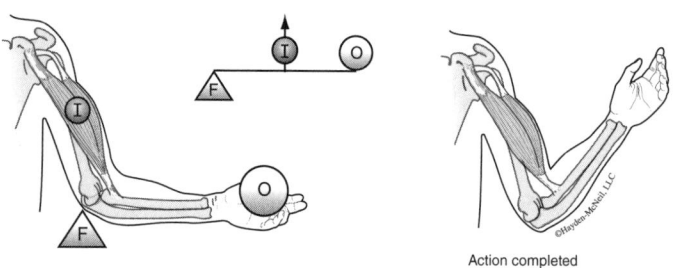

Figure 6-27. Examples of levers in the body.

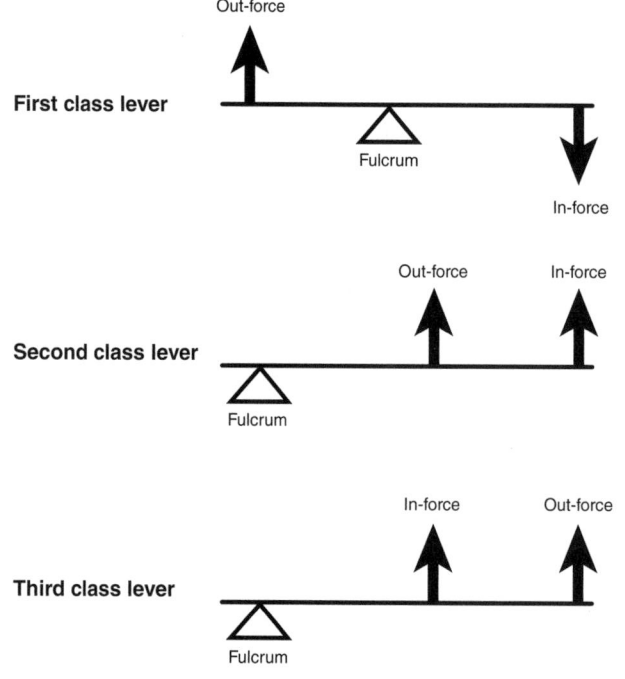

Figure 6-28. Classifications of levers.

Exercise A

Identifying Muscles

Using the chart provided below, find the muscles listed on the provided images, models, and posters. When possible, find the muscle on yourself and perform the action.

Muscle	Origin	Insertion	Action	Relationships
1. orbicularis oculi	maxilla, frontal bone (orbit)	around eye	blinking (closure)	
2. orbicularis oris	maxilla, mandible	lips	closes lips, protrudes lips	
3. masseter	zygomatic, maxilla	mandible	elevates mandible (closes lower jaw, clenches teeth)	
4. sternocleidomastoid	sternum, clavicle	temporal, oc-cipital (mastoid process)	flexes neck, elevates chin, ro-tates head, elevates sternum	
5. zygomaticus major	zygomatic bones	angle of mouth	elevates and abducts upper lip (smiling)	
6. pectoralis major	clavicle, sternum, cart. of ribs	humerus	flexes, adducts, rotates humerus	
7. pectoralis minor	sternal ends of upper ribs	scapula	pulls scapula forward and downward, raises ribs	deep to pectoralis major
8. biceps brachii	two locations on scapula	radius	flexes forearm and shoulder; rotates (supinates) hand	
9. brachioradialis	humerus	radius	flexes elbow	
10. brachialis	humerus	ulna	flexes forearm	deep to lower part of biceps brachii
11. triceps brachii	scapula, two loca-tions on humerus	ulna	extends forearm, (aids in adduction)	
12. deltoid	scapula, clavicle	humerus	abducts upper arm; extends, flexes, and rotates humerus	
13. trapezius	occipital bone; spines of cervical and thoracic vert.	clavicle, scapula	elevates, retracts, depresses, or rotates scapula	most superficial muscle of back
14. latissimus dorsi	spinous processes of S,L,T vert.; ilium	humerus	extends, adducts arm; rotates humerus inward	
15. teres major	scapula	humerus	medial rotates arm, adducts arm, extends arm	
16. supraspinatus	scapula	humerus	aids in abduction of arm, weak flexion of arm, stabi-lizes shoulder	part of rotator cuff
17. infraspinatus	scapula	humerus	lateral rotation of arm; abduction of upper arm, stabilizes shoulder	part of rotator cuff
18. teres minor	scapula	humerus	lateral rotation of arm; weak adduction of upper arm, stabilizes shoulder	part of rotator cuff
19. subscapularis	scapula	humerus	medial rotation of arm, stabi-lizes shoulder	part of rotator cuff
20. pronator teres	humerus and ulna	radius	pronates forearm (and hand)	
21. supinator	humerus and ulna	radius	supinates forearm (and hand)	

Muscle	Origin	Insertion	Action	Relationships
22. extensor digitorum communis	humerus	phalanges	extends fingers and wrist	
23. flexor digitorum profundus	ulna	phalanges	flexes distal joints of fingers	
24. external intercostals	lower margin of upper eleven rib	superior border of rib below	draw ventral part of ribs upward, increasing the volume of the thoracic cavity	
25. internal intercostals	From the cartilages to the angles of the upper eleven ribs	superior border of rib below	draw ventral part of ribs downward, decreasing the volume of the thoracic cavity	
26. rectus abdominis	pubic symphysis	sternum (xiphoid process), ribs	flexes vertebral column, compress abdomen	
27. external oblique	lower ribs	iliac crest, linea alba	compress abdomen, flex and rotate vertebral column (depresses ribs)	most superficial of the lateral abdominal muscles
28. internal oblique	Iliac crest, inguinal ligament, lumbodorsal fascia	lower ribs, linea alba	compress abdomen, flex and rotate vertebral column	middle layer of the lateral abdominal muscles
29. transversus abdominis	inguinal ligament, lumbodorsal fascia, lower ribs	linea alba	compress abdomen	deepest of the lateral abdominal muscles
30. diaphragm	sternum (xiphoid process), lower ribs, lumbar vertebrae	central tendon	pull central tendon downward (increase volume of thoracic cavity)	
31. gluteus maximus	sacrum, coccyx, ilium	femur; fascia	extends, abducts leg, laterally rotates thigh	
32. sartorius	ilium	tibia	flexes thigh; abducts thigh, rotates leg	
33. rectus femoris	ilium	patella (tibia)	extends leg at knee, flexes hip	part of quadriceps femoris
34. vastus lateralis	femur (lateral side)	patella (tibia)	extends leg at knee	part of quadriceps femoris
35. vastus medialis	femur (medial side)	patella (tibia)	extends leg at knee	part of quadriceps femoris
36. vastus intermedius	femur	patella (tibia)	extends leg at knee	part of quadriceps femoris, deep to rectus femoris
37. biceps femoris	ischium, femur	fibula, tibia	flexes knee, and extension and lateral rotation at hip	part of hamstrings
38. semitendinosus	ischium	tibia	flexes and slightly medially rotates leg at knee, extends thigh at hip	part of hamstrings
39. semimembranosus	ischium	tibia	flexes and slightly medially rotates leg at knee, extends thigh at hip	part of hamstrings
40. soleus	fibula, tibia	calcaneus	plantar flexion; (adducts foot)	
41. gastrocnemius	femur	calcaneus	plantar flexion; flexion of leg at knee	

Exercise B

Comparison of the Structures of Cardiac, Smooth, and Skeletal Muscle

You and your partner should obtain slides containing skeletal muscle, smooth muscle, cardiac muscle, and the slide marked Intercalated Disks. For each of the first three, draw what you see. The slide marked Intercalated Disks is also a slide of cardiac muscle, just a different stain was used. This stain makes the intercalated disks found in cardiac muscle much more visible. Use this slide to help yourself differentiate between individual cardiac muscle cells. Draw what you see. You will be asked to show your notes/drawings for participation points.

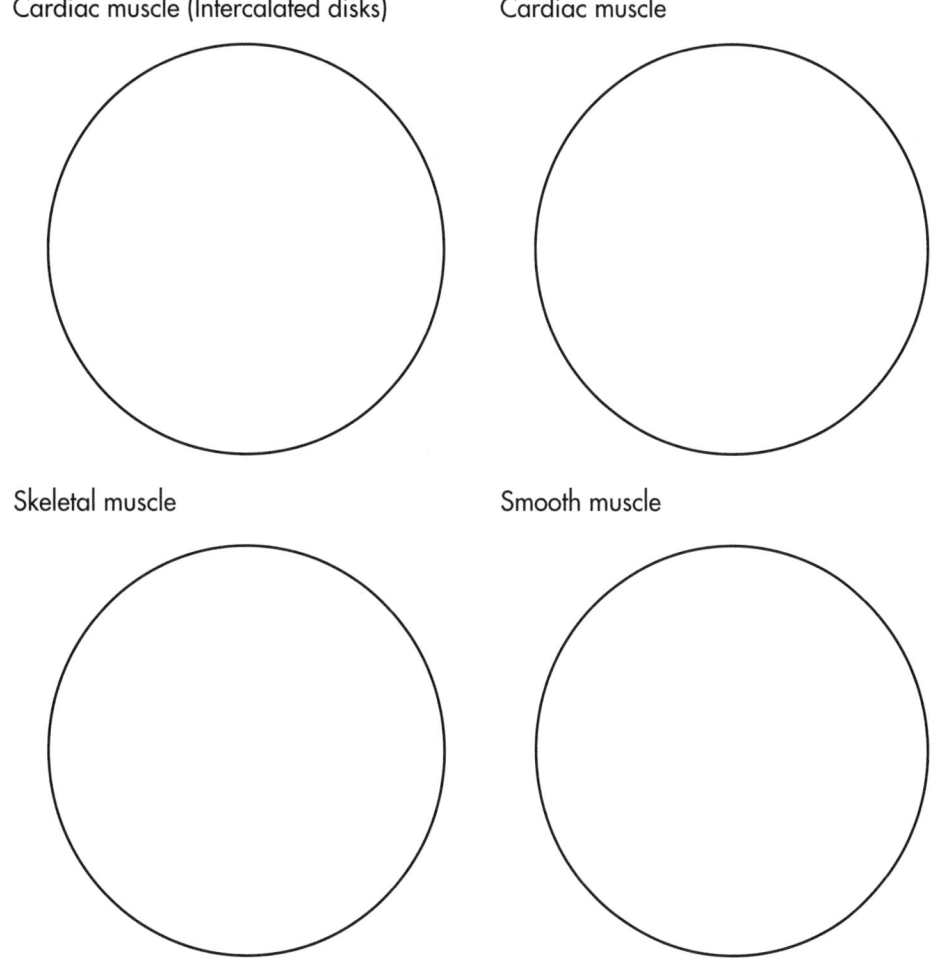

Cardiac muscle (Intercalated disks)

Cardiac muscle

Skeletal muscle

Smooth muscle

Exercise C

Electromyography is a technique that measures the electrical activity of the muscles and the nerves controlling the muscles. The data recorded is an Electromyogram (also known as an 'EMG' or 'Myogram'). There are two methods of recording: needle electrodes inserted through the skin into the muscle, or electrodes placed on the skin surface. The size and shape of the waveform measured provide information about the ability of the muscle to respond when the nerves are stimulated. In the clinical setting, EMG is most often used when people have symptoms of weakness, and examination shows impaired muscle strength. It can help to differentiate muscle weakness caused by neurological disorders from other conditions.

The EMG provides a depiction of the timing and pattern of muscle activity during complex movements. The raw surface EMG signal reflects the electrical activity of the muscle fibers active at that time. Motor units fire asynchronously and it is sometimes possible, with exceedingly weak contractions, to detect the contributions of individual motor units to the EMG signal. As the strength of the muscular contraction increases, however, the density of action potentials increases and the raw signal at any time may represent the electrical activity of perhaps thousands of individual fibers.

Lab Tutor: Electromyography

Before you come to lab please summarize in the spaces below what you believe is the goal of the experiment and any background information that is important to understanding the experiment.

Goal

Background

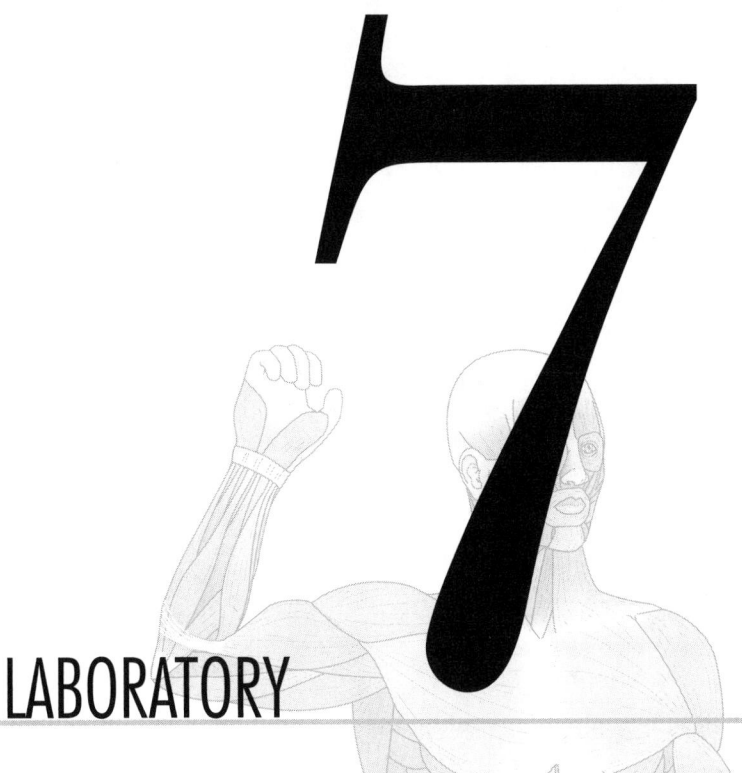

LABORATORY

7

TISSUES IV: NERVOUS TISSUE AND NERVE–MUSCLE INTERACTION

Required Reading: Lectures 10–13

Objectives

1. Summarize the three basic **functions** of the nervous system.

2. Draw a diagram that shows the basic **divisions** of the nervous system.

3. In addition to **astrocytes**, name three other types of **neuroglial** cells and describe the functions that have been suggested for them.

4. Describe all the possible functions of **astrocytes**.

5. Name the three **functional types** of neurons, and sketch the four **anatomical** types of neurons.

6. **Draw** and **label** a neuron (don't forget the dendritic spines).

7. Describe how **substances** and **organelles** move up and down an **axon**. Name the terms used for these processes.

8. Describe a **Schwann cell** and list its functions.

9. List the functions of the **myelin sheath**.

10. Define the **all-or-none** principle of nerve impulse transmission.

11. **Define a synapse—what is it and what is its function? Draw a synapse**, and label its various components.

12. Describe what happens at the synapse when an **action potential** arrives at the presynaptic terminal and after neurotransmitter has been released by exocytosis from the **synaptic vesicles**.

13. Define what is meant by "**presynaptic**" and "**postsynaptic**."

14. Describe, contrast and explain the response of a single muscle fiber and a whole muscle to **electrical** stimulation—define the threshold stimulus and the all-or-none phenomenon.

15. Define a motor unit and describe how motor units are important in controlling the force and rate of muscle contraction.

16. Explain what is meant by **motor recruitment**.

17. Define tetanic contraction, and distinguish it from a twitch.

18. Review the characteristics of skeletal muscle contraction.

19. Investigate the response of skeletal muscle to electrical stimulation.

20. Become familiar with data collection and printing using the LabTutor system.

I. Histology of Nerve Tissue

The nerve tissue of the brain and spinal cord consists of billions of nerve cells or **neurons**, in close association with non-neuronal cells called **neuroglial** cells or just **glial** cells.

A. Neuroglia

Neuroglia cells outnumber neurons by 9 to 1 and make up 50% of the volume of the brain.

1. **Astrocytes**—star-shaped cells found between neurons and blood vessels. Astrocytes make up 50% of all the cells in the brain and have many functions (see notes).

2. **Oligodendrocytes**—resemble astrocytes, but processes are fewer and shorter. They produce a phospholipid **myelin sheath** around axons of neurons in the central nervous system. In the peripheral nervous system, this function is subserved by **Schwann cells**.

3. **Microglia**—the brain's macrophages. They are small cells with few processes. Like macrophages, they may originate from monocytes circulating in the blood. They phagocytize bacteria and cellular debris, and can migrate into an area of damaged nervous tissue.

4. **Ependyma**—line the ventricles of the brain and the central canal in the spinal cord. They may be cuboidal or columnar, and may be ciliated.

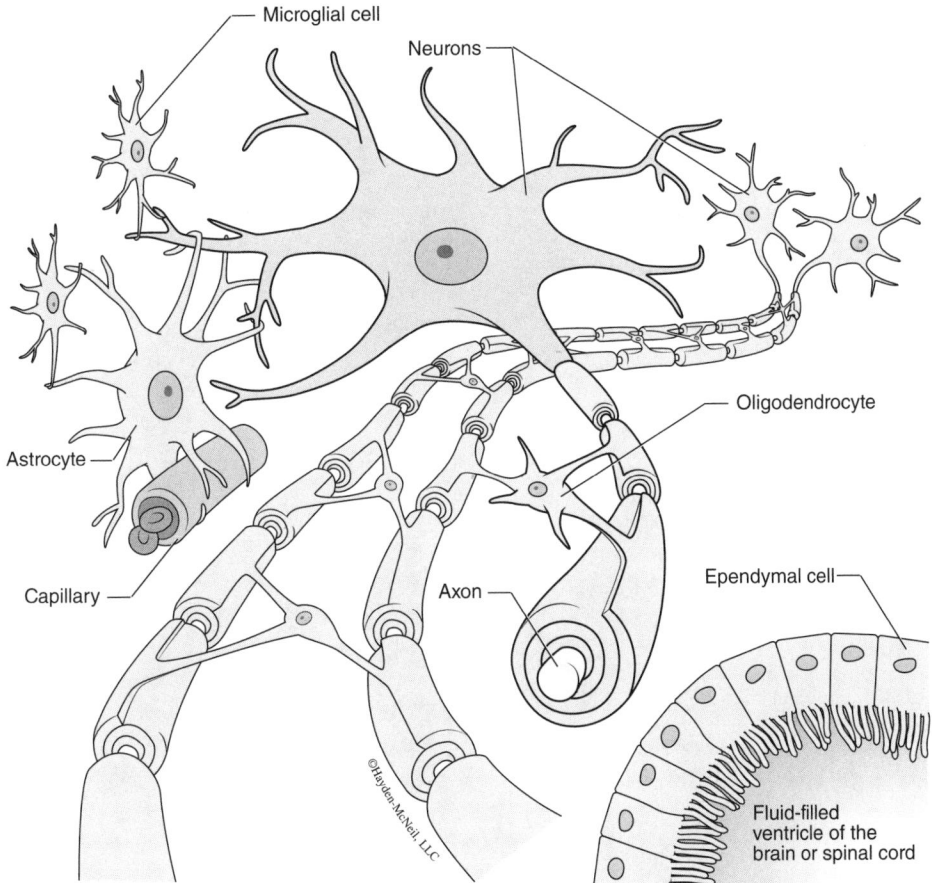

Figure 7-1. Neuroglia.

B. Neurons—Types

A neuron consists of a cell body with processes radiating from it. These processes are called **dendrites** and **axons**. Dendrites have numerous dendritic spines projecting from their surfaces and conduct nerve impulses toward the cell body.

On the basis of *structural* differences, neurons are divided into four types—bipolar, unipolar, multipolar, and pyramidal.

More importantly, neurons can be divided into three types on the basis of *what they do*.

1. **Sensory** neurons—convey sensory information to the central nervous system (brain, spinal cord).

2. **Interneurons**—neurons that convey information from one neuron to another neuron.

3. **Motor** neurons—convey motor commands, usually to skeletal muscles.

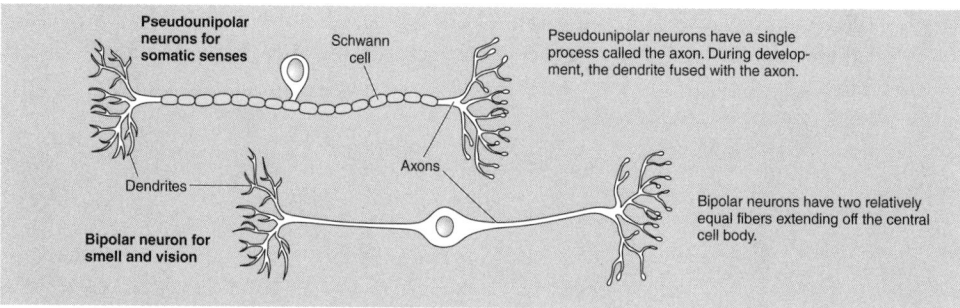

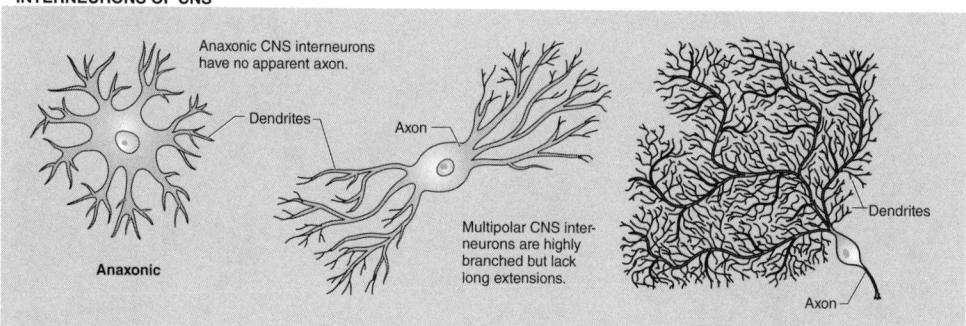

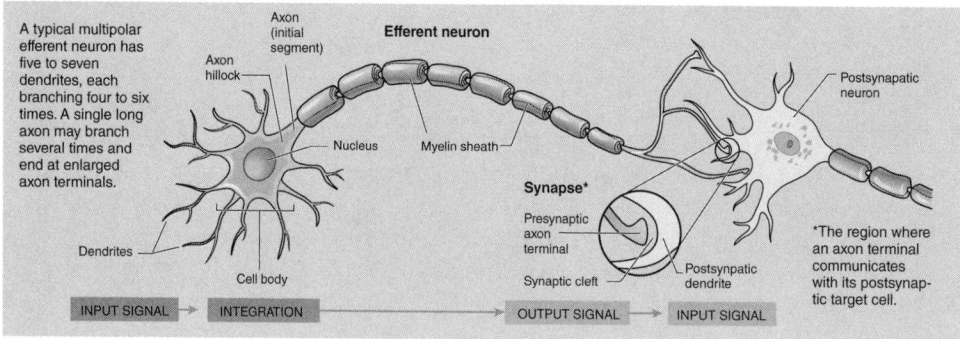

Figure 7-2. Neurons.

C. Neurons—Structure

Neurons have three parts.

1. **Cell body**—in addition to the usual items found in all cells (e.g., mitochondria), neurons contain **neurofibrils** and **Nissl bodies** or **granules**. The latter are modified rough endoplasmic reticulum, and function in protein synthesis.

2. **Dendrites**—short and highly branched. Function is to conduct nerve impulses *toward* the cell body. Have numerous dendritic spines projecting from them.

3. **Axon**—a long thin tubular process arising from the **axon hillock** on the cell body. The axon conducts nerve impulses *away* from the cell body to another neuron or muscle or gland cells. Axons have branches called **collaterals**, which end in **axon terminals**. **The axon terminal has a bulb-like ending called a synaptic end bulb** or **presynaptic terminal**. The presynaptic terminals are in close contact with the plasma membranes of other cells (other neurons, muscle cells, or gland cells). The structure at the region of contact between the presynaptic terminal and the plasma membrane of the receiving cell (the postsynaptic terminal) is called a synapse.

Chemical signaling agents called neurotransmitters are released at the presynaptic terminal and bind to specific neurotransmitter receptors on the plasma membrane of the receiving cell.

Special transport mechanisms convey newly synthesized proteins and organelles along the axon.

- **Axoplasmic flow**—a slow process that carries newly synthesized proteins from the cell body to the axon terminals.

- **Anterograde axonal transport**—a *fast*, ATP-requiring process that transports organelles (e.g., synaptic vesicles, mitochondria) along the axon toward the axon terminals. Axonal transport occurs on the surfaces of micro- or neurotubules.

- **Retrograde axonal transport**—opposite of anterograde axonal transport. Worn out mitochondria can be returned to the cell body via this route. Herpes, polio, and rabies viruses can hitch a ride on this system, and make their way from the surface of the body via the axons of neurons into the cell bodies of the neurons themselves.

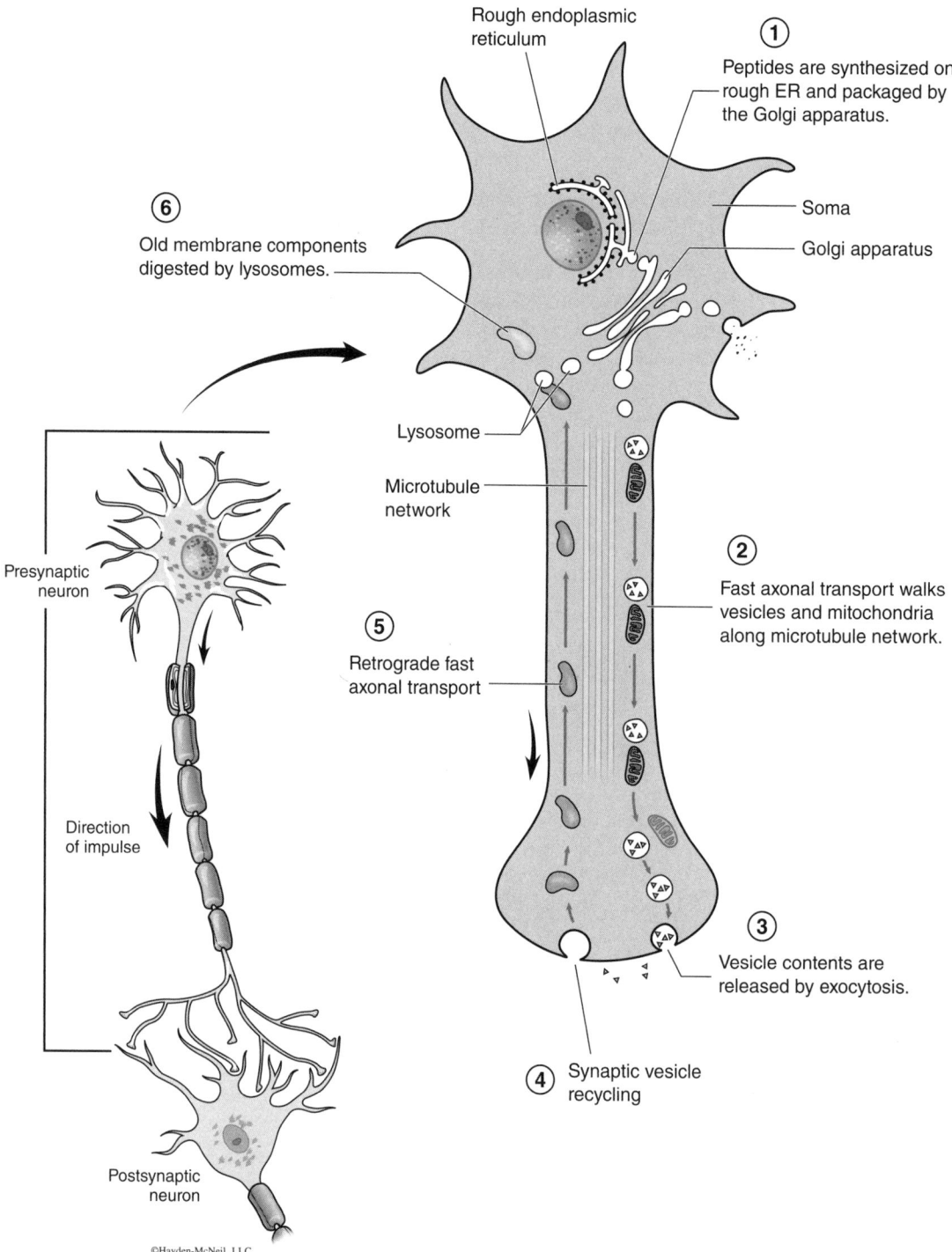

Figure 7-3. Intracellular movements of substances.

In mammals, large-diameter axons are sheathed in a layer of phospholipid. This material is called myelin. Oligodendrocytes form the myelin sheath in the central nervous system, and Schwann cells fulfil this function in the peripheral nervous system. The myelin sheath is interrupted at intervals along its length by patches where the plasma membrane of the underlying nerve axon is exposed. These patches of membrane, which are very rich in voltage-gated sodium channels, are called nodes of Ranvier. Myelin is an electrical insulator. An action potential developed at one node of Ranvier, therefore, depolarizes the next node of Ranvier without having to generate action potentials in the intervening, insulated segment of nerve. The nerve impulse therefore "jumps" from one node to the next, increasing the conduction velocity.

D. How Nerves Are Connected to Skeletal Muscles: The Neuromuscular Junction

The axons of motor neurons make contact with individual muscle fibers at a synapse-like structure called a neuromuscular junction. The sarcolemma at this point is called a motor end plate. The cell bodies of motor neurons are located in the spinal cord or in the brain.

One motor neuron may connect with *many* muscle fibers, but one muscle fiber receives input from only one axon terminal.

A motor neuron together with all the muscle fibers it innervates (= is connected to) is called a **MOTOR UNIT**.

One Motor Unit – A motor neuron and all the muscle fibers it is connected to

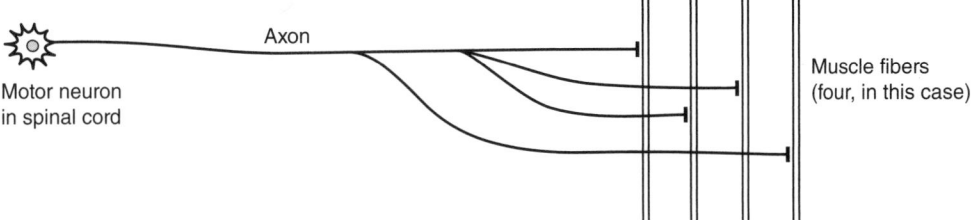

Figure 7-4. Motor unit.

When the motor neuron in the spinal cord is excited, the neurotransmitter acetylcholine is released at all its axon terminals. This generates a wave of electrical depolarization that propagates along the sarcolemma and ultimately causes contraction of the muscle fiber.

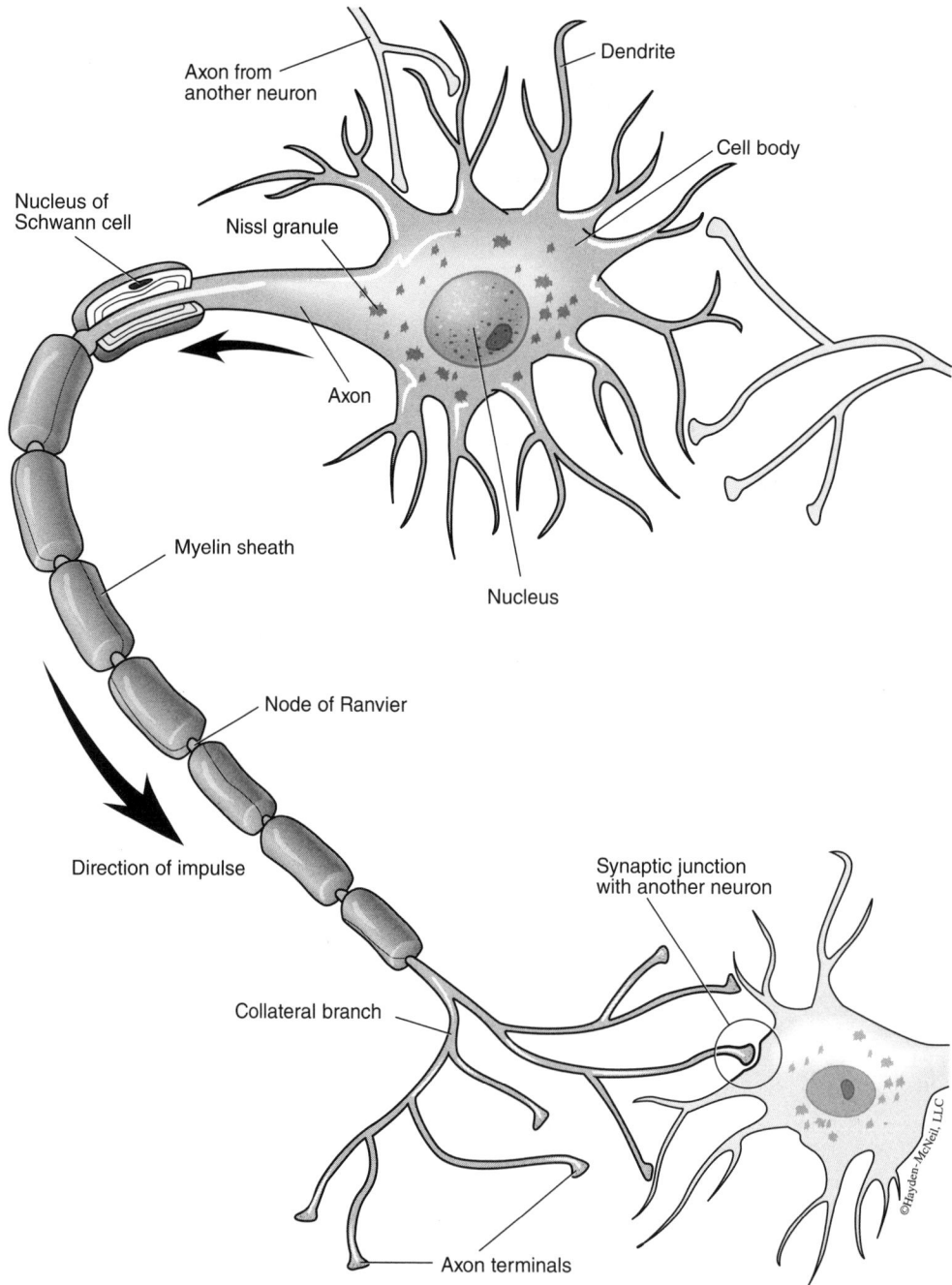

Figure 7-5. The neuron.

The force and speed of contraction of a whole muscle is controlled by the number and sequence of activation of the motor units that innervate its individual muscle fibers. **Increasing the force of contraction of a muscle by progressively increasing the number of motor units activated is called motor recruitment.**

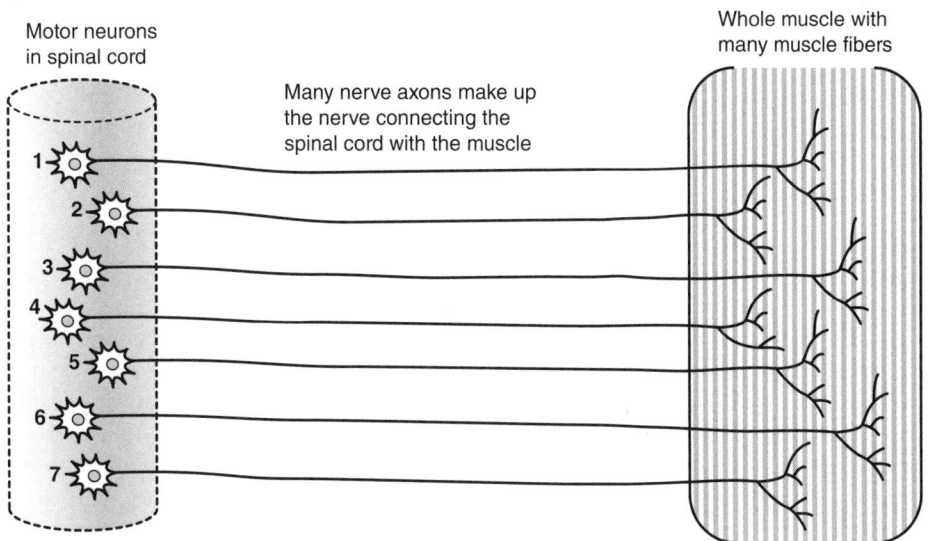

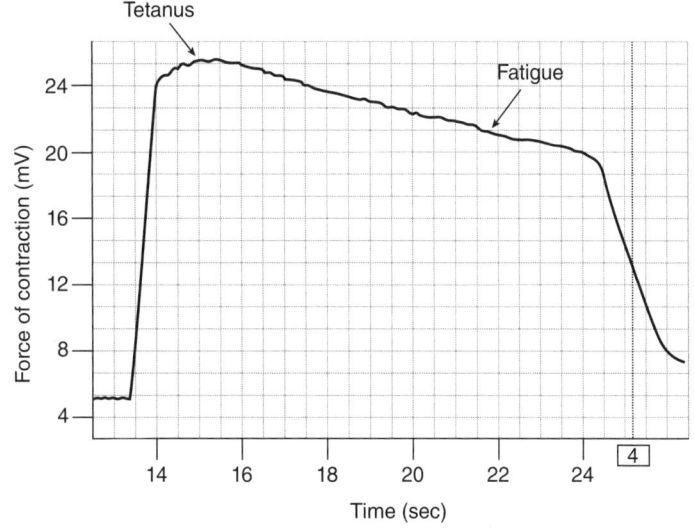

Whole Muscle

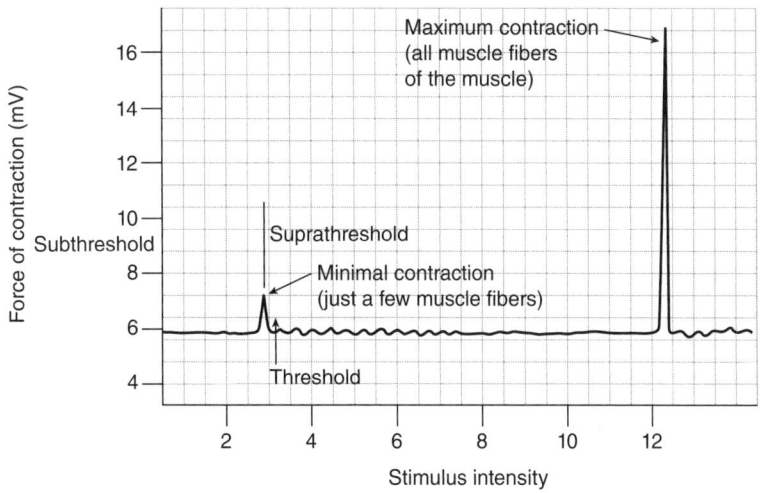

Figure 7-6. Motor recruitment.

Frequency of Muscle Stimulation, Tetanus and Muscle Fatigue

If a skeletal muscle is stimulated so frequently that the individual contractions fuse together the result is a sustained contraction called **tetanus**. Short-term tetanic contractions characterize most of the contractions made by our muscles during voluntary activity, because the motor neurons controlling them typically send out rapid bursts of action potentials when activated.

Muscle fatigue occurs during sustained contraction. You will see your frog muscle fatiguing when you submit it to prolonged tetanus. When fatigue sets in, the force the muscle exerts during tetanus progressively diminishes. In the intact human, there is accompanying discomfort. The causes of this effect are not well understood. One factor may be depletion of muscle glycogen. Eating carbohydrates before a marathon race ("carbohydrate loading") may increase muscle **glycogen** and delay the onset of fatigue. Drinking a solution of glucose during the race may also be beneficial. Other important factors seem to be the accumulation of **lactic acid** and elevation of muscle temperature. Some runners hyperventilate before a race to raise the blood pH so that they can accommodate more lactic acid. The hyperventilation does NOT raise arterial blood oxygen, which is always saturated.

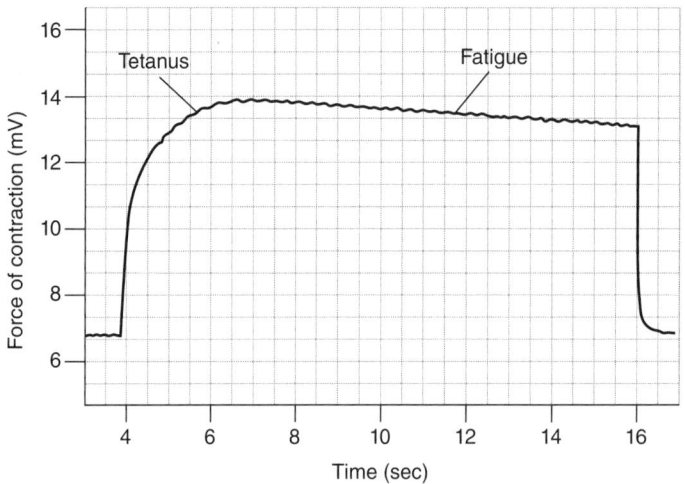

Figure 7-7. Tetanus and fatigue.

Sensory Structures in Muscle and Tendons

Proprioceptive information on muscle length is conveyed to the nervous system by sensory receptors called muscle spindles, and information on muscle tension is provided by Golgi tendon organs.

E. Definition of Threshold Stimulus and All-or-None Phenomenon

Researchers investigating muscle physiology have sometimes worked with a whole muscle (as you will be doing in the lab) or with single muscle fibers dissected out from it. These muscle fibers or the whole muscles can be connected to devices that record contraction when the muscle fiber or muscle is directly stimulated electrically. These devices are called **force transducers**.

Single muscle fibers do not contract until the electrical stimulus is increased from sub-threshold to threshold level. At this point, the fiber contracts with maximum force, which does not increase if the electrical stimulus is increased above threshold (= supra-threshold). There is no partial contraction. The single muscle fiber either contracts or it doesn't. This is called an **all-or-none response**.

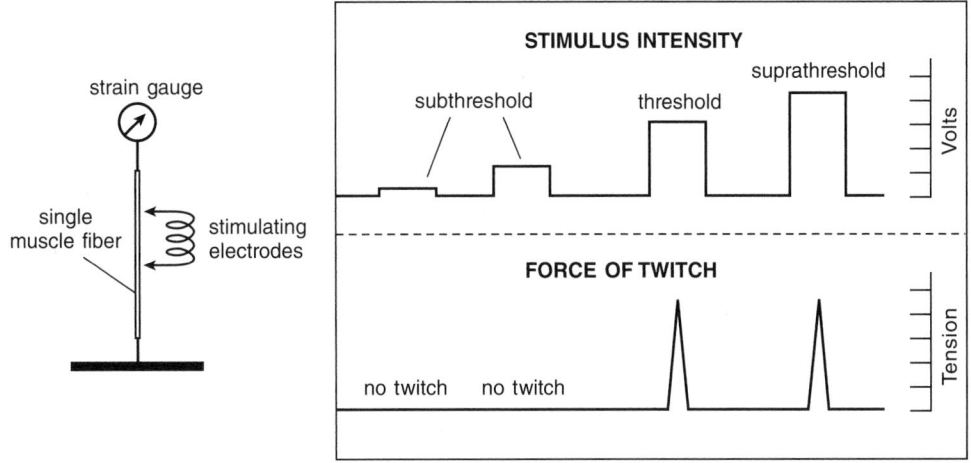

Single muscle fiber goes from no response to maximum response as stimulus is increased.

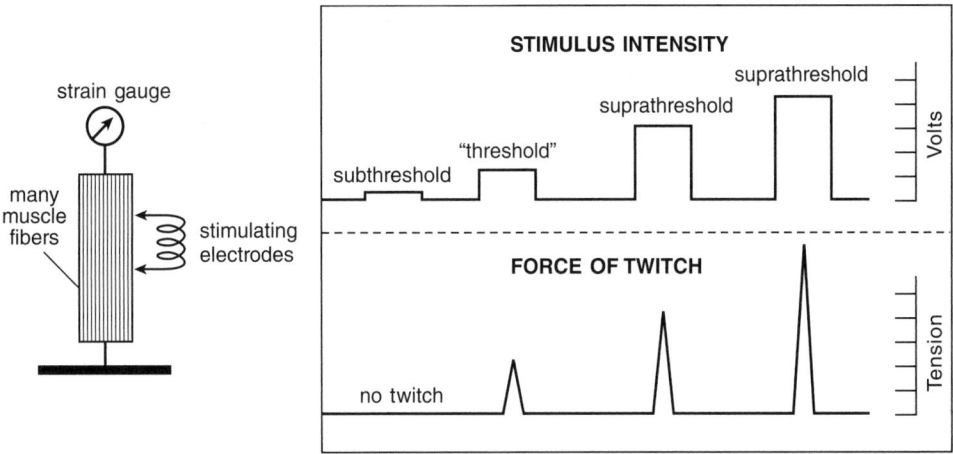

Figure 7-8. Subthreshold, threshold, suprathreshold—Single muscle cell/motor unit vs. whole muscle.

If we do the same experiment with a whole muscle we find a progressive increase in force of contraction as the stimulus intensity is increased. This is because the many muscle fibers that make up the whole muscle have different thresholds. Therefore, as the intensity of the stimulus is increased, increasing numbers of muscle fibers are activated. In other words, in this experiment we have mimicked motor recruitment.

II. Divisions of the Nervous System

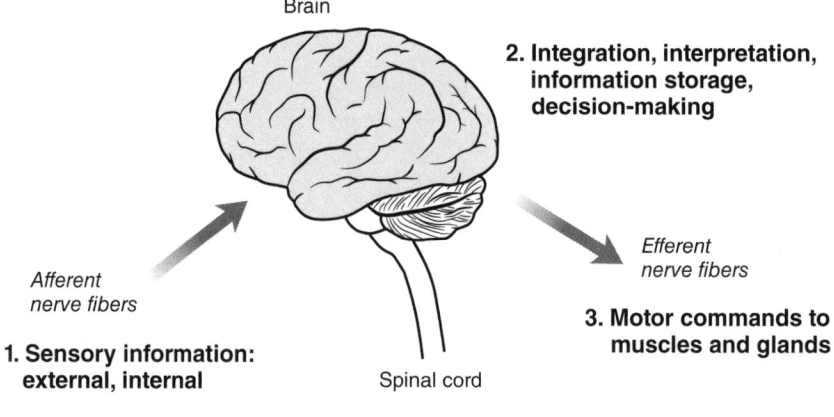

Brain

2. Integration, interpretation, information storage, decision-making

Afferent nerve fibers

Efferent nerve fibers

3. Motor commands to muscles and glands

1. Sensory information: external, internal

Spinal cord

©Hayden-McNeil, LLC

Figure 7-9. Activity of the nervous system.

A. Central Nervous System

Made up of the brain and the spinal cord.

B. Peripheral Nervous System

The nerves that connect the brain and spinal cord with the sensory receptors, muscles, and glands make up the peripheral nervous system. The peripheral nervous system is divided up depending on whether nerve impulses travel from the periphery to the central nervous system (**sensory, afferent** fibers) or from the central nervous system to the periphery (**motor, efferent** fibers: somatic, autonomic).

1. **Somatic efferents**—innervate the skeletal muscles, and are under voluntary, conscious control.

2. **Autonomic efferents**—innervate smooth muscle, the heart (cardiac muscle) and glands—it is not under conscious control, and is therefore involuntary. The autonomic nervous system is divided into the **sympathetic, parasympathetic**, and **enteric** divisions.

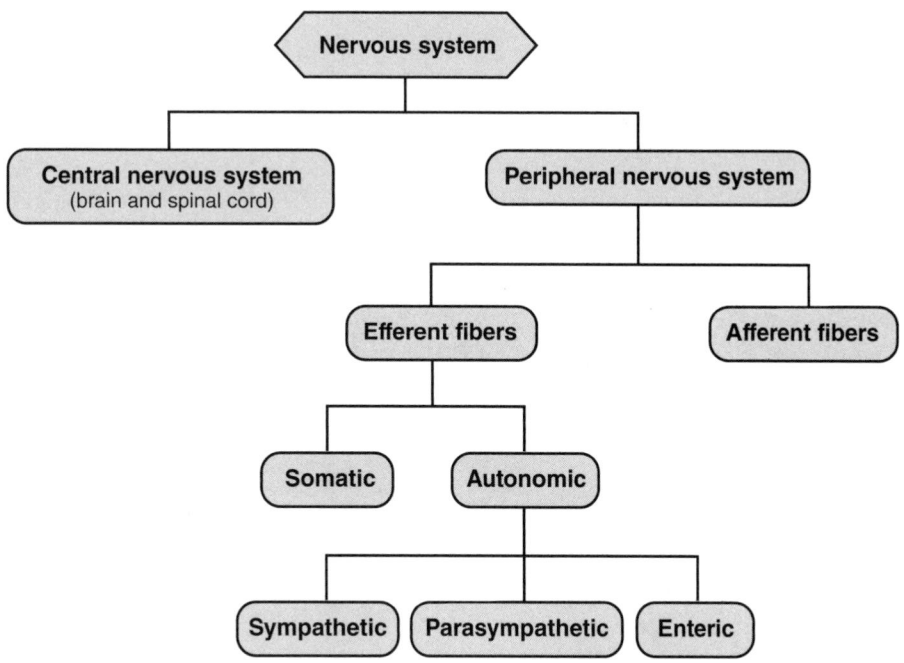

Figure 7-10. Divisions of the nervous system.

III. The Spinal Cord

The central nervous system is made up of the brain and spinal cord. We will deal with the brain in a future lab.

A. Peripheral Nerves—Spinal and Cranial Nerves

The nerves that emerge from the **spinal cord** are called **spinal nerves**. The nerves that emerge from the **brain** are called the cranial nerves. Together, these nerves make up the peripheral **nervous system**.

The spinal cord consists of 31 segments, each of which gives rise to a pair of spinal nerves.

       Cervical—8

       Thoracic—12

       Lumbar—5

       Sacral—5

       Coccygeal—1

The **cervical enlargement** gives rise to nerves for the arms, and the **lumbar enlargement** gives rise to nerves for the legs.

Each spinal nerve emerges from the spinal cord by two short branches, the **dorsal (posterior)** and **ventral (anterior) roots**, which are protected within the vertebral column.

The dorsal root (or sensory root) has an enlargement called the **dorsal root ganglion**. The dorsal root ganglion contains the cell bodies of sensory neurons whose nerve endings are often specially adapted to act as sensory receptors (see Lecture 14). The axons of these sensory neurons enter the spinal cord through the dorsal root and form synapses with other neurons in the spinal cord.

The ventral root (or motor root) is actually composed of a number of **rootlets**, and carries the axons of motor neurons whose cell bodies are located in the gray matter of the spinal cord (see below).

The dorsal and ventral roots merge to form a **spinal nerve** that emerges from the vertebral canal through an **intervertebral foramen**. After emerging from the foramen, the spinal nerve splits into an anterior and a posterior branch. The spinal nerves in the thoracic and lumbar regions also have **rami** (branches) that are part of the autonomic nervous system (we'll talk about the autonomic nervous system later).

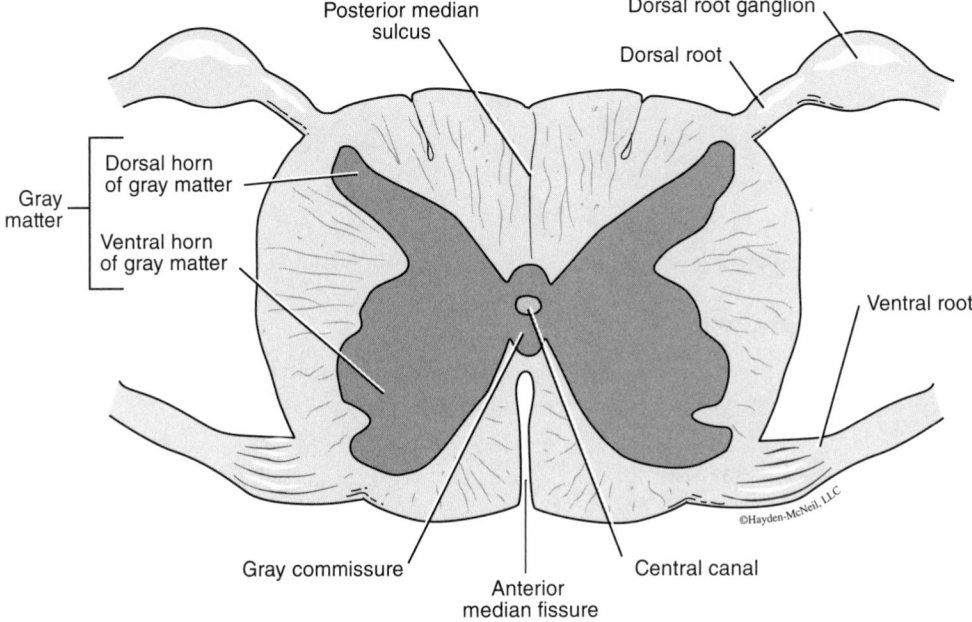

Figure 7-11. Cross section of the spinal cord.

B. Organization of Gray and White Matter in the Spinal Cord

The spinal cord is partially divided into right and left halves by a deep **anterior (ventral) median fissure** and a shallow **posterior (dorsal) median sulcus**.

The spinal cord is composed of gray and white matter. The gray matter, which consists of many cell bodies of neurons with their axons and dendrites, occupies the central region of the cord, and looks like a butterfly or an H in cross section. The two arms forming the top of the H are called posterior (dorsal) **horns**, and the two arms forming the bottom of the H are called the anterior (ventral) horns. The crossbar of the H is the **gray commissure**.

The cell bodies of motor neurons are clustered in the ventral horn gray matter. Other neurons in the spinal cord gray matter are interneurons. Some of these interneurons send axons in the lateral and ventral columns of the white matter for distances ranging from a few, to many segments up and down the spinal cord. Such neurons are called **propriospinal neurons**.

The white matter, consists of myelinated nerve fibers and is divided by the gray matter into anterior (ventral), posterior (dorsal), and lateral **funiculi**.

C. Function of the Spinal Cord: Organization of Neurons and Nerve Fiber Tracts

The major functions of the spinal cord are:

1. It is the major pathway for all information ascending to the brain from the sensory systems of the body and for all commands descending from the brain to the muscles and other effector systems. There are two major ascending tracts conveying information to the cerebral cortex, and a third conveying sensory information to the cerebellum. There are five major descending tracts carrying motor information to the spinal cord.

2. The spinal cord is able to execute certain simple behavioral activities without involving the brain. These activities are referred to as **spinal reflexes**. Neural networks in the spinal cord are also involved in generating the rhythmic pattern of neural activity that controls walking.

LAB EXERCISES—Preparation of the Frog Gastrocnemius

You will be dealing with the frog gastrocnemius without its normal connection to the spinal cord via the sciatic nerve. You will be stimulating the muscle directly by inserting pin electrodes into it. The muscle is provided with nutrients in the form of ions and glucose through the use of Ringer's solution. The composition of Ringer's solution can be found on page 277.

Because of time constraints, the frog has already been set up for you. The frog was first decapitated, then pithed. Although the frog is clinically dead when the head was severed from the body, we destroy the nervous tissue in the isolated head and also in the spinal cord to destroy any spinal reflexes that may confuse your results.

We then skinned the legs and cut the Achilles tendon at the insertion of the gastrocnemius muscle to the calcaneus (heel) bone. The tendon is then attached to the force transducer by a piece of thread. We will be recording the force exerted by the muscle on the force transducer, so the rest of the frog tissue must be secured firmly in the tray with dissection pins.

The setup must be stable, and adjusted so that the thread is taut and will not vibrate when the muscle is stimulated.

When investigating muscle physiology we can study a whole muscle (as you will be doing in the lab), or a single muscle fiber dissected from it. When stimulated electrically, the strength of contraction of these preparations is measured with a **force transducer**.

Single muscle fibers do not contract until the stimulus is strong enough. Weaker stimuli do not cause contraction, and are described as subthreshold. As the strength of the stimulus is increased to threshold level, the muscle fiber finally responds by contracting fully. If the stimulus strength is increased above threshold (suprathreshold), the muscle fiber continues to respond by contracting fully. The single muscle fiber either contracts fully, or it doesn't. There is no such thing as a partial contraction. This is called the **all-or-none response**.

Exercise A—Observing the Neuromuscular Junction

Obtain a slide of the **motor neuron endings**. Observe first under low power, then under high. Below is room to draw what you observe.

Motor Neuron Endings

Branching nerve fibers with motor end plates attached to striated muscle fibers.

Exercise B

Obtain a slide of the **myelinated (medullated) nerve teased**. Observe first under low power, then under high. Locate the cell body of a neuron and look at the processes that extend from the cell body. It is almost impossible to distinguish which are the dendrites and which is the axon unless one can see the Nissl bodies (granules) that usually aggregate at the axon hillock. What do you think the dark purple dots around the neurons are?

Below is room to draw what you observe.

Medullated Nerve Teased

myelin sheath

axon

Node of Ranvier

Exercise C

Neuroglia–Astrocytes

Star-like glial cells in medulla.

Identify cells that terminate on capillary.

Spinal Cord

Explain where cell bodies of motor neurons are located.

Exercise D

Lab Tutor: Frog Leg Muscle

Please summarize in the spaces below what you believe is the goal of the experiment and any background information that is important to understanding the experiment.

Goal

Background

LABORATORY

THE NERVOUS SYSTEM I

Exercises A, B, and C should be done online BEFORE COMING TO CLASS!

Required Reading: Lectures 15–19

READ THE PAGES LISTED BELOW IN YOUR HISTOLOGY TEXT BEFORE COMING TO CLASS, THEN BRING IT TO CLASS.

12TH ED: READ PAGES 170–200, OR
11TH ED: READ PAGES 134–155

Objectives

1. Draw a simple sketch of the brain, and indicate the five main regions of the central nervous system.

2. Review and summarize the Overview of the Main Regions of the Central Nervous System, paying attention both to structure and listed functions.

3. Describe the components of the peripheral nervous system (cranial and spinal nerves), and the structure of a peripheral nerve.

4. Make a diagram showing the three membranes covering the brain—include the subarachnoid space and the arachnoid villi (= granulations).

5. Using a diagram, list and describe the ventricles.

6. Describe the connections between the ventricles and how the ventricles connect to the subarachnoid space.

7. Describe the structure involved in the formation of cerebrospinal fluid.

8. Construct a simple diagram illustrating the flow of CSF.

9. Describe how CSF is absorbed and returned to the blood circulation.

10. List three functions of the cerebrospinal fluid.

11. State one substance that is present in high amounts in blood plasma but is quite low in cerebrospinal fluid.

12. Describe the medulla and the nuclei in it. Name the cranial nerves that originate in it.

13. Describe the pons and the nuclei in it. Name the cranial nerves that originate in it.

14. Describe the midbrain and the structures/nuclei/cranial nerves associated with it.

15. List and diagram the important structures associated with the diencephalon.

16. Describe the *functions* of the thalamus, the hypothalamus, the pineal gland, and the pituitary gland.

17. Describe the connections of the cerebellum to the brain stem.

18. Describe the structure of the cerebellum and make a rough sketch of it in relation to the rest of the brain.

19. Describe the input and output pathways to the cerebellum.

20. List and describe the functions of the cerebellum.

21. Describe the structure of the cerebrum and its various components.

22. Draw the anatomical divisions (lobes) of the cerebral cortex.

23. Identify in a diagram the motor areas of the cerebral cortex, and the areas associated with speech and language (Broca's and Wernicke's areas) and how they are connected.

24. Describe in a diagram the sensory and association areas of the cerebral cortex.

25. Describe the topographic representation of the body in the motor and sensory areas of the cerebral cortex.

26. Tell the story of Phineas Gage and why his accident contributed so much to our knowledge of the workings of the frontal lobes.

27. Briefly describe the limbic system.

28. Describe the different types of memory and describe the consequences of removing the hippocampus.

29. Discuss the concept of how memory may be important in envisioning future thought, actions, plans, and scenarios.

30. Discuss two ways in which memory might be established (LTP, growth of dendritic spines—LTP is associated with changes in dendritic spines).

31. Describe the function of the **corpus callosum**, what happens when it is cut, and what this reveals about the difference between the two cerebral hemispheres.

32. Name the five structures that make up the **basal ganglia**, and name the parts of the brain where they are found.

33. Describe the inputs to the basal ganglia, and their output pathway. Draw a diagram showing the simple circuitry of the basal ganglia.

34. Describe the functions of the basal ganglia.

35. Name and describe *in detail* both the **symptoms** and the **causes** of Parkinson's disease and Huntington's chorea (disease). Be able to diagnose these diseases from a description of the symptoms.

36. Be able to **name and identify the different parts of both a human and a sheep brain**.

37. Define **long-term potentiation** and describe whether it might have a role in memory formation.

I. Introduction

The nervous system has three broad activities.

1. Its sensory systems permit it to **sense** events occurring inside and outside the body.

2. It **interprets**, **integrates**, and may **store** this sensory information (in the form of memories), then it **decides** on an appropriate response, if any.

3. It sends **commands** to muscles and glands (this is called the **motor** function of the nervous system).

The nervous system is divided into the peripheral nervous system and the central nervous system. The central nervous system is divided into the spinal cord and the brain.

The spinal cord contains motor and sensory neurons, most of them connected with the limbs and trunk by means of the **spinal nerves**. The spinal cord contains **interneurons**. It contains the large **ascending tracts** of nerve fibers that transmit sensory information up the spinal cord to the brain. Additionally, it contains large **descending tracts** of nerve fibers that transmit motor commands down the spinal cord from the brain to the muscles. The spinal cord can also execute certain simple behavioral activities without involving the brain (its neural networks contain a program for walking, for example).

The **spinal cord** is actually a continuation of the brain stem. It exits the cranial activity through the **foramen magnum** at the base of the skill and extends into the vertebral canal of the vertebral column.

The **brain** consists of the brain stem, the cerebellum, the diencephalon, and the cerebral hemispheres.

II. Divisions of the Nervous System

The nervous system is divided up as shown in the diagrams.

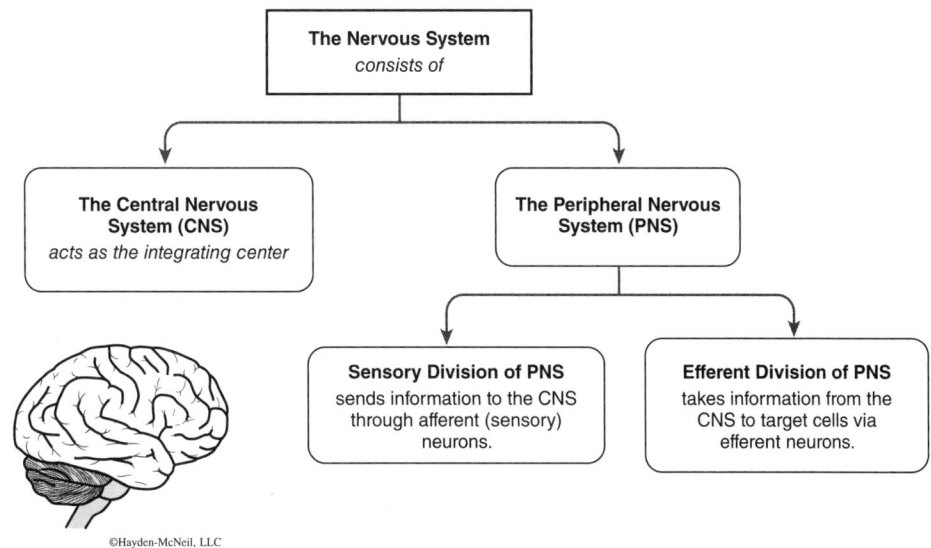

The Nervous System
consists of

The Central Nervous System (CNS)
acts as the integrating center

The Peripheral Nervous System (PNS)

Sensory Division of PNS
sends information to the CNS through afferent (sensory) neurons.

Efferent Division of PNS
takes information from the CNS to target cells via efferent neurons.

©Hayden-McNeil, LLC

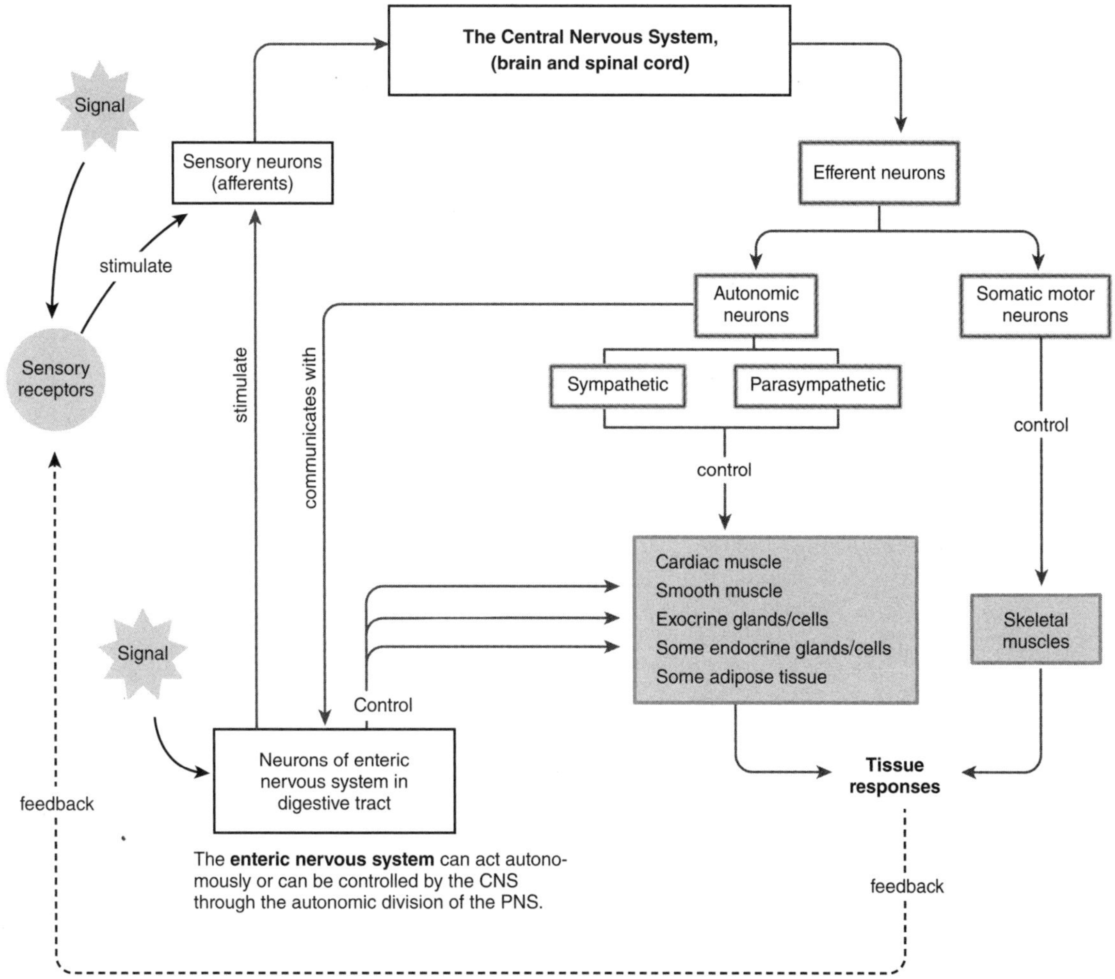

The Central Nervous System, (brain and spinal cord)

Signal

Sensory neurons (afferents)

stimulate

Sensory receptors

stimulate

communicates with

Efferent neurons

Autonomic neurons

Sympathetic

Parasympathetic

control

Somatic motor neurons

control

Cardiac muscle
Smooth muscle
Exocrine glands/cells
Some endocrine glands/cells
Some adipose tissue

Skeletal muscles

Signal

Control

Neurons of enteric nervous system in digestive tract

feedback

Tissue responses

feedback

The **enteric nervous system** can act autonomously or can be controlled by the CNS through the autonomic division of the PNS.

A. Neurons—Types

On the basis of *structural* differences, neurons are divided into four types—bipolar, sensory, multipolar and pyramidal.

More importantly, neurons can be divided into three types on the basis of *what they do.*

1. **Sensory neurons**—neurons that are involved in conveying sensory information to the central nervous system.

2. **Interneurons**—neurons that convey information from one neuron to another neuron. In some parts of the central nervous system, interneurons inhibit or stop other neurons from firing. Such interneurons are said to be inhibitory.

3. **Motor neurons**—neurons that convey motor commands, usually to skeletal muscles.

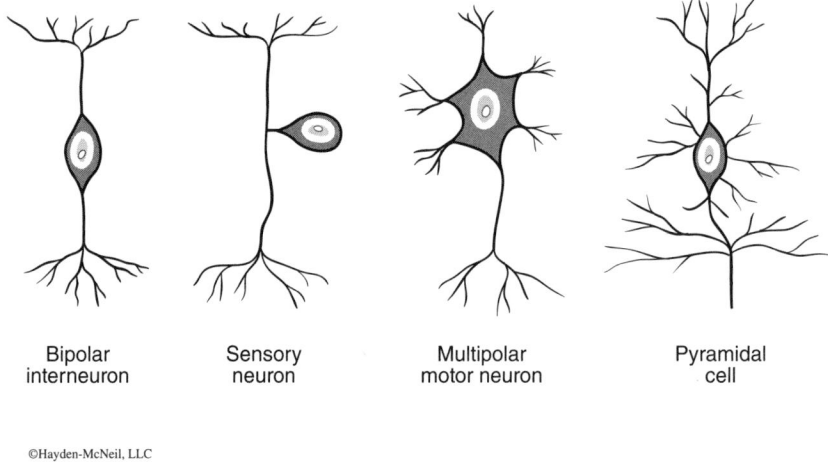

| Bipolar interneuron | Sensory neuron | Multipolar motor neuron | Pyramidal cell |

©Hayden-McNeil, LLC

Figure 8-1. Types of neurons.

III. Some Principles of Organization of Sensory and Motor Pathways in the Brain and Spinal Cord

The following are some points to note about the organization of sensory and motor pathways of the brain and spinal cord.

• Motor pathways consist of **several distinct pathways in parallel**. There is the corticospinal tract, which originates in the cerebral cortex, and also tracts that originate in the brain stem. Sensory pathways also consist of several distinct pathways in parallel. There are the dorsal column tracts and also the spinothalamic tracts.

• Each pathway contains **synaptic relays**.

• Each pathway is organized **topographically**—that is, nerve fibers and neurons from particular regions of the body are grouped together. For example, nerve impulses originating from the hands all travel in groups of nerve fibers that are close to each other, and end up in discrete "hand areas" on the surface of the sensory cerebral cortex. These areas form a "map" of the body surface on the cerebral cortex. Similarly, neurons that are involved in controlling hand *movements* are grouped together in a "hand area" of the *motor cortex.*

- Sensory and motor events on one side of the body are perceived, interpreted and controlled by the cerebral hemisphere on the **opposite side of the body** (the **contra-lateral** side). The sensory and motor pathways (tracts) are therefore *crossed* at some point. The reason for this is not known.

IV. The Spinal Cord Structure

The spinal cord is a column of nervous tissue that passes downward from the brain into the vertebral canal. The spinal cord is said to begin where the nervous tissue leaves the cranial cavity at the level of the foramen magnum.

A. Nomenclature

anterior = ventral

posterior = dorsal

Anterior and **posterior** are basically human terms, used in reference to the upright body. **Dorsal** and **ventral** are basically terms used in animals, in reference to the body on all fours. Since most of the work on the physiology of the central nervous system has been in animals, dorsal and ventral are more often used than posterior and anterior. Sometimes these terms are mixed together. MAKE SURE YOU UNDERSTAND THIS.

B. Peripheral Nerves—Spinal and Cranial Nerves

The nerves that emerge from the **spinal cord** are called **spinal nerves**. The nerves that emerge from the **brain** are called the **cranial nerves**. Together, these nerves make up the peripheral **nervous system**.

The spinal cord consists of 31 segments, each of which gives rise to a pair of spinal nerves.

> Cervical—8
>
> Thoracic—12
>
> Lumbar—5
>
> Sacral—5
>
> Coccygeal—1

The **cervical enlargement** gives rise to nerves for the arms, and the **lumbar enlargement** gives rise to nerves for the legs.

Each spinal nerve emerges from the spinal cord by two short branches, the **dorsal (posterior) and ventral (anterior) roots**, which are protected within the vertebral column.

The dorsal root (or sensory root) has an enlargement called the **dorsal root ganglion**. The dorsal root ganglion contains the cell bodies of sensory neurons whose nerve endings are often specially adapted to act as sensory receptors (see lecture 14). The axons of these sensory neurons enter the spinal cord through the dorsal root and form synapses with other neurons in the spinal cord.

The ventral root (or motor root) is actually composed of a number of **rootlets**, and carries the axons of motor neurons whose cell bodies are located in the gray matter of the spinal cord (see the following page).

The dorsal and ventral roots merge to form a **spinal nerve** that emerges from the vertebral canal through an **intervertebral foramen**. After emerging from the foramen, the spinal nerve splits into an anterior and a posterior branch. The spinal nerves in the thoracic and lumbar regions also have **rami** (branches) that are part of the autonomic nervous system (we'll talk about the autonomic nervous system later).

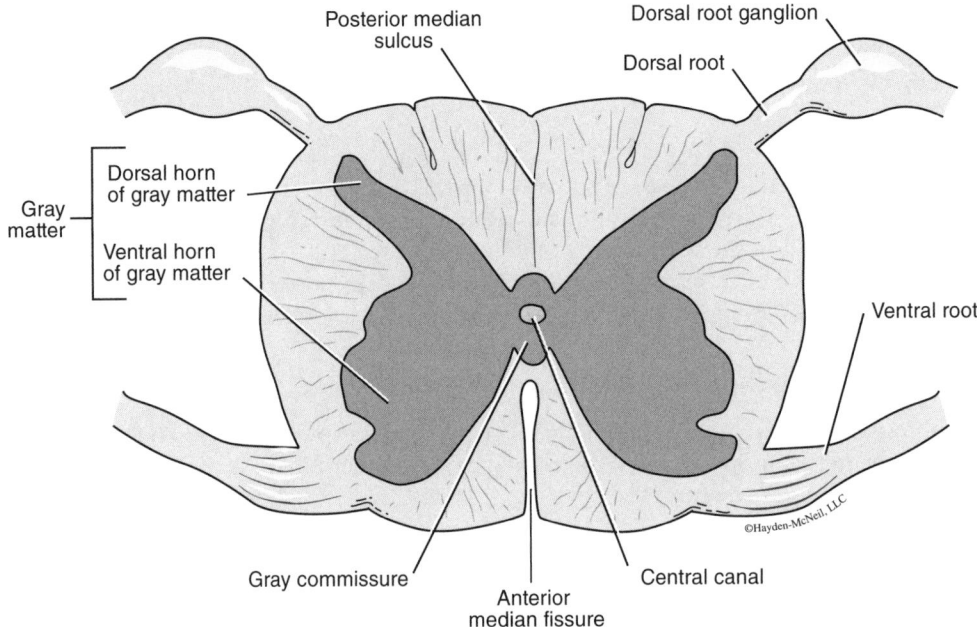

Figure 8-2. Cross section of the spinal cord.

C. Organization of Gray and White Matter in the Spinal Cord

The spinal cord is partially divided into right and left halves by a deep **anterior (ventral) median fissure** and a shallow **posterior (dorsal) median sulcus**.

The spinal cord is composed of gray and white matter. The gray matter, which consists of many cell bodies of neurons with their axons and dendrites, occupies the central region of the cord, and looks like a butterfly or an H in cross section. The two arms forming the top of the H are called posterior (dorsal) **horns**, and the two arms forming the bottom of the H are called the anterior (ventral) horns. The crossbar of the H is the **gray commissure**.

The cell bodies of motor neurons are clustered in the ventral horn gray matter. Other neurons in the spinal cord gray matter are interneurons. Some of these interneurons send axons in the lateral and ventral columns of the white matter for distances ranging from a few, to many segments up and down the spinal cord. Such neurons are called **propriospinal neurons**.

The white matter, consists of myelinated nerve fibers and is divided by the gray matter into anterior (ventral), posterior (dorsal), and lateral **funiculi**.

D. Function of the Spinal Cord: Organization of Neurons and Nerve Fiber Tracts

The major functions of the spinal cord are:

1. It is the major pathway for all information ascending to the brain from the sensory systems of the body and for all commands descending from the brain to the muscles and other effector systems. There are two major ascending tracts conveying information to the cerebral cortex, and a third conveying sensory information to the cerebellum. There are five major descending tracts carrying motor information to the spinal cord.

2. The spinal cord is able to execute certain simple behavioral activities without involving the brain. These activities are referred to as **spinal reflexes**. Additionally (as we have mentioned in the introduction to this lecture), neural networks in the spinal cord are responsible for storing the motor program involved in walking.

V. The Meninges

The brain and spinal cord lie within the cranial cavity and the vertebral canal, respectively. The brain and spinal cord are covered by three membranes that make up the meninges. The outermost membrane is the **dura mater** (means "tough mother"); the middle is the **arachnoid mater** ("spider-like mother"), and the innermost is the **pia mater** ("delicate mother").

The dura mater is composed of fibrous connective tissue containing blood vessels and nerves. It often extends between the lobes of the brain, forming partial partitions. In some areas, it splits into two layers, enclosing the **dural sinuses**.

In the spinal cord, between the dura mater and the wall of the vertebral canal is the **epidural space**. It is filled with fat, connective tissue and blood vessels. The epidural space inferior to the second lumbar vertebra is the site for the injection of anesthetics, such as a saddle block in childbirth.

The arachnoid mater is a thin, spider's web-like membrane lacking blood vessels. Beneath it lies the subarachnoid space that contains **cerebrospinal fluid**.

The pia mater is thin, and contains nerves and blood vessels. It follows the contours of the brain and spinal cord quite closely.

From the cranial cavity, the dura mater extends into the vertebral canal and ends as a blind sac just below the end of the spinal cord.

Clinical Application. A condition known as **meningitis** can be caused by bacteria or viruses. The meninges (usually the arachnoid mater or pia mater) become inflamed. If not treated promptly, death, mental retardation, paralysis, or loss of sight and hearing can occur.

Clinical Application. A severe blow to the head (e.g., a bicycle or motorcycle accident) can rupture meningeal blood vessels. If the blood released from the rupture pools beneath the dura mater, a **subdural hematoma** occurs. Because the blood has no place to go, its accumulation compresses the softer underlying brain tissue. If the increase in pressure is not relieved, brain damage or death can occur.

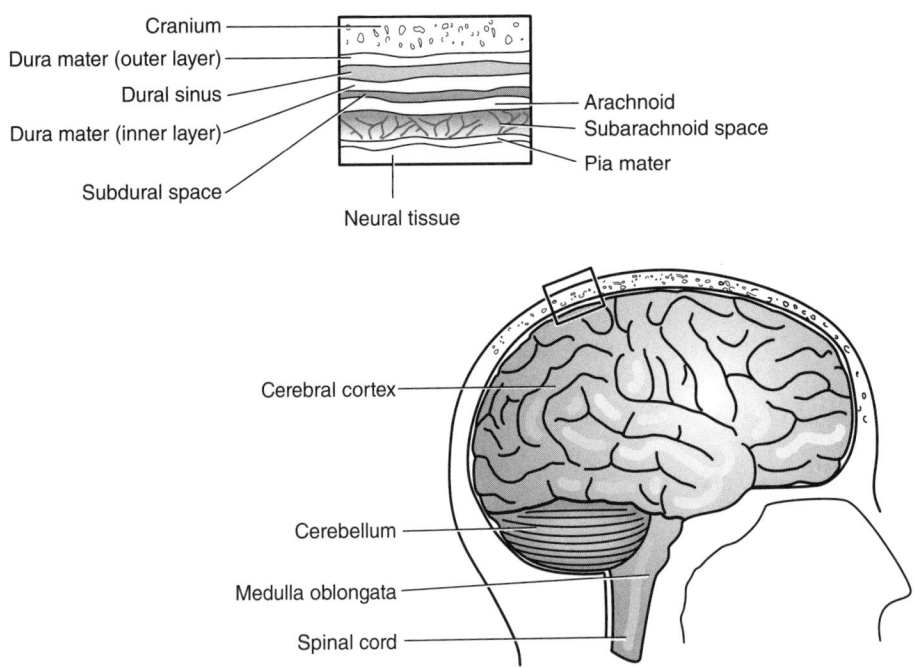

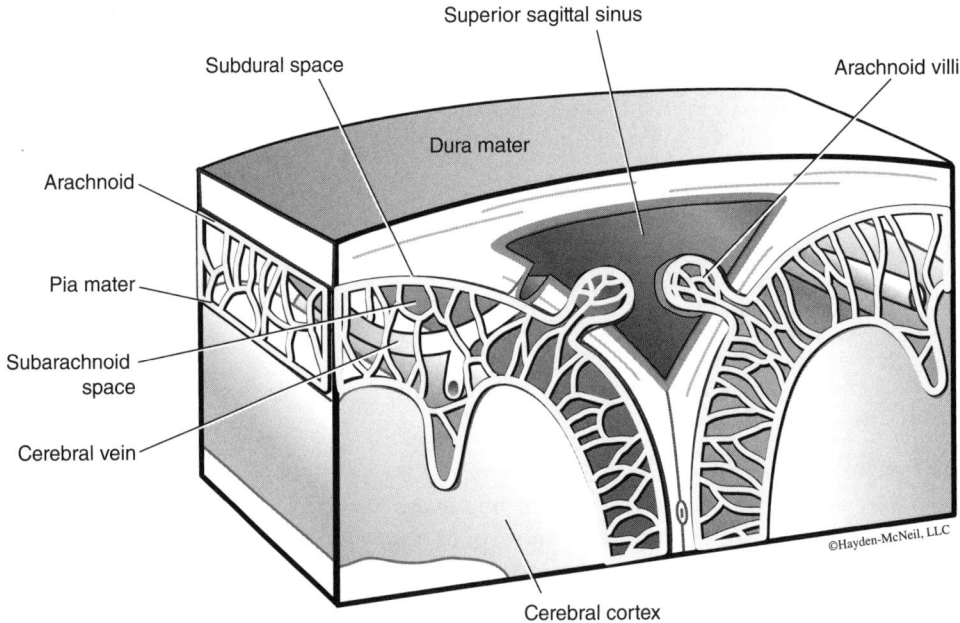

Figure 8-3. The meninges.

VI. Ventricles

The cerebral hemispheres and brain stem are hollow, and contain four interconnected cavities called **ventricles** (see Lecture notes). The ventricles are continuous with the central canal of the spinal cord, and contain cerebrospinal fluid.

1. The first is the right **lateral ventricle**.

2. The second is the left **lateral ventricle**.

3. The **third ventricle** is small. It connects with the lateral ventricles through **inter-ventricular foramina**.

4. The **fourth ventricle** is connected at its anterior end to the third ventricle via the **aqueduct of Sylvius (cerebral aqueduct),** and is continuous with the central canal of the spinal cord at its posterior end. The fourth ventricle has openings in its roof that permit cerebrospinal fluid to pass into the subarachnoid space.

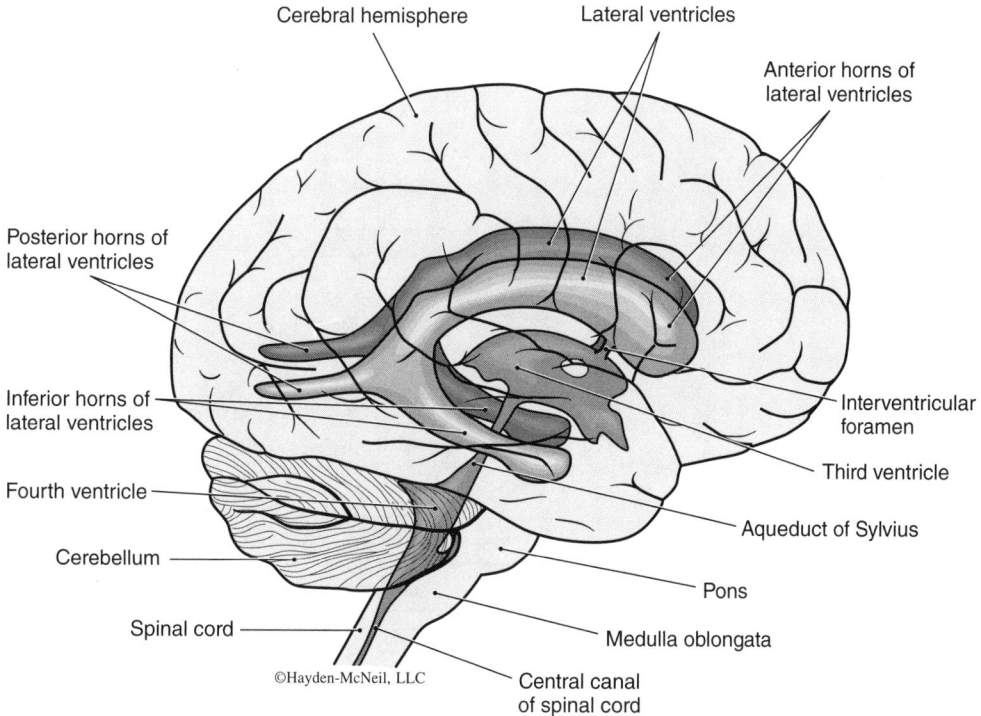

Figure 8-4. Ventricles of the brain.

VII. Cerebrospinal Fluid (CSF)

A. Production of Cerebrospinal Fluid

Most of the cerebrospinal fluid (about 140 ml) is found in the four ventricles, where it is formed as a plasma ultrafiltrate from networks of capillaries called the **choroid plexuses**. The rate of production is about 600–700 ml per day. The choroid plexus consists mainly of capillary networks surrounded by epithelial-like ependymal cells of the neuroglia.

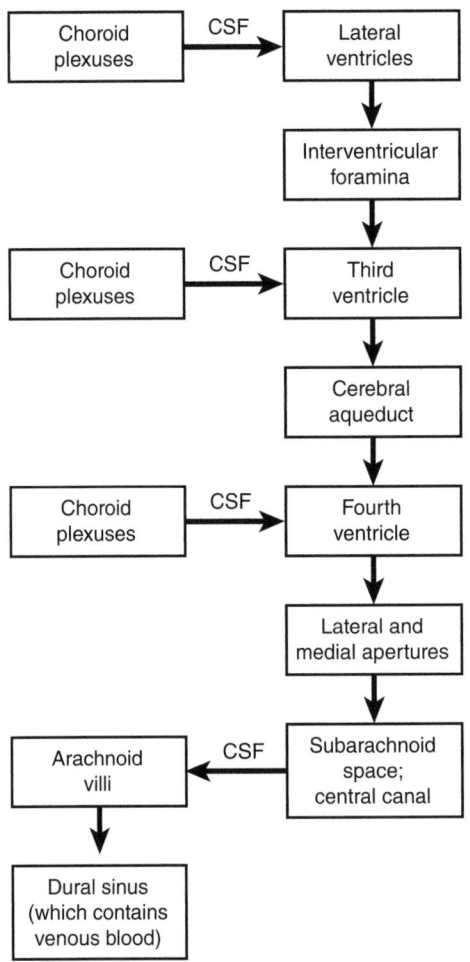

Cerebrospinal fluid flows from the lateral ventricles through the interventricular foramina into the third ventricle. From the third ventricle it flows into the fourth ventricle through the cerebral aqueduct. From the fourth ventricle, cerebrospinal fluid flows into the central canal of the spinal cord and also out of the fourth ventricle into the subarachnoid space. Within the subarachnoid space, cerebrospinal fluid flows over the surface of the pia mater covering the brain and spinal cord.

B. Absorption of Cerebrospinal Fluid

Cerebrospinal fluid is returned to the blood via arachnoid granulations (= arachnoid villi). These are finger-like processes that project into the lumen of the **dural sinuses**, which are filled with venous blood.

C. Functions of the Cerebrospinal Fluid

The cerebrospinal fluid has several functions.

1. Because it is in equilibrium with the brain extracellular fluid, the cerebrospinal fluid is important in maintaining a constant **external environment** for the neurons and neuroglia of the brain.

2. The brain effectively floats in the cerebrospinal fluid, which provides a liquid **cushion** that protects the brain from impact with the bones of the skull when the head moves.

3. The cerebrospinal fluid serves to **remove** waste substances from the brain and transfer them to the blood, and may act to **distribute** some peptide hormones and nutrients.

VIII. The Brain

The brain contains hundreds of billions of neurons that communicate with each other and with other parts of the central nervous system through numerous nerve fibers. The brain serves as a center for receiving sensory information. It also issues commands for movement. Other regions of the brain are also involved in memory and reasoning.

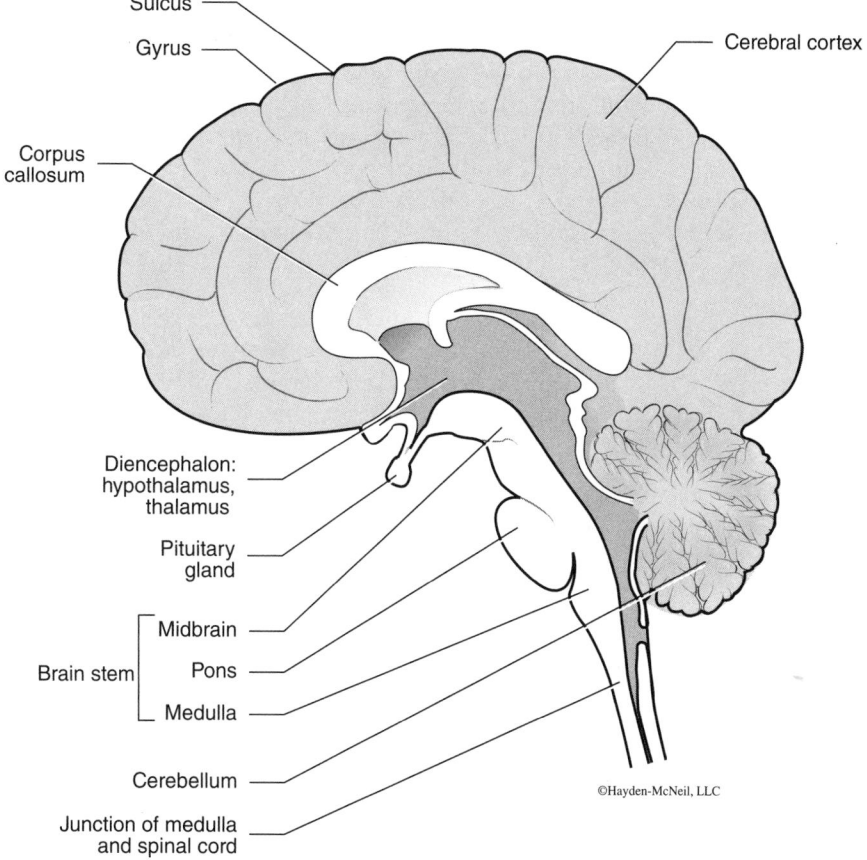

©Hayden-McNeil, LLC

Figure 8-5. Structures of the brain.

A. The Brain Stem

The **brain stem** consists of the medulla, pons, and midbrain. The brain stem contains many nerve fiber tracts and masses of gray matter called **nuclei**.

1.   The **medulla oblongata**, like the spinal cord, consists of a layer of white matter that surrounds a mass of gray matter. The white matter of the medulla consists of ascending and descending tracts that serve as the communication link between the spinal cord and the brain. On the lateral surfaces of the medulla are oval projections called the **olives**. The olivary nuclei connect with the cerebellum. Other nuclei within the medulla function as control centers for many vital processes. Examples are the **cardiac center**, which regulates the heart rate, the **vasomotor center**, which causes the dilation or the constriction of blood vessels, and the **respiratory center**, which regulates rate, rhythm, and depth of breathing. Other nuclei are involved in certain nonvital reflexes such as coughing, sneezing, swallowing, and vomiting.

2.   The **pons** appears as a bulge on the underside of the brain stem and separates the midbrain from the medulla. Through it run the nerve fibers of the middle cerebellar peduncles. Also present are the nuclei for several of the cranial nerves that relay sensory impulses from peripheral nerves to higher brain centers, and nuclei that are involved in the regulation of the rate and depth of breathing.

3.   The **midbrain** is located just above the pons. It contains many myelinated nerve fibers that connect the brain stem and spinal cord with higher parts of the brain. The **cerebral peduncles** are two prominent bundles of nerve fibers on the underside of the midbrain. They contain the corticospinal tracts and the certain sensory fibers. On the upper surface of the midbrain are four rounded eminences (two on each side of the midline) collectively called the **corpora quadrigemina**. The **superior colliculi** contain nuclei responsible for movements of the eyes and of the head and neck in response to visual stimuli. The **inferior colliculi** contain nuclei responsible for movement of the head and neck in response to auditory stimuli.

B. The Cerebellum

The **cerebellum** is important for coordinated smooth movement and posture. Like the cerebrum, it consists of two hemispheres and is made up of an outer layer of gray matter, called the **cerebellar cortex**, and an inner layer of white matter. Like the cerebrum, there are deep masses of gray matter called the fastigial, interposed, and dentate nuclei.

The inferior, middle and superior cerebellar peduncles are nerve tracts that permit communication between the cerebellum and other parts of the brain.

The cerebellum is involved in the execution of smooth, coordinated voluntary movements. It regulates the rate, range, force, direction, and timing of movements by controlling the activities of agonist, antagonist, and synergist muscles.

In this respect, the cerebellum appears to be a device that compares intention with actual movements. When the actual movement deviates from that which has been planned, the cerebellum issues compensatory commands via the motor systems. The cerebellum is involved in posture, balance, and equilibrium. It also has a role in learning motor skills.

C. The Diencephalon

The **diencephalon** is associated with the optic tracts, optic chiasm, infundibulum, pituitary gland, mamillary bodies, and the pineal gland. However, the two major structures are the thalamus and the hypothalamus.

1. The **thalamus** is the major relay and processing station for all information passing to the cerebral cortex. The information may be sensory in nature; it may be from the cerebellum and basal ganglia.

2. The **hypothalamus** contains many nuclei, as well as neuronal receptor cells that monitor the osmotic pressure of body fluids and the body temperature. The hypothalamus is important in homeostasis, such as maintaining the body's water balance. The hypothalamus also controls the autonomic nervous system, directs the release of hormones from the pituitary gland, and is involved in many of the emotional and motivational behaviors associated with the limbic system.

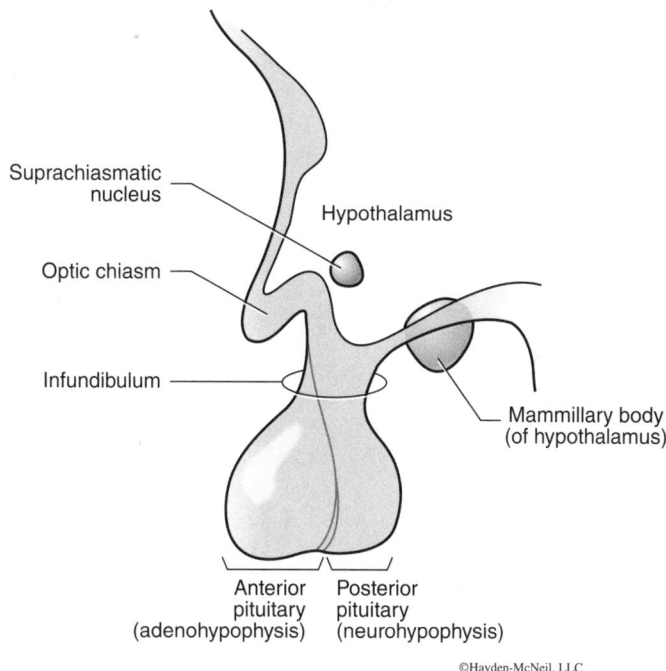

©Hayden-McNeil, LLC

Figure 8-6. Diencephalon—pituitary gland and hypothalamus.

D. The Cerebrum

The cerebrum develops from the anterior portion of the forebrain, and consists of left and right **cerebral hemispheres**. The surface layer of the cerebrum is composed of gray matter (neurons), and is called the **cerebral cortex**. Other areas of gray matter (neurons) are found in masses located deep within the cerebral hemispheres. They make up the cerebral basal ganglia: the **putamen, caudate nucleus**, and the **globus pallidus** (other components of the basal ganglia are found in the midbrain, and consist of the **substantia nigra** and the **subthalamic nucleus**).

The cerebral cortex overlies the cerebral **white matter**, composed of billions of myelinated nerve fibers that conduct nerve impulses into and out of the cerebral cortex, and also between different areas of the cerebral cortex. The **corpus callosum** is a huge band of these fibers that connects the two cerebral hemispheres.

During human embryonic development, the surface area of the cerebral cortex increases enormously, in order to accommodate the increasing numbers of neurons. Consequently, it becomes highly convoluted and folded. The folds are called **gyri** (plural of gyrus). Gyri are separated from each other by grooves called **sulci** (plural of sulcus). Very deep grooves are called **fissures**.

The **longitudinal fissure** separates the right and left cerebral hemispheres. The **lateral fissure** separates the temporal from the frontal lobe. An extension of the dura mater called the **falx cerebri** dips down into this fissure.

Anatomically, the cerebral cortex is divisible into five lobes, mostly named after the skull bones that overlie them.

1. **Frontal lobe**—contains the **precentral gyrus**, which represents the primary motor area.

2. **Parietal lobe**—separated from the frontal lobe by the central groove or sulcus. The **postcentral gyrus** represents the somatosensory area.

3. **Temporal lobe**—separated from the frontal lobe by the **lateral fissure**.

4. **Occipital lobe**

5. **Insula** (Latin for "island")—lies deep within the lateral fissure under the parietal, frontal and temporal lobes. It cannot be seen in an external view of the brain unless the temporal lobe is pulled out and away from the rest of the brain. It is delineated by the **circular sulcus**.

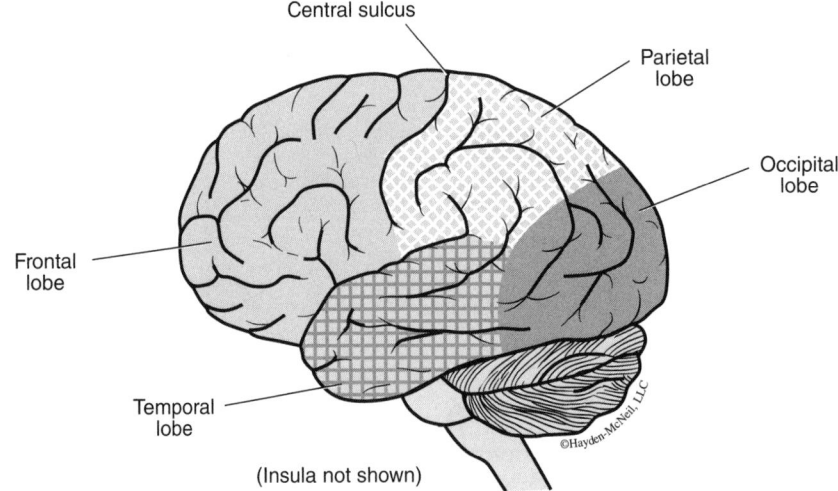

Central sulcus

Parietal lobe

Occipital lobe

Frontal lobe

Temporal lobe

(Insula not shown)

©Hayden-McNeil, LLC

E. The Cerebral Cortex—Functional Areas

The cerebral cortex has areas that have different functions. Large regions of the cerebral cortex are committed to movement (the **motor areas**) and sensation (the **sensory areas**). **Association areas** are involved in our highest intellectual activities and often provide the link between sensation and action. The association areas integrate diverse information, often from many different forms of sensation (sensory modalities) and from other cortical areas.

1. Motor Areas

The motor area contains *primary* and *higher-order* areas. Primary motor areas execute voluntary movements, while higher-order motor areas are involved in the planning of movements. The major primary motor area is located in the precentral gyrus of the frontal lobe. Different parts of this area control movements in different parts of the body, which are roughly mapped on the surface of the cerebral cortex.

The **motor speech** area, or **Broca's area**, is in the frontal lobe (usually on the left side). Neurons in this region control the complex movements of mouth, tongue, larynx, and breathing that make speech possible. Broca discovered this area in the 1860s by noting that patients with damage to the left frontal lobe were unable to speak (i.e., they suffered from Broca's aphasia).

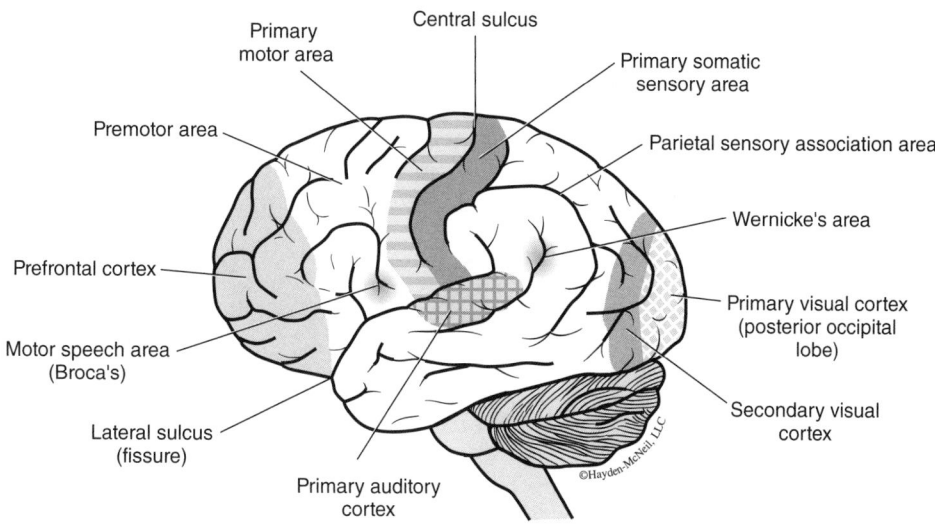

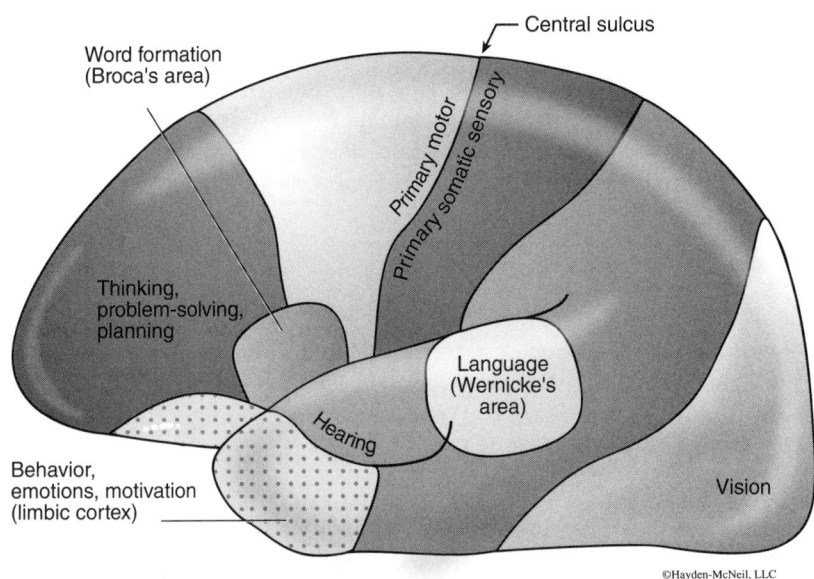

Cerebral cortex functional areas

Wernicke's area is a complex area involved in language reception and comprehension. It is found in the temporal lobe, close to the primary auditory area. It processes both verbal and visual commands. A bundle of fibers called the arcuate fasciculus connects Wernicke's area with Broca's area. A lesion in Wernicke's area does not impair a patient's ability to speak. Such patients often speak fluently, but the words often convey little meaning and they cannot convey the ideas they have in their minds.

The frontal eye field is superior to Broca's area, and is involved in gaze control. Another eye field area is found in the occipital lobes, and seems to be involved in tracking movements of the eyes, as when a spectator watches the ball in a tennis match.

2. Sensory Areas

Primary sensory areas receive information from sensory receptors, while **higher order** sensory areas process more complex aspects of the sensation, and analyze and integrate information that they receive from the primary sensory areas.

The primary **somatic sensory** area is located in the parietal lobe, in the **postcentral** gyrus (B in the diagram). The body surface is mapped roughly on the surface of this gyrus. Damage to this area can lead to loss of fine localization of stimuli, loss of the ability to judge weights, shapes, and textures.

The primary **visual** area is located on the medial surface of the **occipital** lobe, and the primary **auditory** area is located in the superior part of the **temporal** lobe near the lateral fissure. Primary areas for **taste** and **smell** are found in the **parietal** and **temporal** lobes, respectively.

3. Association Areas

Association areas integrate diverse information, often for purposeful action. In consequence they often provide the link between sensation and action. Association areas are found in regions of the parietal, temporal, occipital and frontal lobes. One part of the parietal lobe is known to be important in our awareness of our bodies and where all the parts are located in relation to our surroundings. People with damage to this region may fail to recognize parts of their body as belonging to them. For example, such a person might wake up startled, believing that someone had put a fake leg into bed with them. It was really their own leg they were looking at.

During mammalian evolution the prefrontal association cortex in the frontal lobe expanded dramatically. In human evolution, the development of a distinctively high forehead seems to be associated with the need to accommodate the increasing size of the prefrontal cortex. The prefrontal cortex seems to be involved in the highest intellectual functions that include thinking and problem-solving. It appears to play an important role in personality and emotional drive: it has extensive linkages with the limbic system via the thalamus.

F. Other Components of the Cerebrum

1. The Limbic System

The prefrontal association area is often considered part of the **limbic system**. The limbic system is a loose term for a group of gyri and associated structures (not necessarily cortical) that roughly encircles the corpus callosum and the diencephalon. In turn, the limbic system is encircled by the temporal, occipital, parietal, and frontal lobes.

Functions of the limbic system include self-preservation (feeding, fight, flight), reproduction (mating, care of offspring), emotions, goal-related behavior, motivation, sensations of reward, pleasure and punishment, and memory. The limbic system provides a link between the conscious functions of the cerebral cortex and the autonomic nervous system and endocrine system via the hypothalamus.

Much of the output of the limbic system goes to the **hypothalamus**.

2. Basal Ganglia

The cerebral basal ganglia are masses of gray matter lying deep within the cerebral hemispheres. They are the **caudate nucleus**, the **putamen**, and the **globus pallidus**. Two midbrain structures are also included with the basal ganglia: the **substantia nigra** and the **subthalamic nucleus**. Neurons in the basal ganglia receive major input from the cerebral cortex. The output of the basal ganglia goes via the thalamus back to the cerebral cortex. One of the best understood functions of the basal ganglia is related to voluntary movements.

Clinical Application. Different parts of the basal ganglia facilitate movement, while other parts suppress them. This becomes very apparent when studying two well-known disorders of the basal ganglia—**Parkinson's disease** and **Huntington's chorea.** Refer to lecture notes for more information.

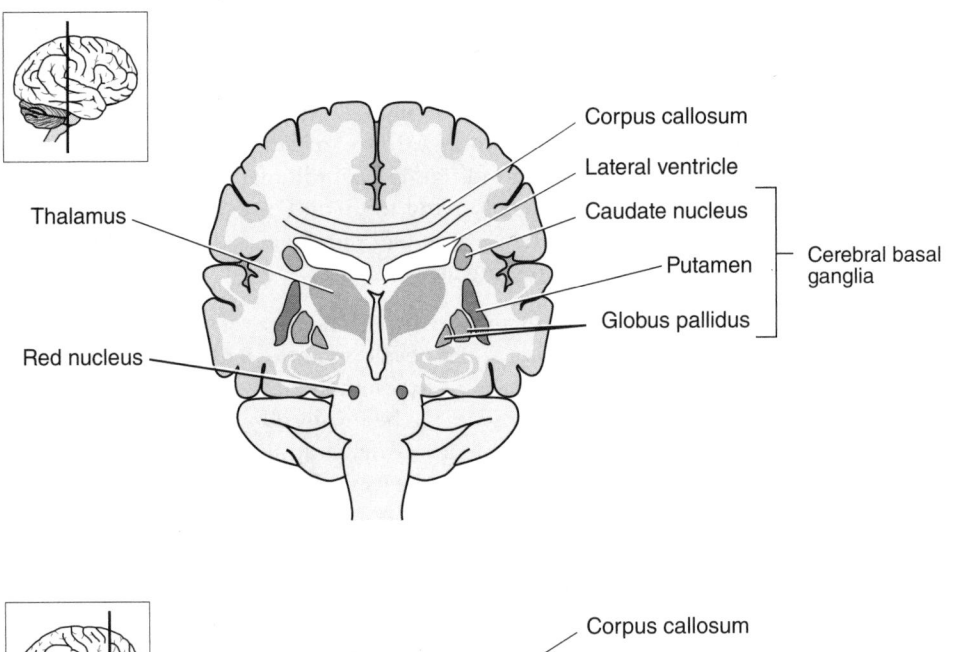

Other components of basal ganglia not illustrated:
- Substantia nigra
- Subthalamic nucleus

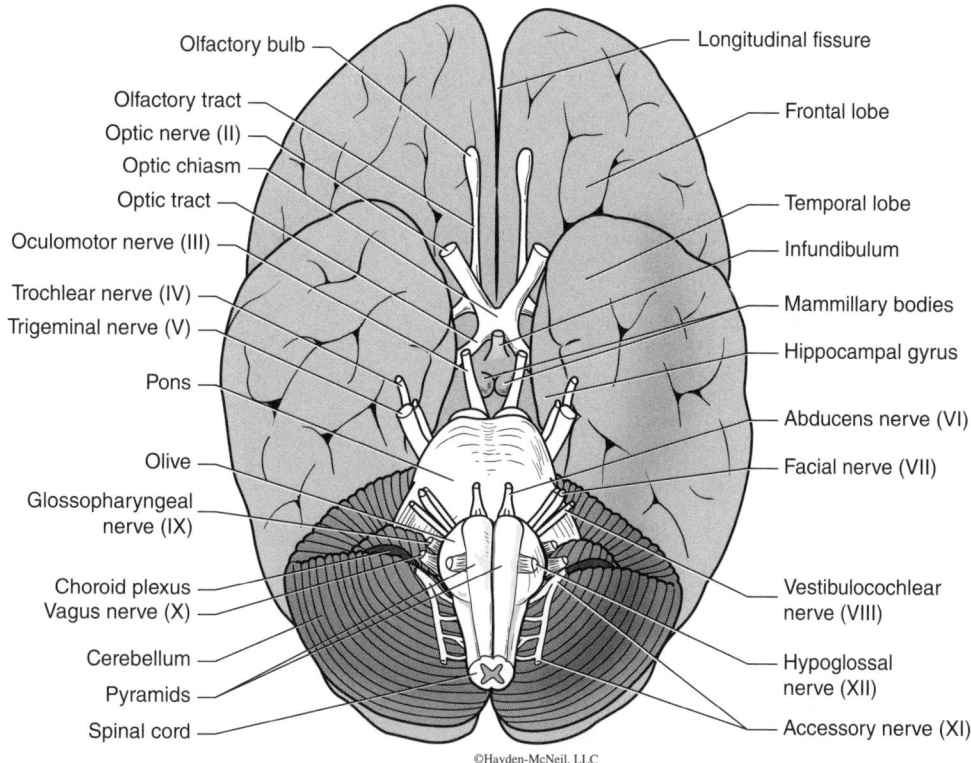

Olfactory bulb — — Longitudinal fissure

Olfactory tract —
Optic nerve (II) — — Frontal lobe
Optic chiasm —
Optic tract — — Temporal lobe
Oculomotor nerve (III) — — Infundibulum
Trochlear nerve (IV) — — Mammillary bodies
Trigeminal nerve (V) — — Hippocampal gyrus
Pons — — Abducens nerve (VI)
Olive — — Facial nerve (VII)
Glossopharyngeal nerve (IX) —
Choroid plexus — — Vestibulocochlear nerve (VIII)
Vagus nerve (X) —
Cerebellum — — Hypoglossal nerve (XII)
Pyramids —
Spinal cord — — Accessory nerve (XI)

©Hayden-McNeil, LLC

Figure 8-7. Brain—inferior aspect.

The twelve cranial nerves are numbered I through XII. Their names are as follows.

I.   **Olfactory** nerves—sensory nerve conveying information from the olfactory cells of the nose.

II.   **Optic** nerves—sensory nerve conveying information from the photoreceptor cells of the retina of the eye.

III.   **Oculomotor** nerves—primarily motor, controlling the eyelids, pupil diameter, and extraocular muscles.

IV.   **Trochlear** nerves—primarily motor, controlling extraocular muscles.

V.   **Trigeminal** nerves (three divisions: ophthalmic, maxillary, mandibular)—mixed, the motor component controlling muscles of mastication and muscles in the floor of the buccal cavity.

VI.   **Abducens** nerves—primarily motor, controlling extraocular muscles.

VII.   **Facial** nerves—mixed, the motor component controls muscles associated with facial expression, the lacrymal glands, and the salivary glands.

VIII. **Vestibulocochlear** nerves (two branches: vestibular, cochlear)—sensory, conveying information from the cochlea (sound) and vestibular apparatus (balance, equilibrium).

IX.   **Glossopharyngeal** nerves—mixed, the motor component controlling muscles in the pharynx involved in swallowing, salivary glands.

X. **Vagus** nerves—mixed, the motor component controls muscles involved in speech and swallowing, with a large autonomic group of nerve fibers that affect heart function, as well as smooth muscle and glands in the viscera of the abdomen.

XI. **Accessory** nerves (two branches: cranial accessory and spinal accessory)—primarily motor, controlling muscles of the soft palate, pharynx, larynx, neck and back.

XII. **Hypoglossal** nerves—primarily motor, controlling muscles that move the tongue.

One of the following mnemonics may help you to remember the cranial nerves.

Oh Once One Takes The Anatomy Final, Very Good Vacations Are Heavenly.

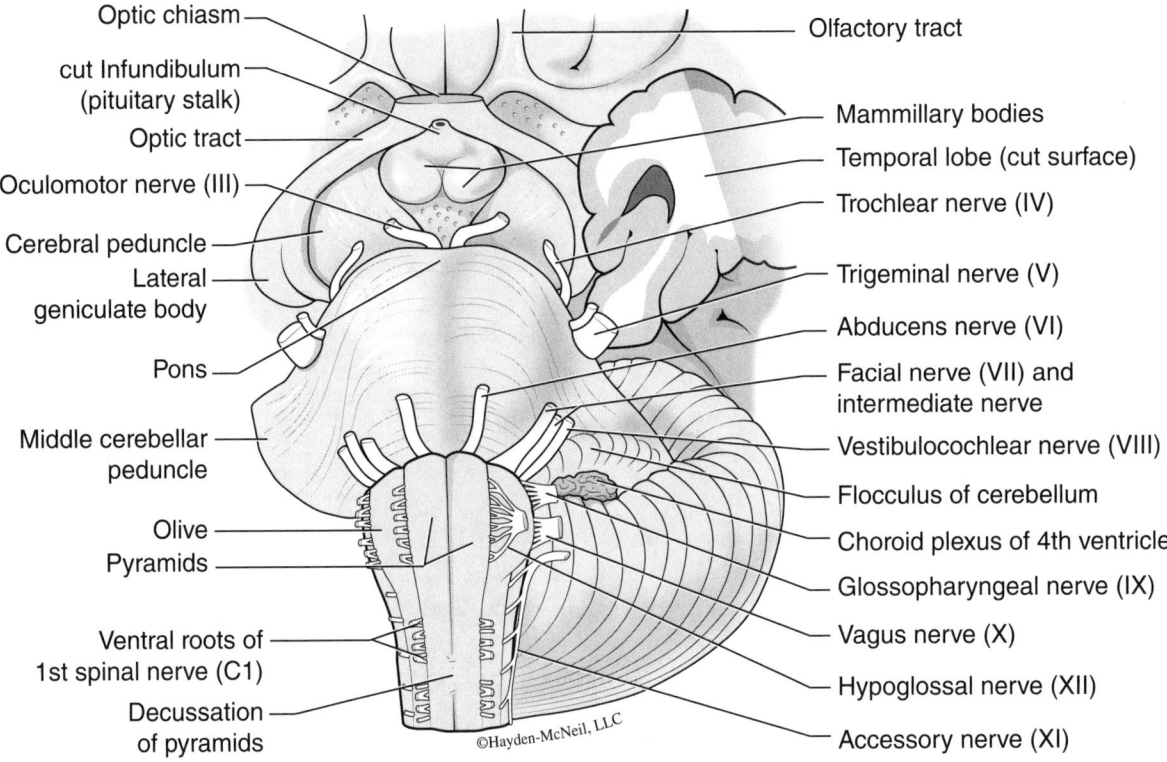

Figure 8-8. Brain stem, anterior view.

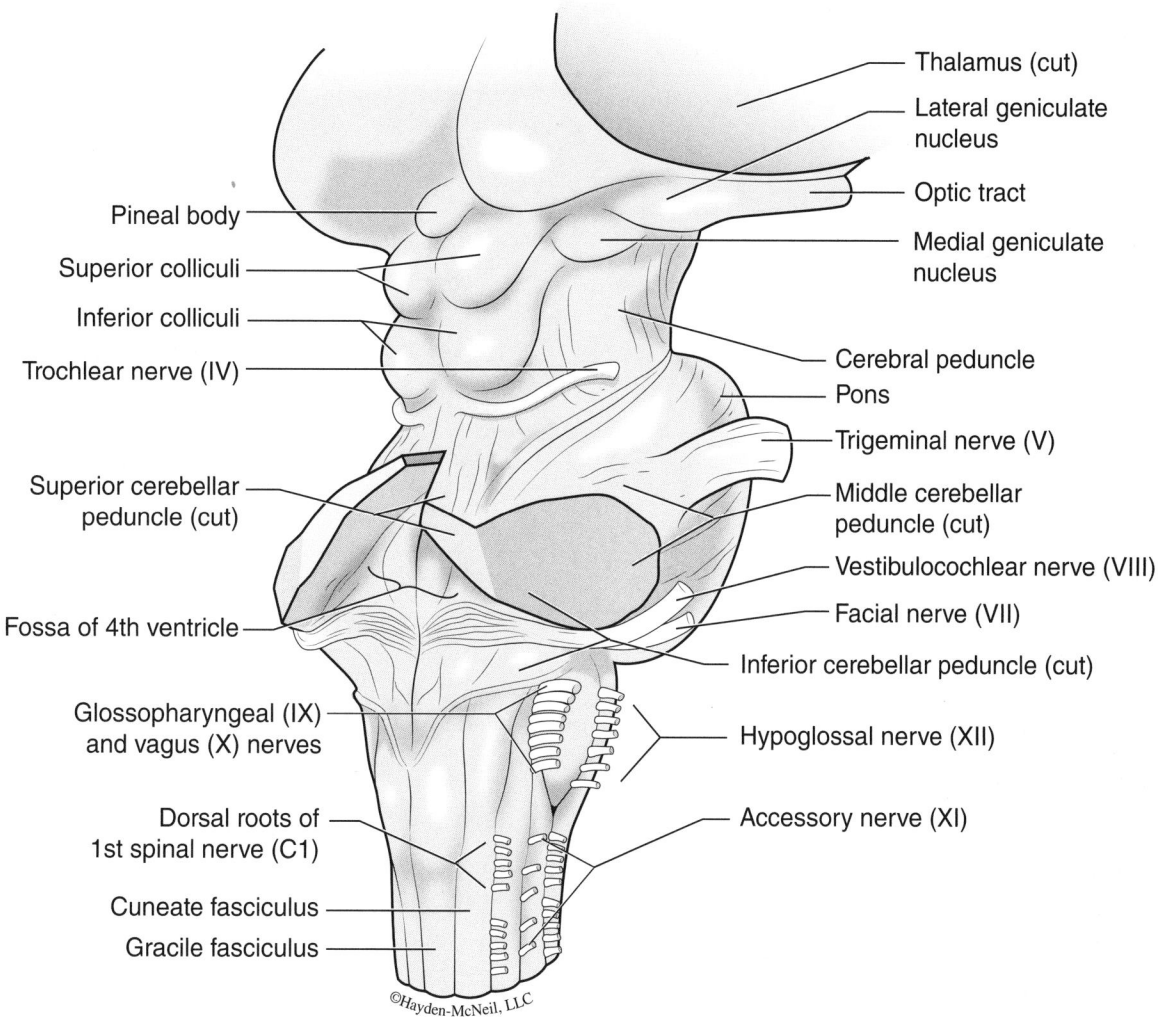

Figure 8-9. Brain stem, posterolateral view.

The Branches and Functions of Cranial Nerves

CRANIAL NERVE (NUMBER)	SENSORY GANGLION	BRANCH	PRIMARY FUNCTION	FORAMEN	INNERVATION
Olfactory (I)			Special sensory	Olfactory foramina of ethmoid	Olfactory epithelium
Optic (II)			Special sensory	Optic canal	Retina of eye
Oculomotor (III)			Motor	Superior orbital fissure	Inferior, medial, superior rectus, inferior oblique, and levator palpebrae superioris muscles; intrinsic eye muscles
Trochlear (IV)			Motor	Superior orbital fissure	Superior oblique muscle
Trigeminal (V)	Semilunar		Mixed	Superior orbital fissure	Areas associated with the jaws
		Ophthalmic	Sensory	Superior orbital fissure	Orbital structures, nasal cavity, skin of forehead, upper eyelid, eyebrows, and part of nose
		Maxillary	Sensory	Foramen rotundum	Lower eyelid; superior lip, gums, and teeth; cheek, part of nose, palate, and part of pharynx
		Mandibular	Mixed	Foramen ovale	*Sensory:* inferior gums, teeth, lips, part of palate, and part of tongue *Motor:* muscles of mastication
Abducens (VI)			Motor	Superior orbital fissure	Lateral rectus muscle
Facial (VII)	Geniculate		Mixed	Internal acoustic meatus to facial canal; exits at stylomastoid foramen	*Sensory:* taste receptors on anterior two-thirds of tongue *Motor:* muscles of facial expression, lacrimal gland, submandibular gland, and sublingual salivary glands
Vestibulocochlear (Acoustic) (VIII)		Cochlear Vestibular	Special sensory	Internal acoustic meatus	Cochlea (receptors for hearing) Vestibule (receptors for motion and balance)
Glossopharyngeal (IX)	Superior and inferior		Mixed	Jugular foramen	*Sensory:* posterior third of tongue; pharynx and part of the palate; receptors for blood pressure, pH, oxygen, and carbon dioxide concentrations *Motor:* pharyngeal muscles and parotid salivary gland
Vagus (X)	Superior and inferior		Mixed	Jugular foramen	*Sensory:* pharynx; auricle and external acoustic canal; diaphragm; visceral organs in thoracic and abdominopelvic cavities *Motor:* palatal and pharyngeal muscles and visceral organs in thoracic and abdominopelvic cavities
Accessory (XI)		Internal	Motor	Jugular foramen	Skeletal muscles of palate, pharynx, and larynx (with vagus nerve)
		External	Motor	Jugular foramen	Sternocleidomastoid and trapezius muscles
Hypoglossal (XII)			Motor	Hypoglossal canal	Tongue musculature

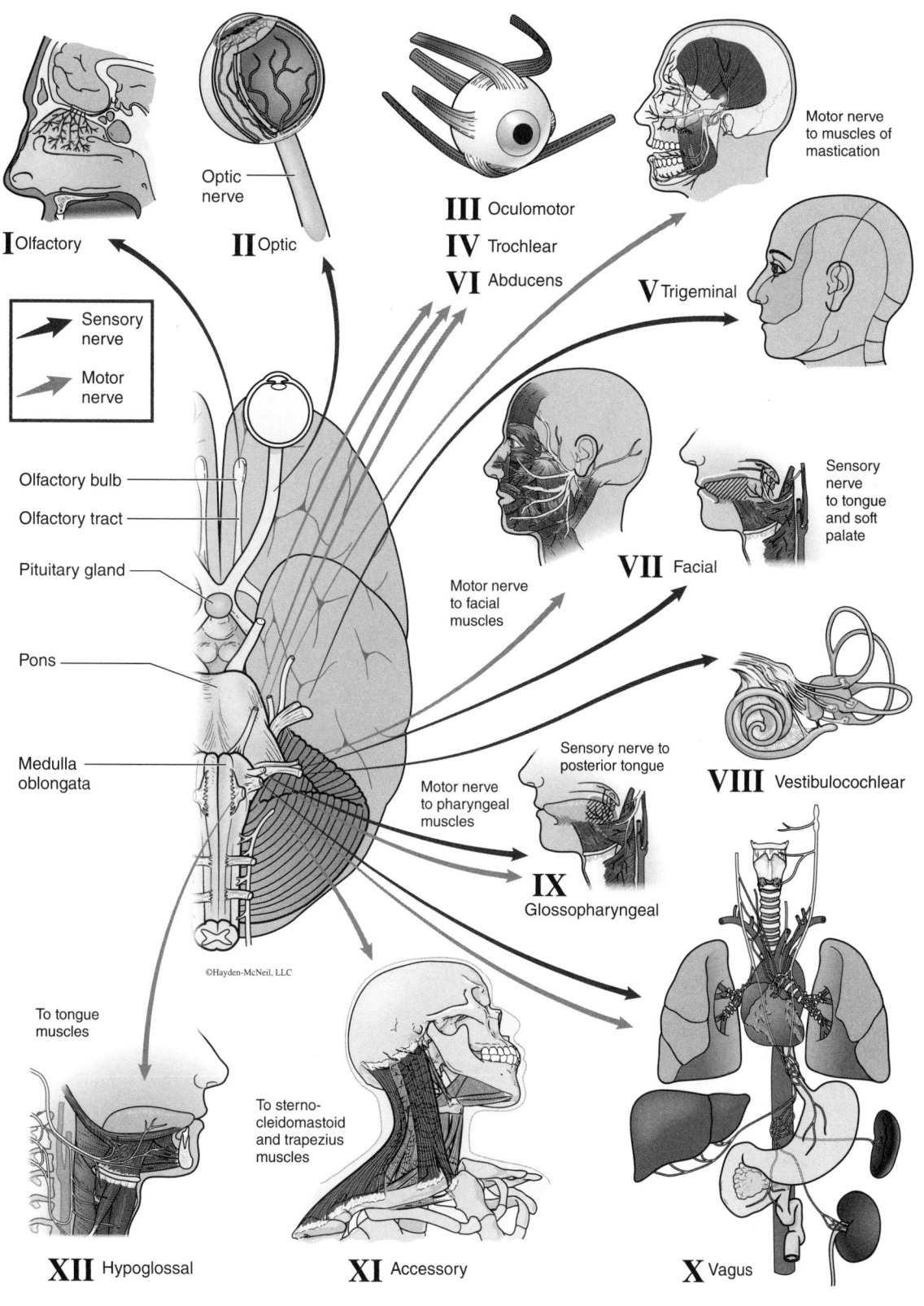

I Olfactory

Optic nerve

II Optic

III Oculomotor
IV Trochlear
VI Abducens

V Trigeminal

Motor nerve to muscles of mastication

Sensory nerve

Motor nerve

Olfactory bulb

Olfactory tract

Pituitary gland

Pons

Medulla oblongata

Sensory nerve to tongue and soft palate

VII Facial

Motor nerve to facial muscles

VIII Vestibulocochlear

Sensory nerve to posterior tongue

Motor nerve to pharyngeal muscles

IX Glossopharyngeal

©Hayden-McNeil, LLC

To tongue muscles

To sterno-cleidomastoid and trapezius muscles

XII Hypoglossal

XI Accessory

X Vagus

IX. Memory

Memory can be divided into **procedural or "knowing how," immediate or working memory**, and **declarative or "knowing that." Declarative memory is divided into short term (recent) memory and long term memory.**

Exercise A

On the diagram of the brain below, label the **central sulcus, lateral sulcus, frontal lobe, parietal lobe, temporal lobe, occipital lobe, primary motor area, somatic sensory area, visual area, auditory area, Broca's speech area,** and **Wernicke's area**.

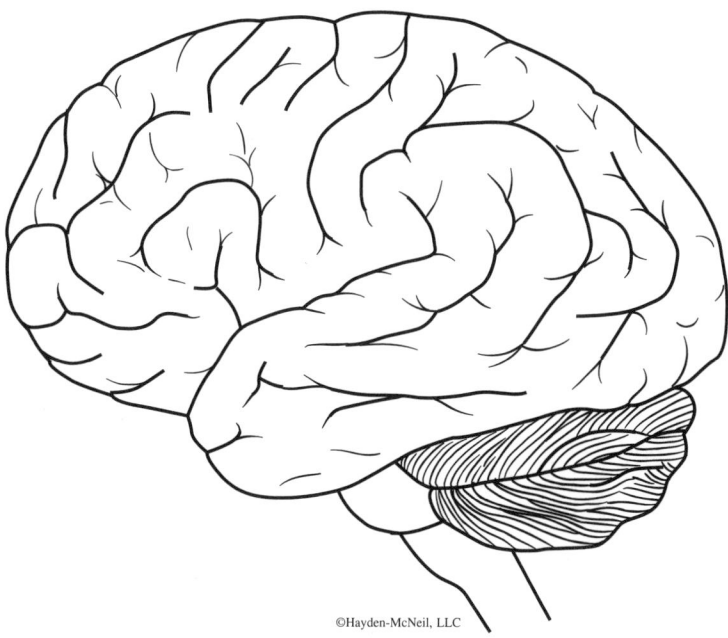

©Hayden-McNeil, LLC

Exercise B

On the diagram of the brain below, label the following anatomic areas: **scalp, skull, thalamus, hypothalamus, pineal, cerebrum, cerebellum, pituitary, pons, medulla oblongata, lateral ventricle, third ventricle, fourth ventricle, corpus callosum,** and **spinal cord.**

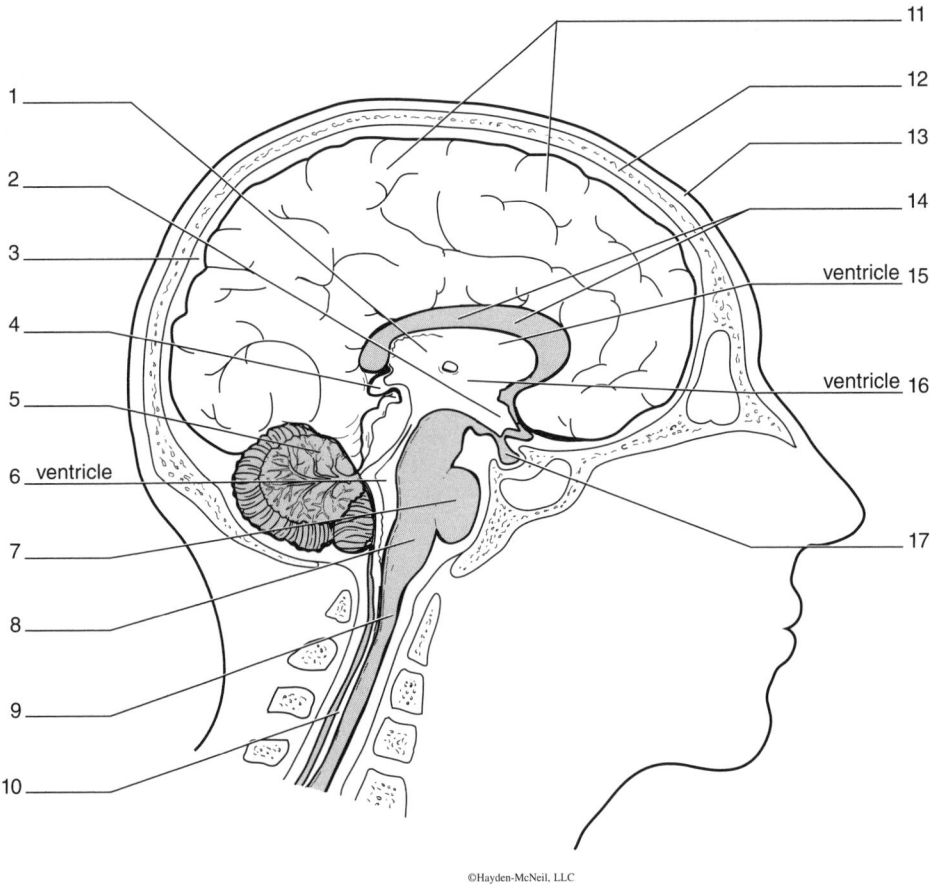

1 _____
2 _____
3 _____
4 _____
5 _____
6 _ ventricle
7 _____
8 _____
9 _____
10 _____

11 _____
12 _____
13 _____
14 _____
ventricle 15
ventricle 16
17 _____

©Hayden-McNeil, LLC

Exercise C

List the function of the parts of the brain listed below.

Meninges	
Cerebral cortex	
Thalamus	
Hypothalamus	
Cerebellum	
Medulla	
Spinal cord	
Superior colliculi	
Inferior colliculi	
Pons	
Midbrain	
Basal ganglia	
Corpus callosum	
Cerebral peduncles	
Pituitary gland	

Exercise D

You and your partner obtain a dissecting pan, a blunt probe, a whole sheep brain, and a midsagittal section sheep brain. Using the diagrams on the following pages, locate the following structures and check the spaces below. This material will be on the quiz and the exam, so be thorough and be ready to answer any questions your TA might have.

Whole Brain:

____ Meninges (remaining layers)

____ Cerebral hemispheres

____ Longitudinal fissure

____ Lobes of cerebrum

____ Cerebellum

____ Medulla

____ Spinal cord

____ Superior and inferior colliculi

____ Olfactory bulbs and tracts

____ Optic chiasma

____ Hypothalamus

____ Infundibulum

____ Pituitary gland

____ Pons

____ Cerebral peduncles

Midsagittal Section:

____ Meninges

____ Cerebral hemispheres

____ Longitudinal fissure

____ Lobes of cerebrum

____ Cerebellum

____ Medulla

____ Spinal cord

____ Superior and inferior colliculi

____ Pineal gland

____ Optic nerve

____ Thalamus

____ Hypothalamus

____ Infundibulum

____ Pituitary gland

____ Pons

____ Corpus callosum

____ Lateral ventricle

____ Cerebral peduncle

____ Arbor vitae

Sheep Brain Dissection Instructions

The brain is covered with a tough membrane.

What is it?

Find the pituitary gland on the inferior side. It will probably be removed when we remove the dura mater.

Locate the openings in the dura mater where the olfactory bulbs are found. Using your scissors, carefully cut laterally around the cerebrum until you arrive back where you started.

Next, on the superior surface, cut down the length of the cerebrum towards the cerebellum (you are basically cutting down the length of the longitudinal fissure) until you reach the transverse fissure. You will notice that the dura mater you are cutting through is thicker than normal. This is because you are cutting through a dural sinus.

Next, turn the brain around. We will be working from the spinal cord forward for a while. Carefully cut the dura mater from the spinal cord up the superior surface of the cerebellum until you reach the transverse fissure. Your two cuts should have just met.

Next, from where the two cuts come together (in the middle of the transverse fissure), cut downward into the fissure until you can carefully "peel" the dura mater away from the brain.

Once the superior and lateral aspects of the cerebrum and cerebellum are free, roll the brain over, so that the inferior side is up. Lift the dura mater gently from the spinal cord end. As you lift it up you should see two nerves connecting from the brain to the dura mater. Cut them.

The last step of removing the dura mater is to carefully trim the dura in front of and behind the optic tracts/optic chiasma. Be careful not to damage them during this process.

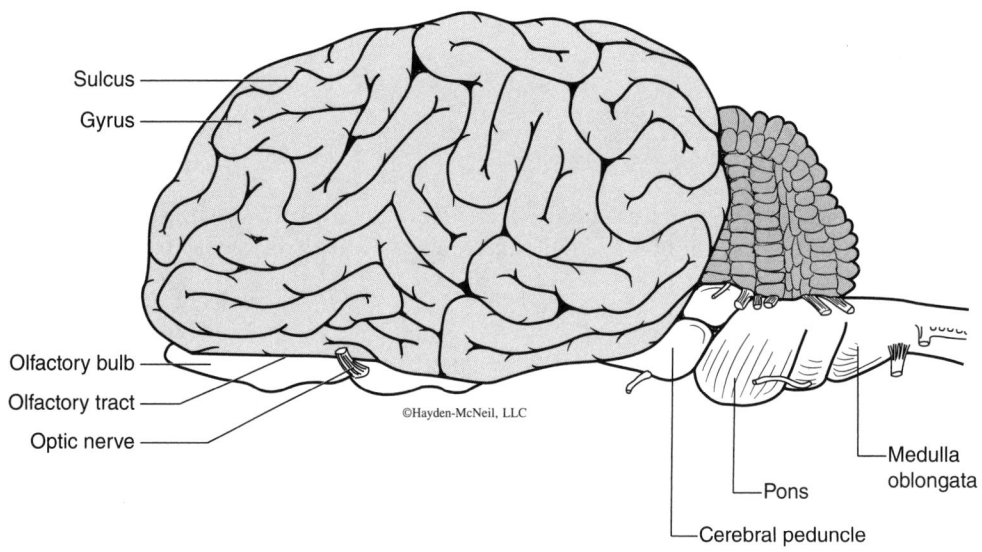

©Hayden-McNeil, LLC

Sulcus
Gyrus
Olfactory bulb
Olfactory tract
Optic nerve
Medulla oblongata
Pons
Cerebral peduncle

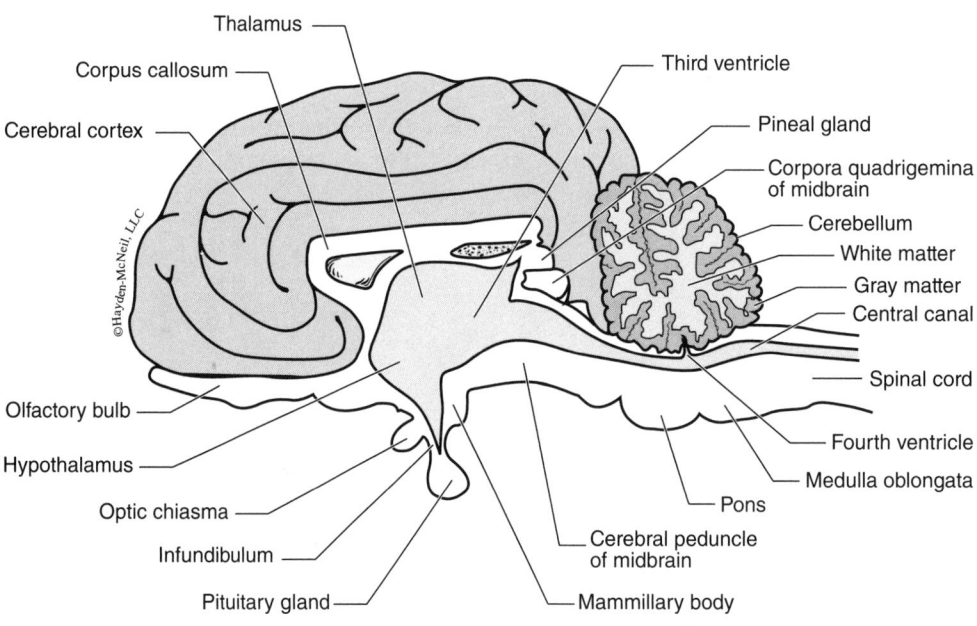

©Hayden-McNeil, LLC

Thalamus
Corpus callosum
Cerebral cortex
Third ventricle
Pineal gland
Corpora quadrigemina of midbrain
Cerebellum
White matter
Gray matter
Central canal
Spinal cord
Olfactory bulb
Hypothalamus
Fourth ventricle
Medulla oblongata
Optic chiasma
Pons
Infundibulum
Cerebral peduncle of midbrain
Pituitary gland
Mammillary body

Anatomy of the Brain

Parts to Review for the Exam

intervertebral foramen	foramen magnum	dura mater
arachnoid mater	pia mater	dural sinuses
epidural space	subarachnoid space	cerebrospinal fluid
4 ventricles	choroid plexuses	arachnoid granulations/villi
dural sinuses	dorsal/ventral roots	diencephalon
corpus callosum	longitudinal fissure	transverse fissure
lateral sulcus	frontal lobe	parietal lobe
occipital lobe	temporal lobe	insula
cerebral cortex	basal ganglia	substantia nigra
subthalamic nucleus	putamen	Broca's area
primary sensory area	primary motor area	hearing area
association area	vision area	cerebellar cortex
superior peduncles	cerebellum	olives
arbor vitae	cerebellar peduncles (3)	pons
midbrain	medulla oblongata	inferior colliculi
corpora quadrigemina	superior colliculi	cerebral peduncles (2)
thalamus	hypothalamus	

9
LABORATORY

THE NERVOUS SYSTEM II

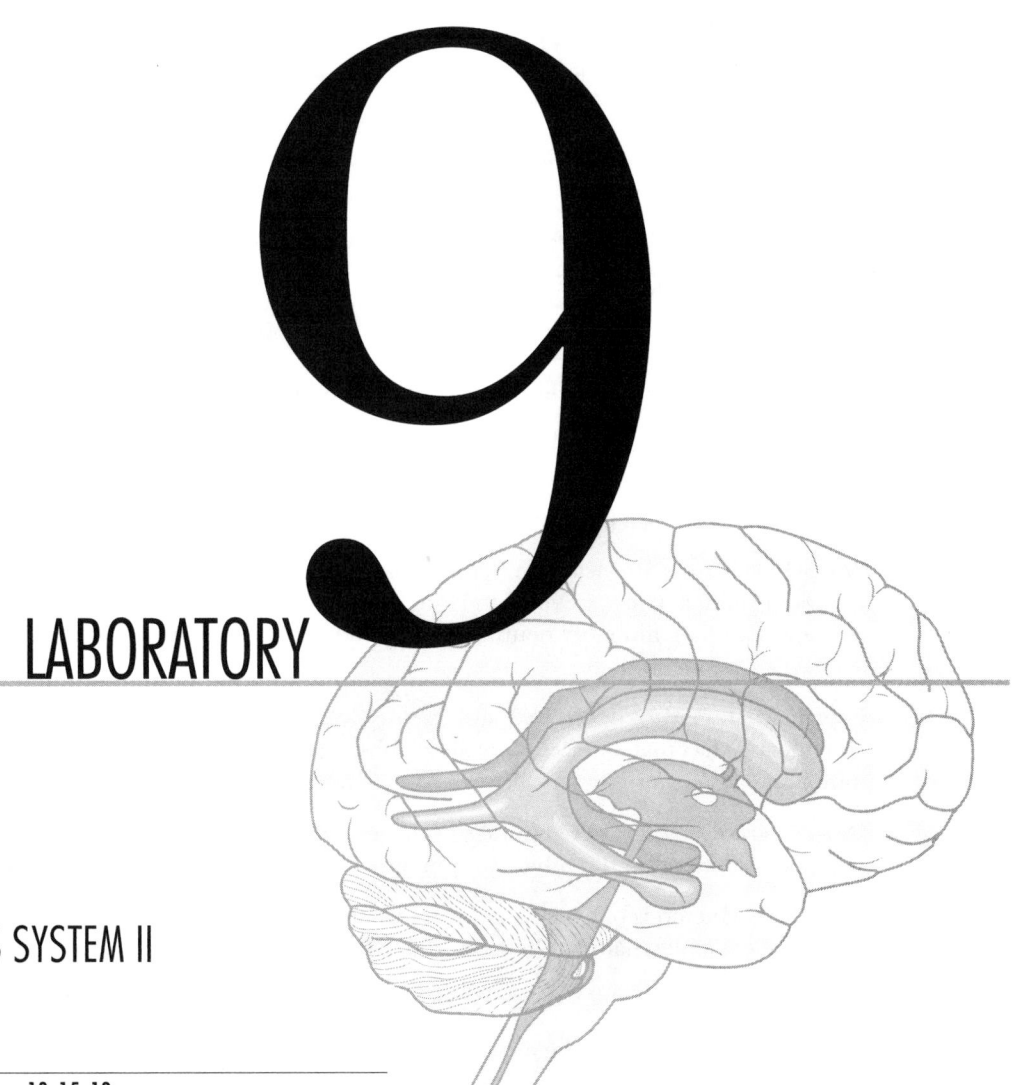

Required Reading: Lectures 13, 15, 19

BRING YOUR HISTOLOGY TEXT TO CLASS.

READ BACKGROUND AND EXPERIMENT FROM LABTUTOR: BRAIN STRUCTURE AND SPINAL REFLEXES.

Objectives

1. What action does an excitatory neurotransmitter have on the **ion channels** and **electrical potential** of the plasma membrane of the postsynaptic (receiving) cell? Use the Goldman-Hodgkin-Katz equation to explain how the channels opened by an excitatory neurotransmitter affect the membrane potential and the excitability of a neuron.

2. Define an **EPSP—draw a diagram** showing the change in membrane potential associated with an EPSP.

3. Name the four major classes of **neurotransmitters**.

4. Name the **neurotransmitters** in each class.

5. Which ion channels are acted on by **inhibitory** neurotransmitters? **Name** an inhibitory neurotransmitter. Use the Goldman-Hodgkin-Katz equation to explain how the channels opened by an inhibitory neurotransmitter affect the membrane potential and the excitability of a neuron.

6. Explain what is meant by an IPSP, and use the Goldman-Hodgkin-Katz equation to account for the fact that an IPSP is not always observed when a neuron is acted on by an inhibitory neurotransmitter.

7. **Draw diagrams** to explain **temporal** summation and **spatial** summation of EPSPs: explain how excitatory and inhibitory input into a neuron is integrated.

8. Describe *two* methods by which a neurotransmitter is **inactivated** after it has had its effect—give examples, naming the neurotransmitter and the method of inactivation.

9. Describe four ways in which **drugs** can act at synapses, and give examples.

10. Draw diagrams explaining the meaning of **convergence** and **divergence** as these terms apply to neural networks.

11. Draw a diagram of a **negative feedback circuit** that includes an interneuron.

12. With diagrams, describe IN DETAIL the structure of the spinal cord, dorsal and ventral roots, dorsal root ganglion, location of motor neurons in the gray matter, and explain the distribution of gray and white matter and how their relative volumes vary in different regions of the spinal cord (not in notes, in lecture only).

13. List the segments of the spinal cord.

14. Explain what is meant by a dermatome, and why dermatomes have clinical importance in the initial neurological examination (no need to memorize them).

15. With a diagram, describe the difference between ascending and descending tracts (pathways) in the spinal cord.

16. Name, draw and describe each of the ascending pathways and their functions.

17. Name, draw and describe each of the descending pathways and their functions.

18. Describe the negative and positive signs resulting from a lesion of the corticospinal tract.

19. List the basic components of a spinal reflex.

20. Describe (with a diagram showing the neurons) the knee-jerk reflex. To what class of spinal reflex does the knee-jerk belong, and what is the importance of this class of reflex in posture and balance?

21. Describe (with a diagram showing the neurons) what is meant by reciprocal inhibition, and why it is important in flexor and extensor movements.

22. Describe (with a diagram showing the neurons) the withdrawal reflex coupled with reciprocal inhibition and the crossed-extensor response.

23. Describe what happens to spinal reflexes when the spinal cord is cut, and explain **why** this happens.

I. Electrical Properties of Cells—the Resting Potential

A. The Electrical Potential Across the Membrane of a Neuron—the Resting Potential

B. The Ionic Permeability of the Membrane of a Resting Neuron

C. Concentrations of Various Ions Inside and Outside the Neuron

Concentrations of MAJOR ions inside and outside a typical neuronal cell are as follows. (Note that concentrations are given in **millimoles**. A mole is the molecular weight in grams, and contains about 10^{23} atoms or ions of the element in question.)

Ion	Inside Cell (millimoles/liter)	Outside Cell (millimoles/liter)	Nernst Potential (millivolts)
Na^+	7	144	+81
K^+	151	4	−97
Cl^-	4	114	−90
Ca^{++}	10^{-7} M	10^{-3} M	+123
Negatively charged proteins	approx. 50	1	

D. Explanation of the Resting Potential

E. Calculation of Membrane Potentials: The Goldman-Hodgkin-Katz (GHK) Equation and the Nernst Equation

We can calculate membrane potential from the Goldman-Hodgkin-Katz equation. Only potassium, sodium, and chloride are shown, but other ions can be added, inserted, or subtracted.

$$E_m = \frac{RT}{F} log_e \frac{P_{Na}[Na_{out}] + P_K[K_{out}] + P_{Cl}[Cl_{in}]}{P_{Na}[Na_{in}] + P_K[K_{in}] + P_{Cl}[Cl_{out}]}$$

R = ideal gas constant; T = absolute temperature (degrees Kelvin); F = Faraday's constant; P = permeability of ion

$[K_{out}]$ = concentration of potassium ions outside the cell

$[K_{in}]$ = concentration of potassium ions inside the cell.

Same applies to sodium

At 37 °C, the term before the bracket can be reduced to 61.5 log_{10}

Since the resting membrane has a very low permeability to sodium and a high permeability for potassium, and if we ignore chloride at this time, the GHK equation simplifies to the Nernst equation, where the only ion that is important in determining the membrane potential is potassium (37 °C). (Walther Hermann Nernst was a German scientist who received the 1920 Nobel Prize in Chemistry for his work in thermochemistry.)

$$E_K = 61.5 \ log_{10} \frac{[K_{out}]}{[K_{in}]} = 61.5 \ log_{10} \ \frac{4}{151} = -97 \ mV$$

Where E_K is the potassium Nernst potential

$[K_{out}]$ = concentration of potassium ions outside the cell

$[K_{in}]$ = concentration of potassium ions inside the cell.

If the membrane were highly permeable to sodium and not permeable to potassium, then we could ignore potassium and the inner surface of the plasma membrane would be positively charged with respect to the outer surface, by the amount of the sodium Nernst potential, which is +81 mV.

$$E_{Na} = 61.5 \ log_{10} \frac{[Na_{out}]}{[Na_{in}]} = 61.5 \ log_{10} \ \frac{144}{7} = +81 \ mV$$

If we are dealing with a negatively charged ion such as chloride, then the equation is written:

$$E_{Cl} = -61.5 \ log_{10} \frac{[Cl_{out}]}{[Cl_{in}]} \quad or \quad E_{Cl} = 61.5 \ log_{10} \frac{[Cl_{in}]}{[Cl_{out}]}$$

If the membrane were permeable to both sodium and potassium, then the membrane potential would be calculated along the lines of the GHK equation as follows:

$$E_m = 61.5 \log_{10} \frac{P_K[K_{out}] + P_{Na}[Na_{out}]}{P_K[K_{in}] + P_{Na}[Na_{in}]}$$

Where P_K and P_{Na} are the permeabilities of the membrane to potassium and sodium, respectively. You can see that if the membrane is not permeable to sodium ($P_{Na} = 0$), sodium drops out of the equation, P_{Na} cancels out and we get the Nernst equation for potassium.

II. The Action Potential of a Nerve Cell

Nerve cells are *excitable*. That is, they can respond to changes in their surroundings.

Some nerve cells are specialized as *sensory receptors*, and are excited when they (or their nerve endings) are exposed to light, heat, pressure, touch, sound, etc. Other nerve cells respond to signals coming from neurons that connect with them by special junctions called *synapses* (next lecture). These signals are often chemical agents called neurotransmitters.

Often a signal (either due to the neurotransmitter or a stimulus such as pressure, touch, sound, etc.) will act to make the inside of the cell membrane less negative with respect to the outside, in which case it is said to **depolarize** the membrane. Depolarization events can occur in graded steps.

When a depolarization event changes the membrane potential to a value called the *threshold*, an **action potential** is generated. At threshold (usually about –55mV), the membrane, which has previously been almost impermeable to sodium ions, starts to become highly permeable to them. In fact, the permeability of the membrane to sodium ions becomes much, much greater than the permeability of the membrane to potassium ions. The sudden increase in permeability to sodium is due to the opening in the cell membrane of **voltage-gated sodium channels**.

Result? When the membrane permeability to sodium increases far above potassium because of these newly opened sodium channels, sodium now dominates the equation for the membrane potential:

$$E_m = 61.5 \log_{10} \frac{P_K[K_{out}] + P_{Na}[Na_{out}]}{P_K[K_{in}] + P_{Na}[Na_{in}]}$$

Consequently, the membrane potential swings away from the potassium resting potential of –97 mV and moves toward the sodium potential of +81 mV.

$$E_{Na} = 61.5 \log_{10} \frac{[Na_{out}]}{[Na_{in}]} = 61.5 \log_{10} \frac{144}{7} = +81 \, mV$$

The sudden depolarization of the membrane caused by an initial threshold depolarization event is the first phase of the **action potential.**

The voltage-gated sodium channels remain open for only a short time, then they start to swing closed. Sodium permeability then drops below potassium permeability, so returning the membrane potential back to its resting condition, which is close to the potassium Nernst potential.

The return of the membrane potential back to its resting value is accelerated because the potassium permeability actually rises above its resting value for a short period of time. The transient rise of potassium permeability is due to the presence of slowly-opening **voltage-gated potassium channels** in the membrane. Since the potassium leak channels are always open, the membrane actually becomes *more* permeable to potassium than it was during the resting phase.

This causes a transient hyperpolarization or overswing at the terminal phase of the action potential. Finally, the voltage-gated potassium channels close, and the membrane returns to the resting potential.

Put simply, the action potential represents a rapid swing of membrane potential from its resting potassium potential toward the sodium potential (which it never reaches), and back again.

During an action potential, the nerve will not respond to further stimuli, and is said to be in its **refractory period**.

Sodium ions that enter the neuron as a result of the slight "leak" at rest and during the generation of action potentials are pumped out by the **ATP-driven sodium pump.**

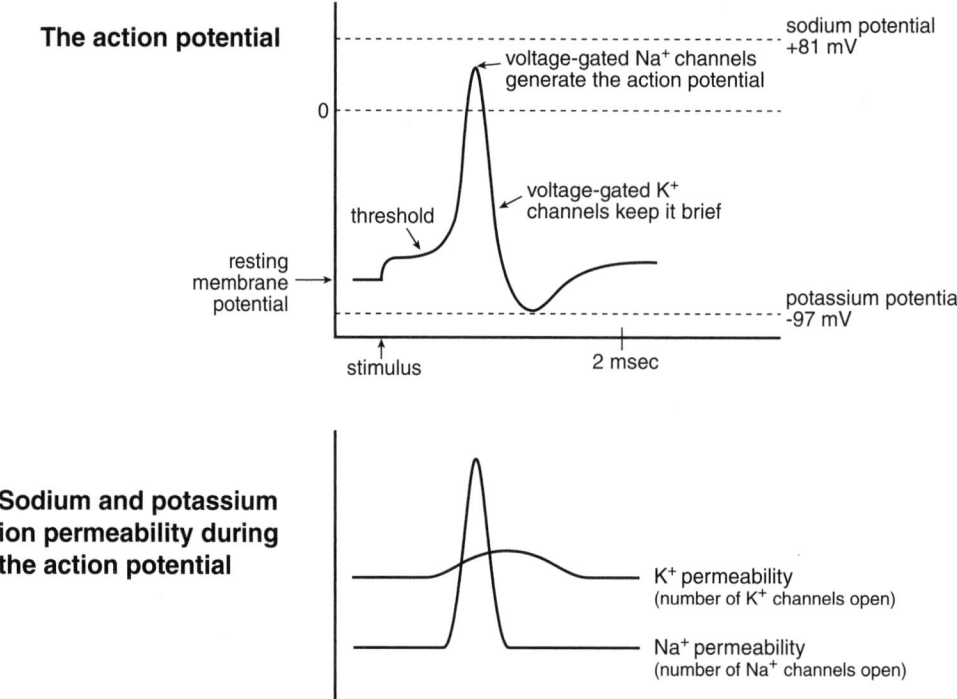

III. Propagation of an Action Potential Along a Nerve Fiber

When an action potential is triggered at the beginning of a nerve fiber, it causes the next region of the nerve fiber membrane to depolarize, also generating an action potential. This is repeated continuously, and the wave of depolarization (i.e., the nerve impulse) travels all the way along the fiber until it reaches the axon terminals.

Behind this wave of depolarization, the nerve fiber repolarizes again, as shown in the diagram.

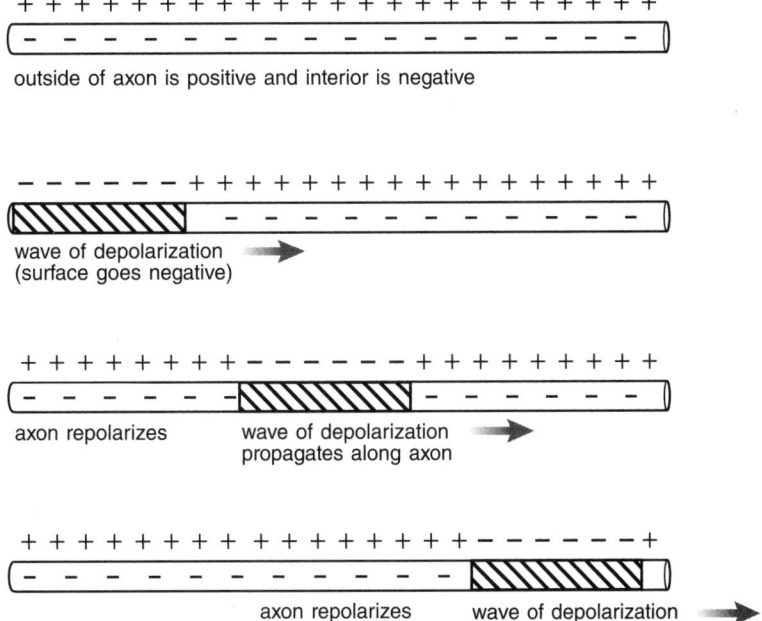

Nerve impulses travel along different nerve fibers at different speeds.

1. Small diameter fibers in mammals have little or no myelin and are slow-conducting.

2. Large diameter fibers in mammals have a thick myelinated sheath and are fast-conducting. The myelin sheath is formed by Schwann cells in peripheral nerves and oligodendrocytes in the central nervous system. It is interrupted at intervals along its length by patches where the plasma membrane of the underlying nerve axon is exposed. These patches of membrane, which are very rich in voltage-gated sodium channels, are called **nodes of Ranvier**. Myelin is an electrical insulator. An action potential developed at one node of Ranvier therefore depolarizes the next node of Ranvier without having to generate action potentials in the intervening, insulated segment of nerve. The nerve impulse therefore "jumps" from one node to the next (**saltatory conduction**—see figure).

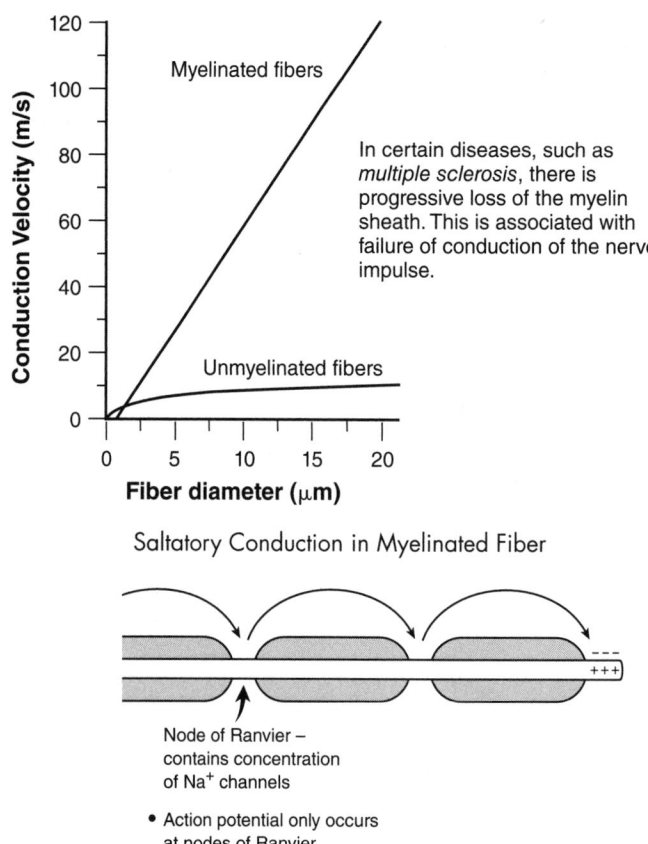

In certain diseases, such as *multiple sclerosis*, there is progressive loss of the myelin sheath. This is associated with failure of conduction of the nerve impulse.

Saltatory Conduction in Myelinated Fiber

Node of Ranvier –
contains concentration
of Na^+ channels

- Action potential only occurs at nodes of Ranvier

IV. How Drugs Act at Synapses

There are many disorders of the nervous system that are tied to neurons that use a particular neurotransmitter. They include Parkinson's disease (dopamine), clinical depression (serotonin, norepinephrine), Huntington's chorea (initially lack of GABA) and neuronal cell death after a stroke (glutamate).

Medications designed to treat these conditions often use four strategies.

1. **Blocking the neurotransmitter receptor**
2. **Blocking the reuptake transporter molecules**
3. **Increasing the amount of neurotransmitter released**
4. **Inhibiting the enzymes that destroy neurotransmitters**

V. Neural Networks

The nervous system is a network of neurons arranged in synaptically-connected sequences called **neural networks** or **neuronal circuits.**

There are many different arrangements of neuronal circuits.

A. Divergence and Convergence

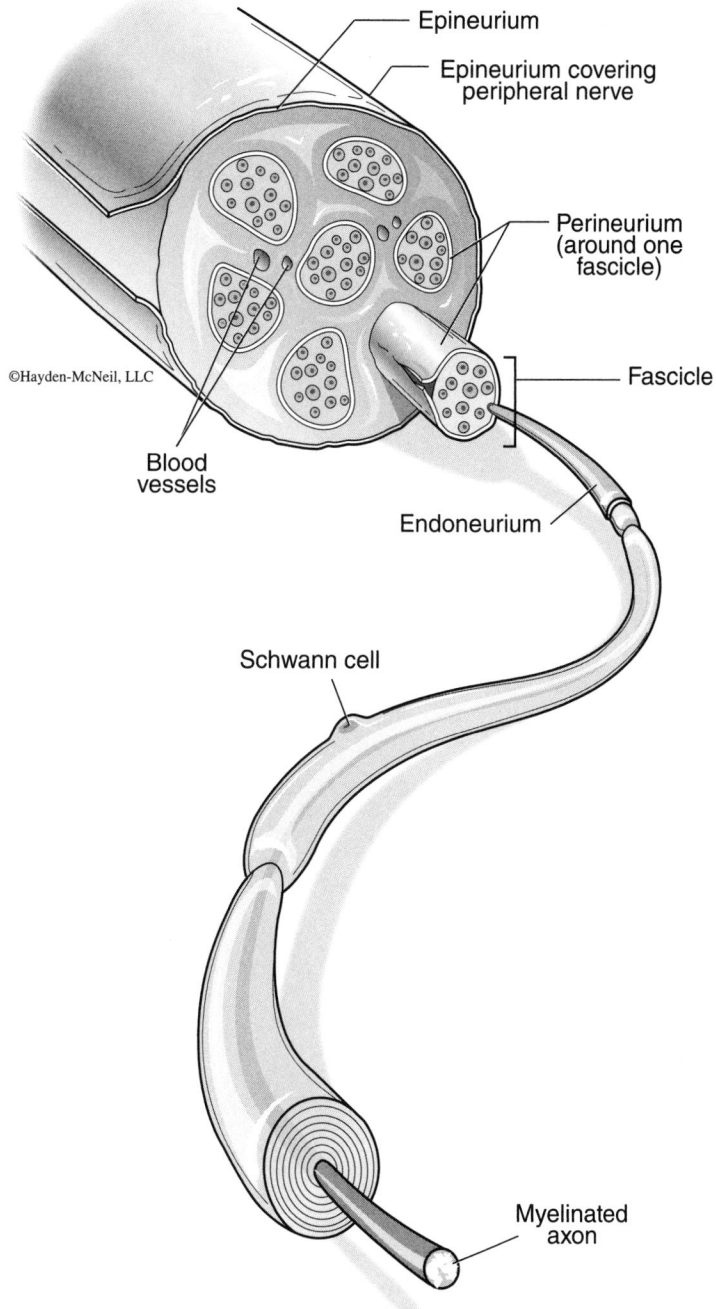

Figure 9-1. Peripheral nerve.

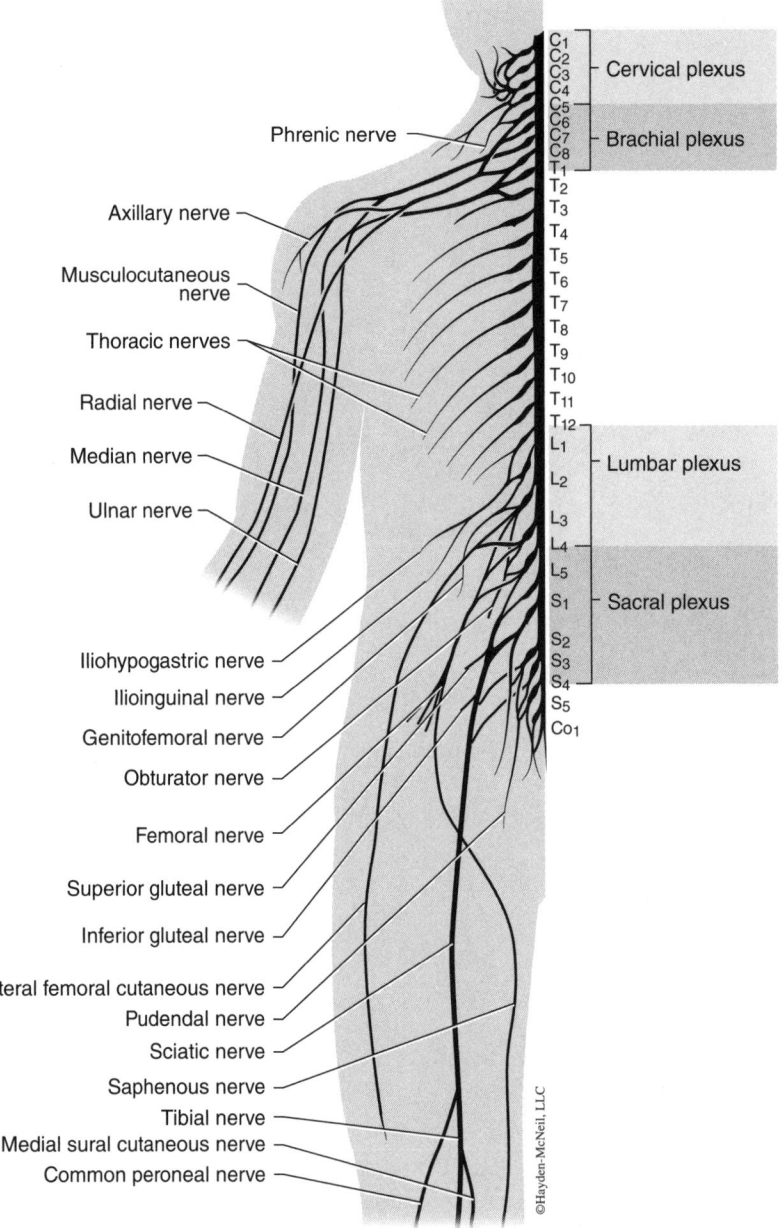

Figure 9-2. Peripheral nerves and nerve plexuses.

The spinal cord consists of 31 segments, each of which gives rise to a pair of spinal nerves.

- **C**ervical   8
- **T**horacic   12
- **L**umbar   5
- **S**acral   5
- **Co**ccygeal   1

The *cervical enlargement* gives rise to nerves for the arms, and the *lumbar enlargement* gives rise to nerves for the legs.

Each spinal nerve emerges from the spinal cord by two short branches, the *dorsal (posterior) and ventral (anterior) roots*, which are protected within the vertebral column.

The dorsal root (or sensory root) has an enlargement called the **dorsal root ganglion**. The dorsal root ganglion contains the cell bodies of sensory neurons whose nerve endings are often specially adapted to act as sensory receptors (see Lecture 14). The axons of these sensory neurons enter the spinal cord through the dorsal root and form synapses with other neurons in the spinal cord.

The ventral root (or motor root) is actually composed of a number of *rootlets*, and carries the axons of motor neurons whose cell bodies are located in the gray matter of the spinal cord (see below).

The dorsal and ventral roots merge to form a **spinal nerve** that emerges from the vertebral canal through an **intervertebral foramen**. After emerging from the foramen, the spinal nerve splits into an anterior and a posterior branch. The spinal nerves in the thoracic and lumbar regions also have **rami** (branches) that are part of the autonomic nervous system (we'll talk about the autonomic nervous system later).

The area of skin innervated by a single dorsal root is called a **dermatome** (see Figure 9-3). Dermatomes are important clinically, because loss of sensation in a particular dermatome indicates the level of a spinal lesion or damage to a spinal nerve root.

Body Region Affected	Spinal Segment
Clavicle	C4
Little finger	C8
Nipples	T4
Umbilicus	T10
Inguinal area	L1
Anterior thigh	L3
Big toe	L5
Lateral side of foot	S1
Perineum	S3–S5

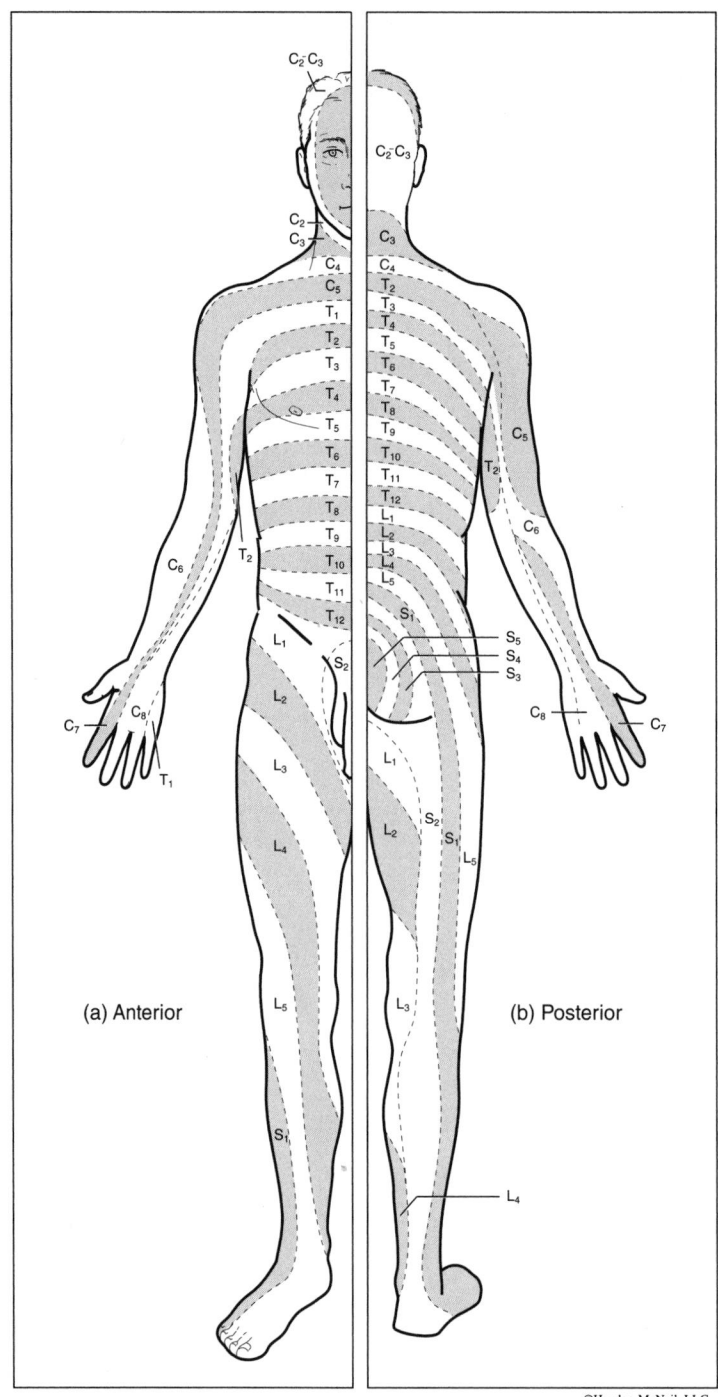

Figure 9-3. Dermatomes.

B. Organization of Gray and White Matter in the Spinal Cord

The spinal cord is partially divided into right and left halves by a deep **anterior (ventral) median fissure** and a shallow **posterior (dorsal) median sulcus**.

The spinal cord is composed of gray and white matter.

The gray matter, which consists of many cell bodies of different neurons with their axons and dendrites, occupies the central region of the cord, and looks like a butterfly or an H in cross-section. The two vertical bars forming the top of the H are called *posterior (dorsal) horns*, and the two vertical bars forming the bottom of the H are called the *anterior (ventral) horns*. The cross-bar of the H is the *gray commissure*.

The cell bodies of motor neurons are clustered in the ventral horn gray matter. Other neurons in the spinal cord gray matter are interneurons. Some of these interneurons send axons in the lateral and ventral columns of the white matter for distances ranging from a few to many segments up and down the spinal cord. Such neurons are called *propriospinal neurons*.

The white matter, consisting of nerve fiber tracts, is divided by the gray matter into anterior (ventral), posterior (dorsal) and lateral *funiculi*.

Points to identify in the very simplified cross section of the spinal cord below are:

- white matter and gray matter
- dorsal and ventral roots
- dorsal root ganglion containing the cell bodies of sensory neurons
- ventral horn gray matter containing the cell bodies of motor neurons

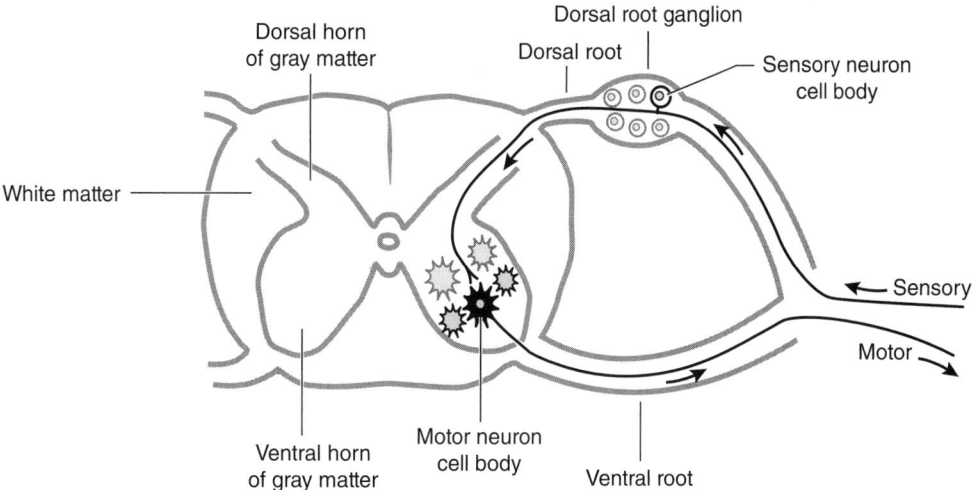

Figure 9-4. Simplified cross-section of the spinal cord.

There are many neurons that have not been shown. Only the sensory and ventral horn motor neurons are diagrammed. The connections illustrated are for the "knee-jerk" reflex.

VI. The Spinal Cord Function—Organization of Neurons and Nerve Fiber Tracts

The major functions of the spinal cord are:

- It is the major pathway for all **information ascending** to the brain from the **sensory** systems of the body.

- It is also the major pathway for all **commands descending** from the brain to the **muscles** and other **effector** systems.

- The spinal cord is able to **execute** certain simple behavioral activities without involving the brain. These activities are referred to as *spinal reflexes*. Additionally (as we have mentioned in the introduction to this lecture), neural networks in the spinal cord are responsible for storing the **motor program** involved in **walking**.

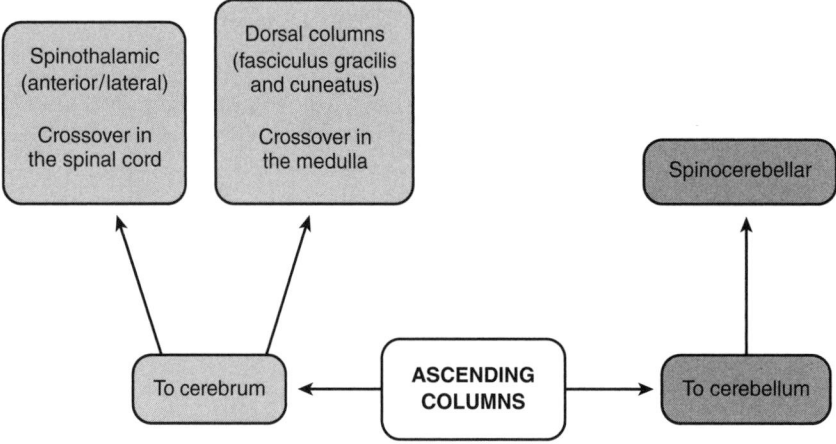

Figure 9-5. Summary of ascending pathways.

A. Ascending Pathways (Tracts)

There are three major ascending systems conveying somatic sensory information to the brain. One of these systems is specifically used for carrying sensory information to the cerebellum.

The first two ascending systems provide an example of the use of parallel pathways. Parallel pathways add subtlety and richness to the sensory experience, and also act as insurance against damage to one of them.

1. The ***dorsal column tracts*** ascend in the *fasciculus gracilis* (gracile fasciculus) and *fasciculus cuneatus* (cuneate fasciculus) of the spinal cord white matter. They synapse with neurons in the ***nucleus gracilis*** and ***nucleus cuneatus*** in the medulla. The fibers from these neurons cross over to the opposite side *in the medulla*, so that signals from sensory receptors on the left side of the body are transmitted to the right side of the brain, and vice versa.

The following sensory information is carried by this system:

a. fine, discriminatory touch
b. vibration
c. kinesthesia, proprioception (limb movement, position)
d. pressure

2. The **anterior and lateral tracts**, which include the anterior and lateral *spinothalamic tracts*, are older on the evolutionary scale than the dorsal column tracts. The anterior and lateral spinothalamic tracts are located in the lateral and anterior funiculi of the spinal cord white matter. Most of the nerve fibers in this system cross over to the opposite side *in the spinal cord*. There is a small contingent of uncrossed fibers, however.

The following sensory information is carried by this system:

a. crude touch (includes tickle and itch)
b. pain
c. temperature

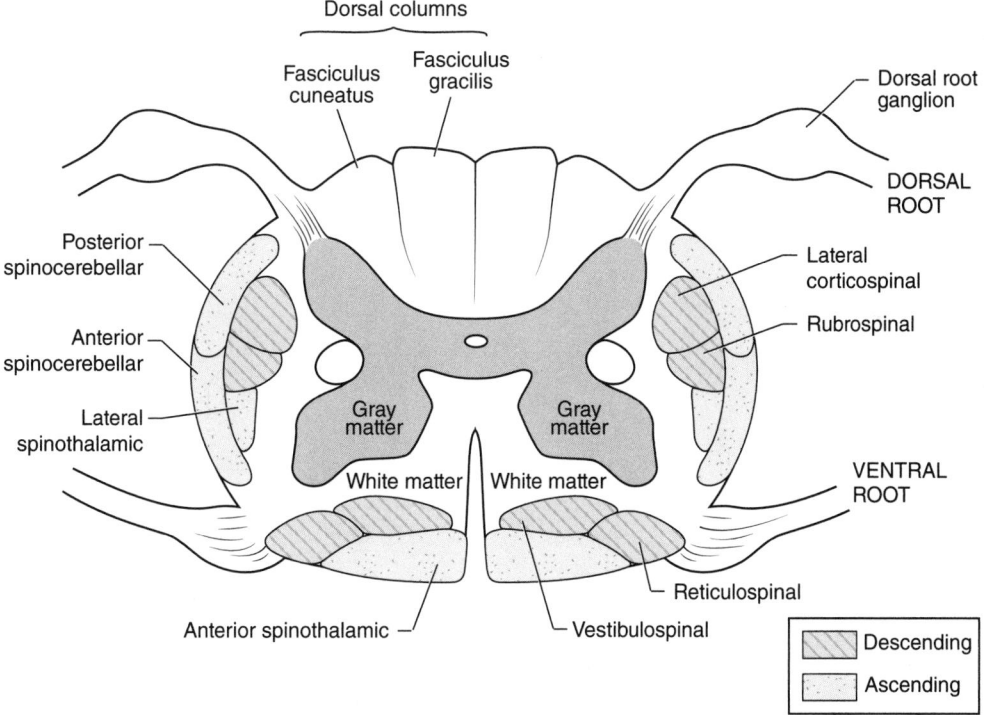

Figure 9-6. The spinal cord.

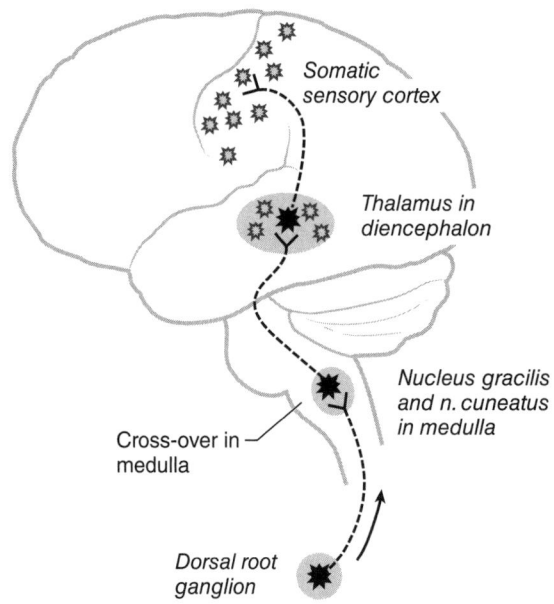

Figure 9-7. Dorsal column tracts (ascending).

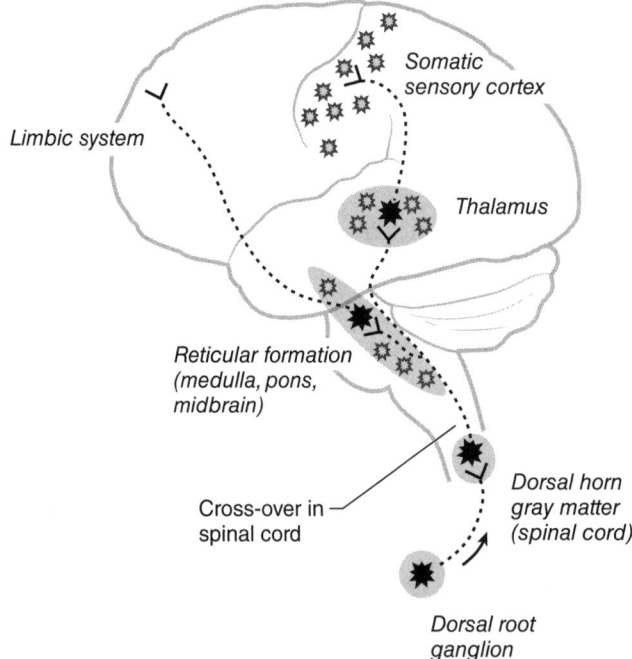

Figure 9-8. Anterior/lateral spinothalamic tracts (ascending).

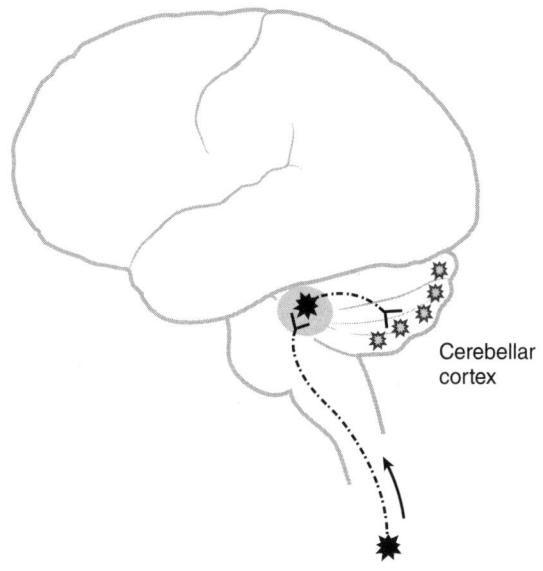

Figure 9-9. Spinocerebellar tracts (ascending).

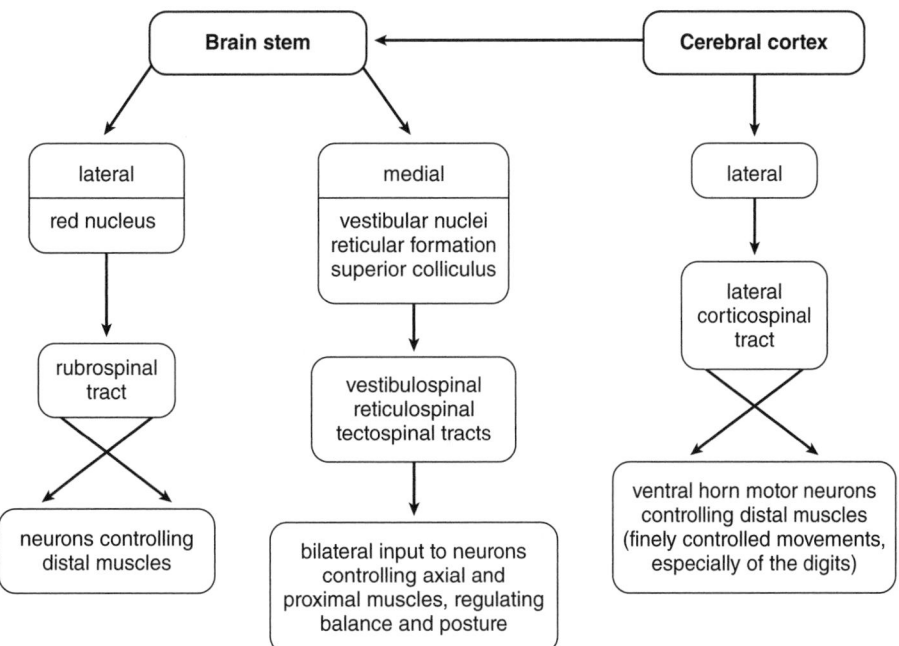

Figure 9-10. Summary of descending tracts.

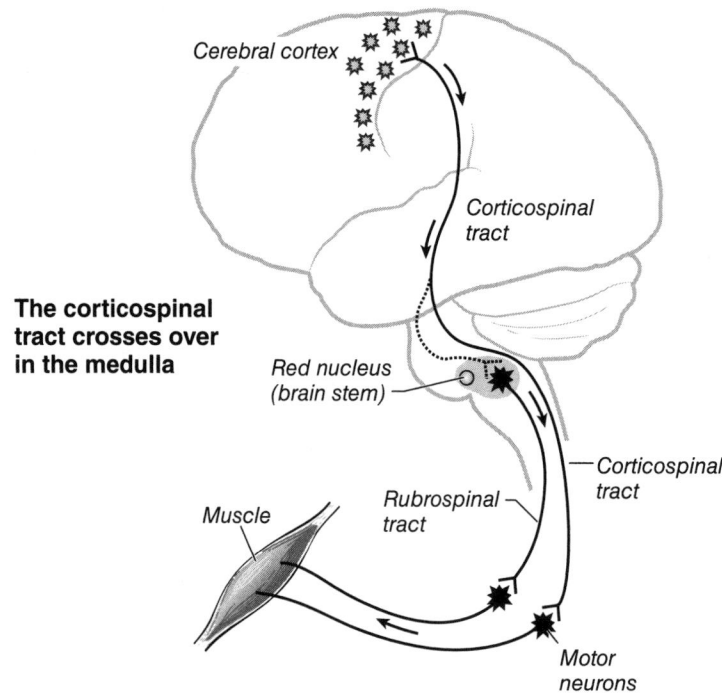

Figure 9-11. Corticospinal and rubrospinal tracts (lateral descending).

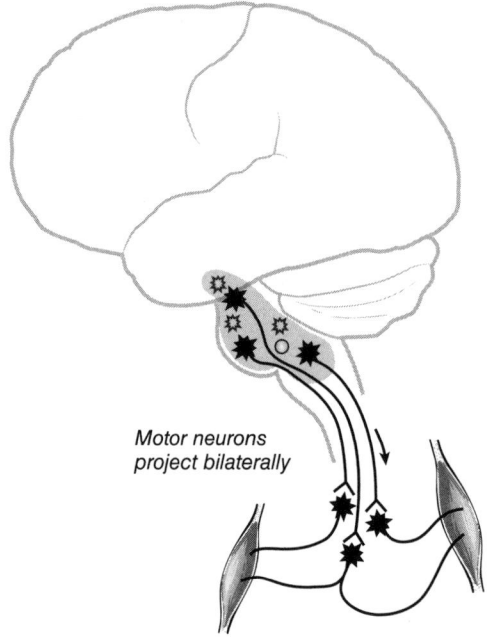

Figure 9-12. Vestibulospinal, tectospinal, and reticulospinal tracts (medial descending).

3. The *spinocerebellar tracts* include the *ventral (anterior) spinocerebellar tract* and the *dorsal (posterior) spinocerebellar tract*. They are located in the lateral funiculi of the spinal cord white matter.

The following information is carried by this system:

a. feedback to the cerebellum of motor signals arriving at the motor neurons in the anterior horns of the gray matter
b. muscle spindle discharges
c. Golgi tendon organ discharges
d. information from the joint receptors
e. input from certain skin tactile receptors that provide clues to joint movements and position.

Via the spinocerebellar tracts, the cerebellum receives important feedback on the progress of ongoing movements.

B. Descending Tracts

The function of various descending tracts will be discussed in a later lecture. They are involved in direct movements, maintenance of posture, modulating ascending sensory systems such as pain, and gating spinal reflex loops.

The three major descending groups of pathways in the spinal cord originate either in the *cerebral cortex* or in the *brain stem*. They include the following tracts, but note that this is not an exhaustive list!

1. Originating in the cerebral cortex, we have the ***corticospinal*** tracts. In humans there is really only one major tract, the *lateral corticospinal* tract. It originates in the cerebral cortex, crosses over in the medulla, and descends in the lateral funiculi. It is sometimes called the *pyramidal tract*. This tract is concerned with commands for finely controlled movements, often involving the hands and digits.

> The *anterior* corticospinal tract, mentioned in many textbooks, is a very minor tract in humans, and may not even exist at all in some individuals.

2. Originating in the **brain stem**, we have the ***reticulospinal, vestibulospinal,*** and ***tectospinal*** tracts (see Lecture 19). The reticulospinal tract originates in the **reticular formation** of the medulla and pons and descends in the medial region of the anterior funiculi. It is not crossed, but neurons receiving input from this tract may project to both sides of the spinal cord.

The vestibulospinal tract originates in the ***vestibular*** nuclei (of cranial nerve VIII, from the ear), and the tectospinal originates in the ***optic tectum*** (= ***superior colliculus***). The optic tectum is involved in controlling direction of gaze, often in response to new objects that appear in the visual field.

The reticulospinal and vestibulospinal tracts are involved in the control of posture and balance.

3. Also originating in the **brain stem**, we have the ***rubrospinal*** *tract*. The rubrospinal tract originates in the ***red nucleus*** (nucleus ruber) of the brain stem, crosses over immediately and descends in the lateral funiculi close to the lateral corticospinal tract. Commands passing down this tract control movements similar to those controlled by the corticospinal tract, but the movements are coarser and not so finely regulated.

C. Lesions of the Corticospinal Tract (Pathway)

Because the corticospinal tract is a very long one, there are many locations from the cortex to the spinal cord where damage can occur.

- **Negative** signs caused by a lesion in the corticospinal tract include **loss** of the ability to make fine movements of the digits and distal limb muscles, and **slowness** and **weakness** of voluntary movements. In this situation, most voluntary commands go through the red nucleus and descend in the rubrospinal tract.

- **Positive** sign—the *Babinski reflex* or *Babinski sign*, described in 1896 by the French neurologist Joseph Babinski. Normally, when the sole of the foot is stroked with the end of a pencil, the foot and toes flex *downward*. When there is damage to the corticospinal tract, however, there is *upward* extension of the big toe, and the other toes fan outward. A Babinski reflex is seen in young infants up to one year, because the corticospinal tract is late to become myelinated.

Normal plantar response

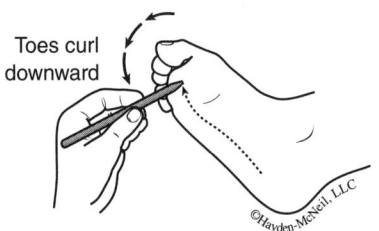

Toes curl downward

Extensor plantar response

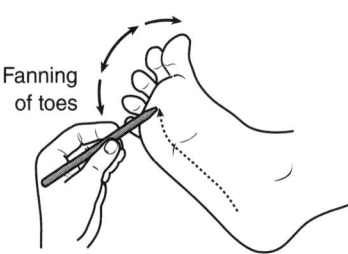

Fanning of toes

Lesion of corticospinal tract causes appearance of Babinski reflex (sign)

Figure 9-13. Normal and extensor plantar responses.

D. Spinal Reflexes

Complex networks of neurons (neuronal circuits) make up the central nervous system. There are many different types of these circuits, most of which will be discussed in lecture. All reflexes are automatic, unconscious responses. They are involved in the maintenance of posture and in such processes as breathing, blood pressure homeostasis, and digestive activities. The simplest reflex is the **spinal reflex**.

A spinal reflex is a simple response to a stimulus, and it activates only neurons in the spinal cord. Spinal reflexes provide an important "background" against which voluntary movements take place and are important in posture. The basic components of a typical spinal reflex are as follows.

1. A **sensory receptor**; functions to sense some change in either the internal or the external environment.

2. A **sensory neuron** attached to the sensory receptor; the nerve impulse is passed from the receptor along this neuron *to* the spinal cord.

3. Sometimes an **interneuron**, which may be either inhibitory or excitatory.

4. The **motor neuron**; receives input from the interneuron and then conveys an impulse to the effector organ (*away* from the spinal cord).

5. The **effector** (**a gland or a muscle**) is outside the nervous system.

The simplest of the spinal reflexes are the stretch reflexes, which are important in maintaining posture. One example is the **knee-jerk (stretch) reflex**, which is initiated by striking the patellar ligament just below the patella. This stretches the quadriceps femoris muscle group slightly and stimulates the muscle spindles in the muscle. The impulse travels along the sensory neuron to the spinal cord where the sensory neuron synapses directly with a motor neuron. In this case, there is no interneuron. The motor neuron then conveys the impulse to muscle, and the muscle contracts.

> Of course, things are not quite as simple as that. It is important to note that while the extensor quadriceps femoris muscles are stimulated, there must be inhibition of the neurons controlling the flexor group of antagonist muscles. This phenomenon is called reciprocal inhibition. Reciprocal inhibition involves an interneuron, and will be discussed further with the withdrawal reflex below. See Figure 9-15.

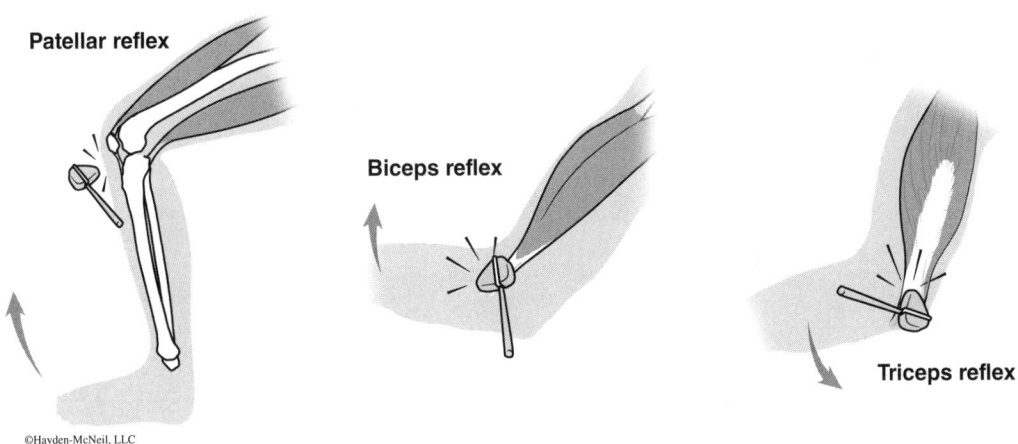

Patellar reflex

Biceps reflex

Triceps reflex

©Hayden-McNeil, LLC

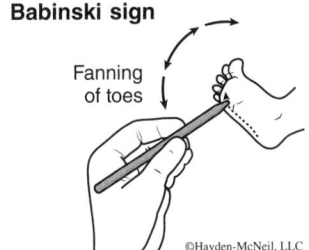

Babinski sign

Fanning of toes

©Hayden-McNeil, LLC

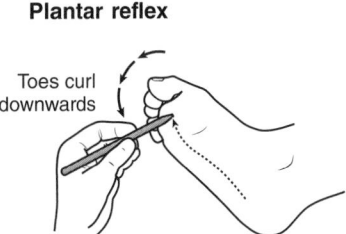

Plantar reflex

Toes curl downwards

Reflexes Important For Diagnostic Testing

REFLEX	SPINAL SEGMENT	STIMULUS	AFFERENT NERVE(S)	EFFERENT NERVE(S)	NORMAL RESPONSE
Superficial Reflexes					
Abdominal reflex	T_7–T_{12} at level of arrival	Light stroking of skin on abdomen	T_7–T_{12} depending on region stroked	Same as afferent	Contractions of abdominal muscles that pull navel toward the stimulus
Cremasteric reflex	L_1	Stroking of skin on upper thigh	Femoral nerve	Genitofemoral nerve	Contraction of cremaster, elevation of scrotum
Plantar reflex	S_1, S_2	Longitudinal stroking of lateral side of sole of foot	Tibial nerve	Tibial nerve	Flexion at toe joints
Anal reflex	S_4, S_5	Stroking of region around the anus	Pudendal nerve	Pudendal nerve	Constriction of external anal sphincter
Stretch Reflexes					
Biceps reflex	C_5, C_6	Tap to tendon of biceps brachii muscle near its insertion	Musculocutaneous nerve	Musculocutaneous nerve	Flexion at elbow
Triceps reflex	C_6, C_7	Tap to tendon of triceps brachii muscle near its insertion	Radial	Foramen rotundum	Extension at elbow
Brachioradialis reflex	C_5, C_6	Tap to forearm near styloid process of the radius	Radial	Foramen ovale	Flexion at elbow, supination, and flexion at finger joints
Patellar reflex	L_2–L_4	Tap to patellar tendon	Femoral nerve	Femoral nerve	Extension at knee
Ankle-jerk reflex	S_1, S_2	Tap to calcaneal tendon	Tibial nerve	Tibial nerve	Extension (plantar flexion) at ankle

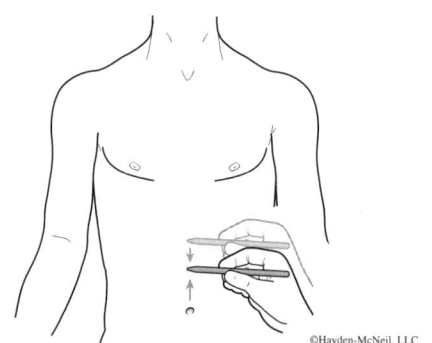

©Hayden-McNeil, LLC

Abdominal reflex

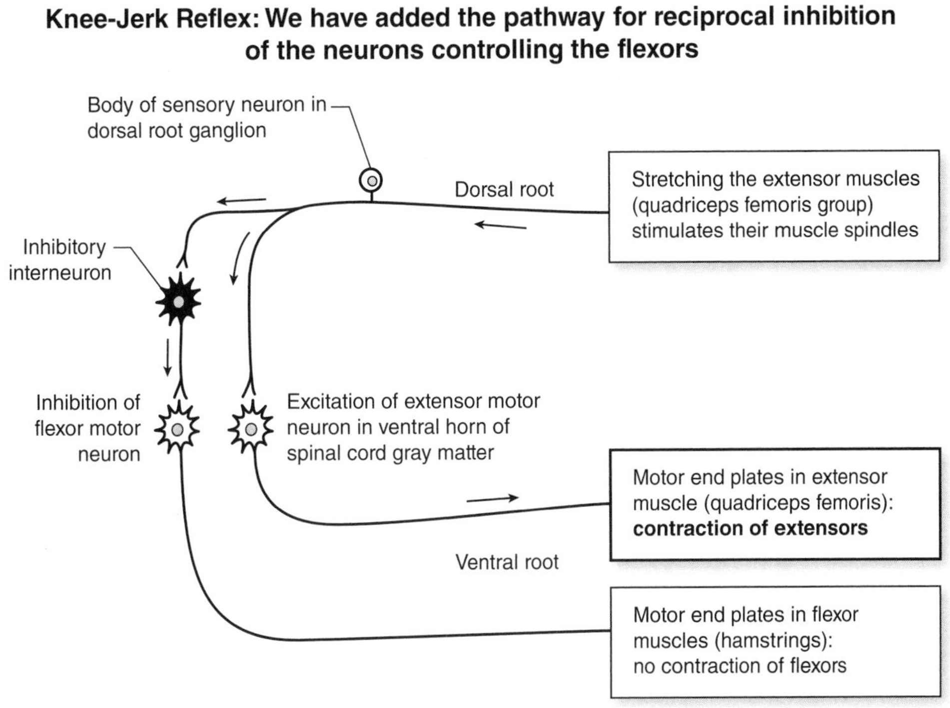

Knee-Jerk Reflex: We have added the pathway for reciprocal inhibition of the neurons controlling the flexors

Figure 9-14. The knee-jerk reflex pathway showing reciprocal inhibition.

The **withdrawal (flexor) reflex** occurs when one touches something painful, such as a hot grill. This involves the withdrawal of the entire hand and arm or leg and foot away from the painful stimulus. If it is the finger, then nociceptors in the finger are stimulated, an impulse travels along a sensory neuron to the spinal cord, the impulses pass to a motor neuron via an interneuron, the impulse is received by its effector organ, the neurons of the flexor muscles are stimulated, and the muscles contract. As with the stretch reflex, reciprocal inhibition occurs, meaning that while the neurons of the flexor muscles are stimulated, there is inhibition of the neurons of the extensor muscles (antagonists). See Figure 9-15.

**Simple Neuronal Pathway for the Flexor or Withdrawal Reflex
with Reciprocal Inhibition -
This reflex operates if your hand or foot receives a painful stimulus.**

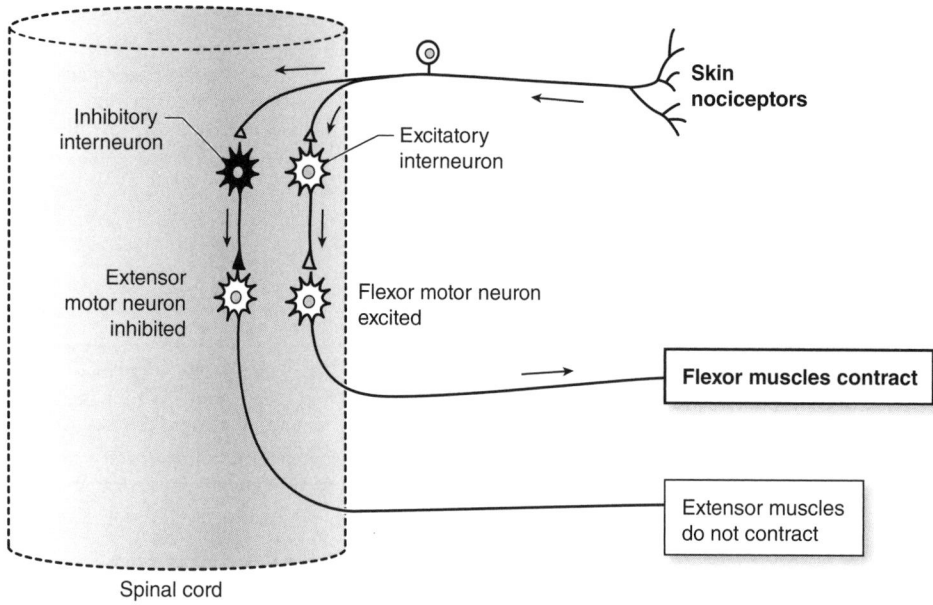

Figure 9-15. Simple pathway for the withdrawal reflex reciprocal inhibition.

In the withdrawal reflex for the legs, something must be added. It is obvious that if your left foot steps on a sharp nail and initiates the withdrawal reflex in the left leg, you will fall down unless you do something supportive with the right leg.

What happens is that although the flexors of the "withdrawing" leg are stimulated, the extensors of the "planting" leg are also stimulated. So in the example above, the flexors of the left leg contract initiating withdrawal while at the same time the extensors of the right leg contract. This causes the right leg to straighten and become more rigid to support the body. This is called the **crossed extensor reflex**. Reciprocal inhibition ensures that the antagonist muscle group on each leg does not interfere with the actions of the prime movers.

**Neuronal Pathway for the Crossed Extensor Reflex
Coupled with the Flexor Reflex and Reciprocal Inhibition -
This reflex operates if you step on a painful object.**

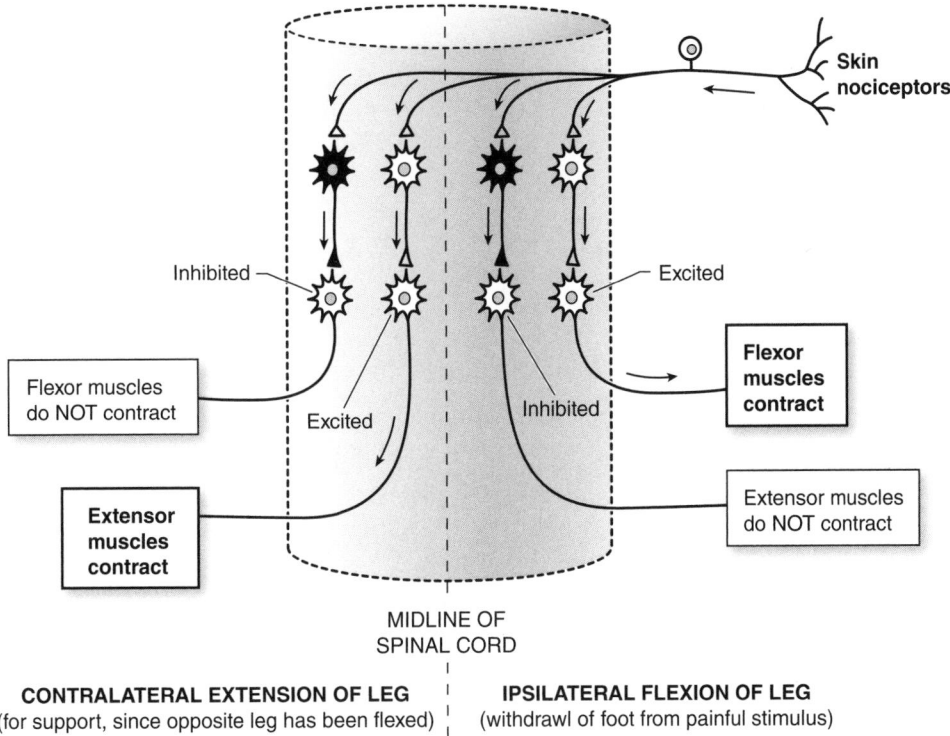

Figure 9-16. Crossed extensor reflex.

E. Spinal Shock

When the spinal cord is cut at the level of the neck or thorax, all spinal reflexes are temporarily lost. The reason is that higher brain centers normally modulate and facilitate spinal reflexes. When the descending nerve impulses from these higher facilitatory centers are lost, the neurons of the spinal reflexes become temporarily insensitive, and fail to respond. During recovery, the spinal reflexes return, often in exaggerated form.

Exercise A

Observe the slides of the spinal cord and ganglion. Identify the following. Draw a figure to assist you for review before the test.

_____ white and gray matter   _____ posterior median sulcus

_____ dorsal and ventral roots   _____ gray commissure

_____ ganglion   _____ central canal

_____ anterior and posterior horns   _____ anterior median fissure

Exercise B

LabTutor: Brain Structure and Spinal Reflexes

Please summarize in the spaces below what you believe is the goal of the experiment and any background information that is important to understanding the experiment.

Goal

Background

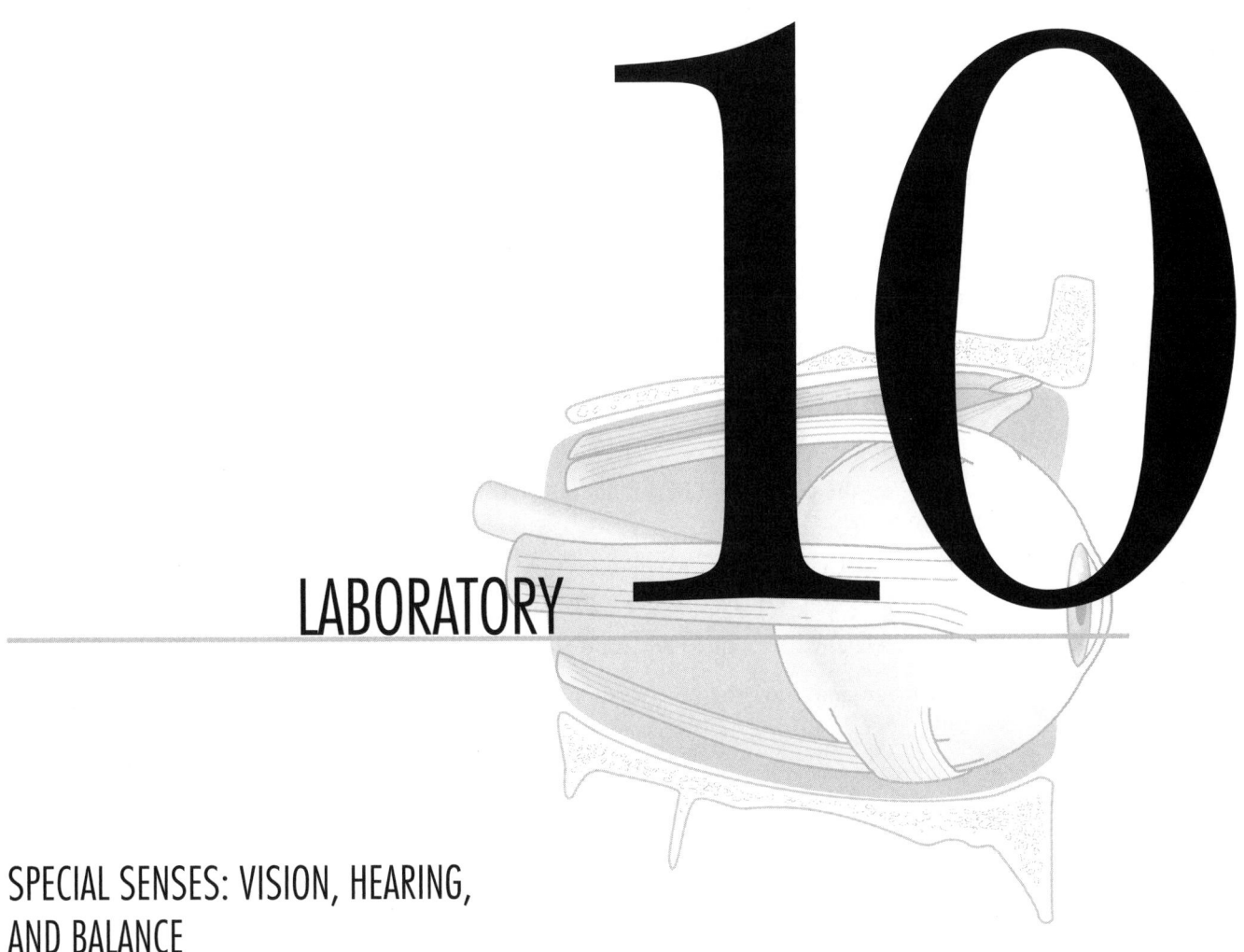

LABORATORY 10

SPECIAL SENSES: VISION, HEARING, AND BALANCE

Required Reading: Lectures 14, 21–22

READ THE PAGES LISTED BELOW IN YOUR HISTOLOGY TEXT BEFORE COMING TO CLASS, THEN BRING IT TO CLASS.

12TH ED: READ PAGES 558–580, OR
11TH ED: READ PAGES 490–507

READ BACKGROUND AND EXPERIMENT FROM BLACKBOARD LAB 10 HANDOUT: OPTICS.

Objectives

1. Name the parts of the **eye** and explain the function of each part.

2. **Draw a diagram** of the **neural retina**, showing the arrangement of the five neural cells found in it.

3. Name the cell layer that makes up the **non-neural** retina.

4. Give the name of the glial cell found in the retina.

5. **Draw a rod**, showing outer segment, mitochondria, nucleus, and synapse.

6. Explain how the **cornea** and **lens** function to form an **image** of the external scene on the retina.

7. Explain what is meant by a **visual pigment**, and explain the importance of vitamin A in vision and in the structure of rhodopsin.

8. Explain how light affects the **membrane potential** of a photoreceptor.

9. **Draw a diagram** to show the nervous connections between the retina and the **visual cortex**.

10. Predict the consequences to vision of cutting **one optic nerve** (refer to the diagram of the visual pathway at the end of these notes).

11. Predict the consequences to vision of cutting **one optic tract** (refer to the diagram of the visual pathway at the end of these notes).

12. Predict the consequences to vision of making a **longitudinal** cut at the **optic chiasma** (refer to the diagram of the visual pathway at the end of these notes).

13. Become better acquainted with **eye structure** through the dissection of a sheep eye.

14. Examine the eye with an **ophthalmoscope**.

15. **Draw a diagram** showing the general plan of **receptor cells** and **pathways** for **hearing** and **balance**.

16. Describe the importance of the sense of **hearing**.

17. Name the **structures** found in the **three parts** of the **ear**.

18. Describe how sound is transmitted from the **external auditory meatus** into the **cochlea**.

19. Describe the anatomy of the **organ of Corti**, and how it **functions** in hearing.

20. State which **cranial nerve** carries **auditory information** to the brain.

21. State which **cranial nerve** carries information from the **vestibular apparatus** to the brain.

22. Name the **sensory ganglion** and **nucleus** in the **medulla** concerned with the **cochlear** pathway; describe the remainder of the pathway to the **auditory cortex**.

23. Name the **sensory ganglion** and **nucleus** in the **medulla** concerned with the **vestibular** pathway.

24. Describe the **importance** of our ability to sense **balance** and **motion**.

25. Name the part of the vestibular system involved in sensing **head tilt**.

26. Name the part of the vestibular system involved in sensing **up** and **down movements** (such as in an elevator).

27. Name the part of the vestibular system involved in sensing **linear horizontal acceleration** or **deceleration** (e.g., when you are in an automobile that speeds up or slows down). Explain how we tell the difference between tilt and acceleration and how this impacts the "heads up" illusion in an aircraft.

28. Name the part of the vestibular system involved in sensing **head rotation**.

29. Name the anatomical components of the **utricle** and **saccule**.

30. Name the anatomical components of the **semicircular canals**.

31. List four sensory mechanisms **in addition** to the vestibular apparatus that are concerned with sensing **balance** and **equilibrium**.

32. Be able to **characterize and distinguish between conductive and sensorineural deafness**.

33. Examine the ear with an **otoscope**.

I. Description and Introduction

Sensory receptors can be specialized:

1. **nerve cells**—the photoreceptors of the eye and the hair cells of the ear are examples

2. **nerve endings**—these nerve endings may be "naked" (for example, pain and temperature) or they may be associated with some kind of special structure (for example, Meissner's corpuscles which respond to touch)

3. **epithelial cells**—taste cells on the tongue fall into this category

In this lab, we shall discuss the structure, properties, and physiological function of sensory receptors. We will also discuss the sensations that are perceived when sensory receptors are stimulated. The main focus of our discussion will be on the **special senses** (**hearing, balance, vision, taste,** and **smell**). However, you need to know the difference between the **somatic senses** and the special senses. The sensory receptors for the special senses are housed in special organs in the head (hearing and balance in the **ear**, vision in the **eye**, smell in the **nose**, and taste in **taste buds** in the tongue), somatic senses involve receptors located in the skin, muscles, tendons, joints, and visceral organs.

Each type of sensory receptor responds to a specific stimulus. Sensory receptors can be mechanoreceptors (touch, pressure, vibration, sound, muscle stretch, etc.), thermoreceptors (warmth, cold), photoreceptors (light), chemoreceptors (taste, smell) or nociceptors (pain). Sensory receptors in the skin, muscles, joints, and visceral organs subserve the **somatic** senses, which include touch, pain, temperature, proprioception, etc.

Somatic senses can also be classified on the basis of where the stimulus takes effect.

1. **Exteroceptive senses** concern changes at the body surface or even at a distance from the body—light, touch, pressure, temperature, pain.

2. **Proprioceptive senses** are mediated by receptors in the muscles, tendons, and joints (receptors in the ear that are involved in balance and in detecting acceleration will be dealt with in the special senses). Proprioceptors respond to changes in muscle length, tendon tension, joint angle, or deep pressure. Proprioceptors are important in guiding body movements.

3. **Visceroceptive senses** or **interoceptive senses** are associated with changes in the internal environment—receptors are found in the visceral organs and even in the brain. The stretch receptors in the walls of the aorta and carotid artery are an example. They provide information on blood pressure.

The special senses are as follows.

1. **Vision**—photoreceptor cells (rods and cones) in the eye

2. **Hearing**—mechanoreceptor (hair) cells in the ear

3. **Balance** (equilibrium)—mechanoreceptor (hair) cells in the ear

4. **Smell** (olfaction)—chemoreceptor cells in the nose

5. **Taste**—chemoreceptor cells in the tongue, epiglottis, the upper third of the esophagus, and on the palate

II. Vision

The eye is the organ of vision. When stimulated by light, changes in the membrane potential of the **photoreceptor cells** (**rods** and **cones**) in the neural retina generate a train of action potentials that are transmitted along the optic nerve to the **lateral geniculate nucleus** of the **thalamus** and from there to the posterior **occipital lobe** of the **cerebral cortex**.

A. Accessory Structures Associated with the Eye

1. **Eyelids**—lined with **conjunctiva**, a mucous membrane that also covers the anterior surface of the eye. The conjunctiva has blood vessels that become prominent when the eyes are "bloodshot."

2. **Lacrimal apparatus**—contains the **lacrimal glands** that produce **tear fluid**. The tear fluid drains into the nasal cavity via the **nasolacrimal** duct. Tear fluid lubricates and moistens the surface of the eye and also contains antibacterial agents such as **lysozyme**.

3. **Extraocular muscles** move the eye. Their origins are in the bones of the orbit and their insertions are in the outer surface of the eye, the sclera.

    a. **Superior rectus**—rotates the eye upward and toward the midline.

    b. **Inferior rectus**—rotates the eye downward and toward the midline.

    c. **Medial rectus**—rotates the eye toward the midline.

    d. **Lateral rectus**—rotates the eye away from the midline.

    e. **Superior oblique**—rotates the eye downward and away from the midline.

    f. **Inferior oblique**—rotates the eye upward and away from the midline.

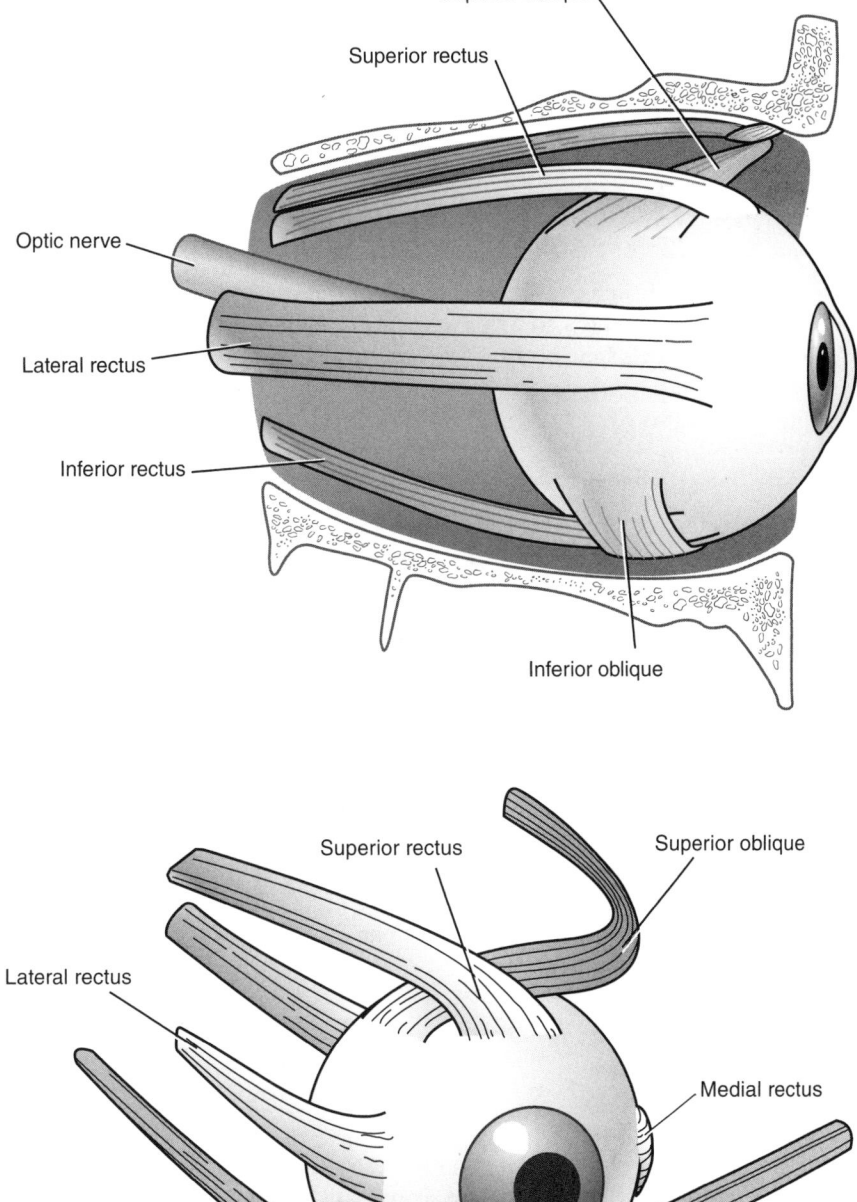

Figure 10-1. Extraocular muscles (right eye).

B. Structure of the Eye

The lens divides the eye into the **anterior** and **posterior** cavities. The posterior cavity is filled with the clear, jelly-like **vitreous humor**. The anterior cavity is filled with a watery fluid called **aqueous humor**, which is secreted by the ciliary body and which drains through the canal of Schlemm. The anterior chamber is divided into the **anterior** and **posterior chambers** by the **iris**.

The eye has three layers, as follows.

1. The Outer Layer—Cornea and Sclera

The anterior portion of the outer layer consists of the transparent cornea. The cornea is the "window of the eye" and also helps to focus incoming light rays on the retina. The cornea lacks blood vessels but has many nerve endings that respond to pain and temperature stimuli. The posterior portion of the outer layer consists of the opaque sclera ("white of the eye"). It is composed of fibrous connective tissue.

2. The Middle Layer (uveal layer)—Choroid, Iris, Ciliary Body

The middle layer is called the **uveal** layer. It is highly vascular (i.e., contains many blood vessels) and usually has melanocytes, which contain granules of the brown-black pigment melanin. The melanin absorbs light and prevents light scattering that could degrade visual acuity (the inside of a camera is black for the same reason).

The uveal layer forms the **choroid** posteriorly and the **iris** and **ciliary body** anteriorly.

The iris gives color to the eye (brown, blue, hazel), and has a hole in its center called the **pupil**. The diameter of the pupil is adjustable, controlling the amount of light entering the eye. It is therefore similar to the iris diaphragm in a camera.

The ciliary body has the **ciliary muscles** and **ciliary processes** on its inner aspect. Fibers called **suspensory ligaments** are attached to the ciliary processes, and serve to hold the **lens** in position. The ciliary muscles adjust the tension in the suspensory ligaments altering the power of the lens and ensuring that images are sharply focused on the retina. The process is called **accommodation**.

The ciliary body also secretes aqueous humor into the posterior chamber, whence it flows through the pupil into the anterior chamber and then leaves the eye via the **canal of Schlemm**.

Clinical Application. If the rate of production of aqueous humor exceeds its rate of removal, the result is a rise of intraocular pressure. This disorder, a condition sometimes associated with aging, is called **glaucoma**. It can result in blindness because the increase in pressure can compress the blood vessels that supply the retina. This condition is treated with drugs that reduce the production of aqueous humor. In the event that the condition is classified as "closed angle glaucoma," the obstructed canal of Schlemm can be opened surgically.

Clinical Application. The aging lens can sometimes become cloudy and opaque, a condition called **cataract**. Treatment involves surgical removal of the affected lens, which is then replaced with an artificial one, or by powerful eyeglasses.

3. The Inner Layer—Neural Retina and Retinal Pigmented Epithelium

Developmentally, the neural retina is an outgrowth of the brain. It is not only sensitive to light, but it can also carry out preliminary processing of the signals generated by the photoreceptor cells. Like the brain, it contains glial cells (**Mueller cells**). There are five different types of neurons in the neural retina. The **photoreceptors** (rods and cones) are actually modified neurons. They contain **visual pigments**, which absorb light and alter the photoreceptor membrane potential, so initiating an electrical signal. The other neurons are classified as **bipolar** cells, **horizontal** cells, **amacrine** cells and **ganglion** cells. The axons of the ganglion cells make up the **optic nerve**, which carries signals to the lateral geniculate nucleus of the thalamus, from where they are transmitted to the occipital lobe of the cerebral cortex. The point where the ganglion cell axons leave the retina is the **optic disk**. Because this area lacks photoreceptor cells it is called the **blind spot**.

The **macula lutea** (yellow spot) is in the central retina. It looks yellow because it contains carotenoid. A depression at its center is called the **fovea centralis**, a region of tightly packed cones associated with high visual acuity. If this area degenerates (e.g., in macular degeneration), it is no longer possible to read the printed word.

The pigmented epithelium is a single layer of melanin-containing cells lying between the neural retina and the choroid. These cells are important in regulating the passage of nutrients from the blood into the retina, in participating in the metabolism of vitamin A and its derivatives, and in removing fragments of membranes that have been shed by the photoreceptor cell outer segments.

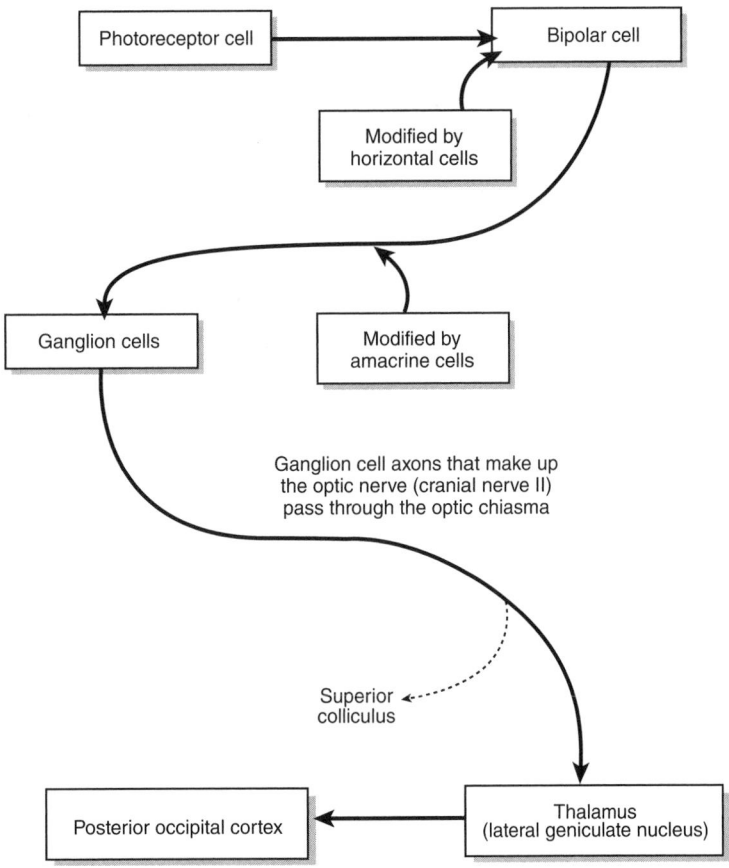

Figure 10-2. Neural pathway—vision.

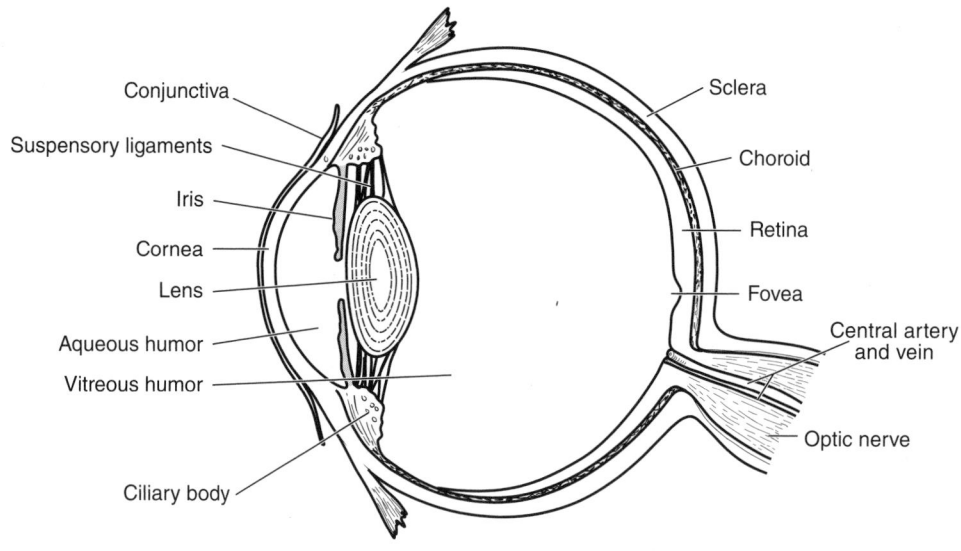

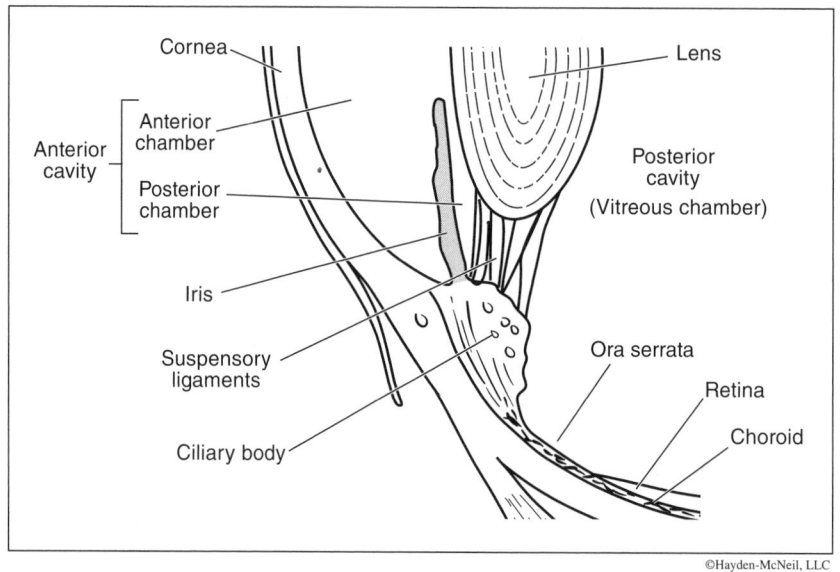

©Hayden-McNeil, LLC

Figure 10-3. Longitudinal section of the eye.

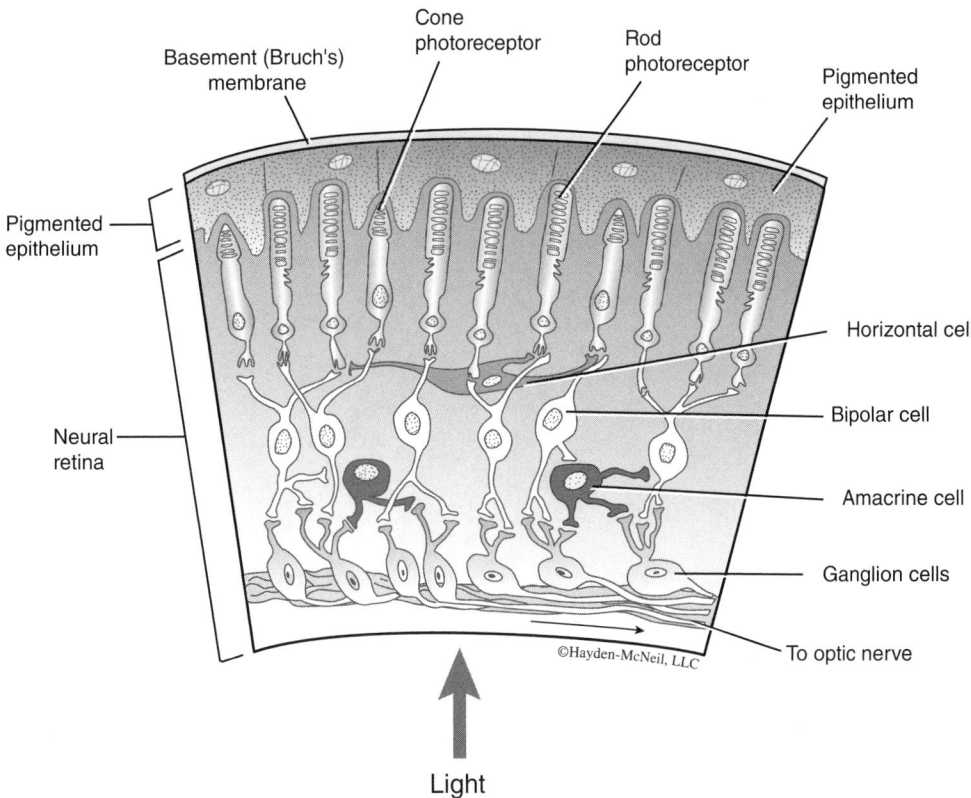

Figure 10-4. The retina.
(Mueller cells not shown)

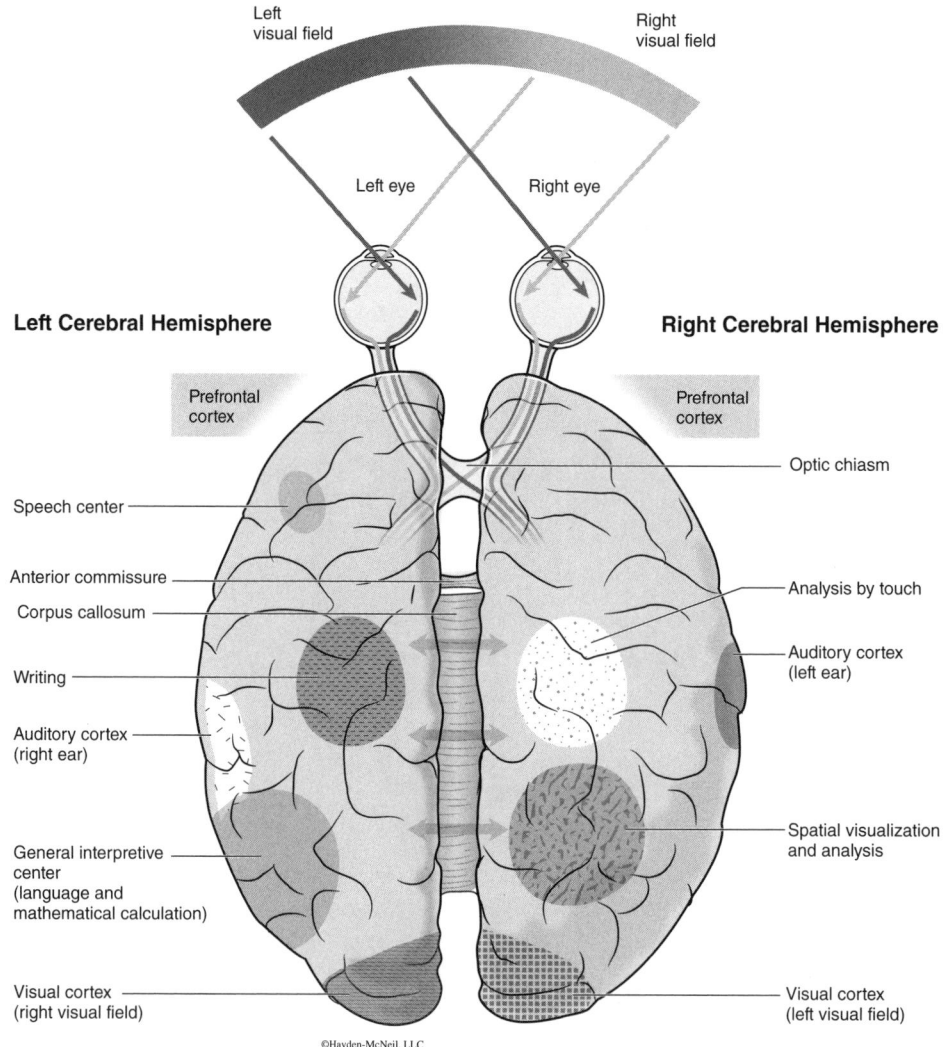

©Hayden-McNeil, LLC

III. Hearing

The external ear and middle ear transmit sound waves to the inner ear, where they are converted to electrical signals that are conveyed to the brain via the cochlear branch of cranial nerve VIII.

A. The External Ear

The external ear consists of the ear flap (**pinna, auricle**) and an S-shaped tube called the **external auditory meatus**, sealed at its inner end by the eardrum or **tympanic membrane**.

B. The Middle Ear (Tympanic Cavity)

Vibrations of the tympanic membrane, which are transmitted by the three **auditory ossicles** (**malleus, incus, stapes**) to the **oval window**, the gateway to the inner ear.

The **Eustachian** (or auditory) **tube** connects the middle ear cavity with the pharynx. It allows the air pressure in the middle ear to equalize with atmospheric pressure.

C. Inner Ear

The complex apparatus of the inner ear is housed in a **bony labyrinth** carved out of the temporal bone.

The **vestibular** apparatus consists of structures associated with the sense of **balance**. It consists of the **semicircular canals**, which respond to head **rotation**, and the **utricle** and **saccule,** which are sensitive to head **tilt** and linear acceleration (the utricle for horizontal acceleration and the saccule for vertical acceleration, as would occur in an elevator).

The **cochlea** is the structure associated with **hearing**. It is a coiled, snail-like structure, partitioned by two longitudinally running membranes into three tubes.

1. **scala vestibuli** (filled with **perilymph**)

2. **scala media** (or cochlear duct, filled with **endolymph**)

3. **scala tympani** (filled with perilymph).

The two membranes are as follows.

- **Reissner's membrane** (the vestibular membrane) is very thin and flexible. It separates the scala vestibuli from the scala media.

- The **basilar membrane** separates the scala media from the scala tympani. On the surface of the basilar membrane, within the scala media, lies the **organ of Corti**, which contains mechanoreceptors called **hair cells**. The hair cells are the auditory receptor cells.

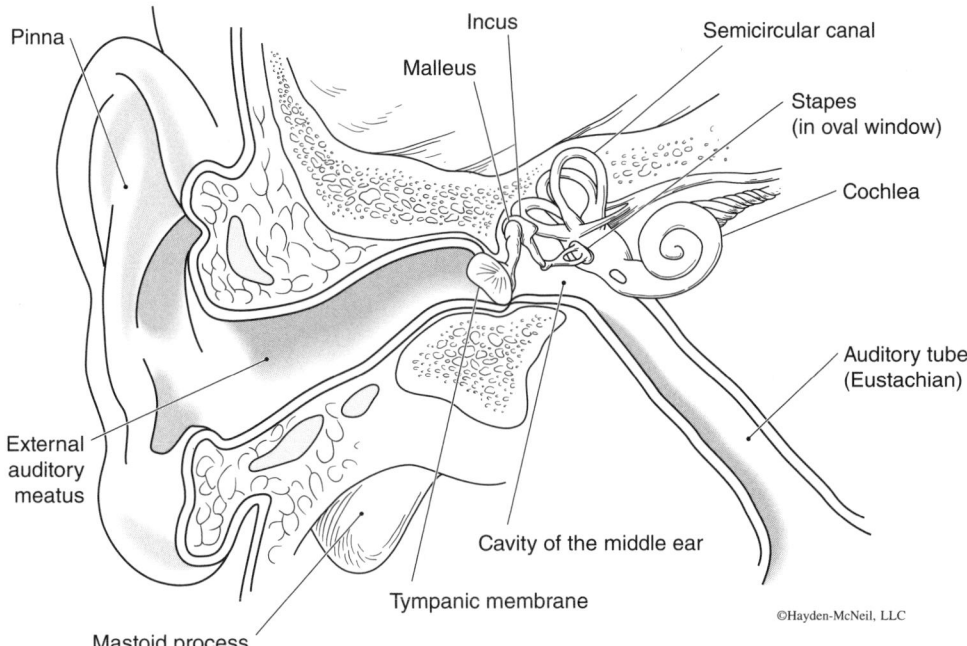

Figure 10-5. The ear.

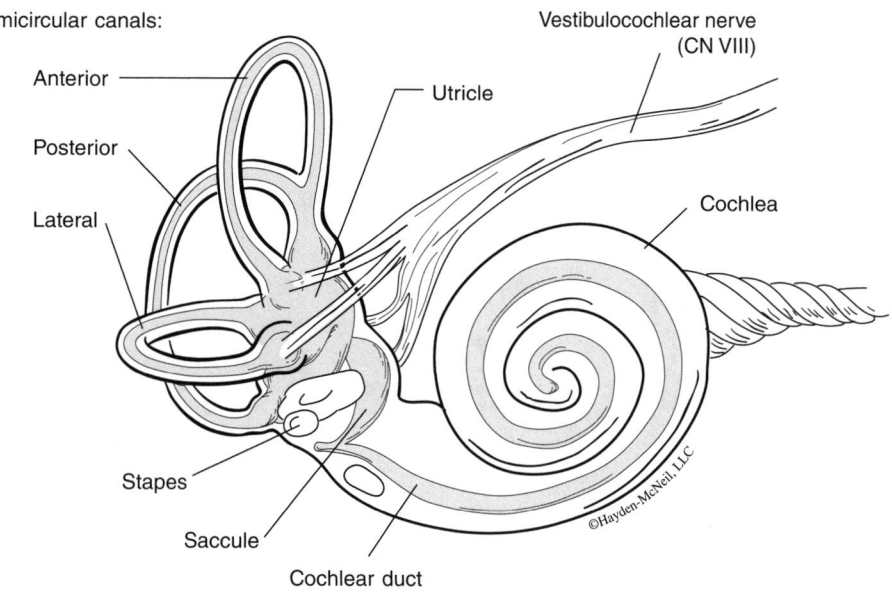

Figure 10-6. The cochlea and vestibular apparatus.

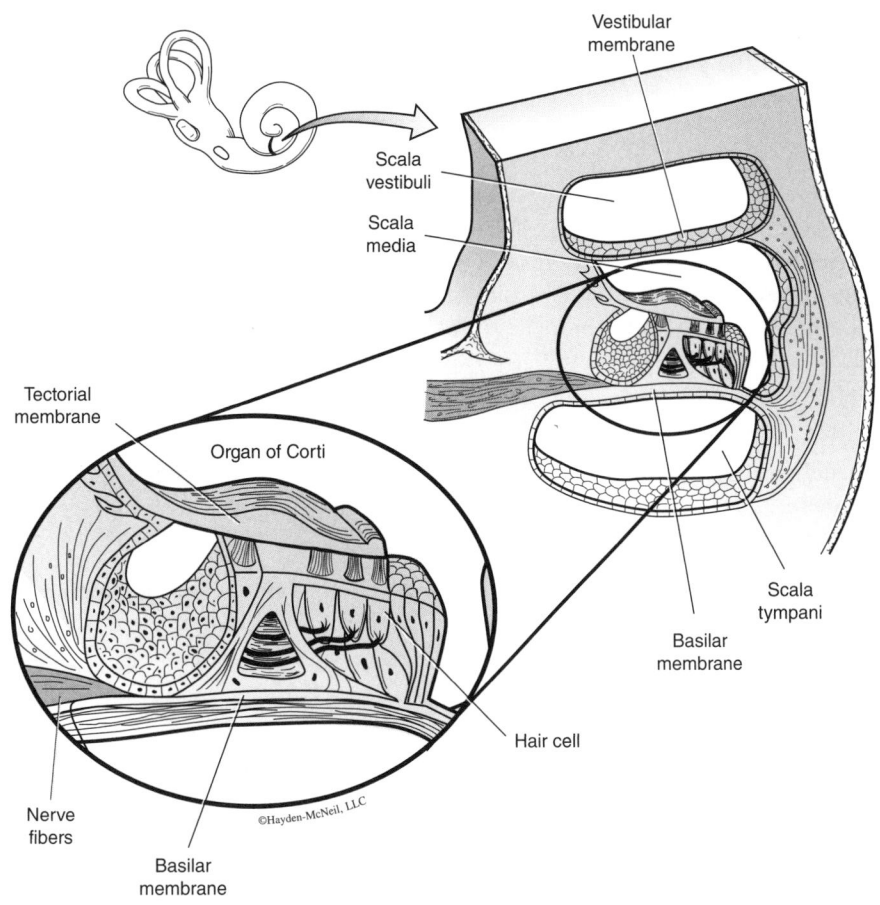

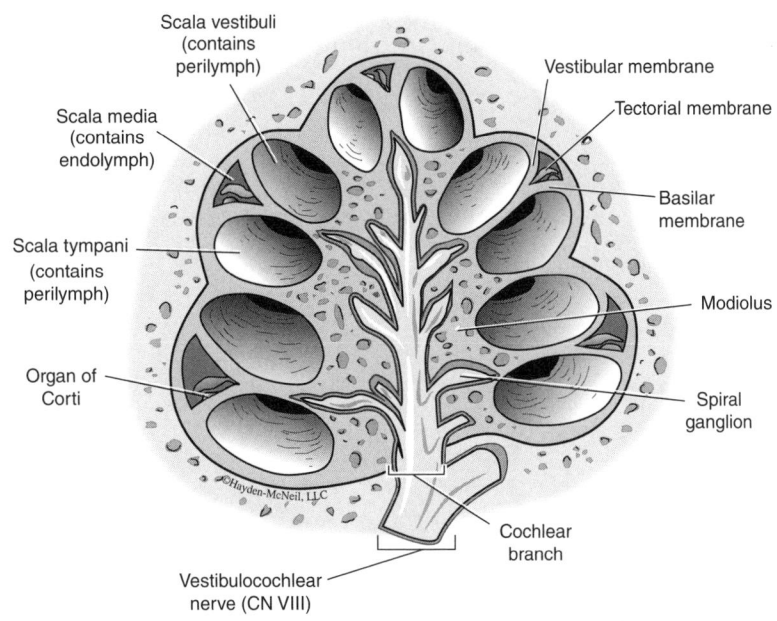

Figure 10-7. Cochlear cross section.

Sound is transmitted through the system and stimulates the auditory receptors as follows.

1. Vibrations of the eardrum are transmitted via the malleus, incus, and stapes to the oval window and thence to the perilymph of the scala vestibuli.

2. Vibrations of the perilymph are then transmitted through Reissner's membrane to the endolymph of the scala media, which causes the basilar membrane to vibrate.

3. Different parts of the basilar membrane vibrate in response to different sound frequencies, enabling us to distinguish between them. Near the oval window, the basilar membrane contains short and stiff collagen fibers that resonate (like the reeds of a harmonica) to high frequencies. Near the apex of the cochlea, the fibers in the basilar membrane are long and more flexible, and resonate only in response to low frequencies.

4. The organ of Corti sits on the basilar membrane. It contains hair cells. The tips of their hairs are embedded in a fixed gelatinous membrane called the **tectorial membrane**. Movements of the hair cells bend their hairs, causing a change in the membrane potential of the hair cells.

5. Afferent fibers of neurons that have their cell bodies in the **spiral ganglion** that make synaptic connections with the hair cells. They respond when there is a change in the membrane potential of the hair cells.

6. The result is a train of nerve impulses that is transmitted via the **cochlear** branch of the **VIII cranial nerve** to the **cochlear nucleus** in the **medulla** and thence to the **thalamus**. From the thalamus, these signals are transmitted to the auditory area in the temporal lobe of the **cerebral cortex**.

> There are also efferent nerve fibers that innervate the hair cells. In some way, they are believed to be able to modulate the response of the hair cells.

7. Finally, the sound vibrations are dissipated after further transmission through the perilymph of the scala tympani to the round window and into the air of the tympanic cavity.

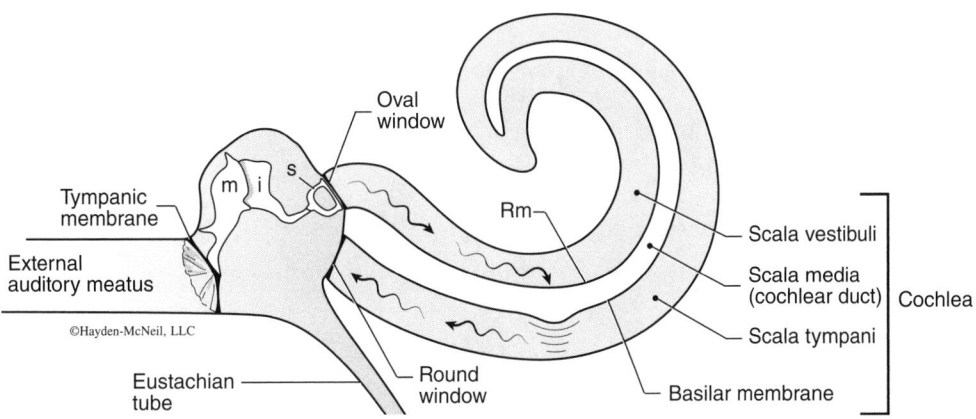

©Hayden-McNeil, LLC

1. Sound waves make tympanic membrane vibrate

2. Vibrations are transmitted via malleus (m), incus (i) and stapes (s) to oval window

3. Vibration of oval window causes perilymph vibration in scala vestibuli

4. Vibration is transmitted through Reissner's membrane (Rm) through endolymph in scala media

5. Basilar membrane vibrates in response to vibration of endolymph in scala media, stimulating hair cells in Organ of Corti (see notes for further details)

6. Vibrations are then transferred via the perilymph in the scala tympani to the round window

7. Vibration of the round window is dissipated in the air of the middle ear

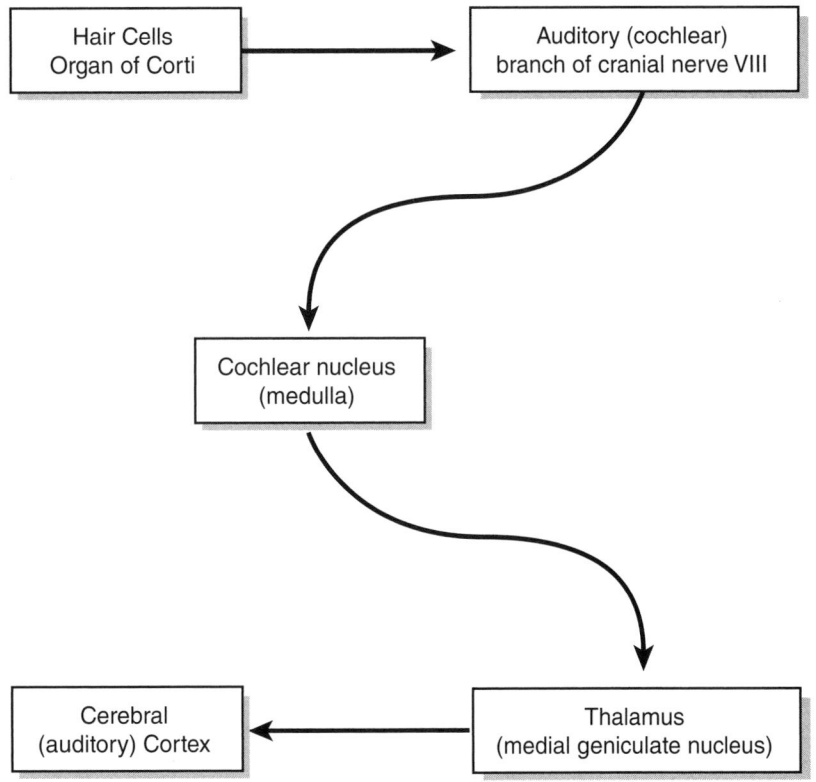

Figure 10-8. Neural pathway—hearing.

D. Hearing Loss

Partial or complete hearing losses can be categorized into two groups. Those that result from the inadequate transmission of sound vibrations to the inner ear are referred to as **conductive**. Those that result from damage to the cochlea or any of the neural structures involved in hearing are called **sensorineural**.

1. Causes of Conductive Hearing Loss

a. Accumulation of dry wax or some other foreign substance in the external auditory meatus.

b. A hardened, torn, or perforated eardrum.

c. Deposition of new bone at the base of the stapes, restricting its motility (this condition can be corrected surgically). The condition is called **otosclerosis.**

2. Causes of Sensorineural Hearing Loss

a. Excessively loud noises—hearing loss may be temporary if the duration of exposure is short; repeated and prolonged exposure can cause permanent damage.

b. Tumor in the central nervous system.

c. Cerebrovascular accident, or stroke—loss of neural function as a result of loss of adequate blood supply to the region in question.

d. Certain drugs, such as the streptomycins.

IV. Balance—The Vestibular System of the Inner Ear

Our ability to sense the balance and motion of our bodies in space is essential in all of the following activities.

*   Standing
*   Walking
*   Running
*   Turning
*   Complex movements
*   Stabilizing eyes during body movements

In a nutshell, the sense of balance tells the central nervous system whether the body is vertical, horizontal, upside down, tilted, accelerating, decelerating, or rotating. The three sets of structures in the vestibular apparatus respond to the following.

*   **tilt** of the head with respect to the direction of gravity—the ear structures involved are the **utricle** and the **saccule.**

*   **linear acceleration and deceleration** (horizontal, as when you are in an automobile, or vertical, as when you are in an elevator)—again, the ear structures involved are the **utricle** and the **saccule.**

*   **rotation**—the ear structures involved are the **semicircular canals.**

All the motor pathways involved in maintenance of balance project via the **vestibulospinal**, **tectospinal**, and **reticulospinal** tracts to the **trunk** and **proximal limb muscles.**

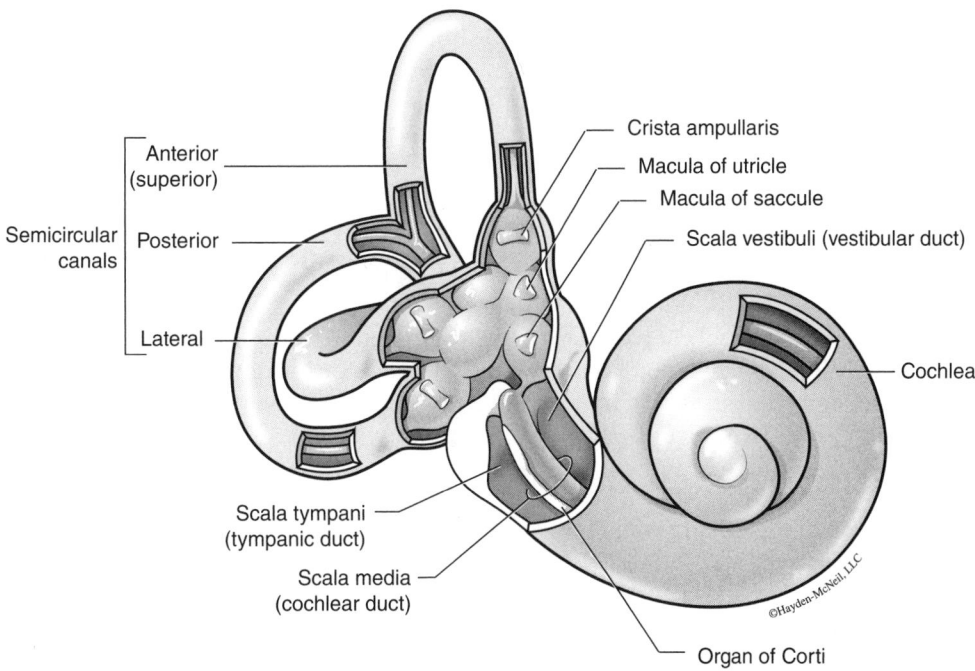

Labels in figure: Anterior (superior); Posterior; Lateral; Semicircular canals; Crista ampullaris; Macula of utricle; Macula of saccule; Scala vestibuli (vestibular duct); Cochlea; Scala tympani (tympanic duct); Scala media (cochlear duct); Organ of Corti; ©Hayden-McNeil, LLC

A. The Utricle and Saccule Detect Head Tilt and Linear Acceleration or Deceleration

The utricle and saccule—the otolith organs—each contain a small patch of hair cells and supporting cells in a sensory area called a **macula**.

The hairs of the hair cells are in contact with the **otolithic membrane**. The otolithic membrane is a sheet of gelatinous material, made twice as heavy as endolymph because it contains many small calcium carbonate crystals—**statoconia** or **otoliths** (= ear stones).

The hair cells are stimulated when their hairs are bent, as occurs when the heavy gelatinous otolithic membrane moves relatively to the hair cell. In the maculae of the utricle and saccule, this happens when the head is *tilted* or when the body moves *horizontally*, or *vertically up and down*. Since the membrane does not project into the lumen of the vestibular apparatus, movements of endolymph caused by angular rotation of the head do NOT affect it.

The utricular macula is oriented so that head tilt and *horizontal* linear acceleration or deceleration causes the hair cells to respond, while the saccular macula is oriented so that *vertical* linear acceleration or deceleration (jumping and falling, moving up or down in an elevator) causes the hair cells to respond.

In summary, the utricle and saccule are important in detecting movements such as falling or accelerating in an automobile, and are the sensory structures involved in maintaining balance when standing still or walking.

Example—suppose you are standing on a platform that is suddenly moved forward. There is the sensation of falling backwards and the body also tends to tilt backwards. The appropriate muscles are activated so that the body leans forward to counteract this effect. Therefore, we do not fall backwards.

B. The Semicircular Canals Detect Head Rotation

There are three semicircular canals. Two of the semicircular canals stand vertically at right angles to each other, and the other is horizontal. In other words, they represent all three planes in space.

Each ampulla of each semicircular canal houses a sense organ called a **crista ampullaris**, or just **crista**.

Each crista is composed of groups of hair cells and supporting cells.

As in the maculae, the hairs of the hair cells extend upwards into a gelatinous mass. In this case, the mass is called a **cupula**.

When the head suddenly begins to rotate in any direction, the inertia of the endolymph in the semicircular canals tends to keep this fluid stationary while the cristae move. The cupula tends to remain stationary with the endolymph, so bending the hairs of the hair cells. Obviously, the direction of bending is opposite to the direction of movement of the head.

Comparison of the Cupula with the Otolithic Membrane

The cupula projects into the endolymph of the semicircular canal, and is deflected by movements of the endolymph caused by head rotation. Unlike the otolithic membrane in the utricle and saccule, gravity has no effect on the cupula, because the cupula lacks otoliths that would make it heavier than the endolymph in which it floats and sways.

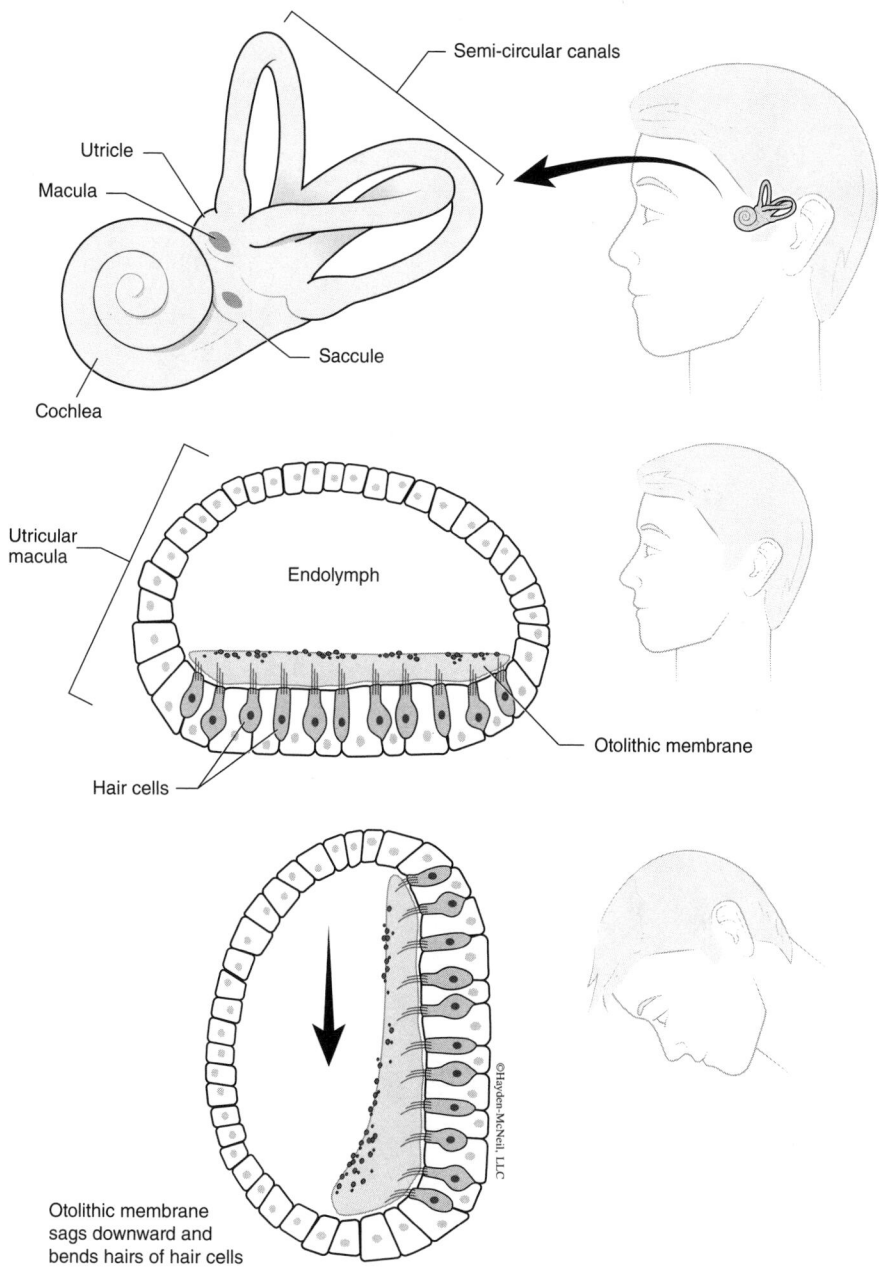

Forward Tilt
Utricular macula is detector
(also detects horizontal linear acceleration)

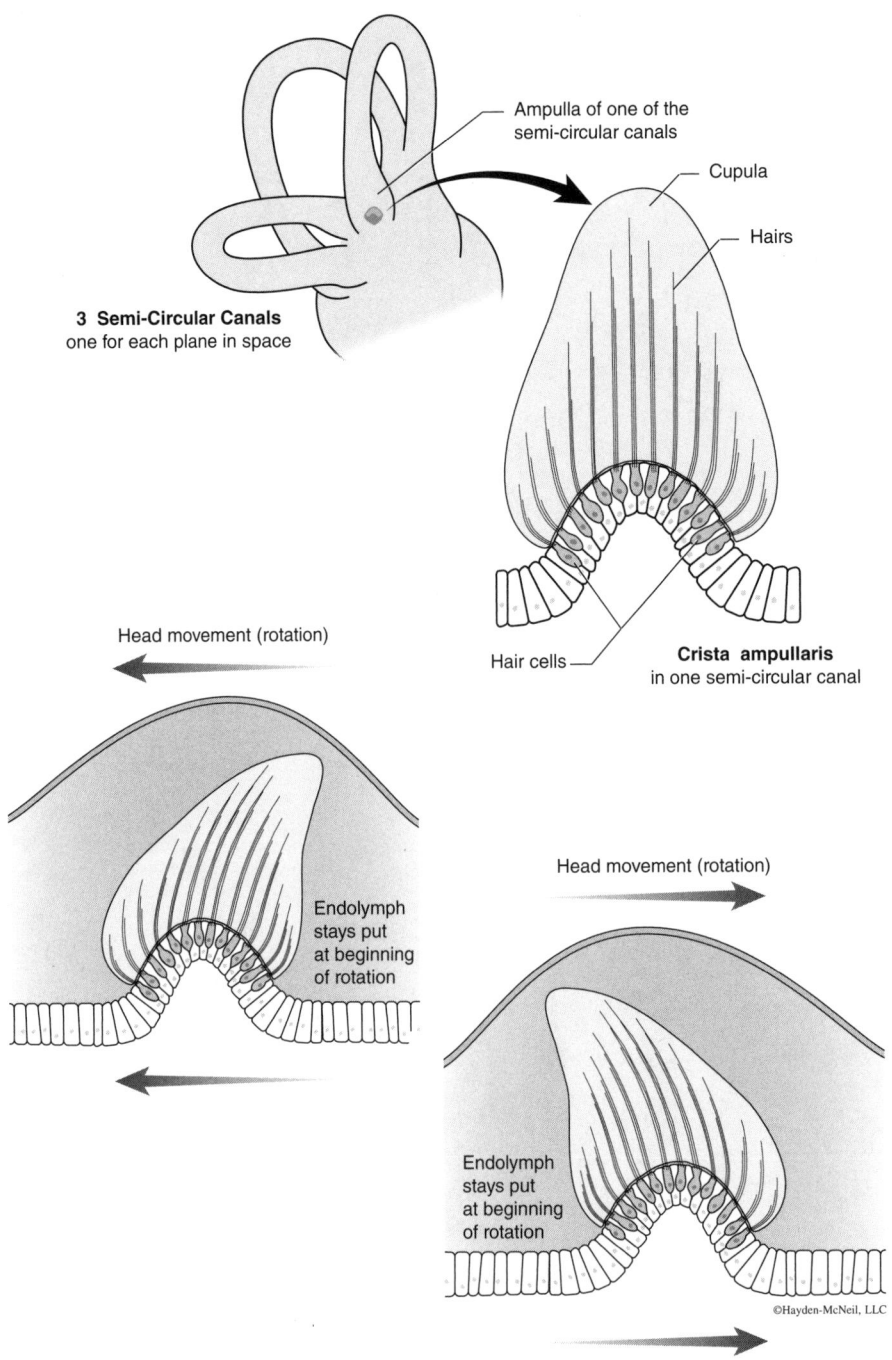

3 Semi-Circular Canals
one for each plane in space

Ampulla of one of the
semi-circular canals

Cupula

Hairs

Hair cells

Crista ampullaris
in one semi-circular canal

Head movement (rotation)

Endolymph
stays put
at beginning
of rotation

Head movement (rotation)

Endolymph
stays put
at beginning
of rotation

©Hayden-McNeil, LLC

Head Rotation
Semi-circular canals and crista ampullaris are detectors

One role of the semicircular canals is in maintaining body balance during the performance of rapid and intricate body movements.

> Example—if a person is running forward in a straight line and by error starts to turn to one side or the other, this rotation movement is detected by the crista ampullaris structures in the semicircular canals and corrections can be made before the person falls off balance.

Another function of the semicircular canals is to maintain a stable image on the retina by stabilizing the direction of gaze, irrespective of head movements.

C. Central Nervous Pathways of the Vestibular System

The hair cells of the vestibular system have synaptic contacts with the dendrites of bipolar neurons with cell bodies in the **vestibular ganglion**. The axons of these neurons and the axons of neurons in the **spiral ganglion** (associated with the cochlea) together make up the vestibulocochlear nerve (cranial nerve VIII).

The fibers in the **vestibular** branch of the eighth nerve make synapses with neurons in a collection of nuclei in the medulla beneath the floor of the fourth ventricle. This collection of nuclei is the **vestibular nucleus** or the **vestibular nuclear complex**.

The output of the vestibular nucleus goes to the following regions of the brain.

- areas that control *eye movements*
- areas that help to control movements of the *head* and *neck*
- via the vestibulospinal tracts to skeletal muscles that control *body posture* in response to head movements
- the *cerebellum* (particularly the vestibulocerebellum)

D. Other Sensory Mechanisms Concerned with Balance

There are many sensory mechanisms in addition to the vestibular apparatus that are concerned with sensing the body's balance or equilibrium. They include proprioceptors that provide information about the relative positions of other body parts (such as bending and extension of the limbs, bending of trunk), and rotation of the neck. Information from exteroceptors conveying pressure sensation from the soles of the feet can tell you whether the weight is distributed equally between the two feet, and whether the weight is forward or backward on the feet. Finally, visual information can also be important, because movement of the body shifts the position of an image on the retina. People with lesions in their vestibular apparatus can still maintain their balance provided their eyes are open and provided they move slowly. If they close their eyes, they lose their balance and fall over.

Exercise A

You and your partner obtain slides of the whole eye. Observe first under low power, then under high. Make sure you locate the sclera, choroid, the three different cell layers of the neural retina, the pigmented epithelium, and the nerve fibers of the ganglion cells. Below is room for you to draw what you observe. You may be asked to show your notes/drawings for participation points.

Exercise B

Sheep Eye Dissection

Materials needed:

- one preserved eye
- dissecting pan
- scalpel
- scissors
- blunt probe
- forceps

1. You and your partner obtain a sheep eye plus all dissecting materials and follow the description below for the dissection of a preserved sheep eye.

2. Identify the **sclera**. The sclera is the white-ish outer layer of the eye and is a tough connective tissue layer. Locate the optic nerve. Leave the optic nerve intact but remove all the muscle and fat that surrounds the sclera. The sclera is continuous with the **cornea** that, with a fresh eye, is transparent allowing one to see the **pupil** and **iris**. In preserved eyes, the cornea is opaque.

3. About 4 mm posterior to the cornea, gently make a stab wound with the point of the scalpel. Extend this incision with scissors by cutting parallel to the edge of the cornea until you have bisected the eye into anterior and posterior halves. You will have cut through the **sclera, choroid,** and **retina.** Make sure you can identify each.

4. The bisection just performed has probably pulled the neural retina away from the retinal pigment epithelium and choroid, giving the inner surface of the eye a brown-black appearance. Both the pigmented layer of the retina and the choroid contain the pigment melanin. Observe the **tapetum lucidum**, an iridescent greenish-blue area located behind the retinal pigment epithelium (which is NOT pigmented at that point). A tapetum is not present in humans but is found in many animals that display "eyeshine," such as sheep, cattle, dogs, and cats.

5. Tip the jelly-like vitreous humor out of the posterior half of the eye. Next, *slowly* invert the anterior portion by putting pressure on the cornea while holding the edges of the eye. While doing the inversion try to observe the delicate fibers (**suspensory ligaments**) which attach the **lens** to the **ciliary body**. Observe the posterior aspect of the **iris** and note the ciliary body. Now, looking at the anterior chamber, identify the **pupil**.

Exercise C

Ophthalmoscopy is a technique that permits you to view the **fundus** of the eye, and can be used to evaluate retinal changes associated with high blood pressure, glaucoma, diabetes, and atherosclerosis. The ophthalmoscope contains a light source and a set of concave lenses to counteract the convex lens of the eye (when the examination is done in an ophthalmologist's office, the pupil of the eye is usually dilated with a mydriatic agent such as an atropine derivative). The room lights should be lowered or switched off and the subject is instructed to look at a specific object straight ahead while the examiner directs light into the eye. The retina, optic disk, macula lutea, and the retinal blood vessels should be visible. Color photographs will be available in lab to help you recognize the parts of these features of the fundus.

Procedure

1. Sit or stand facing your "patient" at your partner's right side.

2. Select "0" on the lens dial **and** the small aperture.

3. Hold the ophthalmoscope vertically in front of your right eye, with the light beam directed toward your partner.

4. Instruct your partner to look straight ahead at a distant object.

5. Position the ophthalmoscope approximately six inches in front of and slightly to the right of your partner and direct the light into his or her pupil. You should see a red "reflex."

6. Keeping the "reflex" in view, move slowly toward your partner until you are really close, approximately **one and one-half to two inches away.** You should be able to see your partner's optic disk. If the disk is not in focus, rotate the lenses in the aperture until the optic disk is clearly visible. Farsighted people will require positive adjustment while nearsighted people will require negative adjustment.

7. Examine the optic disk. Can you see its outline? Can you see blood vessels? Can you find the macula lutea?

8. Continue the observation by asking your partner to look in several directions.

9. Draw what you see below. You may be asked to show your notes/drawings for participation points.

Exercise D

You and your partner obtain a microscope and a slide of the cochlea. Locate the Organ of Corti and in the space below, draw what you observe. Make sure you correctly identify each of the following:

_____ scala vestibuli

_____ vestibular membrane

_____ cochlear duct

_____ tectorial membrane

_____ hair cells

_____ basilar membrane

_____ scala tympani

_____ cochlear nerve

NOTE: The tectorial membrane may have torn away from the Organ of Corti during slide preparation. The slide may not look exactly like the picture.

Exercise E

You and your partner obtain an otoscope and two disposable specula to examine each other's ears. The object is to visualize the eardrum and the shadow of the malleus as it rests against the posterior surface of the eardrum. Pulling the pinna (external ear) upward and backward before inserting the speculum into the external auditory meatus facilitates visualization of the eardrum. Also, the speculum should not touch the walls of the meatus. **Do not reuse specula.**

Procedure

1. Sit or stand at your partner's right side so you are looking right at his/her ear.

2. Hold the otoscope upside down in your right hand.

3. Examine the tympanic membrane. Can you see the outline of the foot of the malleus? Can you see blood vessels? Do you see any scarring of the tympanic membrane or liquid behind it?

4. Draw what you see below. You may be asked to show your notes/drawings for participation points.

Exercise F

Observe the Functional Ear model. Be able to recognize the parts listed below. Use the space provided to sketch the ear.

Auricle		External auditory meatus	
Tympanic membrane		Ear ossicles	
Semicircular canals		Vestibular nerve	
Cochlear nerve		Cochlea	
Temporal bone		Auditory tube	

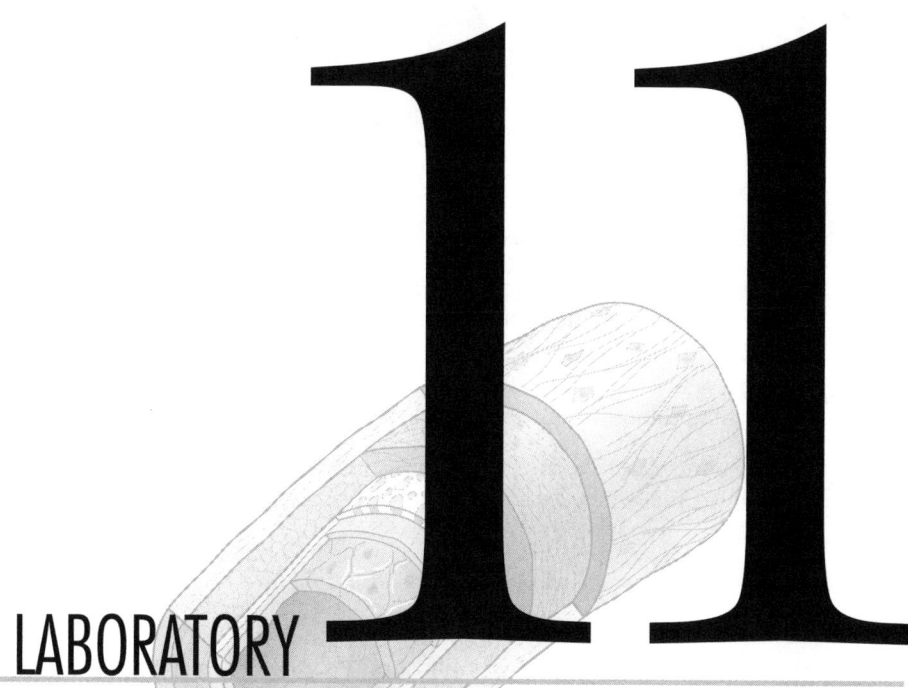

LABORATORY 11

CARDIOVASCULAR SYSTEM I

Required Reading: Lecture 23

READ THE PAGES LISTED BELOW IN YOUR HISTOLOGY TEXT BEFORE COMING TO CLASS, THEN BRING IT TO CLASS.

12TH ED: READ PAGES 216–237, OR
11TH ED: READ PAGES 170–189

Exercises C and E should be done online BEFORE COMING TO CLASS!

Objectives

1. List the seven **functions** of the blood circulation.

2. Draw a labeled diagram showing the basic arrangement of the cardiovascular system, including the systemic and pulmonary circuits, the vessels where oxygenated blood is found and the vessels where deoxygenated blood is found.   Also indicate the vessels that contain blood with high levels of carbon dioxide and vessels that contain blood with low levels of carbon dioxide.

3. List and describe the layers found in the walls of blood vessels, and how they vary between arteries, arterioles, capillaries, venules (muscular and non-muscular) and veins.

4. Explain **vasoconstriction** and **vasodilation**, and why these processes are important.

5. Explain the importance of **vascular endothelial cells** in the cardiovascular system, and list the vasoconstrictor and vasodilators they secrete.

6. List the six main **types** of blood vessels and their structures.

7. Explain two benefits arising from the fact that the large arteries near the heart are very **elastic**.

8. Name the blood vessels that control **peripheral resistance**.

9. Name the blood vessels that control the **capacity** of the circulatory system.

10. Describe the structure of the **heart** and the **layers** of its wall.

11. Name the **valves** of the heart and their locations.

12. Name the **great vessels** entering and leaving the heart.

13. Name the major arteries branching off from the **aorta**, and the regions they supply.

14. Name the major **veins** of the body, and the regions they drain.

I. Introduction

The cardiovascular system consists of a pump (the **heart**) that distributes blood through a series of variously sized tubes (the **blood vessels**) to all parts of the body and then back to the heart.

The circulation of blood fulfills the following seven purposes.

1. Gaseous exchange.

2. Delivery of **major nutrients**, **building materials**, and **"micronutrients"** to tissues and organs.

3. Removal of waste metabolites from tissues and organs.

4. Delivery of hormones from the endocrine glands to distant target tissues (oxytocin, thyroxine, angiotensin, etc.).

5. Defense.

6. Thermal exchange—heat conservation and heat loss.

7. Transports water around the body.

II. Basic Arrangement of the Cardiovascular System

The heart beats about 75 times per minute and ejects about 75 ml of blood with each beat. That means that it pumps about 338 liters per hour.

The cardiovascular system is arranged as follows.

1. The **heart**, which is really two pumps set up side by side. The **right** heart pumps the blood through the lungs (the **pulmonary circuit**) into the left heart. The left heart then pumps the blood through the rest of the body, the **systemic circuit**.

2. Blood is distributed through the pulmonary and systemic circuits by the **arteries, arterioles, terminal arterioles, capillaries, venules,** and **veins**. Blood leaves the heart via the arteries, and returns to it via the veins.

3. The pulmonary circuit receives **deoxygenated** blood from the **right** heart. Blood is **oxygenated** in the lungs, and returned to the **left** heart.

4. The systemic circuit distributes oxygenated blood from the left heart via the **aorta** to the organs and tissues, and returns the blood to the right heart *via* the superior and inferior venae cavae.

5. The systemic circuit consists of a number of circuits arranged *in parallel.* This means that there is wide latitude for altering blood flow through a particular organ without altering the flow through other parts of the system. If they were in series (one after the other), then cutting down the flow in one part would also cut down the flow in all successive parts.

Overview of the General Pattern of Circulation

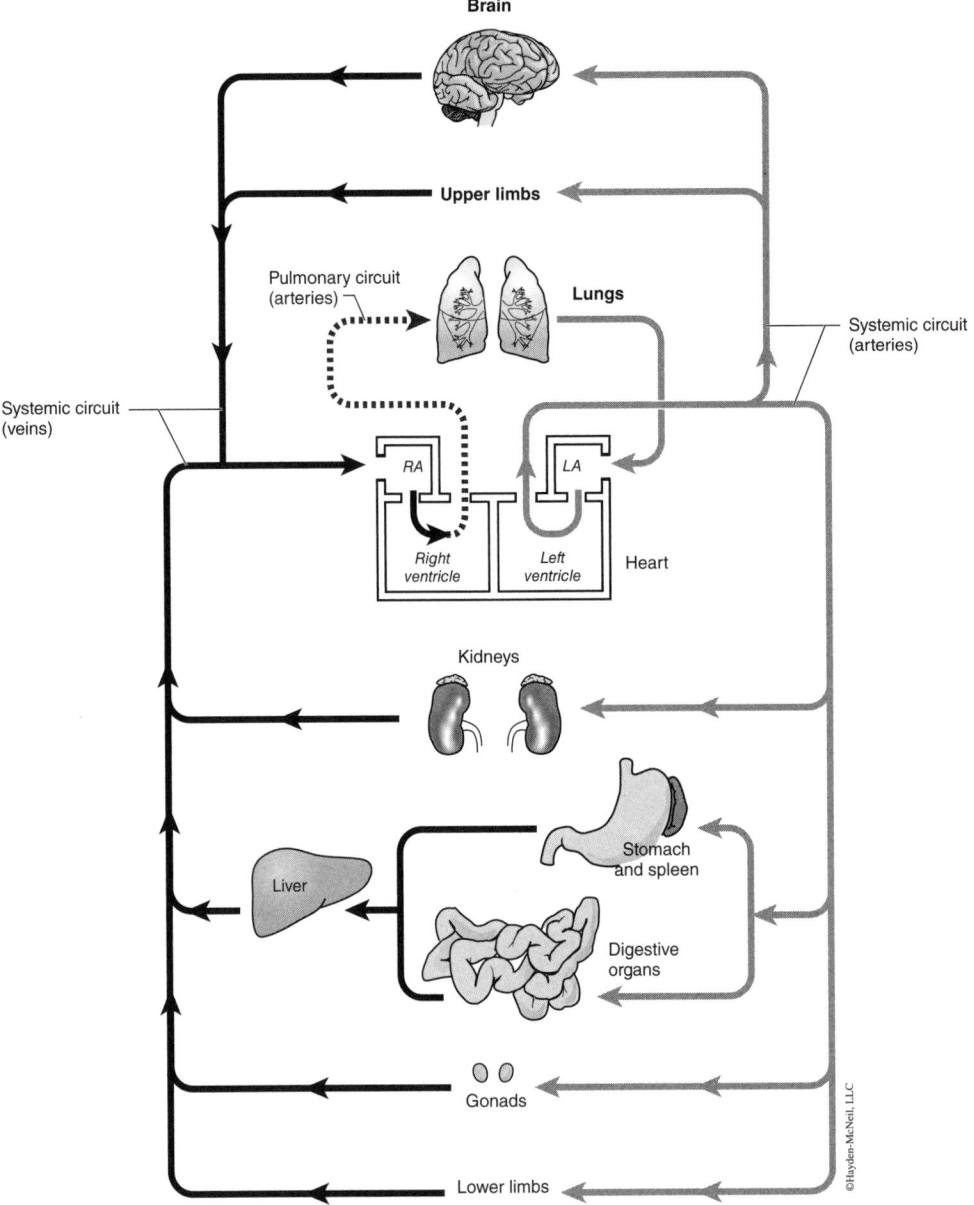

Figure 11-1. Overview of circulation.

There are four important variables that determine the functioning of the cardiovascular system and its response to various life-threatening conditions such as hemorrhage and heart attack. All four come under the control of the autonomic nervous system, principally the sympathetic branch.

1. **Capacity** (the *volume* of the cardiovascular system, which depends on the diameter of the *veins* and *venules*)

2. **Resistance** (diameter of the arterioles)

3. **Heart rate** and **myocardial contractility** (**force** of contraction)

4. **Volume** of blood in the circulation is regulated by the kidneys.

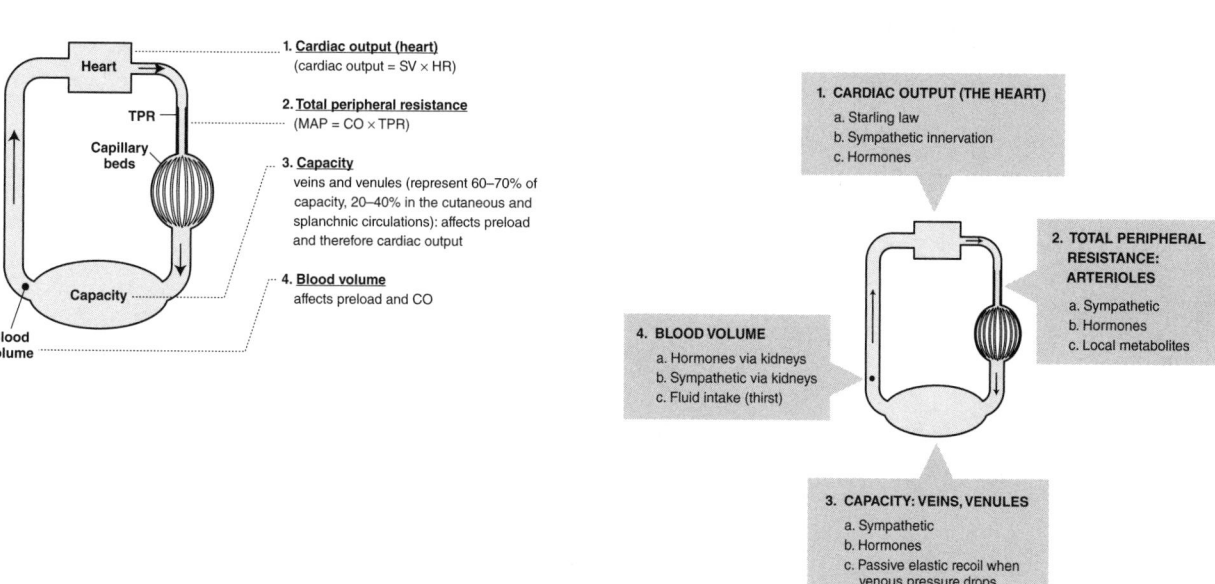

Figure 11-2. The four variables come under a variety of controls, the main one being the sympathetic nervous system.

Wall of Artery and Vein

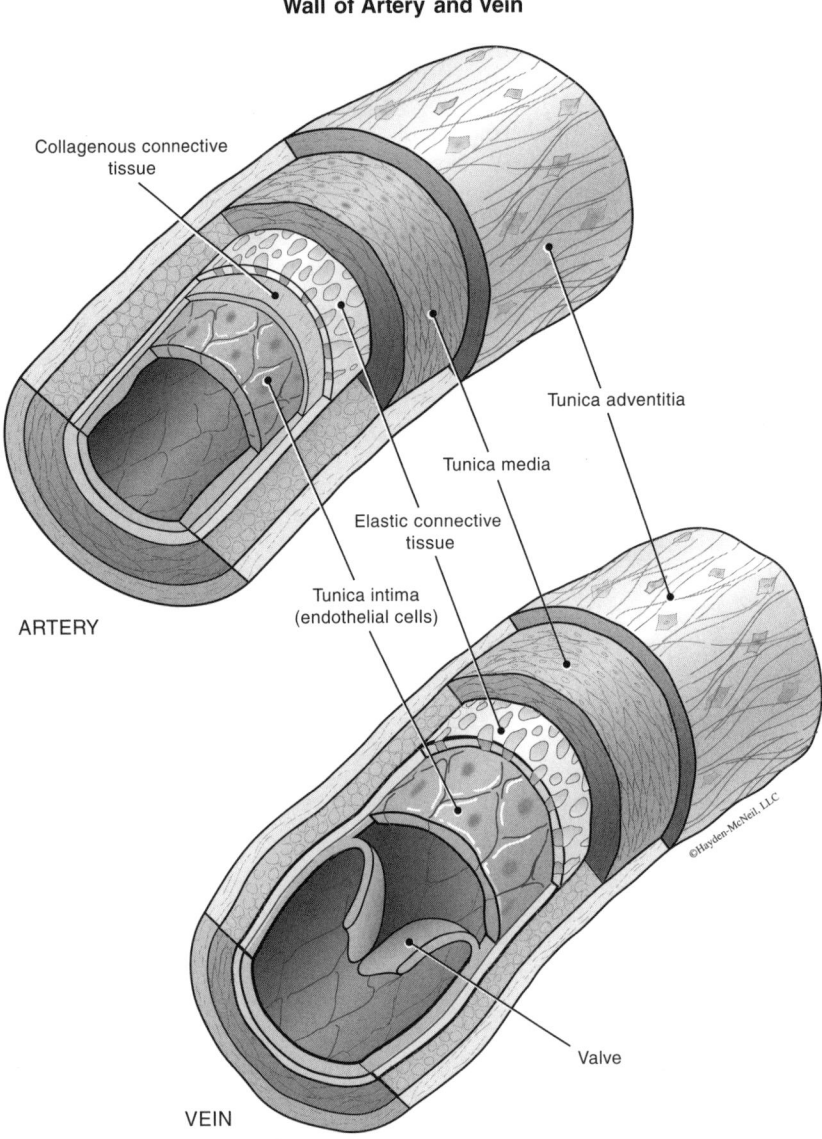

Figure 11-3. Wall of artery and vein.

III. Blood Vessels

There are six types of blood vessels:

1. arteries

2. arterioles

3. terminal arterioles

4. capillaries

5. venules (muscular and non-muscular)

6. veins

Except for the capillaries, the walls of blood vessels have three basic layers.

1. An inner layer of a specialized squamous epithelium called **vascular endothelium**. This layer is called the **tunica intima**.

2. A middle layer composed of smooth muscle fibers, usually with some elastic connective tissue. This layer is called the **tunica media**.

3. An outer layer composed of connective tissue with elastic and collagenous fibers. This layer is called the **tunica adventitia**.

The relative importance of these layers varies according to the type of blood vessel. Capillaries have only the inner layer, and are basically tubes formed from endothelial cells. Arteries, on the other hand, have very thick walls with an abundance of elastic fibers and smooth muscle fibers. Smooth muscle fibers are found in all blood vessels except for capillaries and non-muscular venules.

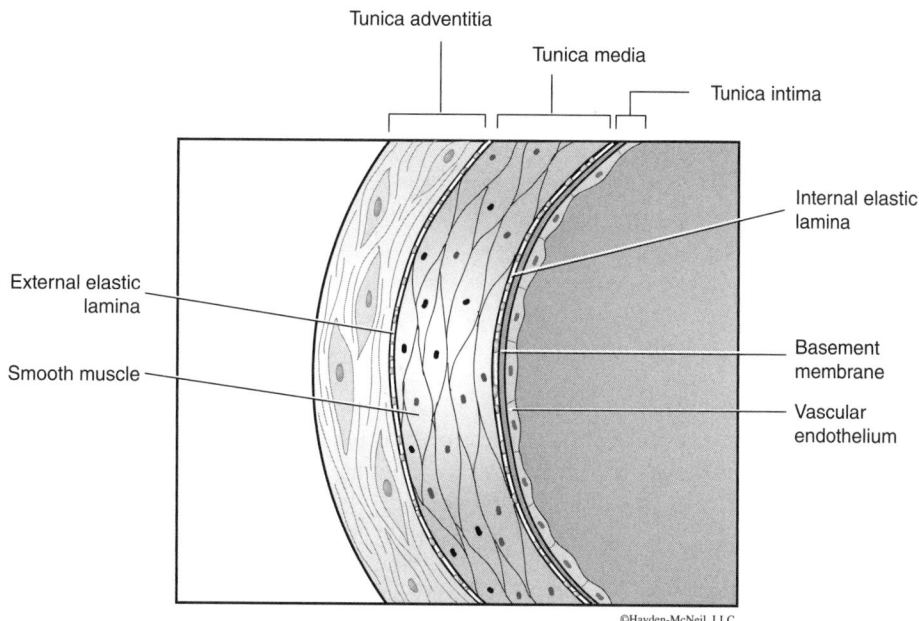

©Hayden-McNeil, LLC

Figure 11-4. Layers of blood vessels.

IV. Vasoconstriction and Vasodilation

Sympathetic stimulation, hormones and metabolic products produce contraction or relaxation of the smooth muscle in the tunica media. If the response is contraction, the result is **vasoconstriction**. If the response is relaxation, the result is **vasodilation**. Vasoconstrictors include the catecholamines norepinephrine and epinephrine, both of which are released from the adrenal gland by sympathetic stimulation. Other important vasoconstrictors are angiotensin II, vasopressin, and endothelin. Examples of vasodilators include nitric oxide and histamine. Histamine is released by mast cells of the connective tissue in response to the injury to the tissue, and is therefore responsible for the redness and warmth of an inflamed area. Metabolic products such as carbon dioxide and acids such as lactic acid also cause vasodilation.

Vasoconstriction and vasodilation control:

1. the flow of blood through organs and tissues (i.e., the arterioles).

2. the resistance of the systemic circuit (also known as the **total peripheral resistance** or TPR; i.e., the arterioles)

3. the total **capacity** of the blood vessels in the cardiovascular system (i.e., the veins and venules).

A. Arteries

The pulmonary arteries and the systemic arteries such as the aorta carry blood away from the heart. The arterial pressure in the systemic circuit is much higher than in the pulmonary circuit. The arteries conduct blood at relatively high pressure *away* from the heart. The tunica media makes up the bulk of the arterial wall, which is very thick and contains an abundance of elastic fibers and smooth muscle.

The ratio of smooth muscle fibers to elastic fibers increases as the distance from the heart increases. The large arteries near the heart (aorta, carotids, common iliacs) have a prominent elastic component in their tunica media. This allows the the arteries to **distend** at each heartbeat and recoil between heartbeats. This smoothes out the pressure wave from the pulse, and between heartbeats their elastic recoil continues to propel blood into the systemic circuit.

In arteriosclerosis, the arteries lose this elasticity and harden.

B. Arterioles

The large arteries make many branches, the diameter of the walls in each branch becoming progressively smaller and smaller. The smallest vessels are called arterioles.

Arterioles are smaller versions of arteries, but the smooth muscle component of the tunica media is very prominent. The arterioles control the blood flow through organs and tissues, and determine the total peripheral resistance.

C. Terminal Arterioles

The terminal arterioles, which develop from arterioles proper, have structures that are intermediate between arterioles and capillaries.

D. Capillaries

Terminal arterioles deliver blood into the capillaries. At the point where the true capillaries originate from the terminal arterioles, one or two smooth muscle fibers encircle the capillary. This is the **precapillary sphincter**, which can open or close the entrance to the capillary.

Capillaries consist of tubes of endothelial cells lying on a basement membrane (basal lamina). They lack media and adventitia. These are the exchange vessels of the circulation, Capillaries deliver nutrients, hormones, oxygen, etc., to the tissues, and remove carbon dioxide and other metabolic products such as lactic acid. The figure shows a typical capillary bed.

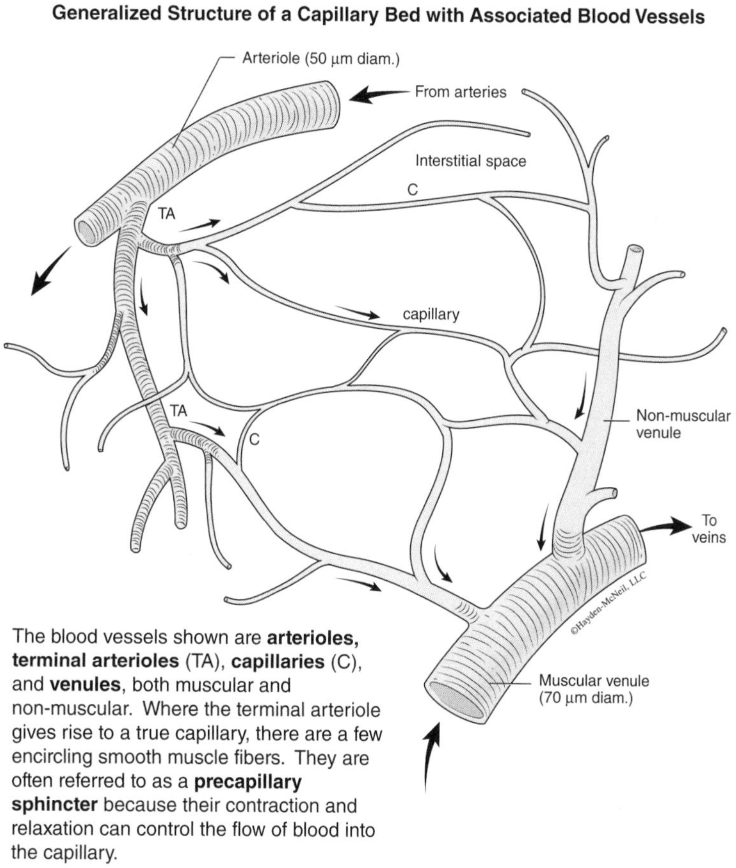

Generalized Structure of a Capillary Bed with Associated Blood Vessels

The blood vessels shown are **arterioles, terminal arterioles** (TA), **capillaries** (C), and **venules**, both muscular and non-muscular. Where the terminal arteriole gives rise to a true capillary, there are a few encircling smooth muscle fibers. They are often referred to as a **precapillary sphincter** because their contraction and relaxation can control the flow of blood into the capillary.

Figure 11-5. Generalized structure of a capillary bed with associated blood vessels.

E. Venules

The pressure of blood in the venous part of the systemic circuit is much lower than on the arterial side. Blood passes from the capillaries into venules, which merge together to form veins. The smallest venules lack smooth muscle in their walls (they are non-muscular venules), but the larger venules (muscular venules) have all three layers. However, their walls are much thinner and are less elastic than the walls of arterioles.

F. Veins

The veins are responsible for returning the blood to the heart to complete the circuit.

Both venules and veins have a large diameter with little elasticity in their walls, which allows them to hold large blood volumes at low pressures. The veins and the venules account for most of the capacity of the circulation. The long veins in the the arms and legs contain flap-like valves. Contraction and relaxation of the surrounding skeletal muscles therefore assists in propelling blood toward the heart.

G. The Heart as a Pump

The heart acts as a double pump. The right heart pumps blood through the lungs to the left heart which then pumps oxygenated blood throughout the body. Therefore, there are two circuits: (1) the **pulmonary circuit**: the right heart to the lungs and back to the heart and (2) the **systemic circuit**: the left heart to the body and back to the heart.

The path of blood through the heart is now complete:

right atrium → tricuspid valve → right ventricle → pulmonary semilunar valve → pulmonary trunk → rt. and lt. pulmonary arteries → lobar branches → pulmonary capillaries → rt. and lt. pulmonary veins → left atrium → bicuspid valve → left ventricle → aortic semilunar valve → aorta → systemic circulation

1. Vessels of the Pulmonary Circuit

Deoxygenated blood in the right ventricle is pumped into the pulmonary circulation through the pulmonary semilunar valve. The first vessel blood enters is the **pulmonary trunk**. The pulmonary trunk then bifurcates (branches) into the **left** and **right pulmonary arteries** that enter the lungs. In the lungs, they divide into **lobar branches** that continue to branch into the **pulmonary capillary** beds. These capillaries surround the alveoli, the site where gas exchange occurs. Oxygenated blood then flows from the pulmonary capillaries into the **pulmonary veins** that drain into the left atrium. There are four pulmonary veins, two from each lung.

2. Vessels of the Systemic Circuit

Oxygenated blood is pumped into the systemic circuit by the left ventricle. The circuit consists of the aorta, its branches that lead to all parts of the body, and the companion system of veins that return deoxygenated blood from the tissues back to the heart.

H. Arterial System

Blood ejected from the left ventricle passes through the aortic semilunar valve and enters the aorta, the largest artery in the body. The aorta is divided into the ascending aorta, the aortic arch, the descending aorta and the abdominal aorta. Three arteries that branch from the aortic arch; the **brachiocephalic**, the **left common carotid**, and the **left subclavian**. The brachiocephalic subsequently branches into the **right common carotid** and the **right subclavian**. The carotids supply the head and neck region while the subclavian on each side branches into the **axillary** artery (armpit). From the axillary artery, blood flows into the **brachial** of the upper arm, then into the **radial** and **ulnar** of the lower arm.

The descending aorta gives rise to numerous small arteries that supply the thoracic wall and the thoracic organs. Below the diaphragm, the descending aorta becomes the abdominal aorta. Branching from the abdominal aorta are the **celiac** artery (which then branches into the **splenic** artery (spleen) and the **hepatic** artery (liver and gallbladder), the **superior mesenteric** (intestinal tract), the **renals** (kidneys), the **gonadals** (ovaries/testes), and the **inferior mesenteric arteries** (colon and rectum).

The abdominal aorta terminally divides into the **right and left common iliacs**. Each common iliac branches into the **internal** and **external** iliacs. From the external iliacs branch the arteries of the leg, the **femoral**, the **popliteal**, and the **anterior** and **posterior tibials**.

I. Venous System

In most cases, the veins that return blood to the heart have the same names as the parallel arteries.

Blood in the leg is drained by the **anterior and posterior tibials**, the **femoral**, and the **great saphenous** (the longest vein in the body). These three veins empty into the **external iliac** which, along with the **internal iliac**, drains into the **common iliac**. Past the common iliacs, is the **inferior vena cava**, one of the great veins of the body that lead directly to the right atrium. As it makes its way to the heart, the **gonadal, renal**, and **hepatic** veins drain into it.

In the lower arm, blood is drained by the **radial** and **ulnar** veins which empty into the **brachial** of the upper arm. The brachial then leads into the **axillary**, which then leads into the **subclavian**, which empties into the **brachiocephalic**, which empties into the second great vein of the body, the **superior vena cava**. The superior vena cava, like the inferior, makes a direct path for the right atrium of the heart.

The head and neck regions are drained by the **internal and external jugulars** (there is a set on each side). Both the internal and external jugulars empty into the **subclavians**. However, where the larger internal jugular joins with the subclavian, the subclavian becomes the **brachiocephalic**.

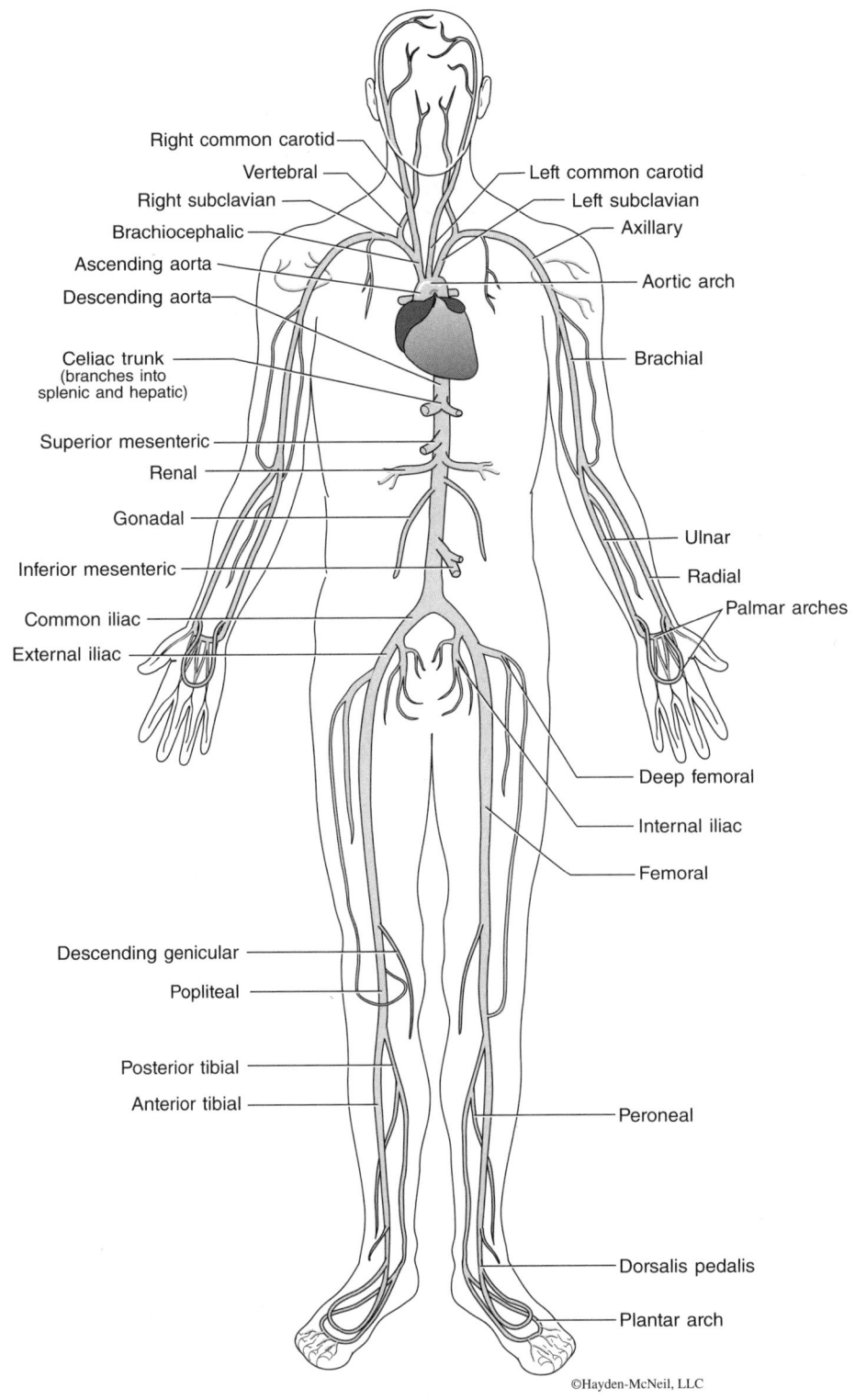

Figure 11-6. The arterial system.

Right common carotid —
Vertebral —
Right subclavian —
Brachiocephalic —
Ascending aorta —
Descending aorta —
Celiac trunk —
(branches into splenic and hepatic)
Superior mesenteric —
Renal —
Gonadal —
Inferior mesenteric —
Common iliac —
External iliac —
Descending genicular —
Popliteal —
Posterior tibial —
Anterior tibial —

— Left common carotid
— Left subclavian
— Axillary
— Aortic arch
— Brachial
— Ulnar
— Radial
— Palmar arches
— Deep femoral
— Internal iliac
— Femoral
— Peroneal
— Dorsalis pedalis
— Plantar arch

©Hayden-McNeil, LLC

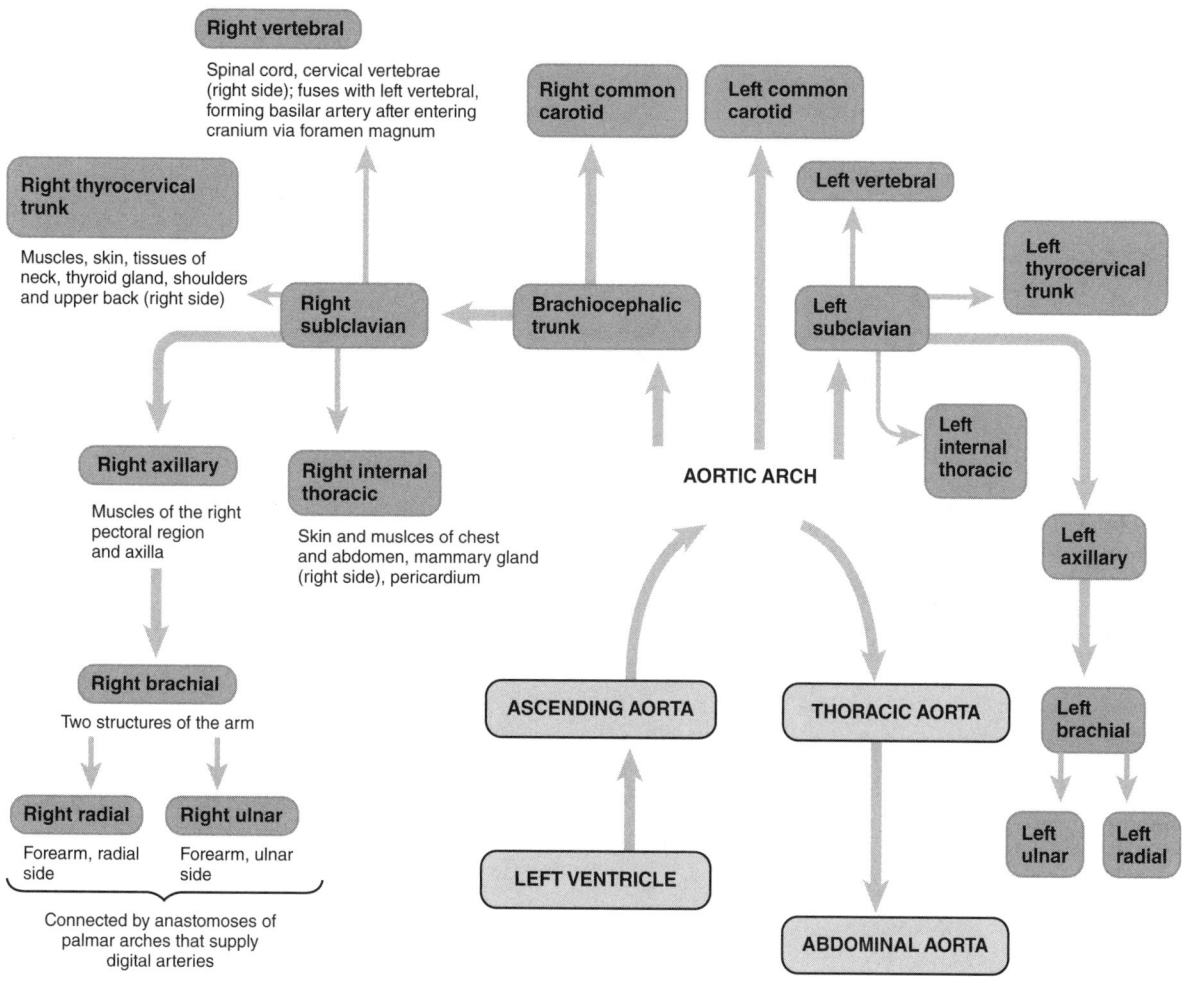

Figure 11-7.

A Summary of the Arterial System

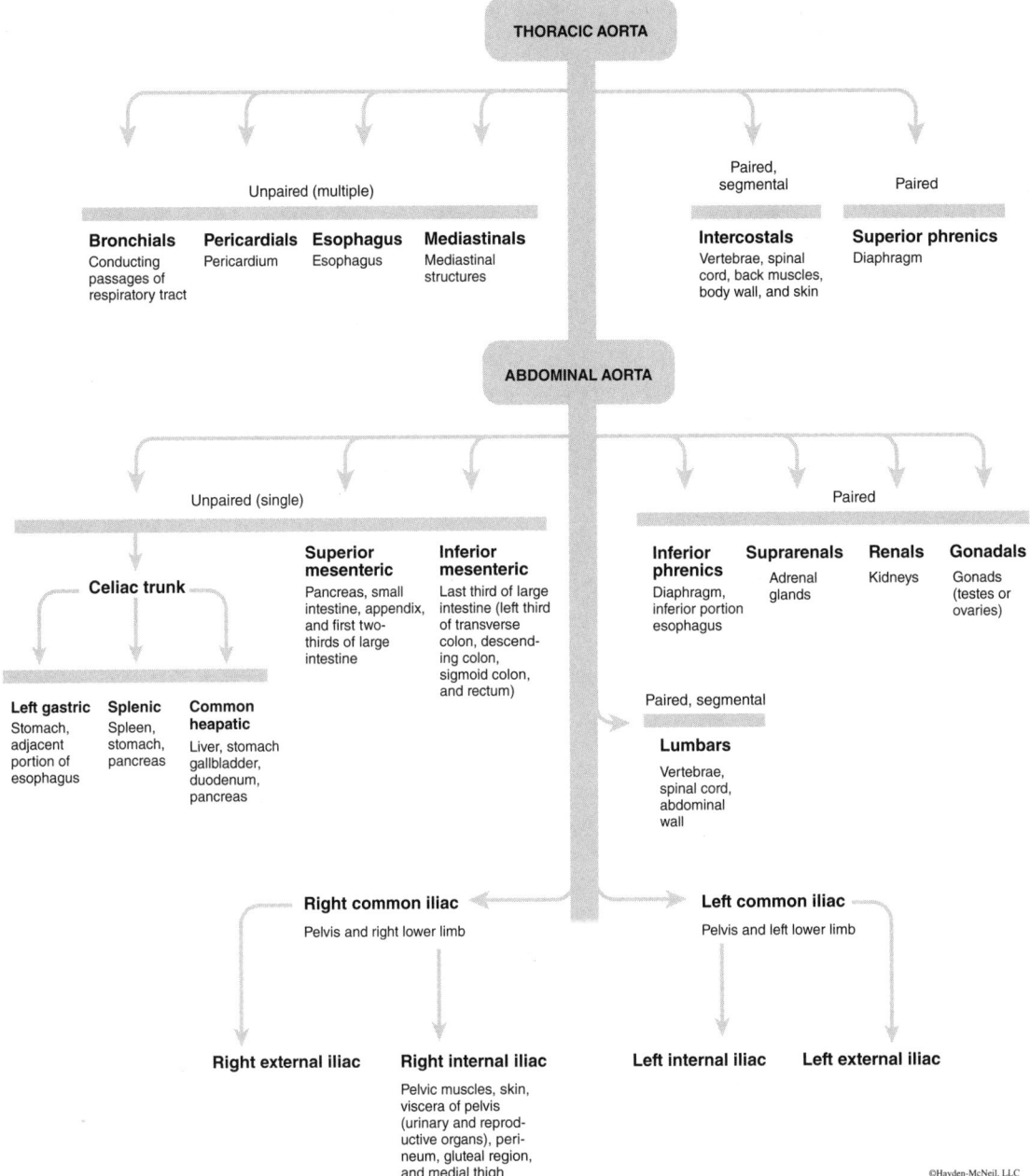

Figure 11-8.

Major Arteries of the Lower Limb

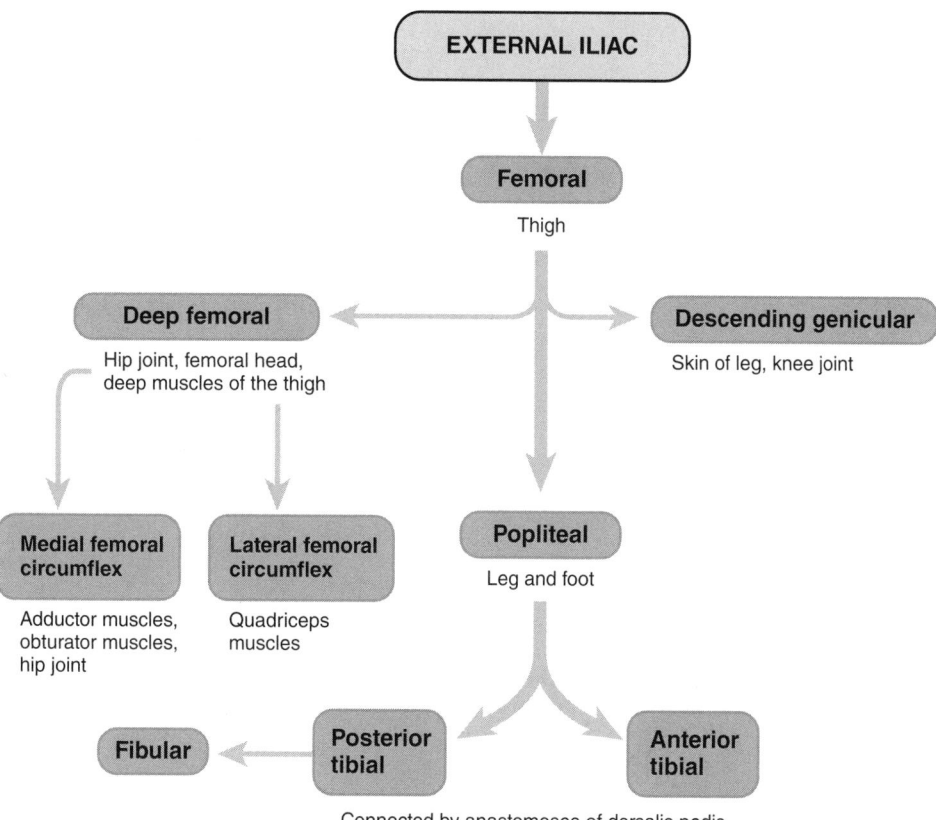

Figure 11-9.

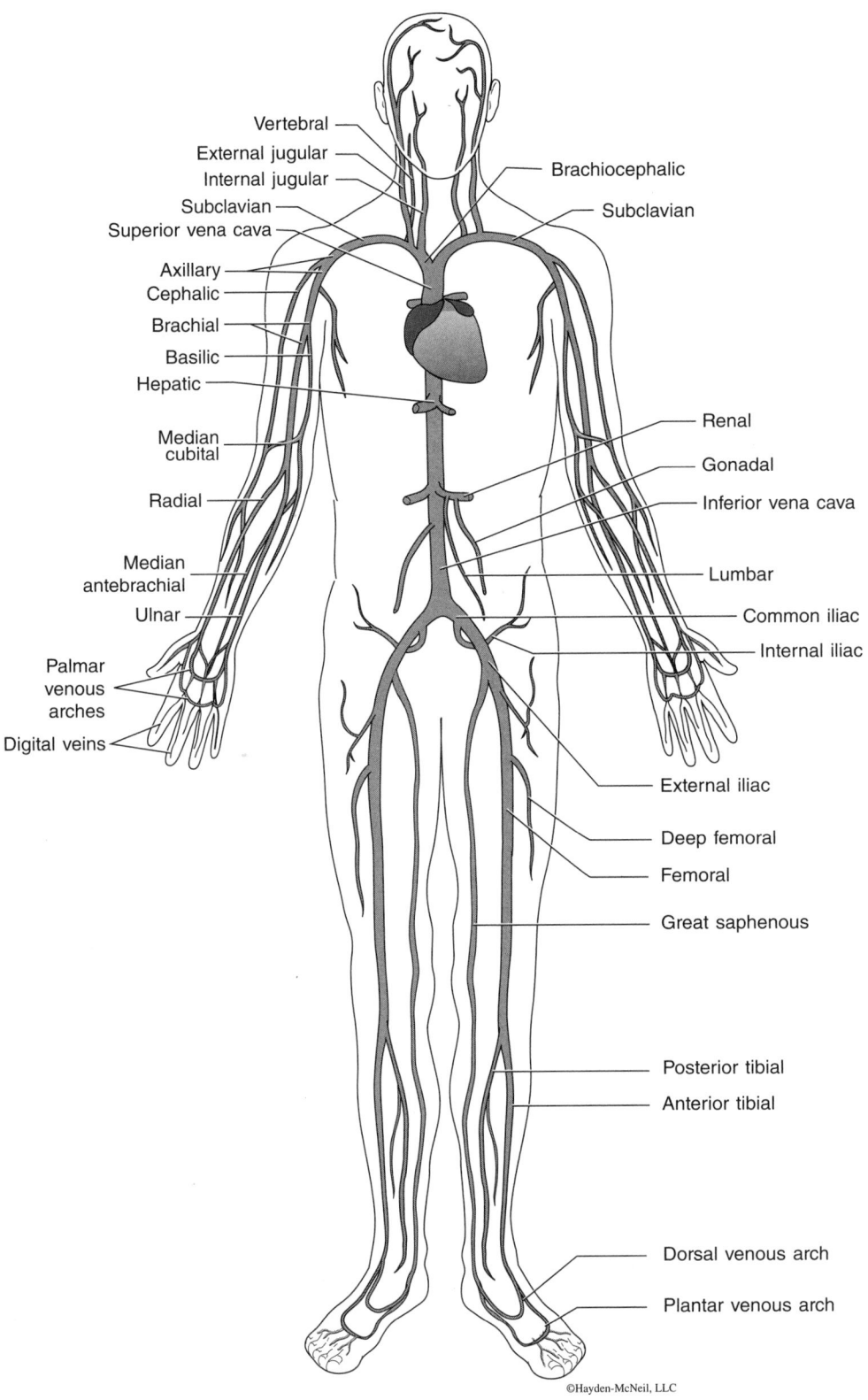

Figure 11-10. The venous system.

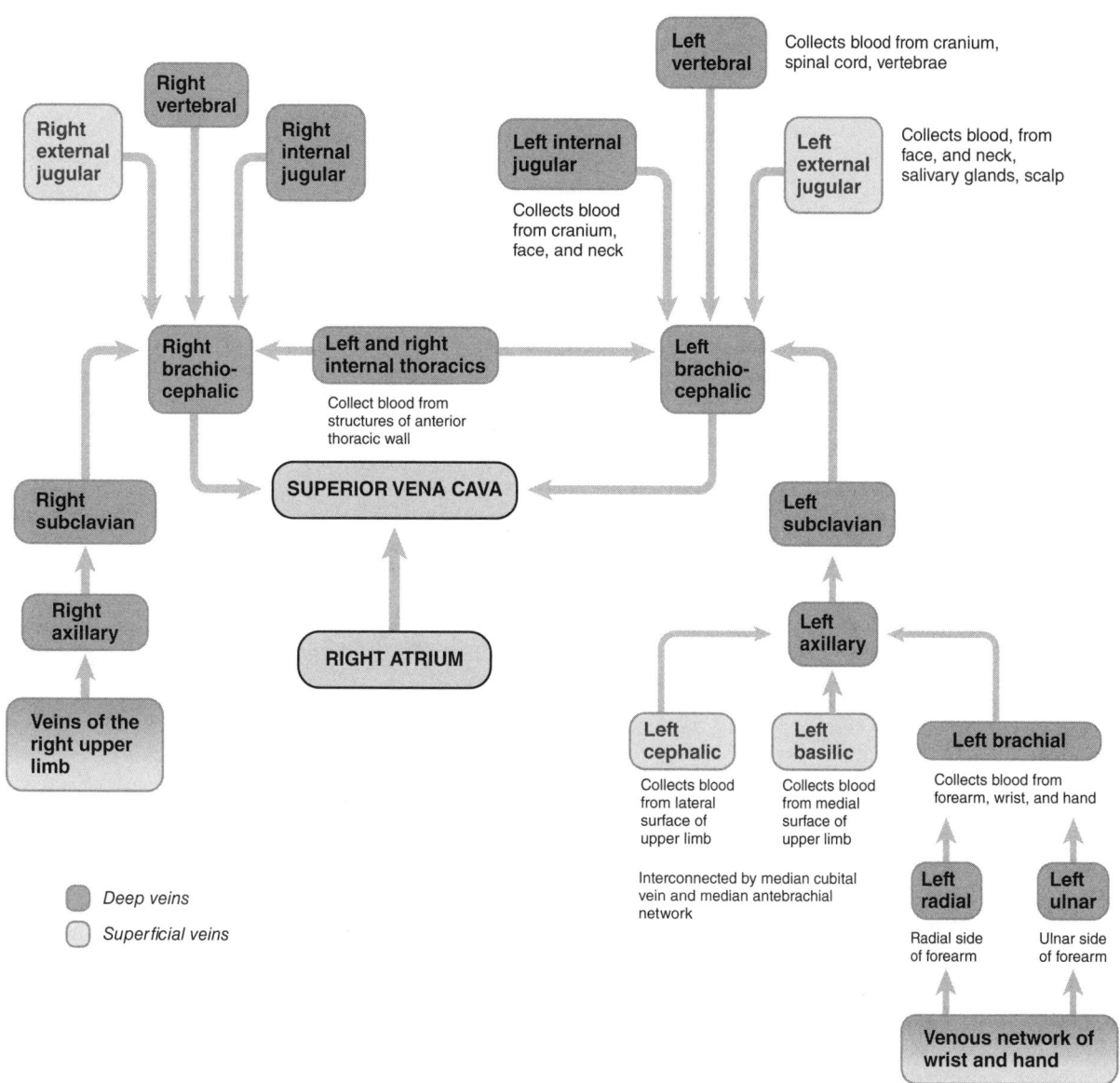

Figure 11-11.

Tributaries of the Inferior Vena Cava

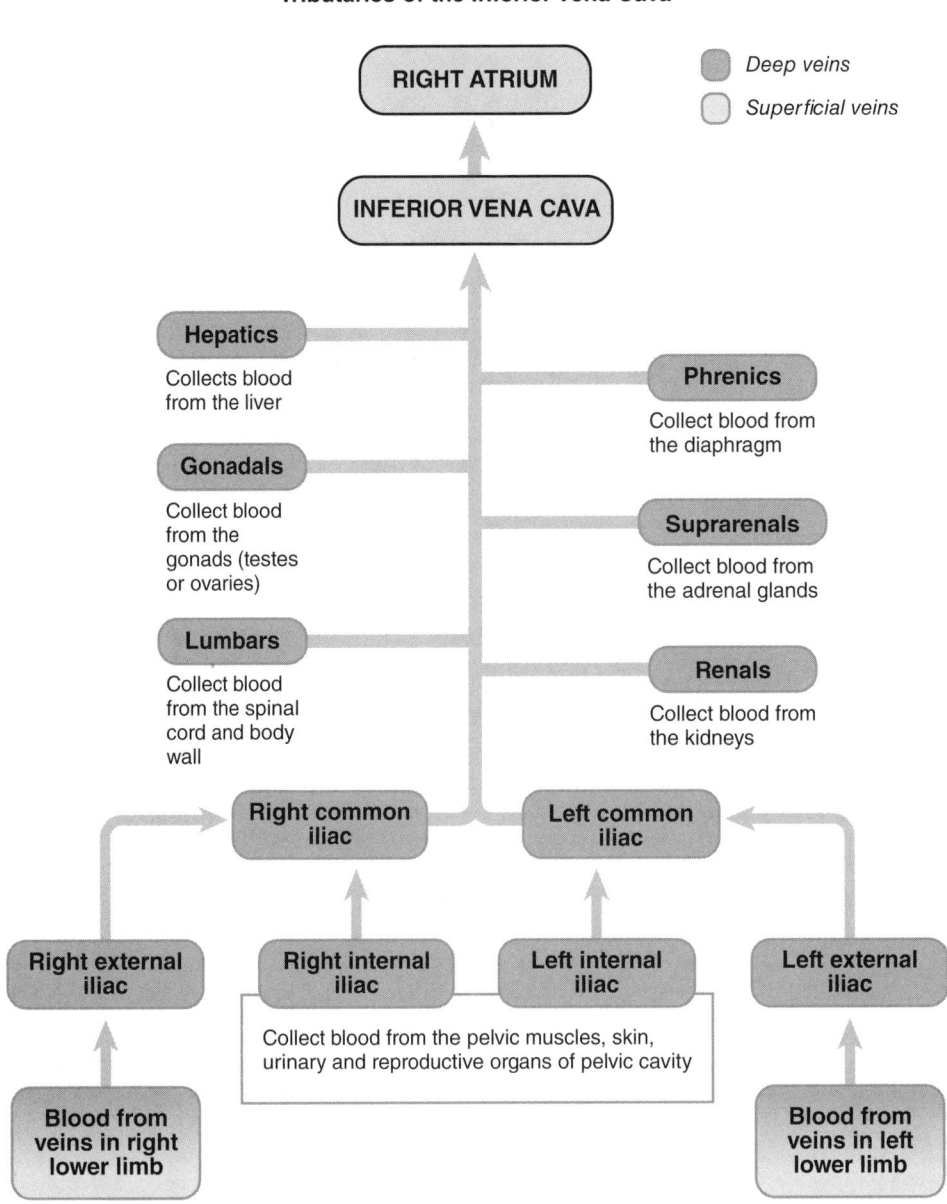

Figure 11-12.

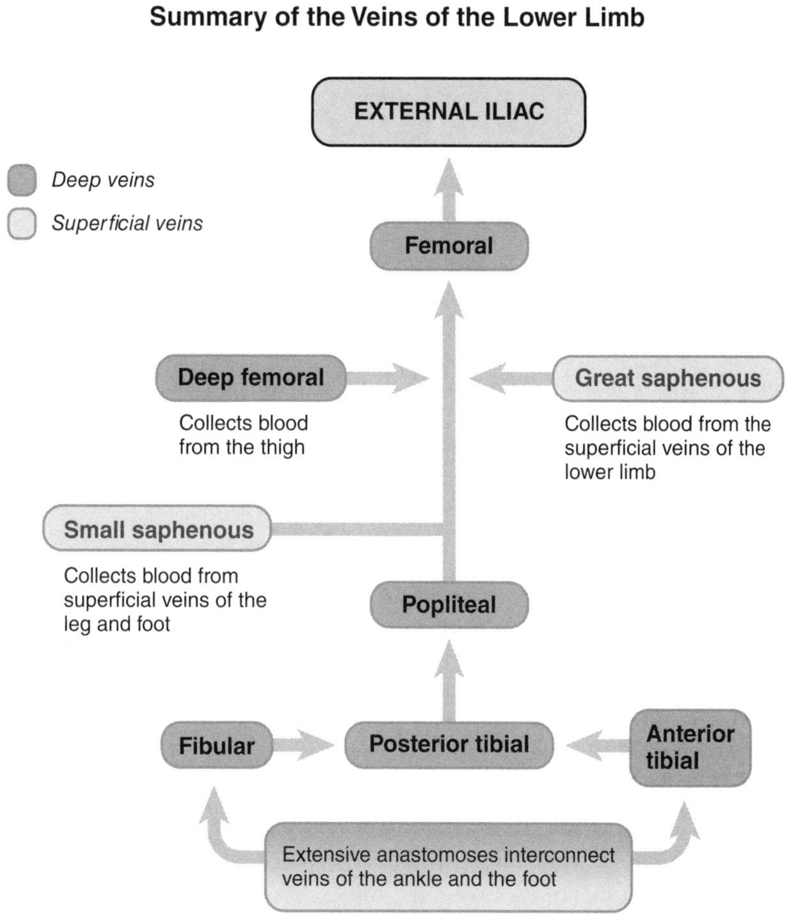

Summary of the Veins of the Lower Limb

Figure 11-13.

V. Blood Supply to the Brain

Four arteries carry blood to the brain, the two **vertebrals** and the 2 **internal carotids**. The vertebrals join together on the inferior surface of the medulla to form the **basilar artery**. Both the basilar and the internal carotids deliver blood to the **circle of Willis**, which, as its name implies, forms a circular circuit on the inferior aspect of the brain. Three pairs of cerebral arteries branch from the circle of Willis and carry blood to the cerebral hemispheres:

middle cerebral—supplies the lateral surface of the parietal and temporal lobes.

anterior cerebral—supplies the medial surface of the frontal and parietal lobes.

posterior cerebral—supplies the medial surface of the temporal and occipital lobes.

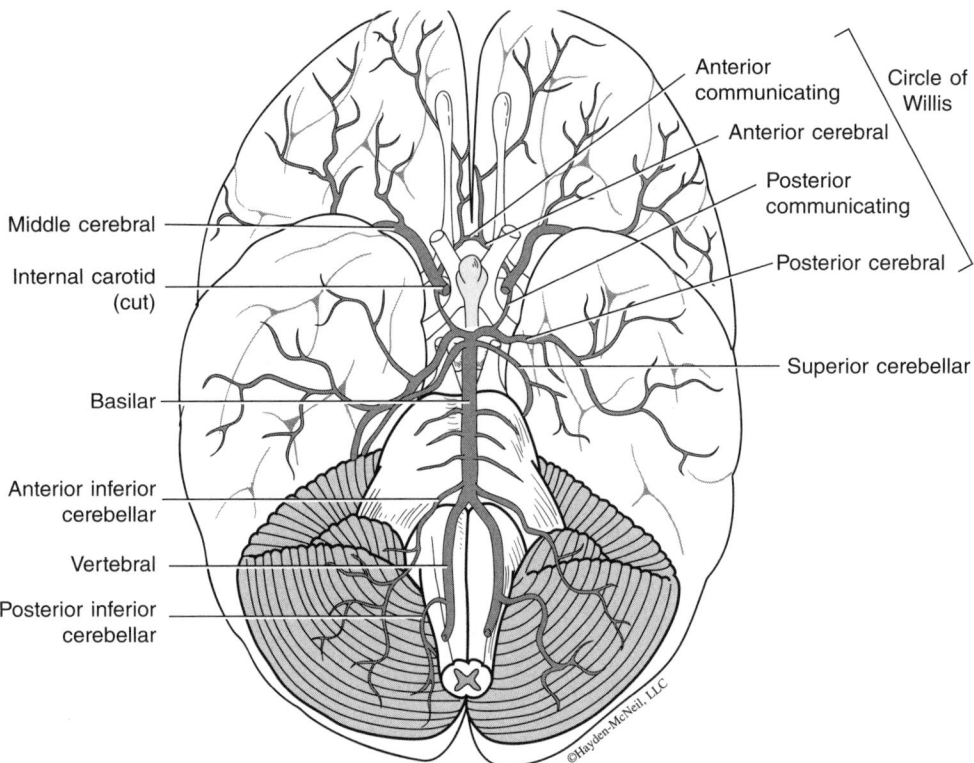

Figure 11-14. The circle of Willis.

Venous drainage of the brain occurs through the **dural sinuses**, which are blood-filled cavities within the dura mater. Blood then empties into the internal jugular veins.

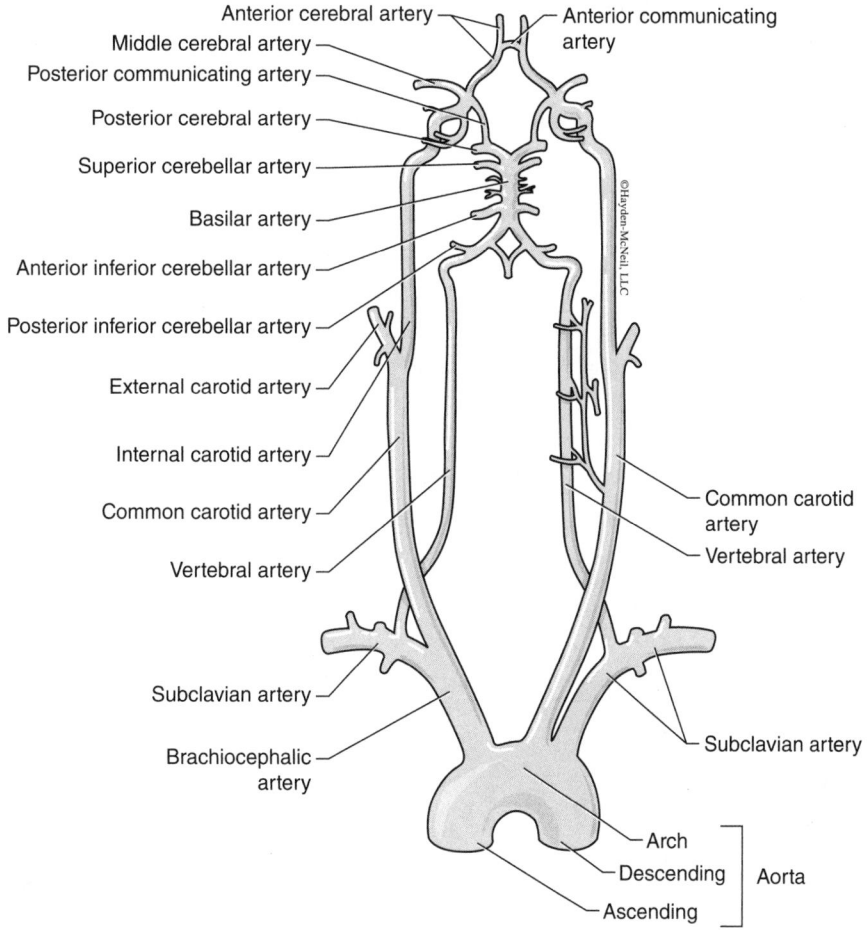

Anterior cerebral artery
Middle cerebral artery
Posterior communicating artery
Posterior cerebral artery
Superior cerebellar artery
Basilar artery
Anterior inferior cerebellar artery
Posterior inferior cerebellar artery
External carotid artery
Internal carotid artery
Common carotid artery
Vertebral artery
Subclavian artery
Brachiocephalic artery

Anterior communicating artery

©Hayden-McNeil, LLC

Common carotid artery
Vertebral artery

Subclavian artery

Arch
Descending
Ascending
Aorta

Figure 11-15.

VI. The Heart

The heart is located in the **mediastinum**, the region between the two lungs.

The heart and the roots of the great blood vessels that emerge from it are enclosed in the **pericardium**, a double-layered serous membrane. The outer layer of the pericardium, called the **parietal pericardium**, consists of an outer layer of dense regular connective tissue and an inner layer of serous membrane. The inner layer of the pericardium (visceral pericardium) is considered part of the heart wall, and is usually referred to as the **epicardium**. Between the parietal pericardium and the epicardium is the **pericardial cavity**, which is filled with a serous fluid secreted by the parietal pericardium. This fluid allows the heart to beat in an almost friction free environment.

The wall of the heart has three layers.

1. The outer **epicardium** (= visceral pericardium).

2. The middle **myocardium**—made up mainly of interlacing bundles of cardiac muscle fibers. These bundles are specially arranged so that the heart acts as a very efficient pump. Cardiac muscle cells are involuntary, striated, and branched.

The inner surface of the myocardium is sculpted into a complex series of ridges and valleys called the **trabeculae carneae**. These prevent the wall of the heart from wrinkling when it contracts.

The myocardium is most developed in the ventricles. It is thinnest in the right ventricle, and is thickest in the left ventricle. This is because the right ventricle the right ventricle pumps blood through the lungs at comparatively low pressure, while the left ventricle does more work by pumping blood to all parts of the body at comparatively high pressure.

3. **Endocardium**—This is the inner layer that lines the cavities of the heart. It consists of a thin layer of vascular endothelial cells overlying a thin layer of connective tissue. The layer of endothelial cells is continuous with the layer of endothelial cells in the blood vessels that emerge from the heart.

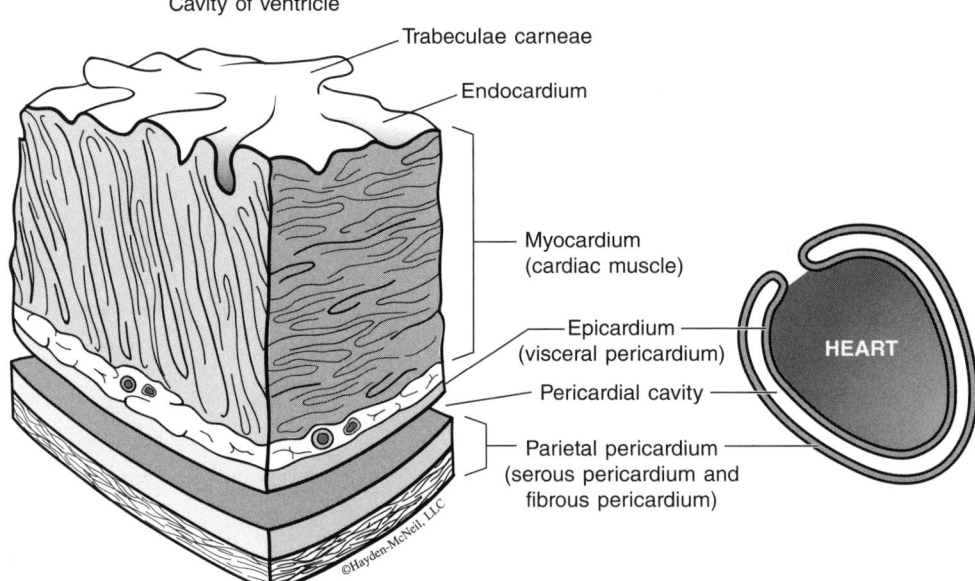

Figure 11-16. The wall of the heart.

A. The Chambers of the Heart

The heart has four chambers, two upper atria (left and right) and two lower ventricles (left and right). The two pumps that make up the left and right hearts are separated from each other by the **interatrial** and **interventricular septa**.

B. Valves of the Heart

A total of four valves guard the openings between the atria and ventricles and between the ventricles and the arterial trunks. The valves ensure that blood passes through the heart in one direction only. **It is important to understand that the opening and closing of these valves is purely passive, and occurs in response to changing pressure differentials across them.**

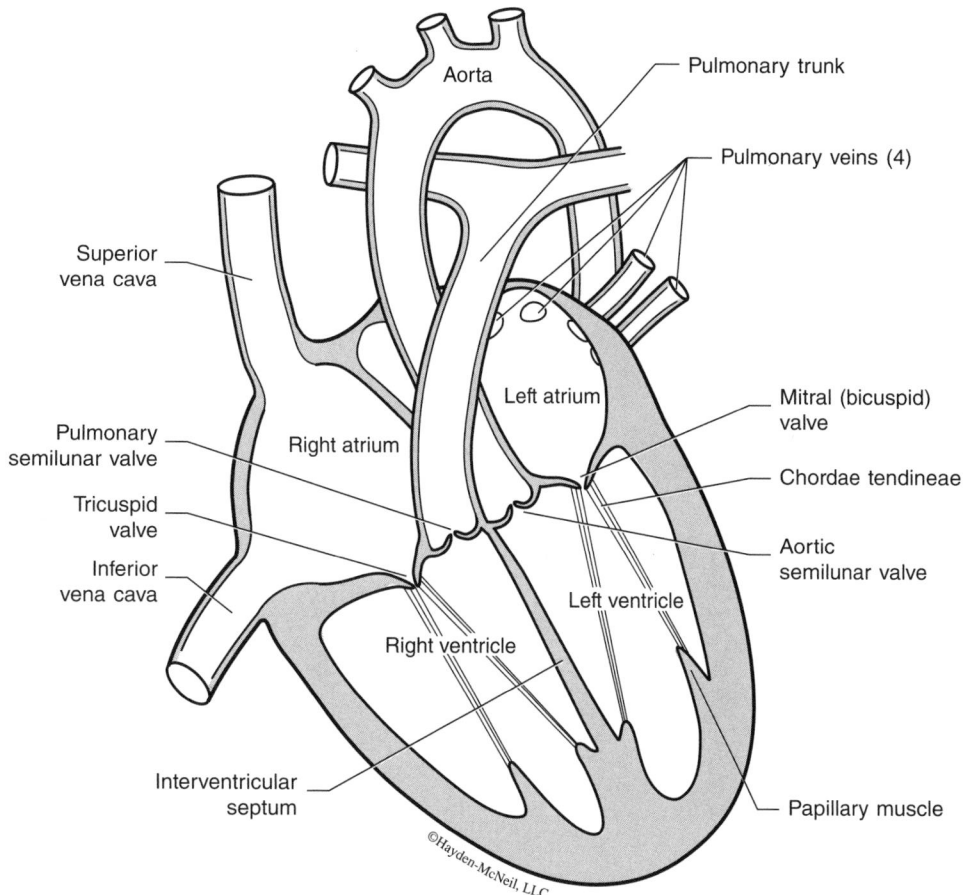

Figure 11-17. Diagram of the heart.

1. **Right side valves**—The right AV valve is called the **tricuspid** valve [an aid to remembering which side this is on is to think of it as the tRI(GHT)cuspid]. It consists of three leaflets. Tendon-like fibrous cords called **chordae tendineae** connect the pointed ends of the leaflets to fingerlike muscular projections (**papillary muscles**) on the inner surface of the right ventricle. The chordae tendineae and the papillary muscles prevent the valve from turning inside out into the atrium when the ventricle contracts.

   The right **semilunar** valve guards the opening from the right ventricle into the pulmonary trunk. The valve consists of three semilunar (half-moon shaped) cusps, and is called the **pulmonary semilunar valve**.

2. **Left side valves**—The left AV valve is called the bicuspid or mitral valve. It has only two cusps, but has chordae tendineae attached to papillary muscles just like the tricuspid valve on the right side of the heart.

   The left semilunar valve guards the opening from the left ventricle into the aorta. Like the pulmonary semilunar valve, this valve has three cusps. It is called the aortic semilunar valve.

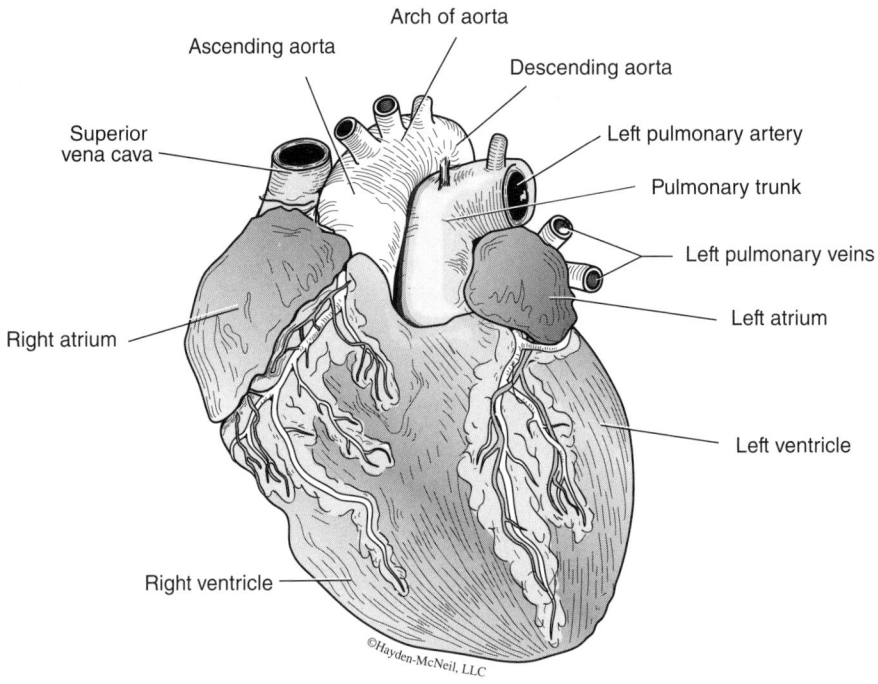

Figure 11-18. The human heart—anterior view.

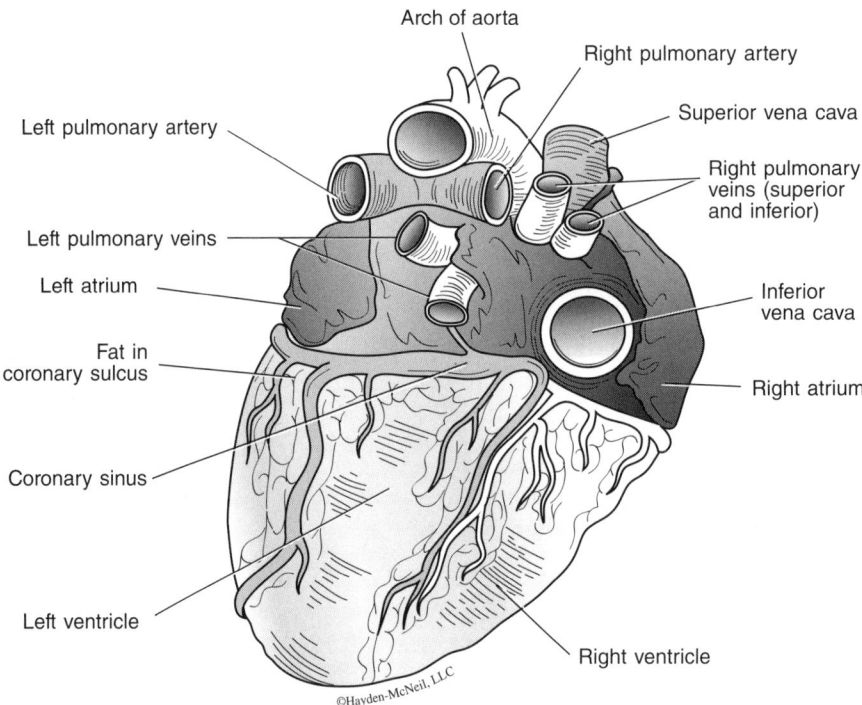

Figure 11-19. The human heart—posterior view.

Sectional Anatomy of the Heart

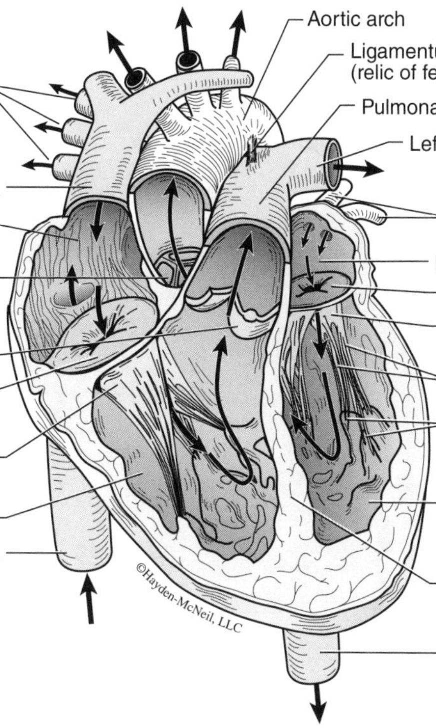

Figure 11-20. The human heart—anterior view (interior).

C. Blood Supply to the Heart—Coronary Circulation

The wall of the heart, like any other tissue, has its own blood vessels. The **right and left coronary arteries** branch from the aorta just distal to the aortic semilunar valve. The left coronary artery supplies blood to the left atrium and both ventricles while the right coronary artery delivers blood to the right atrium and both ventricles. Blood drains into the cardiac veins, which empty into the **coronary sinus**. The coronary sinus then drains into the right atrium.

Exercise A—Dissection of the Mammalian Heart

You and your partner obtain a dissecting pan, a blunt probe, and either the heart of a pig or the heart of a sheep (you need to look at both of them). Using the figure of the heart in the manual, identify the following structures. Before you begin your examination, make sure you have the heart oriented correctly. That means base up, apex down, and a clear distinction of what is right and what is left.

Identify the following:

_____ right atrium	_____ pulmonary semilunar valve
_____ left atrium	_____ aortic semilunar valve
_____ right ventricle	_____ aorta
_____ left ventricle	_____ superior vena cava
_____ tricuspid valve	_____ inferior vena cava
_____ bicuspid valve	_____ pulmonary veins
_____ chordae tendineae	_____ pulmonary artery
_____ papillary muscles	_____ interventricular septum

Hint: In order to identify the veins and arteries of the heart, use your blunt probe or fingers and stick it in an opening leading into the heart. Next, find the end of the probe, determine the chamber in which it is located, and identify the vessel.

Exercise B—Comparison of the Microscopic Structures of an Artery and a Vein

You and your partner obtain a microscope and a slide of an artery and of a vein. Draw what you observe.

Exercise C

Trace the blood flow through the human heart in the figure below. Label the parts of the heart you must move the blood through.

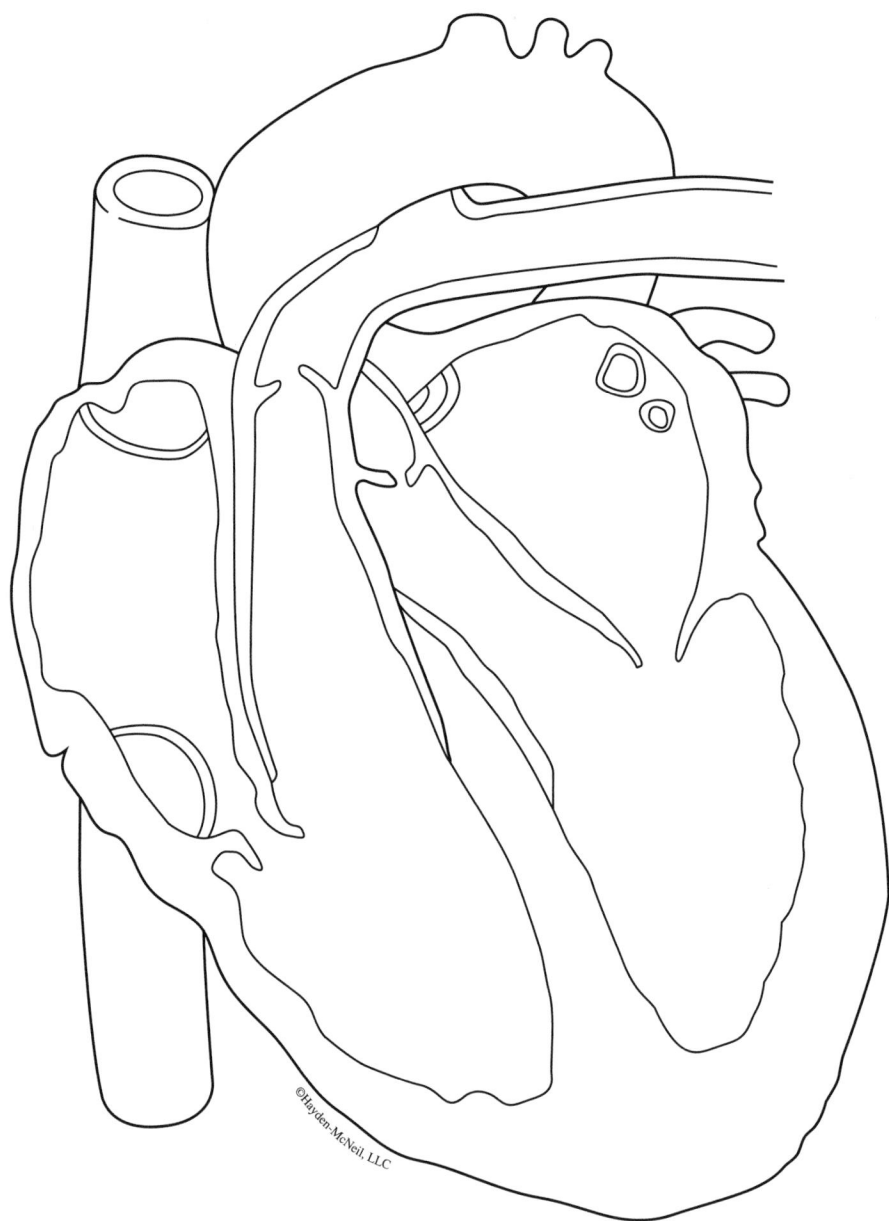

©Hayden-McNeil, LLC

Exercise D—Observation of Microcirculation

Procedure

1. Goldfish were anesthetized by your TAs (they were soaked in methanesulfonate [MS-222]). Wrap the fish (except for the mouth and tail) in dripping wet cotton. (Note: Do not allow the fish to dry out. Keep the cotton protecting it moist!) Place the fish in a Petri dish. Place the dish on the microscope so that the fish's tail is over the hole in the stage. We want to illuminate the capillary beds in this region.

2. Focus on the tail with the low-power objective (10×) of your microscope. Note the movement of blood through the blood vessels. (Examine the capillary circulation.) Identify the arterioles, capillaries, and venules.

Observations

How do you distinguish between the various vessel types?

Sketch the network of blood vessels below and indicate the direction of blood flow.

The smallest vessels are the **capillaries**. They are *just wide enough to permit the passage of a single file of blood cells.* What is the advantage of having red blood cells pass through the capillaries in single file?

Follow the capillary in the direction in which the blood is flowing. It will join a slightly larger blood vessel called a **venule**.

What is the relation between the diameters of the red blood cells and the capillaries?

What is the relation between the diameters of the red blood cells and the arterioles or venules?

What significance might this relation have with regard to the exchange of gases and other products?

Why are exchanges between the surrounding tissues and the blood more likely to occur in the capillaries than in the arteries or veins?

Make notes on the relative velocity of the blood flow in the arterioles, capillaries, and venules. List them as slowest, fastest, etc.

Exercise E

The following is a list of the blood vessels you may be asked to identify. Be sure to be able to identify both right and left arteries and be sure to know which arteries/veins are singular.

Structure name		Structure name	
aorta		anterior tibial vein	
brachiocephalic artery (trunk)		posterior tibial vein	
common carotid artery		femoral vein	
subclavian artery		deep femoral	
axillary artery		great saphenous vein	
brachial artery		internal iliac vein	
radial artery		external iliac vein	
ulnar artery		common iliac vein	
celiac artery (trunk)		inferior vena cava	
splenic artery		gonadal vein	
hepatic artery		renal vein	
superior mesenteric artery		hepatic vein	
renal artery		radial vein	
gonadal artery		ulnar vein	
inferior mesenteric artery		median antebrachial vein	
common iliac artery		brachial vein	
internal iliac artery		median cubital vein	
external iliac artery		basilic vein	
femoral artery		cephalic vein	
deep femoral artery		axillary vein	
popliteal artery		subclavian vein	
anterior tibial artery		brachiocephalic vein	
posterior tibial artery		superior vena cava	
vertebral artery		coronary sinus	
internal carotid artery		coronary artery	
basilar artery		dural sinuses	
circle of Willis		internal jugular vein	
middle cerebral artery		external jugular vein	
anterior cerebral artery		vertebral vein	
posterior cerebral artery			
anterior communicating artery			
posterior communicating artery			

LABORATORY 12

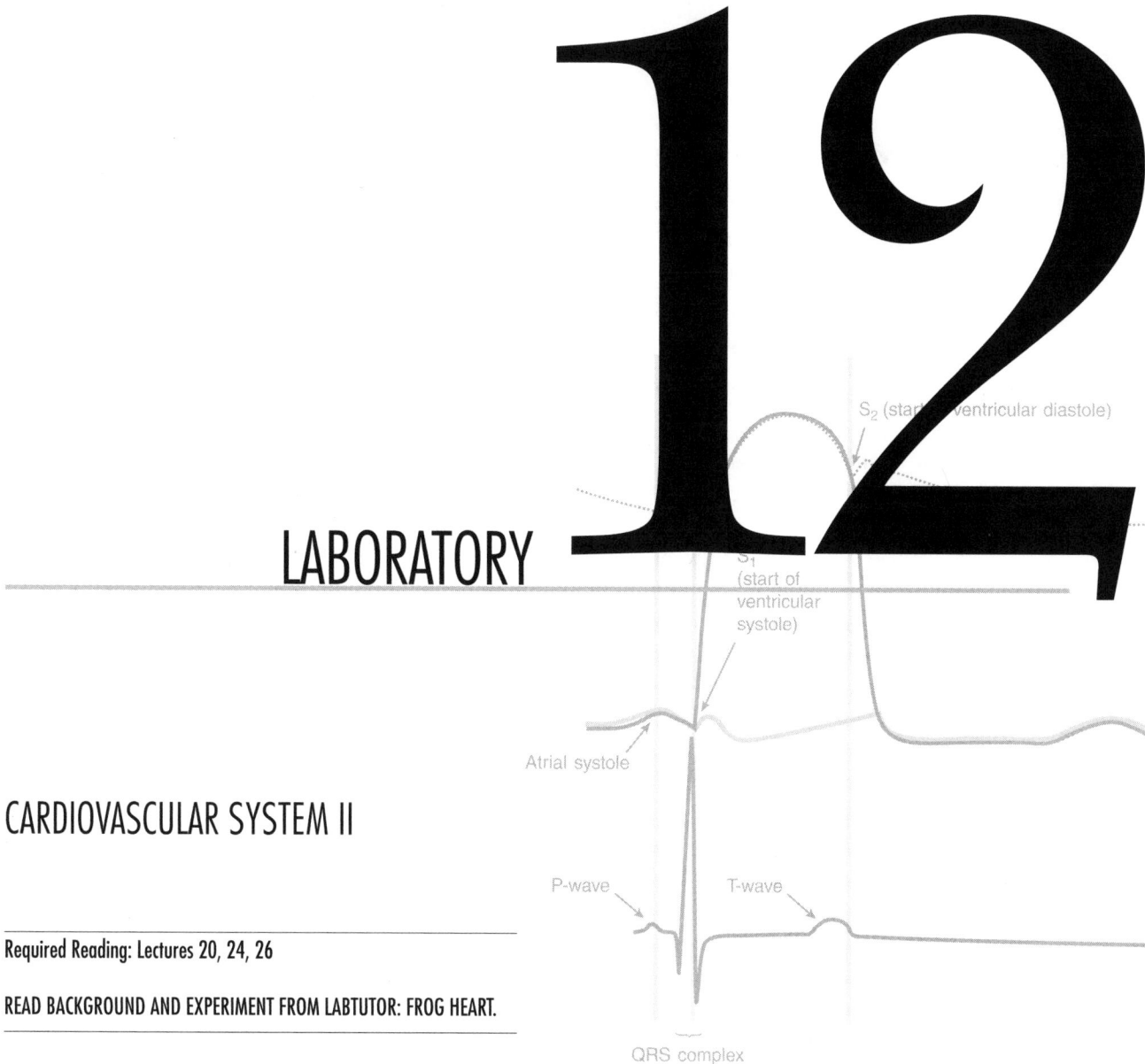

S_2 (start of ventricular diastole)

S_1 (start of ventricular systole)

Atrial systole

P-wave

T-wave

QRS complex

CARDIOVASCULAR SYSTEM II

Required Reading: Lectures 20, 24, 26

READ BACKGROUND AND EXPERIMENT FROM LABTUTOR: FROG HEART.

Objectives

1. Review the autonomic nervous system in Lecture 20.

2. List the **neurotransmitters** found in neurons of the sympathetic branch of the autonomic nervous system.

3. List the **neurotransmitters** found in neurons of the parasympathetic branch of the autonomic nervous system.

4. List the sympathetic and parasympathetic **neurotransmitter receptors**.

5. Compare the actions of the sympathetic and parasympathetic nervous systems on the **cardiovascular system**.

6. Explain how the heart beat is regulated and synchronized.

7. Explain with **diagrams** the action of the **heart valves** during contraction and relaxation of the heart.

8. **Draw a graph** illustrating the changes in **pressure** in the **aorta, left ventricle**, and **left atrium** during the cardiac cycle.

9. Observe and interpret a **record of the output from the force transducer** attached to the beating heart of a frog.

10. Observe and interpret the **effects of temperature and various drugs** on the heart.

I. Autonomic Nervous System, Heart Rate, and Myocardial Contractility

Note: you should be familiar with all aspects of the autonomic nervous system in Lecture 20.

The heart is *innervated* by the sympathetic and parasympathetic branches of the autonomic nervous systems. The action of these two branches is summarized in Figure 12-1.

Central control of the heart is primarily from a region of the medulla called the **vasomotor, cardiac center**. Output from this center controls both sympathetic outflow to the heart and the flow of nerve impulses down the vagus nerve. In turn, the vasomotor center is under higher control from many areas of the brain, including the **hypothalamus, reticular** formation of the brain stem, and the **limbic** system.

Actions of the Autonomic Nervous System of the Heart

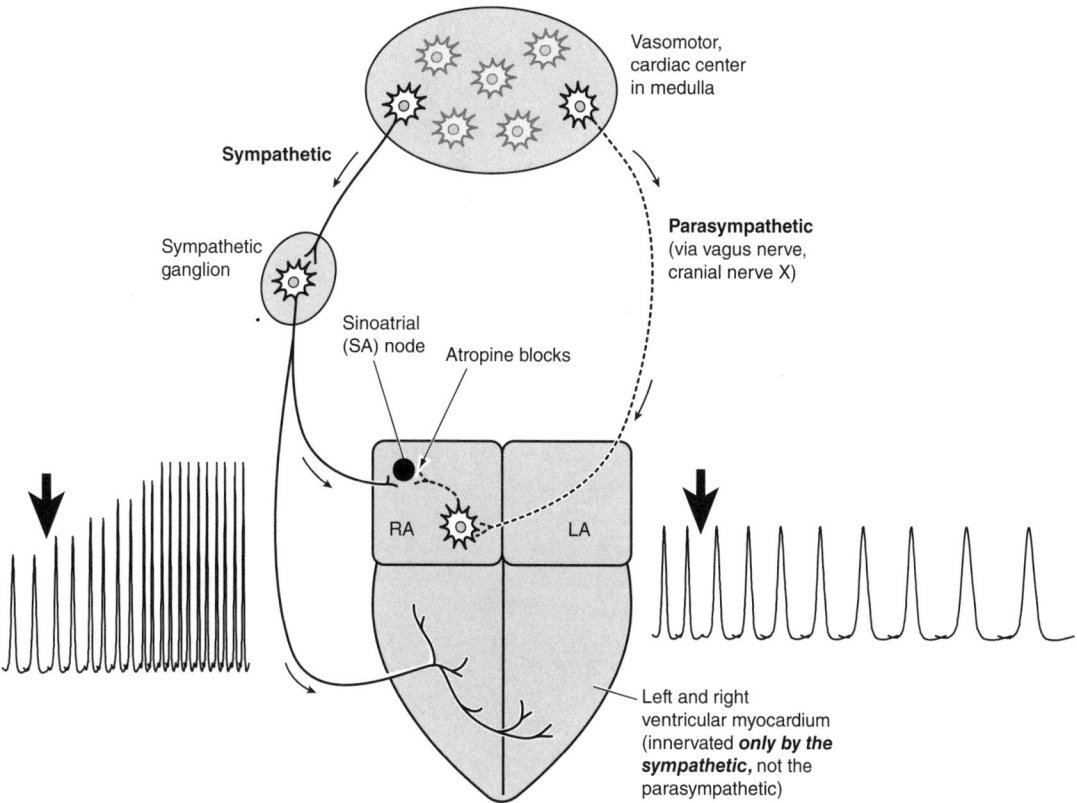

Sympathetic

1. Accelerates heart rate (SA node).
2. Increases force of contraction of the ventricular myocardium.
3. *Norepinephrine* is released at sympathetic nerve terminals and acts on β-*adrenergic* receptors in the pacemaker cells of the sinoatrial node and on cardiac muscle cells of the ventricles.
4. Action of norepinephrine (and epinephrine) on the heart is blocked by β-*blockers*.

Parasympathetic

1. Slows heart rate (SA node).
2. Does *not* alter force of contraction of ventricles because it doesn't innervate them.
3. *Acetylcholine* is released at parasympathetic nerve terminals and acts on *nicotinic* receptors on intramural neurons which also release acetylcholine, which binds to *muscarinic* receptors in the pacemaker cells of SA node.
4. Muscarinic receptors are blocked by *atropine*.

Figure 12-1.

Experiments on the Isolated Heart

A skeletal muscle such as the biceps brachii does not contract unless it receives a nervous command. In contrast, the heart's contraction and relaxation is entirely spontaneous.

This contraction and relaxation can be modulated by the autonomic nervous system and various pharmacologic agents. The sympathetic nervous system increases heart rate, while the parasympathetic nervous system decreases heart rate. This is called a **chronotropic** effect. The sympathetic nervous system also increases **myocardial contractility**, causing the heart to beat more forcefully and reducing the end-systolic volume. This is called the **inotropic** effect.

Norepinephrine (= noradrenalin) is the neurotransmitter released by sympathetic postganglionic nerve terminals in the heart.

Preganglionic sympathetic nerve fibers also cause the release of **epinephrine** (= adrenalin) from neurosecretory cells in the adrenal medulla. Epinephrine is really a hormone that is swept around the body by the bloodstream. Chemically, epinephrine is very similar to norepinephrine, from which it is synthesized by the addition of just one methyl group. The enzyme is *N-methyltransferase*, which is only present in the adrenal medulla.

Norepinephrine   **Epinephrine**

The actions of epinephrine are very similar to norepinephrine. Both of these substances bind to **adrenergic** receptors in the plasma membranes of target cells. **Alpha-adrenergic** receptors are found on the smooth muscle cells of blood vessels, and **beta-adrenergic** receptors are found in the heart and gastrointestinal smooth muscle.

Acetylcholine is the neurotransmitter released at parasympathetic postganglionic nerve terminals. Acetylcholine binds to **muscarinic** receptors in the pacemaker cells of the sinoatrial node and in many other target cells. The **nicotinic** acetylcholine receptor is found on the plasma membranes of neurons in autonomic ganglia and also at the motor endplate of the neuromuscular junction.

Calcium—you also need to know about the important role of calcium in the contraction of cardiac muscle. Calcium enters cardiac muscle during the plateau phase of the cardiac action potential. This increases intra-cellular calcium levels, which has the effect of releasing even more calcium from stores in the sarcoplasmic reticulum. A rise of intra-cellular calcium leads to contraction of cardiac muscle, the effect being mediated by the proteins troponin and tropomyosin (read my notes—you are expected to understand and explain this). When cardiac muscle relaxes, the calcium is either pumped out of the cardiac muscle or back into the sarcoplasmic reticulum.

Certain substances called **calcium channel blockers** can interfere with this intracellular rise of calcium, and can therefore stop cardiac muscle from beating. One example of a calcium channel blocker is **verapamil**. Other substances, such as the cardiac glycosides (e.g., **digitalis**), can increase intracellular calcium levels. This can lead to an increase in myocardial contractility, a useful effect in the failing heart. However, if the dose is too high, these substances can produce "calcium overload," and can stop the heart from beating because it is unable to relax.

As we might expect, a heart that has been removed from the body will continue to beat as long as it is provided with **oxygen** and **nutrients**, such as **glucose**. If it is a mammalian heart, then it must also be maintained at body temperature, about 37 degrees Centigrade (Celsius). The experiments you will be doing will utilize an isolated frog heart.

The Drugs You Will Investigate in the Isolated Heart Preparation

The purpose of these experiments is to investigate the effects of the following agents on the isolated heart:

1. **epinephrine (= adrenalin)**: released into the bloodstream by sympathetic stimulation of neurosecretory (chromaffin) cells in the adrenal medulla. Chemically similar to the sympathetic neurotransmitter norepinephrine. Binds to alpha- and beta-adrenergic receptors in the plasma membranes of target cells (such as those in the sinoatrial node).

2. **propranolol**: a beta-adrenergic receptor blocker, belonging to the class of drugs known colloquially as "beta-blockers." These drugs are used to treat a variety of heart conditions.

3. **acetylcholine**: parasympathetic neurotransmitter that binds to nicotinic and muscarinic receptors in the plasma membranes of target cells.

4. **atropine**: muscarinic receptor blocker.

5. **verapamil**: calcium channel blocker that reduces calcium entry into cardiac muscle cells during the plateau phase of the cardiac action potential. This calcium is needed to release more calcium from the sarcoplasmic reticulum. Calcium ions bind to troponin C, triggering a chain of events that finally leads to the unmasking of myosin-binding sites on the actin molecule.

6. **ouabain**: component of digitalis; inhibits the sodium-potassium ATP-ase, boosting intracellular calcium and increasing myocardial contractility in a failing heart.

7. **phentolamine**: alpha-adrenergic receptor blocker.

Although you will not be using all of them in your investigations, you will be expected to predict and understand the effects of these drugs/neurotransmitters:

II. The Cardiac Cycle

The following are the stages of the cardiac cycle.

Stage 1. Filling

> The atria and ventricles are relaxed. The mitral and tricuspid valves (the A-V valves) are wide open, the aortic and pulmonary semilunar valves are closed. This state is called **diastole**. The pressure in the venae cavae and atria is slightly higher than in the ventricles. Therefore, blood rushes passively from the venae cavae into the atria and on into the ventricles. About 70% of the ventricular filling occurs during this phase.

Stage 2. Atrial systole

The atria contract, topping up the amount of blood in the ventricles by another 30%, filling them completely. The atria then relax, a stage known as **atrial diastole**.

Stage 3. Onset of ventricular systole: isovolumic ventricular contraction

This is the first phase of **ventricular systole**. When the ventricles contract, pressure rises in their interiors and exceeds the pressure in the atria. This causes the A-V valves to close, which occurs passively in response to the pressure differential. As the ventricles contract, the papillary muscles also contract, pulling on and tensing the chordae tendineae. This prevents the A-V valves from turning inside out into the atria.

The ventricles continue to contract with all four valves closed, raising the pressure still more. At this stage, blood is flowing neither into, nor out of the ventricles, and the volume of blood in them does not change.

Stage 4. Ejection

Pressure in the ventricles reaches the point where it exceeds the pressure in the pulmonary arteries and aorta. The semilunar valves open passively, and blood is ejected from the ventricles into the pulmonary and systemic circuits, at first rapidly, then at a reduced rate. As blood is ejected, the pressure in the ventricles starts to fall, an effect that is accentuated when the ventricles cease to contract and enter the phase known as **ventricular diastole**.

Stage 5. Isovolumic relaxation

Pressure in the ventricles drops below the pressures in the pulmonary arteries and the aorta. The result is that the semilunar valves close passively. The pressure in the ventricles continues to fall. At this stage, all four valves are closed and blood is flowing neither into, nor out of the ventricles, and the volume of blood in them does not change.

Stage 6. Onset of filling, Stage 1

Once the pressure in the ventricles falls below the pressure in the atria, the A-V valves open, allowing blood to rush into them and on into the relaxed ventricles. Filling with blood is at first rapid, then its rate is reduced. This phase of reduced filling is sometimes called **diastasis**.

This figure shows the cardiac cycle only for the *left* atrium and *left* ventricle, where blood is ejected into the aorta. The same events are going on simultaneously in the right atrium and right ventricle, where blood is ejected into the pulmonary trunk.

1. Ventricular filling

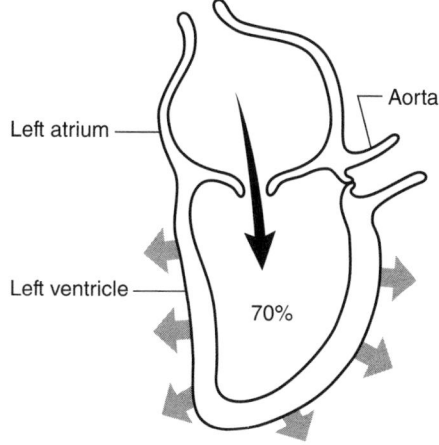

2. Atrial systole

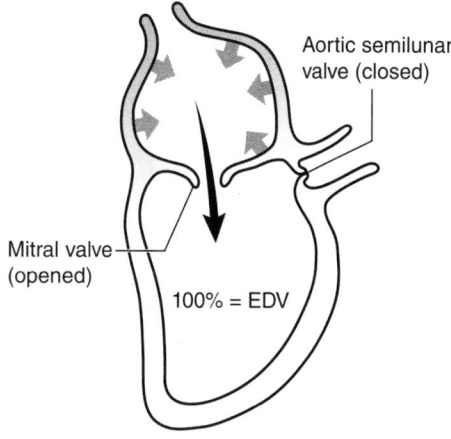

3. Isovolumic ventricular contraction
(no volume change)

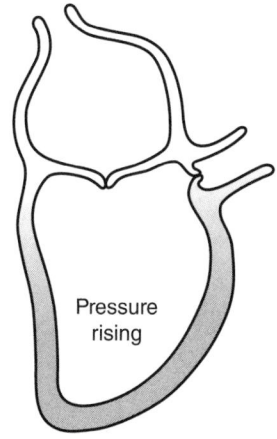

4. Ejection into aorta
(rapid, then reduced)

5. Isovolumic ventricular relaxation
(no volume change)

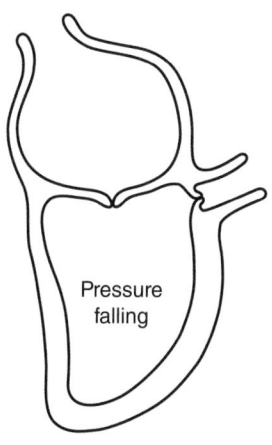

6. Ventricular filling
(rapid, then reduced, diastasis)

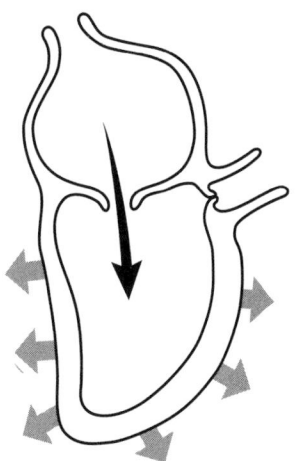

©Hayden-McNeil, LLC

Figure 12-2.

The changes in pressure in the aorta, left ventricle and left atrium during one cardiac cycle are shown in the following figure. Just after the aortic semilunar valve closes, there is a rapid oscillation of aortic pressure that is sometimes called the incisura or dicrotic notch.

Intracardiac Pressure Curves and Stages in Filling and Ejection

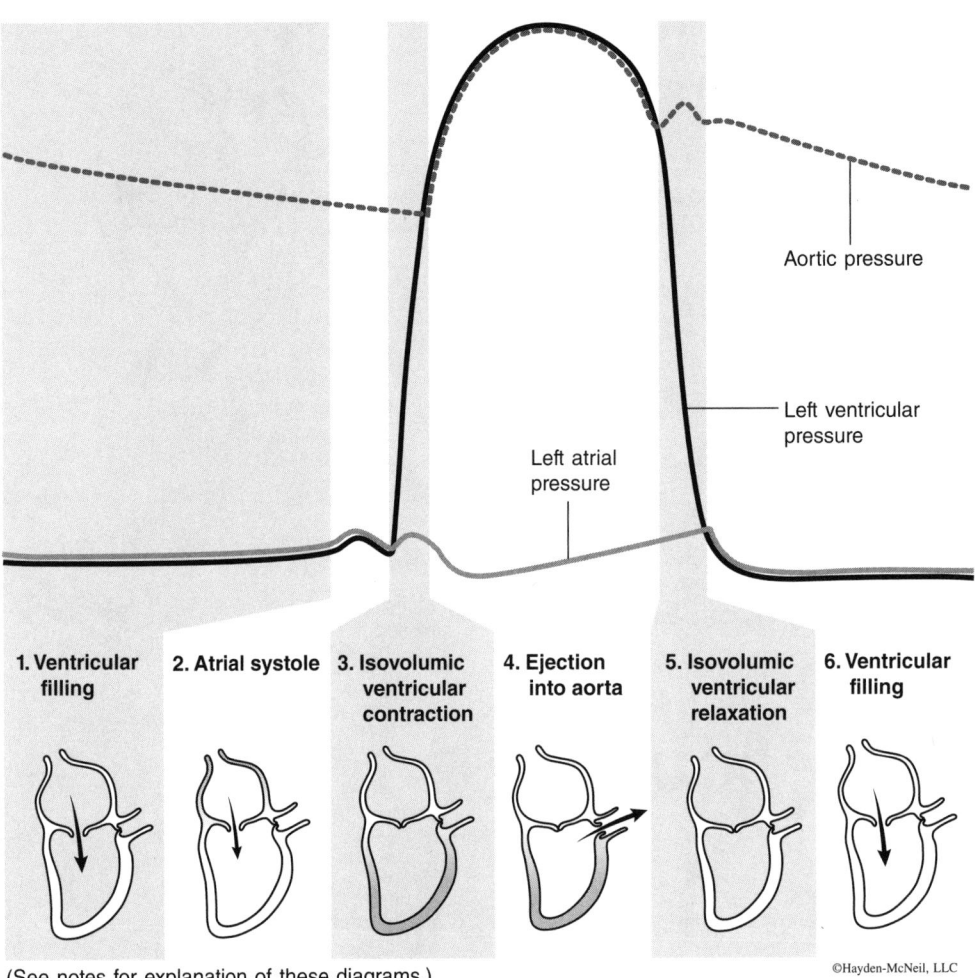

(See notes for explanation of these diagrams.)

©Hayden-McNeil, LLC

Figure 12-3.

III. Four Factors that Determine Blood Pressure

The term **blood pressure** in the context of the present discussion refers to the **mean systemic arterial blood pressure (MAP)**.

The blood pressure is determined mainly by the following four factors (see diagram in Lecture 27).

1. **Cardiac output**—cardiac output = stroke volume × heart rate

2. **Total peripheral resistance**—determined mainly by vasoconstriction or vasodilation of the arterioles

   mean arterial pressure = cardiac output × total peripheral resistance

3. **Capacity of the venous system**—affected by venous constriction and dilation. If the capacity suddenly increases, as might happen with venous dilation, then the blood pressure will drop

4. **Volume of fluid in the circulatory system**—reduced by hemorrhage, increased by **antidiuretics**, which reduce the volume of urine. Certain hormones have an important effect on the volume of fluid in the body. If the volume of fluid in the circulation increases there will be an increase in blood pressure.

Exercise A—Lab Tutor: Frog Heart

Introduction to Experiment

Cardiac muscle differs from skeletal muscle in that is has *inherent rhythmicity*. That is, it contracts and relaxes automatically in the absence of neural stimulation.

Although the heart beats automatically, many chemicals and compounds influence its force and rate of contraction. These include acetylcholine, epinephrine, norepinephrine, etc.

The purpose of our experiment is to determine the effect of epinephrine, acetylcholine, and atropine on the rate and force of contraction of the frog heart. We will use frog heart Ringer's solution to wash the heart and the thoracic cavity between the additions of the various drugs.

Background

The frog heart has two atria but only **one** ventricle. However, in some ways it is similar to the mammalian heart. Stimulation of the **vagus** nerve (cranial nerve X) causes the heart to slow down. This nerve is part of the parasympathetic branch of the autonomic nervous system, and its nerve endings release acetylcholine. The acetylcholine binds to muscarinic receptors on the pacemaker cells of the sinus node. The effect of vagus stimulation or of directly applied acetylcholine is abolished by the muscarinic antagonist atropine.

In parallel to the mammalian heart, the frog heart may accelerate in response to sympathetic stimulation or exposure to epinephrine (very little norepinephrine is present in the frog). However, the actions of epinephrine are complicated by variation in the frogs' sensitivity at various times of year. It is usually reported, for example, that in spring and early summer there is only a slight response. The responses get progressively stronger as the season progresses. So the response to epinephrine in your frog preparation may not be very strong or may not be observable at all.

A. Preparing the Frog Heart

Because of time constraints the frog has already been set up for you. The frog was first decapitated. A frog is clinically dead as soon as its head is severed from its body. We then pithed the frog by inserting a probe down its spinal cord to destroy any spinal reflexes.

Two horizontal incisions were made along the lower abdomen and just above the sternum. A third was made vertically, connecting the first two.

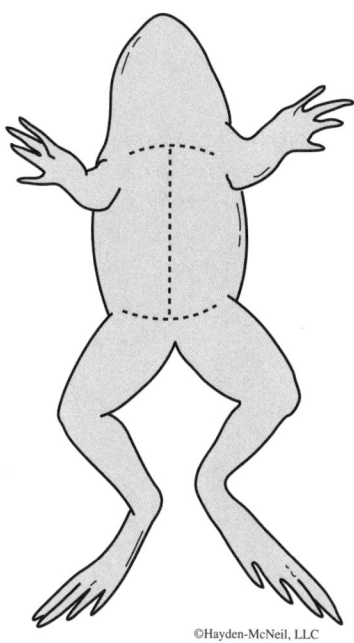

Figure 12-4.

The TAs cut through the pericardium to gain access to the heart. We pierced the heart at its apex with a steel needle attached to a length of filament. The needle was bent to form a hook, so that the heart wouldn't slip loose.

The other end of the filament was tied to the **force transducer** on the ring stand (the force transducer has already been connected to the **amplifier box**). The filament must be taut, so that we do not have any disturbance during the recording. The heart is at an angle to the force transducer to reduce the chance of tearing the heart tissue.

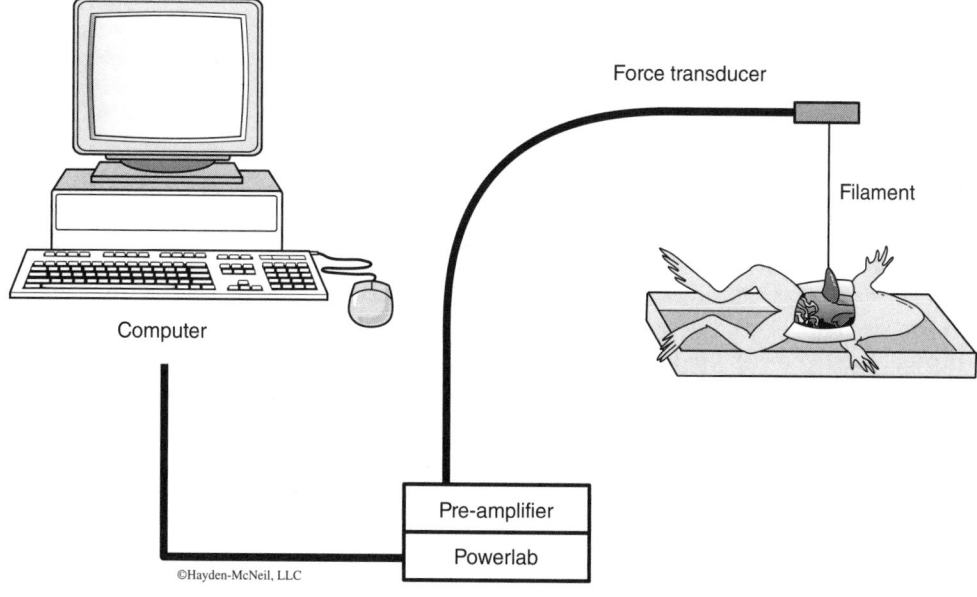

Figure 12-5.

The purpose of connecting the frog heart by a filament to the force transducer is to record the contractions of the atria and ventricle that are produced as two successive peaks in the recordings.

The atrial contraction appears as a small peak on the screen and the ventricular contraction as a larger peak that follows the atrial peak. The following are examples of heart contractions that we obtained from two different frogs. Both the rate and amplitudes of these contractions differ. The amplitude of the atrial beat is enhanced in the second set of recordings by the tension and orientation of the heart setup.

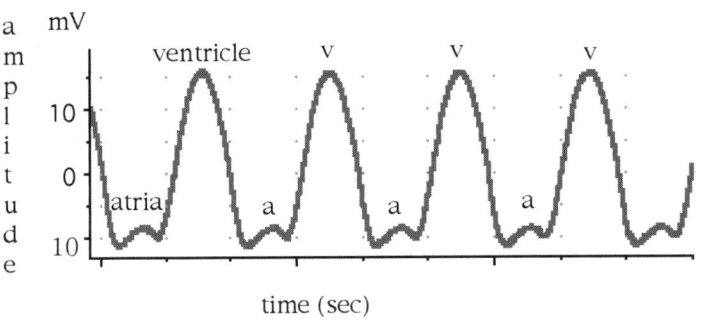

Figure 12-6.

OR

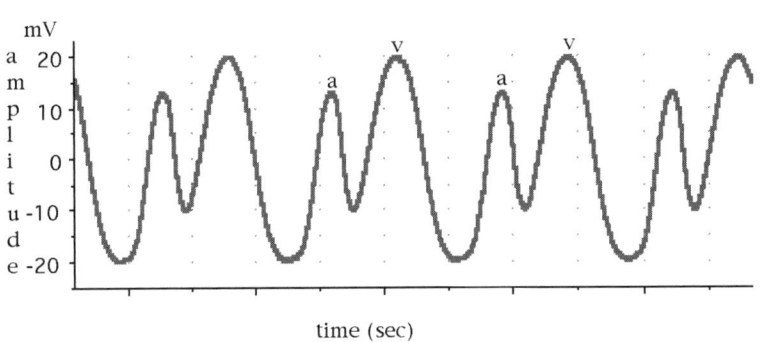

Figure 12-7.

The **height** (**amplitude**) of these peaks is directly related to the strength of the contraction. The **rate** (**frequency**) can be determined from the time lapse between ventricular peaks. You will be making these calculations.

The **conduction time** from the atria to the ventricle is the time between the atrial and ventricular peaks in the recording of each cycle. In this way, the effects of various drugs on the **strength of contraction, frequency of heartbeats**, and the **A-V conduction time** through the heart can be determined.

Atropine, epinephrine, and acetylcholine are dangerous drugs. Be very careful not to spill any of the solutions. Do not allow the solutions to come into contact with the skin. Wear gloves at all times!

Be very cautious in applying these drugs, because they are very potent and may stop the heart completely if an overdose is given. Acetylcholine is especially potent. If the heart does stop, apply epinephrine to restore the beat. After the effect is recorded, rinse the heart with frog Ringer's and allow the heart to return to normal before the next drug is applied.

B. Doing the Experiment and Collecting the Data

WARNING: You **must** wear gloves when handling any of the drugs in this experiment. **Alert** your TA immediately of any spills of these drugs on any surface or especially on clothing or skin.

What is frog Ringer's solution?

This solution is used to bathe the heart and also to make up your drugs. Its components and their concentrations are given below.

	g/liter distilled water
Sodium chloride	6.50
Potassium chloride	0.14
Sodium bicarbonate	0.16
Glucose	2.00
Calcium chloride	0.21

This solution approximates the extracellular fluid composition in the frog, and it also contains glucose, which is used as a fuel for muscle contraction.

LABORATORY 13

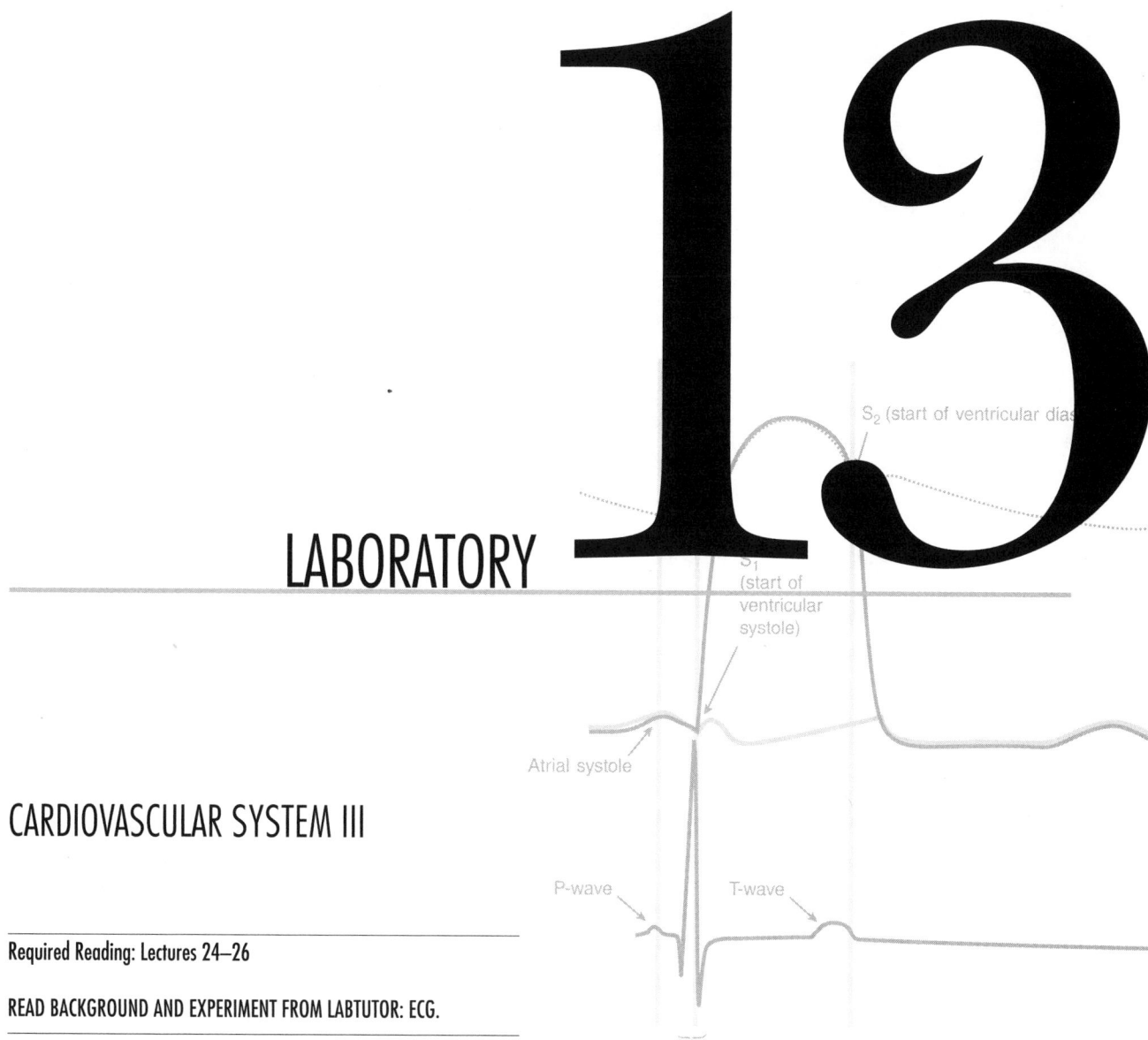

S_2 (start of ventricular dias...

S_1 (start of ventricular systole)

Atrial systole

P-wave

T-wave

QRS complex

CARDIOVASCULAR SYSTEM III

Required Reading: Lectures 24–26

READ BACKGROUND AND EXPERIMENT FROM LABTUTOR: ECG.

Objectives

1. Describe how **blood pressure** is measured in humans; name the **instrument** most commonly used in the doctor's office.

2. List the **heart sounds**, and how they are produced.

3. Define what is meant by a **murmur**, and give examples of the causes of **systolic** and **diastolic** murmurs.

4. List and define **11 important parameters** that relate to the functioning of the heart, and **give equations** for calculating them.

5. List the four important factors that affect **cardiac output**.

6. Define **preload**.

7. Define **afterload**, and list three factors that affect it.

8. Define **myocardial contractility**, and three factors that increase it.

9. Explain **Starling's Law of the Heart**.

10. Describe how the **sympathetic** and **parasympathetic** branches of the autonomic nervous system affect the **heart and blood vessels, and the effects (if any) on the mean arterial pressure, capacity and cardiac output.**

11. Describe the electrical conduction system of the heart and the sequence of events that follows depolarization of cells in the **sinoatrial node**.

12. Describe how an electrocardiogram is **recorded** and list the **twelve leads**.

13. **Draw an electrocardiogram**, label its components, and describe what they represent.

14. Relate the waves of the **electrocardiogram to the pressure waves in the heart, to the opening and closing of the valves, and to the heart sounds.**

15. Define a cardiac **arrhythmia** (dysrhythmia).

16. Following what event might you see an elevated or depressed **S-T segment**, possibly with an **inverted T wave** and an **increased Q wave**?

17. Explain the **resistance** of the circulatory system and how it affects mean arterial pressure.

18. Explain the **capacity** of the circulatory system.

19. **Draw a diagram** of the circulatory system, and indicate the peripheral resistance and capacity components.

20. List four factors that determine **blood pressure**.

21. Describe the two basic **systems** that govern blood pressure.

22. Explain the **baroreceptor reflex**, and describe its functional importance.

23. **Draw a diagram** illustrating how the baroreceptor reflex operates if blood pressure suddenly increases above normal.

24. **Draw a diagram** illustrating how the baroreceptor reflex operates if blood pressure suddenly decreases below normal. List the possible causes of a decrease in blood pressure.

25. Record the electrocardiogram, list the waves of the electrocardiogram (sketch it from memory), and how these waves correlate with the mechanical events during the cardiac cycle.

26. Measure the finger pulse, measure pulse rate from these data and from an electrocardiogram, and carry out an experiment to understand the anatomy of the blood supply to the fingers.

27. Carry out a simple experiment to demonstrate the operation of the baroreceptor reflex when standing up from a prone position.

I. Introduction

In this laboratory, we will observe and measure the finger pulse, heart sounds, blood pressure, and ECG.

II. Heart Sounds

The sounds of the cardiac cycle are heard with the aid of a stethoscope, and the technique is called **auscultation**. Instead of a stethoscope, a microphone can be used, and the sounds recorded to produce a **phonocardiogram**.

The two major sounds emitted by a normally functioning heart are S_1 and S_2. Two other sounds (S_3 and S_4) are difficult to hear in a normal heart, although they can be detected with a microphone. They can sometimes be heard in certain heart disorders, such as congestive heart failure.

1. **The first heart sound, S_1,** occurs at the onset of ventricular systole. It is due to the **closure of the A-V valves** (the mitral and tricuspid valves). The mitral valve closes slightly ahead of the tricuspid valve, generating two components to S_1 that are called M_1 (mitral) and T_1 (tricuspid). There are certain locations of the stethoscope bell that enable us to hear M_1 and T_1 more clearly.

2. **The second heart sound, S_2,** occurs when the **semilunar valves close**, and marks the end of ventricular systole. The aortic valve closes slightly ahead of the pulmonic valve, generating two components to S_2 that are called A_2 (aortic) and P_2 (pulmonary). These two components of S_2 can be heard more clearly at certain locations on the chest wall.

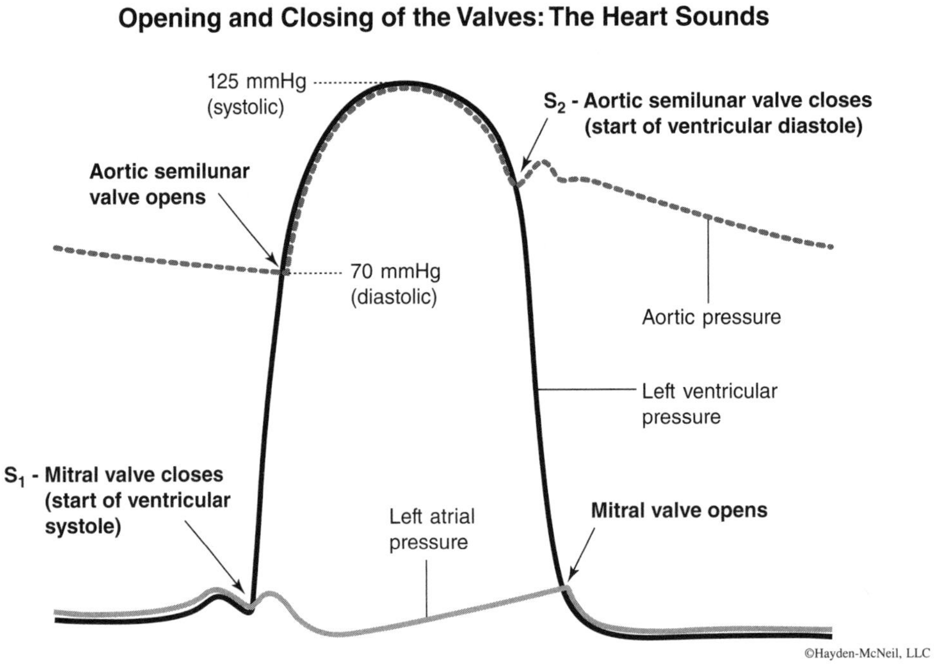

Opening and Closing of the Valves: The Heart Sounds

125 mmHg
(systolic)

S_2 - Aortic semilunar valve closes
(start of ventricular diastole)

**Aortic semilunar
valve opens**

70 mmHg
(diastolic)

Aortic pressure

Left ventricular
pressure

S_1 - **Mitral valve closes
(start of ventricular
systole)**

Left atrial
pressure

Mitral valve opens

©Hayden-McNeil, LLC

Figure 13-1.

Murmurs

It is unlikely that we will hear heart murmurs in the lab. Murmurs are abnormal sounds that may be heard during ventricular systole or diastole. There are many types, but we shall describe just two. See diagram below.

1. **Systolic murmurs**—a systolic murmur can occur when the tricuspid or mitral valves do not close properly during systole. This causes blood to regurgitate into the corresponding atrium during ventricular systole and during isovolumic ventricular relaxation, a time when the A-V valves should be tightly closed.

2. **Diastolic murmurs**—a diastolic murmur can occur when the aortic or pulmonic (pulmonary) valves do not close properly. This allows blood to regurgitate into the ventricles during ventricular diastole, a time when the aortic and pulmonic valves should be tightly closed.

Heart Murmurs

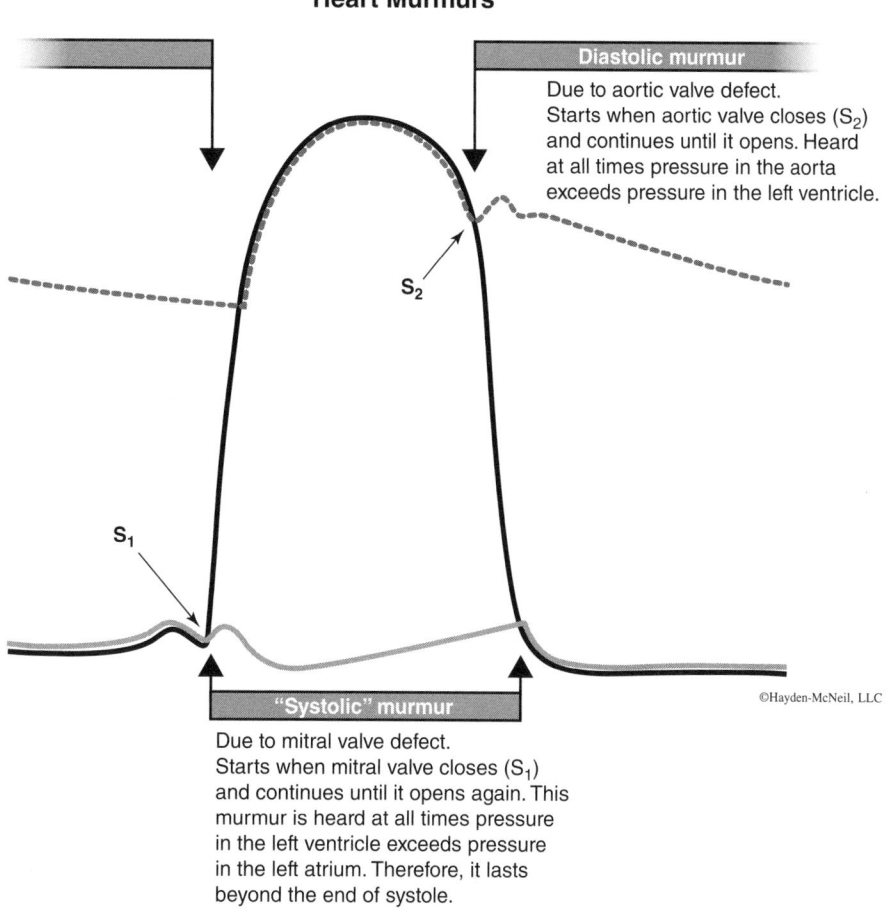

Diastolic murmur

Due to aortic valve defect. Starts when aortic valve closes (S$_2$) and continues until it opens. Heard at all times pressure in the aorta exceeds pressure in the left ventricle.

S$_2$

S$_1$

©Hayden-McNeil, LLC

"Systolic" murmur

Due to mitral valve defect. Starts when mitral valve closes (S$_1$) and continues until it opens again. This murmur is heard at all times pressure in the left ventricle exceeds pressure in the left atrium. Therefore, it lasts beyond the end of systole.

Figure 13-2.

III. Correlation of the Waves of the ECG with the Events of the Cardiac Cycle

The electrical events precede the mechanical events. Therefore, atrial systole occurs during the declining phase of the P-wave, and the onset of ventricular systole on the declining phase of the QRS complex. At this point, we hear S$_1$ as the mitral valve closes.

The remaining correlations between the ECG and the cardiac cycle are illustrated in the following figure.

The Electrocardiogram, Cardiac Cycle, and the Intracardiac Pressure Curves

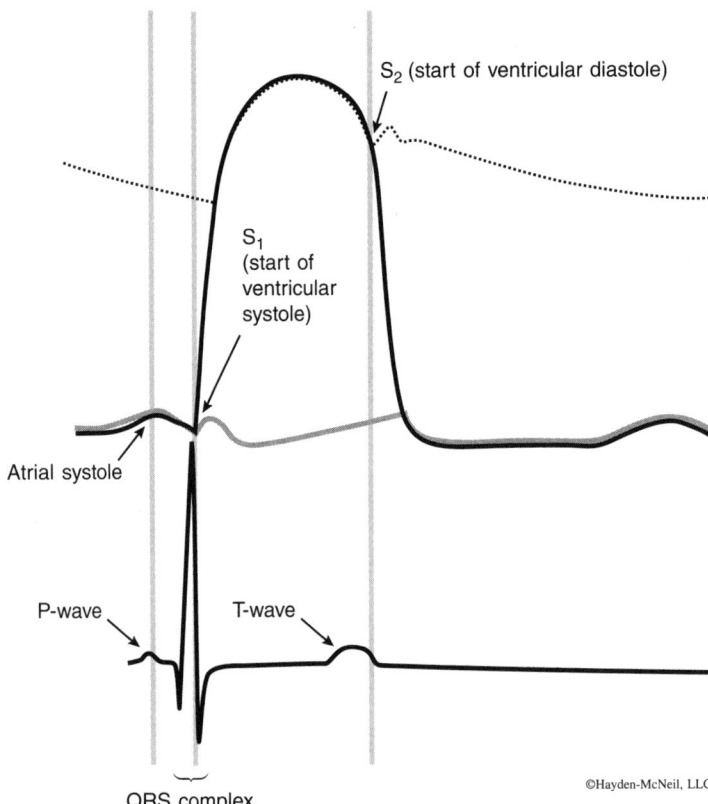

Figure 13-3.

IV. List of Important Parameters

Be warned that examination questions in lecture and in the laboratory may involve knowing what these parameters represent, and also carrying out calculations with them.

Parameter	Measured in	Example
1. Heart rate (HR)	beats per minute	70
2. Cardiac output (CO)	liters per minute	5.6
3. Stroke volume (SV)	ml per beat	80
4. End diastolic volume (EDV)	ml	145
5. End systolic volume (ESV)	ml	65
6. Diastolic aortic pressure	mm mercury	65
7. Systolic aortic pressure	mm mercury	125
8. Mean blood pressure	mm mercury	85
9. Pulse pressure	mm mercury	60
10. Total peripheral resistance (TPR)	mm mercury per liter per min	15.2
11. Ejection fraction		0.55

Calculations

a. **Stroke volume** = end diastolic volume – end systolic volume

b. **Pulse pressure** = systolic aortic pressure – diastolic aortic pressure

c. **Mean blood pressure** (mean arterial pressure) = diastolic aortic pressure + 1/3 pulse pressure

d. **Cardiac output** = heart rate × stroke volume

e. **Total peripheral resistance (systemic vascular resistance)** = mean blood pressure/cardiac output

   Mean blood pressure (mean arterial pressure) = total peripheral resistance × cardiac output

   This is an important equation that helps you to understand **hypertension**. Generally, in hypertensives there is an increase in total peripheral resistance without much change in cardiac output.

f. **Ejection fraction** = stroke volume/end diastolic volume. A low ejection fraction (under 0,6) indicates that the heart is pumping inefficiently and may be failing.

V. Factors That Affect Cardiac Output

Cardiac output is the amount of blood pumped by the heart per minute. It is an important index of heart function. During a heart attack, for example, there is usually a drop in the cardiac output.

Four factors are important determinants of cardiac output.

1. Preload—the Amount of Blood Returning to the Heart, End-Diastolic Volume

This is known as **Starling's Law of the Heart**, after the English physiologist Ernest Starling.

Force of contraction and cardiac output increase with increasing preload (end diastolic volume) until the cardiac muscle fibers in the myocardium are overstretched and Starling's law fails (this can occur in congestive heart failure). Starling's law ensures that the heart pumps out the same volume of blood that it receives from the veins.

2. Afterload—Resistance to Ejection of Blood from the Ventricles

For the left ventricle, the resistance to ejection (afterload) is affected by the:

1. **Pressure in the aorta**—the higher the pressure, the higher the resistance, and the tougher it is for the heart to pump against it (like pumping up a bicycle tire)

2. **Total peripheral resistance (systemic vascular resistance)**—a major determinant of mean arterial pressure. Total peripheral resistance depends on arteriolar diameters, which are affected by vasoconstriction and vasodilation.

3. **Pathological changes** that lead to a narrowing (**stenosis**) of the aortic valve or the aorta itself.

3. Heart Rate

Since the cardiac output is the heart rate multiplied by the stroke volume, any factor that changes the heart rate is likely to change the cardiac output. This is illustrated in the following table.

Condition	Heart Rate (beats/min)	Stroke Volume (ml)	Cardiac Output (liters/min)
Rest	60	92	5.5
Exercise	90	97	8.7
	100	109	10.9
	120	112	13.7

In this table, the heart rate **doubles** during exercise (from 60 to 120 beats per minute). However, the cardiac output **more than doubles** because of an increased **stroke volume**, and goes up from 5.52 liters per minute to 13.74 liters per minute.

4. Myocardial Contractility (cardiac inotropic state)—Strength of Contraction at a Given Fiber Length

Myocardial contractility (cardiac inotropic state) is the force of contraction of the cardiac muscle at a **given fiber length**.

Myocardial contractility does not change during the operation of Starling's law of the heart, which is the result of increased force of contraction when the fibers **increase in length** during stretching.

Myocardial contractility is increased by a number of factors. They include:

1. **Norepinephrine** and **epinephrine** (increase the heart rate as well)

2. **Increased extracellular calcium**

3. **Digitalis**, which increases intracellular calcium.

VI. Blood Pressure Measurement in Humans

In the present context, blood pressure represents mean arterial pressure (MAP). In hospital intensive care units, needles or catheters may be introduced into peripheral arteries, or into the heart chambers, and the pressure measured directly with strain gauges or similar devices. Ordinarily, however, the blood pressure is measured indirectly by means of a **sphygmomanometer**. This consists of an inflatable bag contained in an inextensible cuff. The cuff is wrapped around the arm (occasionally the thigh), and inflated to a pressure somewhat in excess of arterial systolic pressure. This pressure is determined by a measuring device called a manometer. The pressure is then released slowly. When the pressure falls just below the systolic level, small spurts of blood escape through the brachial artery. They may either be detected by *palpating* (feeling with your fingertips) the radial artery at the wrist, or by listening with a **stethoscope** applied to the skin of the antecubital space over the brachial artery. This latter method is called **auscultation**. The sounds that are first heard are called **Korotkoff sounds**. The Korotkoff sounds disappear once the cuff pressure drops below diastolic pressure.

Systolic blood pressure is the maximum arterial pressure developed during cardiac systole. Diastolic blood pressure is the minimum arterial pressure observed during cardiac diastole. You will see blood pressure numbers written as 120/80 mmHg, indicating that the systolic pressure is 120 mmHg and the diastolic pressure is 80 mmHg. On most automatic blood pressure recording devices, the mean arterial pressure (MAP) is given as well.

According to three professional bodies, normal blood pressures are defined as follows.

Professional Body	Classifications	Systolic Values (mmHg)	Diastolic Values (mmHg)
European Society of Cardiology (ESC), 2013	Optimal	<120	<80
	Normal	120–129	80–84
	High Normal	130–139	85–89
	Grade I Hypertension	140–159	90–99
	Grade II	160–179	100–109
	Grade III	>179	>109
	Isolated Systolic Hypertension	>139	<90
Joint National Committee (JNC 7), 2003	Normal	<120	<80
	Pre-Hypertension	120–139	80–89
	Hypertension	≥140	≥90
National Institute for Health and Care Excellence (NICE), 2011	Normal	<140	<90
	Stage I Hypertension	≥140	≥90
	Stage II Hypertension	≥160	≥100
	Severe Hypertension	≥180	≥110

Meier *et al.*
Meier *et al. BMC Medicine* 2013 **11**:211 doi: 10.1186/1741-7015-11-211

Hypotension is blood pressure that's lower than 90/60 mmHg.

1. Four Factors that Determine Blood Pressure

The term **blood pressure** in the context of the present discussion refers to the **mean systemic arterial blood pressure (MAP)**.

The blood pressure is determined mainly by the following four factors (see diagram in Lecture 27).

1. **Cardiac output**—cardiac output = stroke volume × heart rate

2. **Total peripheral resistance**—determined mainly by vasoconstriction or vasodilation of the arterioles

   mean arterial pressure = cardiac output × total peripheral resistance

3. **Capacity of the venous system**—affected by venous constriction and dilation. If the capacity suddenly increases, as might happen with venous dilation, then the blood pressure will drop

4. **Volume of fluid in the circulatory system**—reduced by hemorrhage, increased by **antidiuretics**, which reduce the volume of urine. Certain hormones have an important effect on the volume of fluid in the body. If the volume of fluid in the circulation increases there will be an increase in blood pressure.

Viscosity of the blood can be important in some conditions, such as polycythemia, where the blood contains abnormally large numbers of red cells.

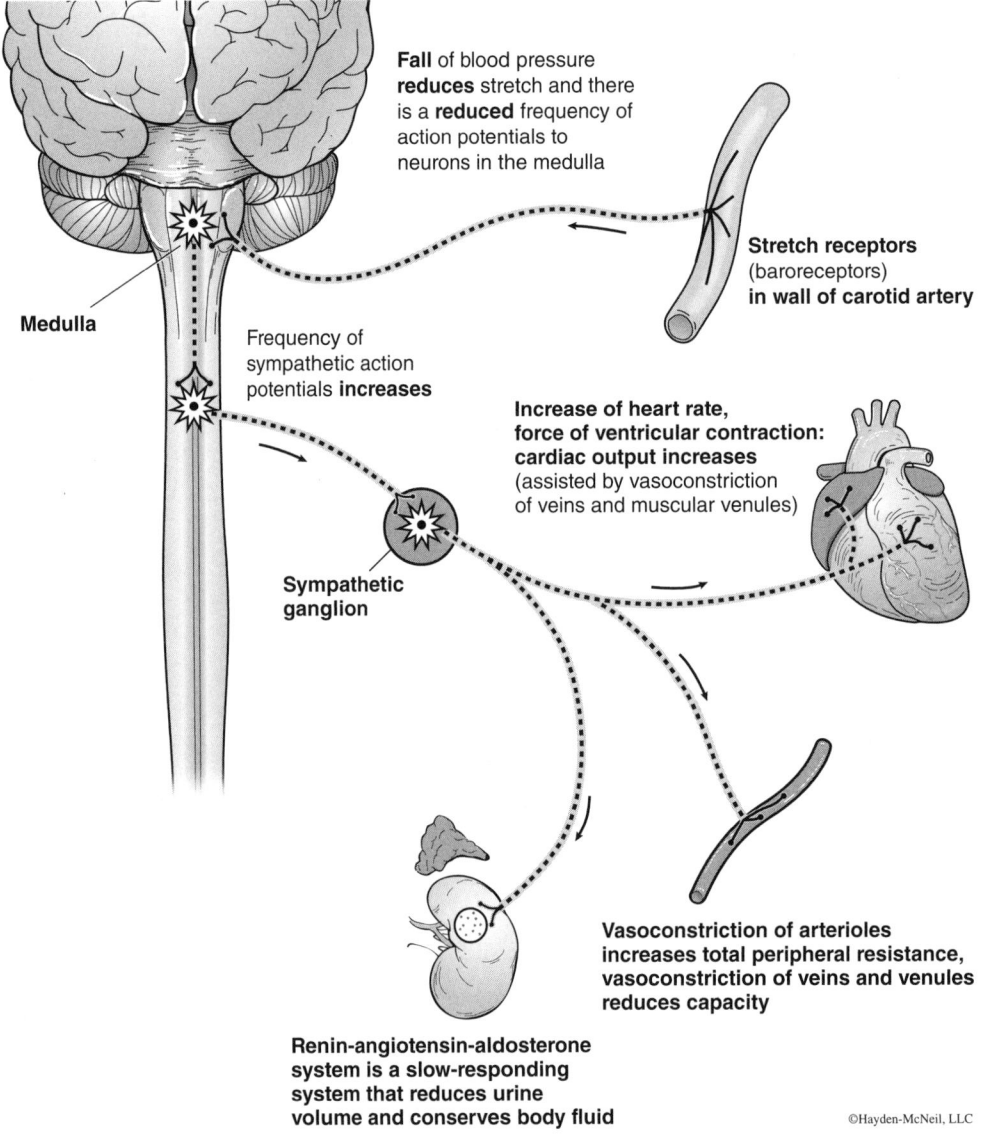

Fall of blood pressure **reduces** stretch and there is a **reduced** frequency of action potentials to neurons in the medulla

Medulla

Frequency of sympathetic action potentials **increases**

Stretch receptors (baroreceptors) **in wall of carotid artery**

Increase of heart rate, force of ventricular contraction: cardiac output increases (assisted by vasoconstriction of veins and muscular venules)

Sympathetic ganglion

Vasoconstriction of arterioles increases total peripheral resistance, vasoconstriction of veins and venules reduces capacity

Renin-angiotensin-aldosterone system is a slow-responding system that reduces urine volume and conserves body fluid

©Hayden-McNeil, LLC

Figure 13-4. The *baroreceptor reflex* for controlling blood pressure.

VII. The Cardiac Pacemaker and Conduction System

Contraction of the myocardium is triggered by rhythmic depolarization of the cells in the sinoatrial node. The wave of depolarization initiated by these cells spreads to the ventricles via specialized myocardial cells that make up the conduction system of the heart. The sequence of events is described in your lecture notes and in the diagram below.

After the myocardium has become depolarized and has contracted, the process of repolarization begins. In humans, the apical surface of the myocardium repolarizes a little earlier than the basal region.

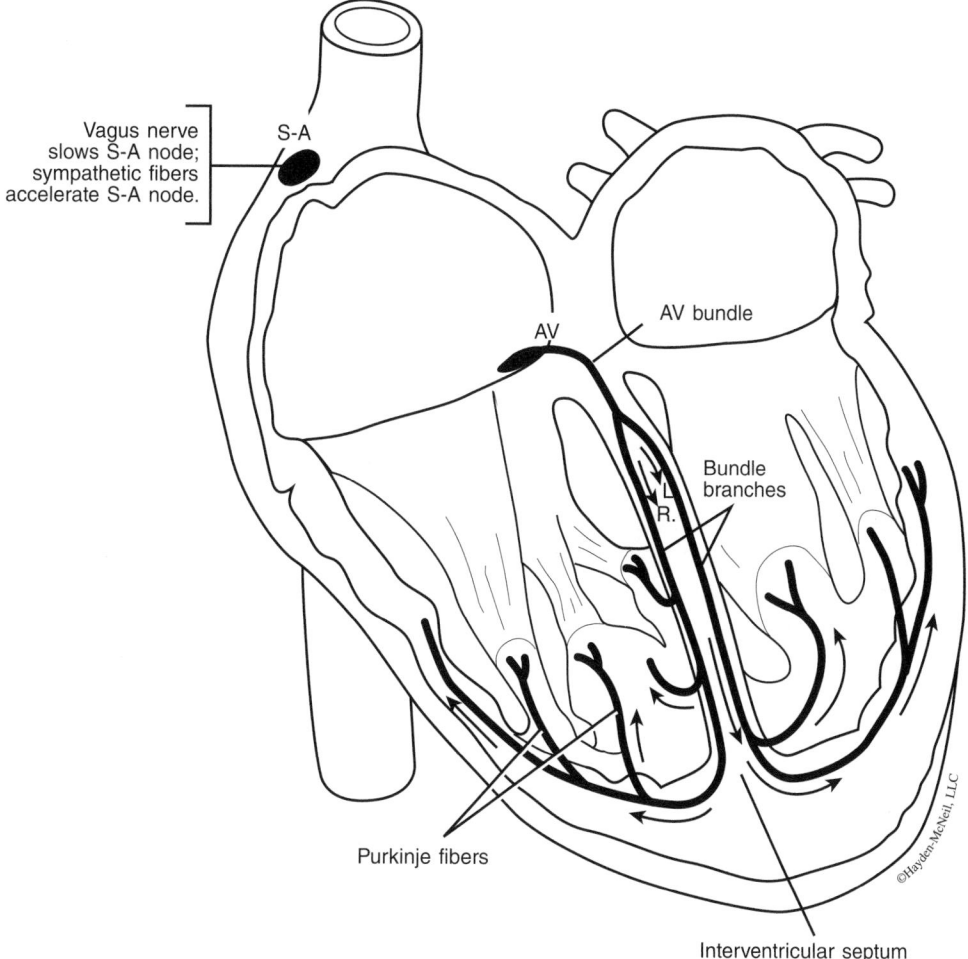

Figure 13-5. Cardiac conduction system.

VIII. Recording the Electrocardiogram

The pulsating electrical activity that occurs as the heart muscle contracts and relaxes sets up a flow of current in the chest that may be detected by attaching electrical leads to the skin at a number of standard locations on the surface of the body.

An **electrocardiogram** can be recorded through any one of *twelve* leads.

- The **three standard limb leads** are designated I, II, and III. They are attached to the two wrists and the left leg (a "ground" lead is usually attached to the right leg).

- Six chest or precordial leads are attached to specific points on the **chest wall**, and are designated V1 through V6.

- Three other leads are referred to as **augmented** leads (aVL, aVR, and aVF).

The leads are connected through a specially designed electrical circuit to a sensitive and stable amplifier (you will see this in laboratory).

The output of the amplifier goes to a **recording** device that can be an oscilloscope, computer, or a pen that moves over a strip chart recorder. In our laboratory, the output goes into the computer, and the data can be printed out.

Abnormalities in the ECG reflect abnormalities in the heart. By carefully examining the ECG, it is possible to determine whether the patient has a cardiac problem, where it is, what it is, and what to do about it.

1. Components of the Electrocardiogram

A typical electrocardiogram (see figure) consists of the following five major components, the origins of which are shown in the table on the following page.

1. **P wave**

2. **Pause (the P-R interval)**

3. **QRS complex**

4. **T wave**

5. **S-T segment**

You are expected to know what these components represent in the cardiac cycle, and there will be questions on them in the lecture examination and in the laboratory tests. They are summarized in the following table.

Component of ECG	Origin
P wave	Depolarization of the atria, indicates S-A node function. The **onset of the P wave precedes the onset of atrial contraction.**
P-R interval	Indicative of the time it takes for the impulse to pass through the A-V node into the ventricles (atrioventricular conduction time).
QRS complex	Depolarization of the ventricles—the QRS duration indicates the time in which ventricular depolarization occurs. **The onset of the QRS wave precedes the onset of ventricular contraction.**
T wave	Repolarization of the ventricles, at which time they are ready to be stimulated again.
S-T segment	The part of the electrocardiogram between the S-wave of the QRS complex and the T-wave. Its elevation or depression with respect to the baseline can be important in diagnosing a myocardial infarction.
PQRSTP	One complete cardiac cycle.

There is also a wave representing atrial repolarization, but it is buried in the much larger QRS complex wave that is caused by ventricular depolarization.

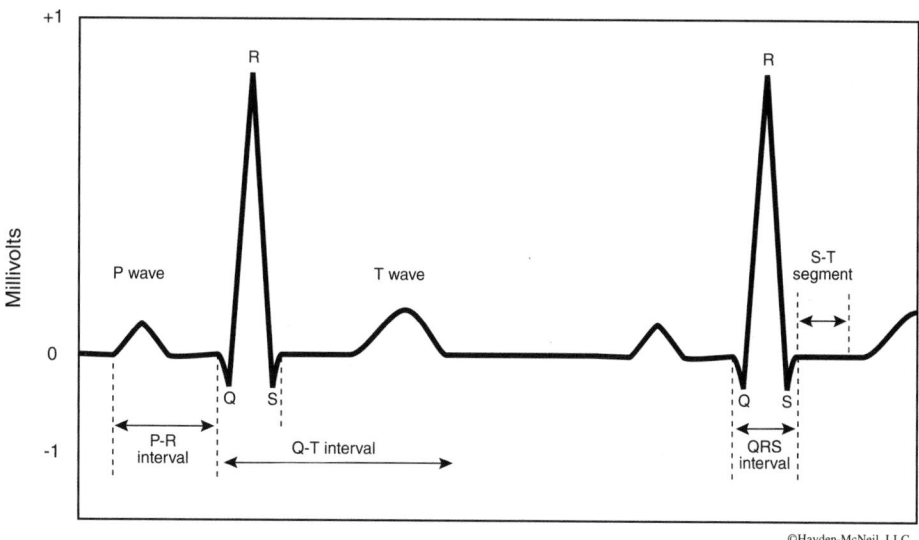

©Hayden-McNeil, LLC

Figure 13-6. A normal electrocardiogram.

2. Changes in the Electrocardiogram Following a Myocardial Infarction

A myocardial infarction is death of cardiac muscle tissue following loss of its blood supply. The coronary arteries provide blood to the myocardium, and in coronary artery disease (CAD) they may become narrowed or completely blocked. If the blockage is caused by a blood clot, it is referred to as a thrombosis. Myocardial ischemia is the first consequence of these events. Myocardial ischemia means that the myocardium is receiving insufficient blood flow (i.e., oxygen) to satisfy its metabolic demands. If myocardial ischemia is prolonged, it leads to a myocardial infarction, commonly referred to as a heart attack.

Following a myocardial infarction, it is possible that changes will be observed in one or more of three regions of the electrocardiogram.

1. **ST segment**—the ST segment can be important diagnostically, and may be elevated. This is referred to as a STEMI (ST elevated MI). Under some circumstances, the ST segment may be depressed.

2. **T-wave**—the T-wave may be inverted.

3. **Q-wave**—the Q-wave may increase in size (cardiologists sometimes speak of this as a "Q-wave infarction").

Except for the Q-wave changes, the ECG gradually returns to normal after a period of time that can last up to several months.

3. Cardiac Arrhythmias (Dysrhythmias)—Some Examples

A **cardiac arrhythmia** (also known as a dysrhythmia) is an abnormal cardiac rate or rhythm.

Dysrhythmias may be caused by a variety of conditions. Conditions that cause dysrhythmias include lack of oxygen, drug effects, electrolyte imbalance, and myocardial or conduction system damage due to myocardial ischemia.

We expect you to learn the different dysrhythmias from the **lecture notes for lecture 25**.

Dysrhythmias may arise from factors operating in the following areas.

A. Sinus node

   1. Sinus tachycardia

   2. Sinus bradycardia

B. Atria

   1. Atrial flutter/Atrial fibrillation

C. A-V nodal (junctional)

D. A-V block and bundle branch block

E. Ventricles

   1. Premature ventricular contractions (PVCs)

   2. Ventricular tachycardia

   3. Ventricular fibrillation

EXPERIMENTS

Exercise A

Auscultation of Heart Sounds

1. Clean the earpieces of the stethoscope with alcohol prep pads and allow the alcohol to dry.

2. Don the stethoscope, and place the bell of the stethoscope on the thorax, just to the sternal side of the left nipple, and carefully listen for heart sounds. The first will be a longer, louder sound than the second, which is short and sharp.

Exercise B

Blood Pressure Determination

You must take two blood pressure readings, the **systolic pressure**, which represents the pressure in the arteries at the peak of ventricular ejection, and the **diastolic pressure**, which reflects the pressure during ventricular diastole (relaxation). Blood pressures are reported in millimeters of mercury (mmHg) with the systolic pressure appearing first and the diastolic pressure second. A reading of 120/80 translates to a systolic pressure of 120 mmHg and a diastolic pressure of 80 mmHg. Normal blood pressure varies from person to person depending on age, gender, weight, and health factors.

The sphygmomanometer is an instrument used to obtain blood pressure readings by the ausculatory method. It consists of an inflatable cuff with an attached pressure gauge.

The cuff is placed around the upper arm and inflated to about 180 mmHg, a pressure which should occlude circulation into the forearm. Cuff pressure is gradually released, and the examiner listens with a stethoscope for characteristic sounds called the **sounds of Korotkoff**. These sounds indicate the resumption of blood flow into the arm. The pressure at which the first soft tapping sounds can be detected is recorded as the systolic pressure. As the pressure is slowly reduced further, blood flow becomes more turbulent, and the sounds become louder. As pressure is reduced still further below diastolic pressure, the artery is no longer compressed and blood flows freely and without turbulence. At this point, the sounds of Korotkoff can no longer be detected. The pressure at which the sounds disappear is recorded as the diastolic pressure.

Procedure for taking blood pressure readings:

1. Work in pairs to obtain brachial artery blood pressure readings. Obtain a stethoscope, alcohol prep pads, and a sphygmomanometer. Clean the earpieces of the stethoscope, and check the cuff for the presence of trapped air by compressing it against the laboratory table.

2. The subject should sit in a comfortable position at the laboratory table with the left arm supported on the bench (approximately at the level of the heart). Wrap the cuff around the subject's left arm just above the elbow with the inflatable area on the medial arm surface. The cuff may be marked with an arrow; if so, the arrow should be positioned over the brachial artery. Secure the cuff by tucking the distal end under the wrapped portion or by bringing the two Velcro areas together.

3. Palpate (feel) the brachial pulse, don the stethoscope, and place its diaphragm over the pulse point.

4. Inflate the cuff to approximately 150–200 mmHg pressure, and slowly release the pressure valve. (**THE CUFF SHOULD NOT BE INFLATED FOR MORE THAN ONE MINUTE**. If you have any trouble obtaining a reading within this time, deflate the cuff, wait 2 to 3 minutes and try again.)

5. Watch the pressure gauge as you listen for the first soft thudding sounds of the blood spurting through the partially occluded artery. Record or note this pressure (systolic pressure), and continue to release the pressure. You will notice first an increase, then a muffling of the sound. Note the pressure at which the sound becomes muffled or disappears (diastolic pressure). Often times, there is some controversy as to when the sound disappears. In any case, use your best judgment.

6. Make two blood pressure determinations, and record your results below.

First trial:

Systolic Pressure _____ Diastolic Pressure _____

Second trial:

Systolic Pressure _____ Diastolic Pressure _____

7. Compute the **pulse pressure** for each trial. The pulse pressure is the difference between the systolic and diastolic pressures and indicates the amount of blood forced from the heart during systole, or the "working" pressure.

Pulse Pressure = Systolic Pressure – Diastolic Pressure

Pulse Pressure:

first trial _____ second trial _____

Exercise C—LabTutor: ECG and Peripheral Circulation

Recording an ECG

The three standard limb leads are attached to the two wrists and to the left leg. A ground lead is commonly attached to the right leg. We will not be recording from the nine other leads.

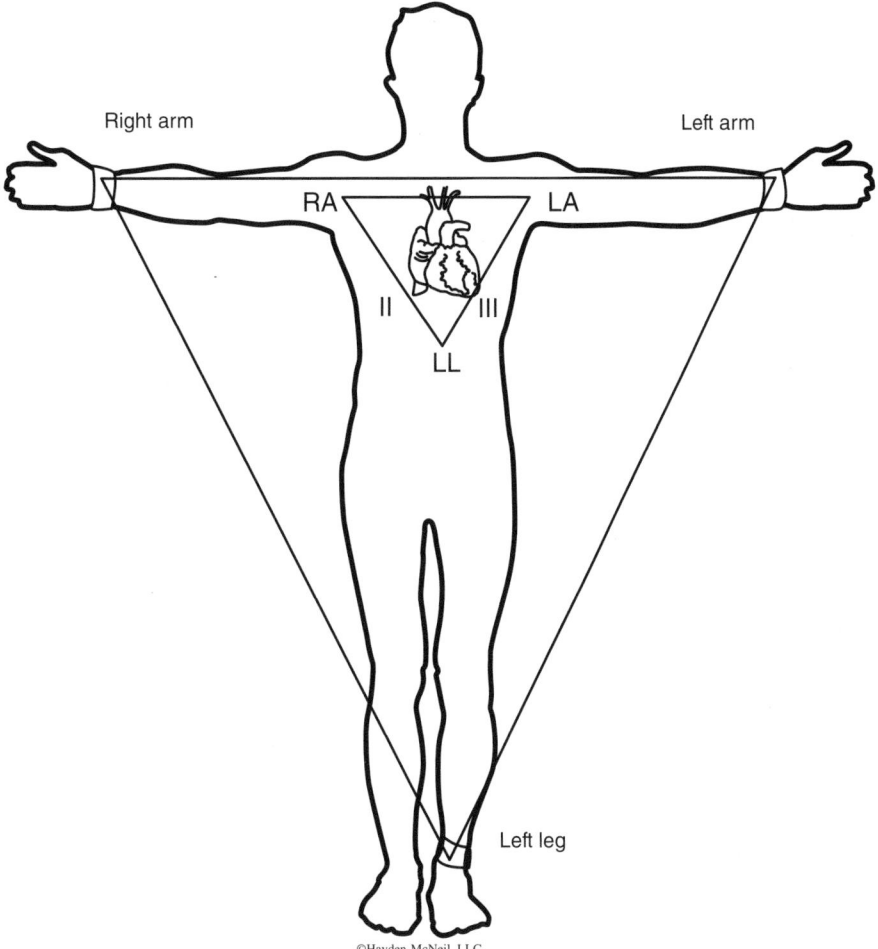

©Hayden-McNeil, LLC

Figure 13-7. Standard limb leads.